Racism and Anti-racism in Ireland

Edited by
Ronit Lentin and Robbie McVeigh

First published 2002
by
Beyond the Pale
BTP Publications Ltd
Unit 2.1.2 Conway Mill
5-7 Conway Street
Belfast BT13 2DE

Tel: +44 (0)28 90 438630
Fax: +44 (0)28 90 439707
E-mail: office@btpale.com
Website: http://www.btpale.com

British Library Cataloguing-in-Publication Data.
A catalogue record for this book is available from the British Library.

ISBN 1-900960-16-8

Cover Photograph: Derek Speirs / Report

Dedications

In memory of Ettie Steinberg,
the only Irish person
to have been
murdered in Auschwitz
and
Zhao Liu Tao
murdered in Dublin, 24 January 2002.

And in memory of John O'Connell,
friend and comrade and tireless campaigner against racism.

The most ambitious aspiration of the 1916 Proclamation
was the commitment to
'cherish the children of the nation equally'.
We dedicate this book to our children – in the hope and expectation
that they will be cherished equally alongside all other children of their generation –
black and white, settled and Traveller, Jew and gentile, citizen and refugee.

Contents

Acknowledgements

Thanks to the Department of Sociology, Trinity College Dublin, for supporting this project financially. Thanks to all the contributors and to Drazen Nozinic for his editorial assistance.

1.

Situated racisms: A theoretical introduction

Robbie McVeigh and Ronit Lentin

Declaration on Race and Racial Prejudice *Article 2*:

1. Any theory which involves the claim that racial or ethnic groups are inherently superior or inferior, thus implying that some would be entitled to dominate or eliminate others, presumed to be inferior, or which bases value judgements on racial differentiation, has no scientific foundation and is contrary to the moral and ethical principles of humanity.

2. Racism includes racist ideologies, prejudiced attitudes, discriminatory behaviour, structural arrangements and institutionalised practices resulting in racial inequality as well as the fallacious notion that discriminatory relations between groups are morally and scientifically justifiable; it is reflected in discriminatory provisions in legislation or regulations and discriminatory practices as well as in anti-social beliefs and acts; it hinders the development of its victims, perverts those who practise it, divides nations internally, impedes international co-operation and gives rise to political tensions between peoples; it is contrary to the fundamental principles of international law and, consequently, seriously disturbs international peace and security.

3. Racial prejudice, historically linked with inequalities in power, reinforced by economic and social differences between individuals and groups, and still seeking today to justify such inequalities, is totally without justification. (UNESCO, 1978)

Introduction

On Monday 21 January 2002, Zhao Liu Tao, a 29-year-old Chinese man was attacked, along with two friends, by a group of Irish youths on his way home in Drumcondra, Dublin. The youths hurled racial abuse at the Chinese students before a scuffle broke out. Zhao Liu Tao was hit repeatedly on the head with an iron bar and was admitted to hospital where he died on Thursday 24 January. Zhao Liu Tao's death was widely reported as Ireland's 'first racially-motivated murder'. Certainly it marked a terrible new phase in the evolution of racism and anti-racism in Ireland. The murder has hardly been mentioned by the press after the initial reports and the garda inquiries have been low key, but the popular myth that racism is not a problem in Ireland had been brutally and irrevocably dispelled.

The refusal to acknowledge any problem had dominated attitudes towards racism in Ireland for decades. For example, it was not until December 2000 that Ireland finally ratified the Convention on the Elimination of All Forms of Racial Discrimination (CERD). It came into force in Ireland on 28 January 2001. Ireland had signed the Convention in 1968 but it had failed to ratify despite increasing pressure to do so throughout the 1990s. The ratification was, of course, a positive move. It was also an enormous tribute to those who had continued to pressurize the government to sign the convention. Like much United Nations material, the Convention is both legalistic and verbose. Nevertheless, it is the most important international declaration on racism. Like the definitive UNESCO *Declaration on Race and Race Prejudice* cited above, it provides a common language for the understanding of what racism is around the world. Moreover, it signifies the repudiation of racism by the world community:

> In one international declaration, covenant and convention after another since the United Nations was founded, States have accepted that all members of the human family have equal and inalienable rights, and have made commitments to assure and defend these rights. Racial discrimination, nevertheless, remains a stumbling block to the full realization of human rights. In spite of progress in some areas, distinctions, exclusions, restrictions and preferences based on race, colour, descent, national or ethnic origin, continue to create and embitter conflict, and cause untold suffering and loss of life. The fundamental injustice of racial discrimination, no less than the dangers it represents, has made its elimination a target of action by the United Nations (United Nations 2001).

This book responds to the issues that this position raises in Ireland – questions about the 'fundamental injustice' of racism in Ireland as well as the 'dangers it represents'. In the 1990s, Irish racism began to be theorised by social scientists in Ireland, particularly since the arrival of increasing (though still relatively very small) numbers of migrants, refugees and asylum-seekers. These analyses highlight the racialisation of Irishness in relation to 'old' ethnicities such as Travellers, Black Irish people and Jewish people. However, despite the plethora of newspaper articles and radio and television programmes on new manifestations of racism in Irish society, and beside a few journal articles, NGO publications and a handful of booklets, there is no authoritative academic text that students and other interested parties can refer to in the Irish context. This book aims to fill this theoretical and pedagogical gap.

This book situates racisms in Ireland, and makes sense of how and why Irish society has become racialised. More simply, it asks how it is possible that racism has become normalised in Ireland. In the process of normalising racialisation, shocking things have been said in recent years about minority ethnic groups.[1] These verbal attacks have not usually come from organised fascist or racist movements like in other European countries, but have emerged from 'ordinary' journalists, politicians and writers. Moreover, there has been no shortage of people eager to defend the right to say such things.

Thus, in 1996, Mary Ellen Synon, a former *Sunday Independent* journalist, was able to write in that newspaper: 'Traveller life is without the ennobling intellect of man or the steadying instincts of animals. This tinker "culture" is without achievement, discipline, reason or intellectual ambition' (Synon, 1996). In 1997, the highly acclaimed veteran Irish author Francis Stuart was able to declare in the Channel Four television documentary *A Great Hatred* (quoting from his own autobiography): 'the Jew is the worm that got into the rose and sickened it' (Sebag Montefiore, 1997). In 1998, the Fine Gael County Councillor John Flannery proposed that all Travellers be 'tagged with microchips like cattle' in order to monitor their movement. Travellers, he claimed, 'expected everything to be done for them while giving little in return' (Murray and Varley, 1998). The Immigration Control Platform has emerged, devoted to the project of keeping Ireland free of refugees and immigrants, and calling on the government of Ireland to opt out of the Geneva Convention so that Ireland is no longer obliged to accept asylum-seekers. There also have been numerous serious attacks, including stabbings, as part of a general trend of verbal and physical harassment of people of colour and asylum-seekers in Irish cities. In late 1999, a major crisis at the Dublin Refugee Application Centre due to overcrowding and lack of accommodation for incoming asylum-seekers, prompted the chairman of the Eastern Health Board, Dáil member Ivor Callely, to call on the government to 'get tough' on asylum-seekers and 'throw out' illegal immigrants, claiming Ireland is becoming a 'soft target' for illegal immigrants and demanding 'strong leadership' to stem the tide of immigrants 'coming into the State to cash in on the benefits' (Donoghue, 1999: 1). Callely's statement caused anger and embarrassment and resulted in a counter-statement from the Minister of State in the Department of Justice, Equality and Law Reform, Liz O'Donnell, who called the government's asylum policy 'doom laden' and 'a shambles' (Haughey, 1999a: 6). However, the fact that the statement was made by a TD who is in charge of the largest Health Board in Ireland, part of whose brief is to look after asylum-seekers' health and accommodation needs, is an indication of the racist undertones of Ireland's immigration and asylum policies, an argument made forcibly by Tracy (2000) and in several publications of the Irish Refugee Council (IRC, 2000; Fanning *et al*, 2000). A needs analysis survey conducted by the African Refugee Network published in October 1999 showed that 89.7 per cent of the respondents experienced racism in Ireland; racism included verbal abuse (68.75 per cent), physical abuse (25 per cent) and being arrested (6.25 per cent). 79 per cent of the respondents said they were refused service in pubs and nightclubs (African Refugee Network, 1999). An Amnesty International survey, *Racism in Ireland: The Views of Black and Ethnic Minorities* (AI, 2001), found that 78 per cent of the sample had experienced racism and 81.5 per cent agreed that the government is not doing enough to combat racism.

Racism has moved from the margins of Irish political life to the centre – it is now 'common sense' to show concern about the relatively small number of asylum-seekers in Ireland. Yet this occurs in a country that, throughout the 1980s alone, exported more undocumented workers to the USA than the entire refugee population currently resident in Ireland. In 1997, a poll carried out for the European Commission, which found worryingly high levels of hostility to immigration, also found that 55 per cent of Irish people defined themselves as 'racist', although this was lower than the two-thirds of Europeans who do so (Smith, 1997: 6). This book contextualises these developments theoretically, politically and experientially.

Our contextualisation of racism is necessarily complex but it begins from a simple premise: racism is about racialised violence. This involves more than racist attacks on the street by individual bigots, and entails organised, structured, institutionalised violence. This is as true in Ireland as anywhere else. Examples of physical violence abound. According to asylum-seekers, speaking in 1998, 'there have been 17 serious attacks, including stabbings, in the past two months... The level of xenophobia is rising, yet I have never heard anyone in the government condemn racism in public'. The attacks included a brutal kicking along a busy Dublin street of Mary, a pregnant asylum-seeker from Angola (who had given birth in June 1998 to an Irish child); a stabbing in May 1998 of the Nigerian asylum-seeker Akeem Salami Shodiya and his two friends by a gang of youths as they walked along O'Connell Street; and an assault in April 1998 with a smashed bottle by a group of youths not far from the city centre Halfpenny Bridge against the 17-year old Zairean asylum-seeker Landeau, whose political prisoner mother had died in jail and whose father was assassinated before his eyes. The wound to his head needed 16 stitches. The result of these assaults is that asylum-seekers like Mary, Akeem and Landeau stay indoors, terrified to set foot outside (Nic Suibhne, 1998: 32).

In June 2000, as David Richardson, a white Englishman, and his Black wife and son who was working in Dublin, were walking home outside Trinity College Dublin, they were attacked by a group of white Irish men, shouting 'niggers out', 'black bastards' and 'monkeys', and stabbing David so that he had to spend several weeks in intensive care. On August 17, the stabbed man's son, Christian, having been called a 'Black bastard' by passers-by, decided to resign his Dublin IT job and leave Ireland. Since arriving back in England, he said, he felt 'less tense and more relaxed than in the last couple of weeks', as he had been feeling 'a bit scared' living in Ireland (Halloran, 2000: 4).

Asylum-seeker John Tambwe of Ireland's African Refugee Network, angered by the extensive media attention for the incident, due, as he claims, to Mr Richardson being *white*, says this happens all the time: 'I have suffered all sorts of racial abuse. Once someone spat in my face. Some fellows urinated in my letterbox. I have been called "nigger" countless times, and had my apartment spray-painted with obscenities' (Sweeney, 2000: 10). Tambwe also reports racist discrimination by bouncers in nightclubs and restaurants and by service providers such as ambulance drivers, racist graffiti and casual racist abuse yelled by passers-by.

There is no doubt that verbal attacks lead directly to violent physical attacks on refugees. People who call for refugees to be put out of the country are calling, whether intentionally or not, for human beings to be attacked and killed. Equally, however, a government which shows such alarm at the tiny numbers of refugees, which puts in place overtly racist immigration controls, which says 'we' cannot take any more refugees, is setting up a system which incites the same violence. It is this reality of organised, institutionalised violence that separates racism from national chauvinism or xenophobia.

Racism is not about petty differences between individuals or nations – it is about genocide. The lesson from the Nazi Holocaust, but also from colonisation, is that the ultimate logic of racism is genocide, slavery and institutionalised violence. The attitude of fascist groups such as Reclaim Dublin and their propaganda that 'Blacks bring drugs and prostitution', is common to many European cities. However, it is extremely worrying that ordinary Irish people are either shrugging off the existence of growing racism or joining the extremists in arguing that Ireland is 'too small' to accept large numbers of refugees or that accepting a larger number of refugees and migrants might bring about racism. In the same token, most Irish people are not contradicting the claim by the Minister for Justice that a large percentage of asylum applicants are 'bogus' and therefore targets for deportation.

Despite the well-meaning resistance to 'hierarchies of oppression', racism still appears high up in the matrix of subordination as one of the 'big three', along with classism and sexism. Perhaps this is because each of these is experienced constantly – whatever side of the power asymmetry one is on. For example, able-bodied people are constantly empowered by able-bodied chauvinism, yet they are not necessarily conscious of this empowerment; heterosexual people are empowered by heterosexism, yet this may not always figure in their sense of self. Class, 'race' and gender are there all the time, 'in one's face', whatever one's class, ethnic or gender identity may be. Ethnic difference is different because it is less tangible than the other two and because so many people still believe there is something 'genetic' and 'natural' about phenotypic differences between people. Some people will insist that class is an objective truth rooted in relationship to the means of production; some people will insist that gender is an objective truth rooted in biological sex differences; but, once biological racism is discarded, ethnicity becomes quintessentially subjective. It is never fixed, nor 'Black and white', but located within a complex matrix of definitions of self and other.

Of course, we know that class and gender are socially constructed in the same kind of way as 'race'. But we also 'know' whether we are men or women and, whether we are working class or middle class. It is much harder to 'know' whether we are white (or not-Black) or Black (or not-white) or settled (or not-Traveller) or Traveller (or not-settled) or Irish (or not-British) or not-Irish and so on. Each of these parts of our identities is already multi-faceted. 'Knowing' you are a Jew, say, already implies intra-ethnic difference: you may be an Irish Jew or a French Jew, but, even as a French Jew, you may originate from the Maghreb or from Alsace, you may be orthodox or secular, you may be Ashkenazi, Sephardi or Mizrahi, thus complicating the matrices of your ethnic identit(ies). 'Race' or ethnicity cannot be 'known' in the same way as class or gender. In this sense ethnicity is quintessentially dialectical because it never *is* except when it simultaneously is *not*. In other words, ethnicity is about constantly (re)negotiating and maintaining boundaries, and about inclusion and exclusion, where inclusion always excludes and differentiates between who is allowed and who is not allowed to belong to the collectivity.

For example, anti-Irish racism is different for Irish people in the USA, Britain and the north of Ireland and the south of Ireland. Equally, however, racism is different for the same person in each of these contexts. The same Jewish person in New York or Dublin or Tel Aviv or Hebron; the same African person in Johannesburg or Khartoum or London or Moscow; the same South Asian person in Bombay or Kenya or Guyana or Scotland; the same Chinese person in Indonesia or Hong Kong or China or Belfast. This proves definitively that racism has nothing to do with some putative quality of the racialised individual or with his or her culture. If Irish people induced anti-Irish racism, then it would exist beyond countries with a legacy of British colonisation. If Jews induced antisemitism, then it would not exist in countries where there are no Jews. If refugees induced racism then Ireland would still have less racism than most western countries, since its record of accepting refugees has been so poor. In each of these examples it becomes clear that racism is a quality of, and caused by, a racist society rather than by racialised minorities.

While there is a need to situate racism in Ireland theoretically, our guiding principle is that racism cannot be abstracted from people's lived experiences. Racism is a complex social phenomenon which needs to be theorised in ways which can respond to this complexity, but it is also about the personal stories of 'knowing, because experiencing subjects' (Stanley, 1993), about biographies and auto/biographies, through which social processes such as racism become manifest and tangible. We are all located somewhere within different intersections of racialised matrices and our location encourages us to theorise and write in particular ways. Therefore, both the editors, as authors of this introduction, and the contributors to this collection, are not merely theorists of racism and anti-racism. We have all experienced various aspects of racism and are all also anti-racism activists. We all approach the specificities of Irish racism from a situated positioning, using our 'intellectual auto/biographies' (Stanley and Wise, 1993) as an analytic tool. This is social theory grounded in lived experience rather than abstracted from it. It is also social analysis written *by* people rather than *about* people. As such it is a sobering testament to the continuing struggle against racism in Ireland – a vigorous assertion of the fact that racism is neither 'normal' nor 'natural', and, more importantly, that it is resistible.

As editors, we both come to the study of racism with a deep long-standing political commitment to the anti-racist struggle. Neither of us fears accusations of bias. Rather, we would readily admit to our politics informing our academic analysis. Nor do we worry about accusations that writing another academic book is the least important task when so much else remains to be done. Since we both believe in the unity of theory and practice, we feel that providing academic knowledge is vital in order to supply students and researchers with much needed information and theory, and also in order to theoretically ground our anti-racism politics.

Indeed, this creative dialectic between political and academic analysis of racism continues to run through anti-racist work. While it is not always recognisable by academics, political struggle continues to inform academic analysis. Take for example the critical notion of *institutional racism*, which has moved back centre-stage in discussions of racism following the publication of the report of the inquiry into the murder of Stephen

Lawrence in Britain (see Anthias, 1999; Yuval-Davis, 1999). The term 'institutionalised racism' has permeated academic analysis over the past thirty years. We now even find some police forces able to admit that they are 'institutionally racist'. The concept, however, was rooted in the theoretical work of the Black Panther movement in the USA. It is useful to invoke Stokely Carmichael's original definition of institutional racism and remember how different it is from safer and more academic notions:

> Racism is both overt and covert. It takes two closely related forms: individual whites acting against individual Blacks, and acts by the total white community against the Black community. We call these individual racism and institutional racism... When white terrorists bomb a Black church and kill Black children, that is an act of individual racism, widely deplored by most segments of society. But when in that same city – Birmingham, Alabama – five hundred Black babies die each year because of the lack of proper food, clothing, shelter and proper medical facilities, and thousands more are destroyed or maimed physically, emotionally, and intellectually because of conditions of poverty and discrimination of the Black community, that is a function of institutional racism (Carmichael, 1967: 3-4).

This kind of analysis continues to have more immediate resonance with the reality of racism for Travellers, people of colour and refugees in Ireland than any amount of theorising around racial discourse or 'identity politics' (McVeigh and Binchy, 1998).

We start from the premise that the emergence of the current phase in Irish racism is neither 'natural' nor inevitable. It has to be explained and linked to broader ideas about the very concept of Irishness itself. This develops the notion of the *specificities* of Irish racism. Racism is not a given; its existence in Irish society (as elsewhere) needs to be *situated*. In particular, we have to make sense of racism in Ireland in terms of the contradictory location of Ireland in racialised discourses. In recent years Irish racism has appeared in new and frightening forms focusing on refugees and asylum-seekers and on in-coming people of colour. However, these new forms developed out of older manifestations of Irish racism such as antisemitism,[2] anti-Traveller racism and racism against Black-Irish people.

Despite the problematic tendency to dilute the concept of racism to apply to hatred of foreigners – xenophobia, and to all forms of ethnic discrimination, which some authors have named 'ethnicism' (Essed, 1991; and in the Irish context Boucher, 1998), applying the term merely to colour-based hatred and discrimination runs the risk of reifying 'race' beyond social constructions of collectivity, belongingness, origin or destiny. The term 'racism' has entered common usage in the wake of Nazi racialisation of Jews and Roma (pejoratively known as 'Gypsies'). The horrific consequence of this racialisation was the annihilation of a third of Europe's Jews and a large proportion of Europe's Roma people. By naming antisemitism and anti-Gypsyism 'racism', do we run the risk of conferring upon Jewish or Roma people a 'racial' connotation assigned to them by Nazi ideology?

According to Miles (1989: 46), after 1945, the term racism was used precisely in order to prevent the discourse of 'race' as a biological, immutable category, from being used for similar political purposes in the future. Therefore we feel fully justified in naming anti-Travellerism, antisemitism, as well as hatred of refugees – all racialised in popular and official discourse – racism. Racism, we believe, is any distinction, exclusion, restriction or preference based on 'race', colour, descent, as well as national or ethnic origin, which inferioritises or excludes a collectivity using mechanisms of power.

So, how does Ireland sit in terms of this broader analysis of 'race', racialisation and racism? The history of Irish racism is paralleled by the history of racism against Irish people. Through centuries of colonisation, Irish people experienced attempted genocide, slavery, forced emigration, starvation and war – in short, almost every form of institutionalised and racialised violence, which provided the basis for historical and contemporary forms of anti-Irish racism. Thus, we see Ireland and Irishness racialised in different and contradictory ways. Ireland is empowered by its whiteness, by its Europeanness and by the advancement of Irish blocs in other countries such as the USA. Each of these processes actively encourages a specific racialisation of Irish consciousness, not least in the countries of the diaspora, where Irish people were actively involved in racialised encounters with members of other ethnic groups. Ireland is also disempowered, however, by its colonial history, by its location on the periphery of Europe, by emigration, by dependency. These experiences have seen Irish people racialised and disempowered by anti-Irish racism. They also give Irish people an immediate personal reason for challenging racism in its diverse forms. In this sense Ireland is quintessentially 'between two worlds' – both perpetrator and survivor of racism, both thoroughly racist and determinedly anti-racist.

A discussion of racism and Irishness throws light on other racialised encounters because of Ireland's particular structural location. This discussion suggests that analyses of racism have to be sensitive to intra-ethnic differences and inequalities, and in particular differences of class, gender and (dis)ability. It is our intention to situate racism firmly within this intersection of subordinations. But the discussion must also be sensitive to inter-ethnic differences. Racism is not just something done by white people to Black people – it also structures relationships between different racialised groups. This book interrogates nuances of racialised relations between different ethnic groups, for example the resistance, by Romanian refugees, to sharing hostel space with a group of Roma in Wexford city.

In a sense, Ireland is an 'ideal-type' of the cutting edge of debate and analysis around 'race' and racism in the new millennium. Racism is not static precisely because it is about power. Recent debates have moved away from old and simplistic dichotomies – Black/white, colonised/coloniser, First World/Majority World – and towards recognising the contradictory and overlapping nature of ethnic identity and racialisation at the beginning of the twenty-first century. One of the key challenges for anti-racist analyses is to engage with the changing quality of contemporary racism without retreating to relativism and postmodernism. It is still possible to locate the asymmetries of power that are central to racism and which distinguish it from prejudice, ethnicism, or from xenophobia and national or regional chauvinism.

The second section of this introduction sketches the development of sociological approaches to the study of racism, from the sociology of 'race relations' to a sociology of racisms, in the plural. The third section examines the racialisation of 'Irishness'. The fourth section provides an annotated bibliography of racism and anti-racism in the Irish context, and the final section concludes with some comments on continuity and change.

Towards a sociology of racism

The impulse to theorise 'race' and ethnicity came from two key sources: first, the great anti-imperialist struggles, which had been defined by the link between 'race' and empire; second, the struggles of people of colour within the countries of the metropolis. In the USA Du Bois's *The Souls of Black Folk* (1903 [1965]) developed the ideas of earlier African-American radicals like Frederick Douglass and Sojourner Truth. There was also an overlap here as many colonized peoples developed their analysis as students and/or political exiles in the capitals of Europe. Here the analyses of liberation movements began the process of interrogating colonial science and its notions of 'Race'. A whole series of classic texts appeared in this genre including Frantz Fanon's *The Wretched of the Earth* (1969) and *Black Skins, White Masks* (1970), Albert Memmi's *The Colonizer and the Colonized* (1990), Aimé Césaire's *Discourse on Colonialism* (1972) and Amilcar Cabral's *Revolution in Guinea: an African People's Struggle* (1969).

'Race relations' as a distinct paradigm of *white academic* research began in the 1920s with studies of segregation, immigration, race consciousness and assimilation by American sociologists and anthropologists following the seminal work of Robert Park (Park, 1925; Stanfield, 1985, 1993). Park, who explored the contexts within which ideas of race become socially meaningful, was instrumental in breaking with previous biologistic concerns with inter-racial relations. These concerns had been associated with social Darwinism and were based upon a pseudo-scientific notion of 'race'. Park, who insisted that 'race' was primarily a *social* rather than a *biological* category, regarded 'race relations' as:

> the relations existing between peoples distinguished by marks of racial descent, particularly when these racial differences enter into the consciousness of the individuals and groups so distinguished, and by doing so determine in each case the individual's conception of himself as well as his status in the community... Race relations, in this sense, are not so much the relations that exist between individuals of different races as between individuals conscious of these differences (Park 1950: 81).

This approach was developed by a number of theorists who came to regard 'race relations' as a distinct category of social relations and therefore to argue that the sociological analysis of 'race relations' was valid and important in understanding the nature and extent of racism. This developing sociology made reference to 'race relations situations' in the 'First World' as well as in the colonies and former colonies of the 'Third World' (Banton, 1977; Van den Berghe, 1978).

Racism and constructions of 'race'

Although there is broad acceptance that 'races' as such do not exist, the notion of 'race' is still being widely used in popular and social scientific discourses. Any attempt to map a sociology of racism must therefore relate to the changing perceptions of the concept of 'race' in contemporary social sciences. It can be argued that it is social scientists, in their anxiety to use categories and sub-divisions, and by presenting 'race' as a category, who have contributed a great deal to the invention of racism, and to its formulation as doctrine and scholarly theory (Wieviorka, 1995: 3). We will present a trajectory from a sociology of 'race relations', through Marxist and neo-Marxist approaches, postmodern and cultural studies approaches, and feminist approaches that focus on the intersection of gender and race/ethnicity, towards a sociology of racisms, in the plural.

Despite plenty of historically specific accounts of racialised encounters in different societies, there has been an insufficient historical perspective regarding the position of 'race' and racism within social relations (cf. Malik, 1996; Solomos and Back, 1996; Back and Solomos, 2000; Gilroy, 2000). According to Gilroy, letting old visual signatures of 'race' go is not easy, but it opens new anti-racist hopes (Gilroy, 2000: 43). In order not to isolate contemporary racism from past understandings, particularly of the idea of 'race', it is crucial to contextualise it within several historical factors. These factors include: ideas about 'race' and their impact on racist discourses; slavery as shaping racial ideas and social relations; the development of 'scientific' ideas and discourses about 'race'; the role of colonialism and imperialism as forms of racial domination; the role of Nazi state racism in developing ideas of genocidal 'racial purity'; and the impact of migration and the movement of labour as shaping ideas about 'race' in advanced industrialised societies.

The term racism became a prominent discourse in the European social sciences in the wake of the Holocaust, when it became imperative for some academics and scientists, as well as political activists, to reject the way in which 'race' had been used in Nazi Germany (Miles, 1989: 43). However, racism is not a new phenomenon and has a history of representations of the Other through processes of inclusion and exclusion (cf. De Beauvoir, 1949, 1993). Those who designate certain populations as the Other also establish criteria by which they themselves are represented as the norm. In the act of defining African as 'Black' and 'savage' and excluding them from their world, Europeans in the eighteenth and nineteenth centuries represented themselves as 'white' and 'civilised'. The discourse of 'race' used to inferioritise and exclude was employed, with inverted meanings, to include and superioritise. If Africans were represented as a 'race', then Europeans too were a 'race', albeit a superior one. The racialised Other was not only created in the colonial context but also within nation states, most notably in the case of Jews and Roma. These representations, neither static nor unitary, occurred long before European colonialism; hence, for instance, the representations of Africans within the Greco-Roman world during the third and second centuries BC. However, representations of the Other have not been based solely on somatic differences, but also on cultural traits; hence for example European representations of Muslims as barbaric, exemplified in Huntington's (1997) 'clash of civilisations' theory, which came into popular use during the US war against Afghanistan.

From this perspective it becomes clear that there are very immediate problems with the concept of a 'race relations' theory. Despite the many caveats employed by authors writing within the 'race relations' paradigm, it seems inevitable that the idea of 'race' becomes 'a fact' in the course of working with it as an autonomous social relation. Thus racism comes to be seen as a consequence of the interaction between so-called 'races' even when the scientific illegitimacy of the concept of 'race' is being emphasised in such analyses. Paul Gilroy (1998), in an article called 'Race ends here', argues explicitly that contemporary theorising about 'race' is complicit in the reification of racial difference. He posits the contradictions and limitations of anti-racist discourses and calls for a major re-thinking of strategies for tackling racial thinking and practices. It is crucial to remember, according to Gilroy, that 'race' is absurd as a principle of power, particularly in the age of molecular biology and body imaging: 'there will be individual differences, but that is not "race"' (Gilroy, 2000: 42).

Another critic of the 'race relations' research agenda is Robert Miles, for whom the object of analysis is not 'race relations' but rather racism, which he views as central to the process of capital accumulation (Miles, 1982; 1986). According to Miles, 'after "race relations" there is indeed another way of looking at social relations, a way that does not need to employ the idea of "race" as an analytical concept' (Miles, 1993: 1). While for 'race relations' theorists such as John Rex (1970) it is sufficient that the term 'race' is used in everyday talk as a basis for social action for him to address it analytically, Miles sees 'race' as an ideology that hides real economic relations.

Rather than accept the notion of 'race' as a given, Miles develops the idea of racialisation to refer to 'those instances where social relations between people have been structured by the significance of human biological characteristics' (Miles, 1989: 75). For Miles, the politics of 'race' are narrowly confined to the struggle against racism: it is not race but racism that is 'the modality in which class is lived and fought through' (Miles, 1988: 466; see also Hall, 1980: 314). Although Miles's linking racial to class differentiations may lead to class reductionism, his insistence on the intersection of racism with political and social regulation, making 'race' above all a *political* construct, is to be applauded.

Mac an Ghaill (1999) locates the shift between what he calls materialist identity politics and the politics of differentialist cultural difference in the emergence of identity as a key concept in late modernity. He suggests that the disintegration of older social collectivities – such as social class – has brought about a shift from essentialist understandings of ethnic identities to a more fluid sense of plural identities (Mac an Ghaill, 1999: 40-1). However, far from abandoning class analyses, Mac an Ghaill argues that new theoretical and empirical work of racialised minority ethnic groups and de-racialised ethnic majorities need to re-engage critically with earlier theoretical issues of class analysis in relation to the state, migration and social control. This approach must address concerns of the working class in an age of mass unemployment, mass migration and the emergence of an 'underclass' experiencing multiple exclusions (Mac an Ghaill, 1999: 6). Some theorists (e.g. Goldberg, 1990, 1993), concerned to avoid uniformity and homogeneity, have suggested incorporating post-structuralism into analyses of racism. One of the main results of this shift is the growing concern with *culture* as a focus of analyses of ethnicity in metropolitan settings. This emphasis on culture has engendered studies of racialised discourses in the media, literature, art and popular culture (e.g. Chambers, 1990; Cohen, 1992; Hall, 1992a; Brah, 1993; Hall, 1997) to examine the production and re-production of the social phenomena of racism. A number of studies recorded press coverage of racial questions and media portrayal of minority ethnic groups (e.g. Hall *et al*, 1978; van Dijk, 1991). If there has been a key trend in recent years, it is probably the movement towards a more complex ethnicisation of race and racism (see, for example, Donald and Rattansi, 1992; Bhabha, 1994; Werbner and Modood, 1997; Cohen, 1999; Hesse, 2000). However, arguing against the facile replacement of 'race' with 'ethnicity' or 'culture', Paul Gilroy argues that 'the culturalist versions of racial discourse – though superficially more benign than the cruder force of biological 'race' theory – are no less vicious or brutal than those on the receiving end of the cruelties and terrors they promote' (Gilroy, 2000: 34).

If, however, we are to theorise what has been dubbed 'cultural racism', we must note Salman Rushdie's *The Satanic Verses* (1989) as a focal point in understandings of cultural racisms in Britain: the attempt by some Muslim leaders in Britain and elsewhere to mobilise politically around the publication and the ensuing Iranian fatwa on Rushdie resulted in a heated debate about 'the future of race relations' in Britain (e.g. Modood, 1992). The rise of the political Right in Britain during the 1980s and 1990s occasioned a *new racism*, which Fanon had already referred to as *cultural racism*, which, linking racism with ethnicity and nationalism, presumed that Blackness and, say, Englishness, are reproduced as mutually exclusive (Gilroy, 1987: 55-6).

The sociology of 'race relations' was now being criticised for being conservative and Eurocentric in its failure to record the experiences of members of racialised ethnic groups and for seeing such groups as no more than the objects of other people's beliefs and behaviours. Tariq Modood (1992) develops this line of criticism to argue that the sociology of race relations occludes 'ethnicity', which 'race relations' theorists tend to regard as a 'quasi-group' whose existence depends upon its treatment by a dominant group. According to Modood, theorists such as Rex give little indication of how ethnographies of ethnic 'quasi-groups' relate theoretically to his paradigm of race relations as class conflict, and give no theoretical guidance on the relationship between the modes of being of an ethnic (quasi-) group and social domination and racial inequality. 'Race relations', according to Modood, is a misnomer, 'for there is no group interaction, only an analysis of white racism regardless of what is happening in the internal life of the non-white groups' (Modood, 1992: 50-1).

Modood further argues against the British race relations paradigm which privileges *colour* in determining the sociological profile of any non-white group which produces what he terms 'racial dualism', or the tendency to categorise everyone as either 'black' or 'white'. However, unlike Anthias and Yuval-Davis (1992) who problematise the categories 'black' and 'white', to include intra-racial ethnic groupings (particularly in relation to class and gender), Modood tends to merely add the category 'Asian' and/or 'Muslim' into the equation when speaking of Britain, a category which, like 'black' or 'white' is too general to include all the intra-ethnic groupings it may contain. Modood argues that colour, as well as class and culture, are all distinct dimensions of 'race'; thus the 'more distant an individual or group is from the norm of white middle-upper class British Christian/agnostic, the greater the marginality and exclusion' (Modood, 1992: 54; see also Werbner and Modood, 1997).

Feminist approaches to racism

A crucial theoretical intervention in the sociology of race comes from US and British feminists, members of minority ethnic groups (e.g. Carby, 1982; Amos and Parmar, 1984; Minh-ha, 1989; Hill-Collins, 1990; hooks, 1990; Williams, 1991; James and Busia, 1993; Bhavnani, 2001). While some early feminist work criticises the gender-neutrality of race sociologists, some of the more powerful critiques highlight Western feminism's focus on patriarchy as well as the ethnocentrism and racism within feminism itself (e.g. hooks, 1981; Amos and Parmar, 1984; Mohanty *et al*, 1991; in the Irish context see Janjua, 1997; Lentin, 1998a; 1998b). They argue that it is arrogant to assume any discussion of feminist theory without examining 'our many differences'. The black American writer Audre Lorde (2001: 89-92) rejects the tokenistic call by white women that women of colour (or in the case of Ireland, Traveller women and other minority women) educate them by sharing their experiences (see also McDonagh, 2000). According to the black American writer bell hooks, 'to black women the issue is not whether white women are more or less racist than white men, but that they are racist... Sexist discrimination has not prevented white women from assuming the dominant role in the perpetration of white racial imperialism, but it has not prevented white women from absorbing, supporting, and advocating racist ideology or acting individually as racist oppressors in various spheres of American life' (hooks, 2000: 376). As a result of debates in British feminist journals such as *Spare Rib* and *Feminist Review*, feminist sociologists (e.g. Anthias and Yuval-Davis, 1992; Brah, 1996) have been focusing on the *intersection* between racism and sexism and between gender, class and racial positionings in specific socio-economic contexts. This has engendered work on the position of migrant and racialised women and the impact of migration and nationality legislation on Black and ethnic minority women. Nira Yuval-Davis and Floya Anthias (1989, 1992; Yuval-Davis, 1997) have theorised gender and racialisation, linking constructions of gender to racism and to nationalist projects (see also Lutz *et al*, 1995, for example). Yuval-Davis argues that women are often in an ambivalent position within nations and ethnic groups:

> On the one hand, they often symbolise the collectivity's unity, honour and the raison d'etre of specific national and ethnic projects, like going to war. On the other hand, however, they are often excluded from the collective 'we' of the

body politic, and retain an object rather than subject position... In this sense the construction of womanhood has a property of 'otherness'. Strict cultural codes of what it is to be a 'proper woman' are often developed to keep women in this inferior position (Yuval-Davis, 1997: 47).

In the Irish context, the late Indian-Irish feminist Gretchen Fitzgerald (1992) was the pioneer with her seminal work *Repulsing Racism* published as part of the Attic Press 'Lip' series. Other contributors to the debate on the gendered aspects of racism in Ireland were Victorian Chan (1996), Shalini Sinha (1997) and Shahida Janjua (1997) who all wrote about the position of feminists of colour in Ireland.

Beside academic writings on gender and race, fiction and essays by Black and minority women (e.g. Morrison, 1988 and 1992) 'give voice' to Black women as does research on slavery and colonialism (e.g. Corcoran Nantes, 1997; Thomas, 1997; Bakare-Yusuf, 1997, to give but very few examples) and on the sexuality of minority women and the often unconscious sexualisation of racism (e.g. Cohen, 1988; 1993; Marshall, 1996).

Racism and inequality

Much sociological and public policy research has understandably focused on the way in which racist ideologies and practices structure social inequalities, despite the fact that *racism* and *racial discrimination* are not necessarily synonymous. Many writers warn against the 'conceptual inflation' (Miles, 1989) of using the blanket term *racism*, or *institutionalised racism* to explain all such inequalities. Anthias and Yuval-Davis (1992) posit racism as occurring when the construction of 'otherness' is used in order to either exclude or exploit. Wieviorka (1997) argues that racism includes both elements: inferioritisation, leading to a social relation of domination, and differentiation, leading to the rejection of the Other, and ultimately to violence and even genocide. Floya Anthias (1999) links the concept of institutionalised racism with notions of 'unwitting racism' as it exists in cultures of powerful organisations such as police forces.

The bulk of research in industrialised societies has concentrated on racially and ethnically based inequalities in housing, employment, education, and social welfare and on measures to combat these inequalities, rather than on 'unwitting' forms of institutionalised racism. Of primary importance here is the role which processes of discrimination play in the racialisation of poverty. One of the most important features of recent policy debates about 'race' have centred on the question of the 'underclass'. This term was first coined by Myrdal (1962) to mean a group of people at the bottom of the class structure, permanently removed from the labour market and with no economic power, usually taken, in the USA, to mean the Black urban poor. In Britain there has been growing interest in the underclass, due to work by Charles Murray and other neo-conservatives who fuel fears that Britain's 'inner cities' may follow the American example. Similar fears, albeit not directly related to the creation of an 'underclass', are voiced in Ireland in relation to the housing of refugees in city centre or rural areas. See, for example, *Irish Times* columnist Kevin Myers arguing in 1998 that allowing more refugees into Ireland would cause ghettoising and racism: 'We can listen and we can learn from the experiences of others. We must have controls over immigration... And we should certainly not expect the least advantaged and least educated communities in Dublin and elsewhere to be the sole unassisted hosts of ghettos and newcomers. Down that road lies certain disaster' (Myers, 1998: 15).

Much of the equal opportunities literature in the British context tends to be based on the 'race relations industry' where there is a huge amount of research generated by the Race Relations Act and its related Commission for Racial Equality (CRE) alongside local and regional council initiatives on racial equality. Modood *et al*'s *Ethnic Minorities in Britain* (1997) is the contemporary classic in this genre and the latest in the line of reviews of the effectiveness of race relations as required by the Race Relations Act (1976). Ireland is also beginning to witness the onset of a 'race relations' industry, as argued in chapters 14 and 15, in the form of government-led anti-racism awareness programmes, anti-racism training programmes and a growing body of research which positions ethnic minorities under a microscope of separatist interrogation.

Racism and anti-racism

Recently the new politics of 'race' have meant that social scientists have begun theorising what is popularly called anti-racism (e.g. Cohen and Bains, 1988; Anthias and Yuval-Davis, 1992; Gilroy, 1990; Cohen, 1992; Rattansi, 1992; Goldberg, 1993; Solomos, 1993; Wieviorka, 1997; Modood, 1997; Modood and Werbner, 1997; Bonnet, 1997, 2000). The main questions asked by social scientists in this regard are what is meant by anti-racism in the contemporary political environment, and what strategies need to be engaged in to tackle racism. Contemporary anti-racism is a controversial concept despite the legacy of anti-racist movements in the 1950s and 1960s, during the high point of anti-colonialist and anti-imperialist movements in many majority world countries. The impact of Nazism and the Holocaust has been another influence on the resolve of anti-racists to act against the activities of expanding extreme Right and neo-Nazi movements in several European countries. However, anti-racism has been under-researched in the social sciences and as a result, the term tends to be used rather indiscriminately (see Alana Lentin, 2000).

In recent years, with the recognition of the complexities of ethnic make-up as well as the deconstruction of the formerly homogeneous categories 'black' and 'white', there has also been a renewed focus on antisemitism (see for example the Institute of Jewish Policy Research's journal *Patterns of Prejudice* and annual publication *Antisemitism World Report* as well as contributors to Cheyette and Marcus's collection *Modernity, Culture and 'The Jew'*, 1998; in the Irish context see Keogh, 1998; Goldstone, 1999; 2000).

Other new developments of particular interest for us are works on anti-Irish racism, in particular Hickman and Walter's (1997) empirical work for the CRE, which lays to rest the debate around whether or not anti-Irish racism exists in British society. This work develops earlier, more political and theoretical work (Curtis, 1984; Hickman, 1995; see also Mac an Ghaill, 1999). Together with work on anti-Gypsyism and Islamophobia, this work highlights the capacity of so-called 'white' minority groups to experience racism. At the same time, the old categories of 'black' have been deconstructed to include other people of colour (see work on 'new ethnicities', particularly emanating from the Centre for New Ethnicities Research at the University of East London, but also Anthias, 1992; Hall, 1992b; Back, 1996; and Brah, 1996, among others).

Racism and popular culture

It is impossible to understand contemporary racisms without understanding the cultural mechanisms that enable their expression. Although there is not a lot of research on the role of popular culture in promulgating racism, there is considerable research on the role of the media in shaping the images of 'race' and in encouraging racism (e.g. van Dijk, 1991, 1993; see also Guerin, and White, in this volume).

Following Bauman's argument, which links racism with modernity (in his seminal *Modernity and the Holocaust*, 1989, Bauman uses sociological tools to argue that the Holocaust was a direct consequence, rather than an aberration, of modernity), Solomos and Back (1996) argue that racist ideas have gone hand in hand with technological advancement. Popular culture is of course not uniform in its role in popularising racial imagery. Instead it is both 'the locus for the expression of racism' and a 'site where the efficacy of racist images can be challenged'.

There was a clear link between racism, popular culture and propaganda in Germany during the Third Reich. Nazi popular culture needs to be viewed through the lens of Auschwitz (Adams, 1992): representing Jewish victims in Nazi posters and cartoons as decadent and as vermin contrasted with the re-invention of the Aryan character within art, film, sculpture and architecture. According to George Mosse (1985: xii), racism during Nazi times was 'a visual ideology based upon stereotypes... racism classified men and women: this gave it clarity and simplicity essential to its success'. Likewise, Hall (1997) demonstrates how racialised images in advertising, popular literature and cinema helped maintain the cultural hegemony of British imperialism.

Paul Gilroy (2000: 75) stresses the link between Nazi antisemitic ideology and anti-black racism and between 'the genocidal terrors perpetrated inside Europe and the patterns of colonial and imperial slaughter that preceded them under Europe's colours but outside its continental boundaries'. Indeed, images of Black minorities after 1945 reflect the ambivalence about Black presence in European societies as posing serious moral and political dangers. Media discourses in recent years present the shift from colour coded racisms and a preoccupation with 'racial crime' to a dual representation of minority ethnic groups as both 'a problem' and as experiencing injustice and discrimination that are 'morally offensive' (Hulme, 1986; Gilroy, 1987). At its most basic, photography, as used by the news media and the advertising industry, serves to foreground racial and ethnic difference as can be seen, for instance, in media representations of Black sports people (Hall, 1997). New technology cultural media such as the Internet (a major recruiting instrument for far right organisations), but also advertising, television and the cinema, can serve to express contemporary racisms and at the same time convey 'critical discourses that unsettle and undermine racist regimes of representation' (Solomos and Back, 1996: 200).

The Racialisation of Irishness

The development of racism is never an accident. There are particular reasons for its existence and reproduction. In the Irish context there are different processes that serve to explain the development and role of racism in Ireland (McVeigh, 1992a). The beginnings of an answer to the question why Irish people are racist can be found in the fact that racism assumes specifically Irish forms. However, this does not suggest that all racism in Ireland is rooted in the characteristics of Irishness. Clearly, from the earliest examples of the racialisation of European consciousness, Irish people have been part of and learnt from more general trends. Thus, as early as 1757, the influential Irish philosopher Edmund Burke was able to speculate on the topic of 'darkness terrible in its own nature' in his famous essay on the sublime and the beautiful. Burke relates the story of a boy who was born blind and then gains his sight after a cataract operation. He provides an early example of the assumed 'naturalness' of racism and racialised otherness:

> Among many remarkable particulars that attended his first perceptions and judgements on visual objects … the first time the boy saw a Black object it gave him great uneasiness; and that some time after, upon accidentally seeing a Negro woman, he was struck with great horror at the sight. The horror, in this case, can scarcely be supposed to arise from any association (Burke, 1909: 121).

So, at one level, the racialisation of Irish consciousness was little different from that which occurred across Europe from the beginning of European colonial expansion. In addition, as we have argued above, racism is also affected by class and gender and other structuring elements which are present in any society – in this sense too Irish racism is little different from other forms of European racism.

Irish racism is also structured, however, by other elements and forces that are peculiar to Ireland and to Irishness. There are two overlapping processes here – firstly, the *racialisation of Irishness* and, secondly, the development of the *specificity of Irish racism*. The racialisation of Irishness saw a specific positioning of Irishness – both subjectively and objectively – in hierarchies of race and ethnicity. The specificity of Irish racism is intimately connected to the particular dynamics of racism within this process of racialisation in Ireland and among Irish people. A key defining component here was the existence of anti-Irish racism, which has always crucially structured the way in which Irish people themselves are racist (see McVeigh's chapter 9 in this volume). This has encouraged a specific form of *subordinate privilege* of Irishness – for example, Irish people often benefited from their role within the British Empire yet remained clearly subordinate within the imperial chain. Irish people have 'made it' economically and politically as an ethnic group in the USA, yet remain outside the 'WASP' establishment.

There are a number of different dimensions to Irishness, north and south, which encourage the racialisation of Irishness and account for the specificity of Irish racism (McVeigh, 1992a, 1996). Broadly, these can be dichotomised in terms of *historical legacy* and *contemporary location*. The attention to historical legacy recognises the specific location of Ireland in terms of the wider colonial expansion that first gave rise to racism. Of particular importance, obviously, was the relationship of Ireland to British imperialism and its attendant racism. The peoples of Bombay and Belfast, Dublin and Durban were bound together by their supposed role within the great chain that was the British Empire. The Irish Diaspora also took place in this context and established Irish blocs in each of settler colonial formations created by British colonialism – in North America, Australasia and South Africa. This created Irish settler blocs which in turn created racialised interfaces between Irish people and other colonised and indigenous people – Native Americans and African Americans in the USA, Chinese and Aboriginal Australians in Australia, and so on.

Equally, however, it created a racialised interface between these Irish blocs and the dominant white, British settler bloc. The attention to the contemporary location of Ireland, north and south, draws on this historical legacy but also sees different and newer reasons for racialisation. For example, Irishness may be still influenced by Britishness but it also learns from other European and North American sources. The position of Ireland, north and south, inside a 'Fortress Europe' built by the European Union to exclude the peoples of the Majority World is one such source. This gives the Irish a new structural relationship with other colonised peoples and potential 'immigrants', a relationship that is immediately racialised. Likewise the empowerment of Irish emigrant blocs in countries of settlement like the USA and Australia makes them capable of new forms of racism.

The much-vaunted 'Celtic tiger' phenomenon (denoting the economic boom of the 1990s in the south of Ireland) has marked the gap between Ireland and other former colonial formations. It is not an accident that the rise in racism in Ireland has accompanied a growing prosperity for sections of the Irish people. In combination then, the historical legacy and contemporary location create a specific dialectic that begins to explain contemporary Irish racism.

The historical legacy and the racialisation of Irishness

Through much of their history Irish people have necessarily made sense of the world through the filter of other people's perceptions of that world. Historically, this means that Ireland experienced and learned from British racism in the high colonial period. As the rest of world became racialised in its use of discourse, so did Ireland. Irish people found a specific place in the British colonial process. While British imperialism was the principal cause of the Irish diaspora, it also created the colonial polities within which settlement took place. Other Irish people worked directly in the service of the British Empire – as soldiers but also as missionaries and administrators. In combination these processes led to the establishment of Irish blocs in Britain, in the USA and Canada, in Australia and New Zealand, and in South Africa. These Irish communities were placed and continue to exist in specific relations to indigenous peoples and to other immigrant groups.

The gradual empowerment of Irish emigrant blocs saw a parallel racialisation of their relationship with other minority ethnic groups. Each of these relations has assumed specifically racist forms. Firstly, there was an immediate encounter between

Irish people and indigenous people. It was an Irish emigrant – General Phillip Sheridan from Killinkere in County Cavan – who gave voice to the genocidal maxim 'the only good Indian is a dead Indian'. The Irish also found themselves in new relationships with other ethnic blocs in different settler colonial societies. For example, the Irish-American community found itself in a particular relationship with African Americans. It is not insignificant that an Irish name, 'Lynch', came to characterise racist murder. This is emblematic of a wider struggle between African Americans and Irish Americans (Ignatiev, 1995). Certainly it is striking how quickly starving Irish refugees found a location in the American labour market which reinforced ethnic solidarity and encouraged many of them to become racist and pro-employer. Irish people colluded in the segregation and de-skilling of the African American community; there was no simple solidarity between Irish famine refugees and African Americans despite the Irish experience of colonial oppression.

We find subsequent American racism replete with traces of Irishness. There is no doubting the ethnicity of Joseph McCarthy – architect of 'McCarthyism', US xenophobia at its worst – or Eugene 'Bull' Connor – most notorious of all the southern US opponents of Black civil rights, nor the avowed antisemitism of senator Joseph Kennedy, UN ambassador and father of President John F. Kennedy.

Sometimes the Irish dimensions to expressions of racism were explicit – and often in bizarrely contradictory ways. For example, policing was racialised in terms of the specific role of the American Irish community but it was also racist in its treatment of Black people. This racialised interface is not just significant in terms of Black/Irish relations in the countries of the Diaspora – the experiences are also important in the construction of minority ethnic people in Ireland. This process remains extremely important as the Irish Diaspora continues. This diasporic racism is often 'repatriated' through continuing contact with Ireland, especially when Irish emigrants return home. This repatriated racism has always been 'made sense' of in specific ways through particular forces in Ireland. One historical example of the repatriation of racism is Fr John Creagh, director of the Limerick Redemptorist arch-confraternity who, after spending some years in England and France, imported French antisemitism to Limerick. The consequence (as discussed by Lentin, chapter 10 in this volume) was the 1904-6 Limerick pogrom, which resulted in the decimation of the Jewish community in Limerick. The Limerick pogrom also provides a good example of how Irish racism can be reworked out through sectarian division. Louis Hyman (1972) records how:

> With two or three exceptions, the community was pauperised. The Protestants of the city espoused its cause and opened relief funds, but this only intensified the rancour of the Redemptorists and of the Community of the Holy Family. The attack mounted and, through no fault of their own, the Jews became a kind of buffer between two antagonists; they asked that no further subscriptions be canvassed among Protestant sympathisers, and the anti-Jewish campaign in the press was ignored (Hyman, 1972: 214).

This is illustrative of the way in which racism became fused with other forces in Ireland. Another infamous example is Arthur Griffith's justification of John Mitchel's well-documented racism. While Mitchel's racism was a product of the Diaspora, Griffith brought it very firmly 'back home'. In his introduction to Mitchell's *The Jail Journal*, Griffith attacks those who attempted to 'excuse' Mitchel's views on slavery:

> His views on Negro-slavery have been deprecatingly excused, as if excuse were needed for an Irish nationalist declining to hold the Negro his peer in right (Griffith, 1982: 368).

Griffith also proved an active antisemite during the Limerick pogrom of 1904-6. If Griffith's racism is an example of the way that nationalism – an internal, Irish discourse – can reproduce racism, there are plenty of examples of how Irish Unionism is equally capable of generating racist ideas. The ease with which Enoch Powell – prime mover of the 'new racism' in Britain in the 1960s – was adopted by the Ulster Unionist Party as MP for South Down from 1974 until 1987 is an obvious example (McVeigh, 1998b: 19-22). There are elements within Irish Nationalism and Unionism which reinforce different oppressions rather than challenging or showing solidarity with them. Moreover, there are elements of Irish nationalism and unionism which encouraged racism through inherent xenophobia. Each of the competing nationalisms on the island of Ireland – Irish, British, Ulster – has been capable of actively reproducing racism.

The relationship between nationalism and racism assumed new forms, as each nationalism assumed a level of political autonomy in Ireland – in the south this culminated in independence from Britain, in the north in devolved government. This new autonomy created new opportunities for empowerment. For starters there is the ethnic homogeneity of 'Irishness' itself as constructed, for example, by the 1937 Constitution of the Republic of Ireland. According to Kelly (1988: 211), Ireland's Taoiseach Eamon de Valera, the architect of the Constitution, was 'unquestionably both courteous and not only just but generous in his approach to minority traditions, but his Constitution seems almost deliberately designed to alienate them'. The preamble to the Constitution,[3] according to the Constitution Review Group (1996: 4), is 'overly Roman Catholic and nationalistic in tone'. Dermot Keogh (1988) documents de Valera's complex consultation process with Catholic church leaders to ensure that the Constitution was based on Catholic principles, despite the recognition, in Article 44, of 'non-Catholic Christian denominations, the Jewish Congregation... (and) other religious denominations existing at the date of the coming into operation of this Constitution'. The resulting document conflates Irish identity with Irish-Catholic identity and constructs difference in religious, rather than ethnic terms (Lentin, 1998a: 10). In the north, the hegemony of unionism allowed little space for any minority communities – Irish, Jewish or Traveller (Farrell, 1980; Noonan, 1998; Warm, 1998). Northern Ireland Prime Minister James Craig had infamously celebrated: 'All I boast of is that we are a Protestant Parliament and a Protestant State' (cited in Hepburn, 1980: 165); this was a cold house for more than Catholics.

In the case of antisemitism, political prejudice dovetailed neatly with the religious antisemitism of the Catholic Church. Until Vatican Two in 1965 the Church ruled that

Jews were collectively responsible for the death of Jesus (Hyman, 1972: 347; see also Mac Gréil's surveys, 1978, 1996; and Lentin, chapter 10 in this volume). If Catholicism carried an inherent antisemitic racism (see Keogh, 1998 and Goldstone, chapter 11 in this volume), it also manifested elements of anti-black racism in a specifically religious phenomenon. This is illustrated by the collections for 'Black Babies', which were until recently a ubiquitous feature of Irish church propaganda. The 'Black Babies' phenomenon conditioned Irish Catholic people to regard black people in a particular way – as passive victims who could only be saved by the good offices of the Catholic Church. However, the experiences of black-Irish children in Catholic institutions run by religious orders such as the Christian Brothers and Sisters of Mercy have not received any specific attention even during the late 1990s media coverage of the abuse of children in the orphanages and children's homes run by these orders. For instance, Christine Buckley, a Nigerian-Irish former inmate of the Sisters of Mercy's Goldenbridge orphanage was called, among other things, 'Black bastard' by the nuns, but her racialisation went unnoticed in the substantial media coverage of the filmed account of Goldenbridge (Louis Lentin, 1996).

While the Catholic Church in Ireland may not have been implicated in the process of western military and political imperialism and its accompanying racist ideology, it certainly was implicated in a specifically Catholic western religious imperialism. The relationship of the Protestant bloc in Ireland to western imperialism, particularly, of course, British imperialism, was even less ambiguous. Although Presbyterian radicalism at the turn of the eighteenth century ensured that Belfast would not benefit from the slave trade, subsequent developments within the Protestant bloc produced general support for, and involvement in, the process of British colonialism. This encouraged a more thorough racism among some unionists and loyalists and still surfaces in different ways that are, once again, often articulated to sectarianism. This ill-focused racism has also manifested in the overlap between loyalism and British racist and fascist groups (McVeigh, 1998b: 22-3). Once again we see how racism has been fused with internal Irish processes – Protestant and Catholic, unionist and nationalist, religious and political. Thus, we have to move beyond explaining Irish racism in terms of simply learning from elsewhere. This is even more clearly illustrated by the existence of older racisms in Ireland directed against Travellers, Jews and Black Irish people.

Endogenous Irish racism

While racism in Ireland has become pronounced in the late 1990s with the moral panic provoked by the arrival of (very few) asylum-seekers and refugees to Ireland south and north (see Nozinic, chapter 4 in this volume), we do not understand it as a new phenomenon. Rather, Ireland was never the monoculture it told itself it was. Racism against existing indigenous minorities, in particular Travellers, Jews and black Irish people, had always existed. Indeed, the tendency to target racist intentions and actions as originating by the presence of incoming outgroups is easier than attributing it to the 'host' majority, as Phil Cohen argues: 'The Other has to be imagined, even if not represented. The discourse of ethnocentrism and xenophobia can handle that task only as long as it is still plausible to locate the Other as coming form outside rather than inside' (Cohen, 1993: 18).

Even numerically, contemporary Ireland can no longer be thought of, and think of itself, as a monoculture. Because an ethnicity question has not yet been included in the census of population in the Republic of Ireland (it was included in the 2001 census in the north), numbers of members of minority ethnic groups can only be guestimates. According to McVeigh (1996: 22), there were some 45,000 people of colour in Ireland north and south in 1996. The Irish-Jewish community north and south probably numbered approximately 1,800 people at the beginning of the 1990s (according to the latest census figures in 1991 there were 1581 Jewish people in the south and 230 in the north. Since then, several hundred young Jews have emigrated from the south, but several hundred Jews have arrived as labour migrants, particularly in the high tech industries, again, figures can only be guessed). The Irish Traveller community numbers around 30,000 people in both parts of Ireland. In combination, we estimate that there were some 75,000 minority ethnic people in Ireland, around 1.5 per cent of the population in 1996. Since 1997, with a net in-migration (albeit made up mostly of returning Irish emigrants) of 66,000 (compared with 200,000 emigrants in the 1980s; Wren, 2000: 14), and with the arrival of some 38,662 asylum-seekers (based on the number of asylum applications from 1991 to the end of November 2001; source: Office of the Refugee Application Commissioner, 2001, personal communication) plus a number of people of colour from other EU states and a growing number of undocumented workers from elsewhere, we can hazard a guess that at the end of 2001 there were at least 200,000 members of minority ethnic groups in Ireland, north and south, although we must re-emphasise, these figures can only be guestimates.[4]

In preparation for the 2002 census in the south, a limited nationality question was piloted; people were asked whether they are Irish, Irish Traveller, British or 'other ethnic origin' (Mac Connell, 1999: 2). Such a question might have given the Central Statistics Office more accurate information of the number of Travellers in the south, but it leaves those who do not fall into the three first definitions scope for self-definition. It also implies, for instance, that one cannot be 'Traveller' and 'Irish', nor both 'Irish' and 'British' at the same time. However, it was decided not to include an ethnicity question in the south in the 2002 census. Asking an ethnicity census question is problematic, precisely because of the shifting, multi-layered, multi-faceted nature of ethnicity, but without a more clearly defined ethnicity question, arriving at an accurate estimate of the number of minority ethnic people is impossible, nor is it possible to plan for appropriate service provision for members of minority ethnic groups (for a discussion of some of the issues involved, see Bochain, 1990).

Much of the racism in Ireland is now focused on the Other 'inside' – it is an 'endogenous' racism. Anti-Traveller racism is perhaps the definitive example of this. Travellers are an indigenous, nomadic, minority ethnic group in Ireland (McCann *et al*, 1994; O'Connell, chapter 2 in this volume). The prejudice, discrimination and violence experienced by Travellers can clearly be characterised as racism (DTEDG *et al*, 1993; McVeigh, 1992b). The issue of anti-Traveller racism has been brought into sharp focus by a number of unrestrained attacks on Travellers. Witness Mary Ellen Synon describing Traveller 'lifestyle' under the banner headline 'Time to get tough on tinker terror "culture"':

> It is a life of appetite ungoverned by intellect. It is a life which marauds over private property and disregards public laws. It is a life of money without production, land without cost, damage without compensation, assault without arrest, theft without prosecution, and murder without remorse. It is a life worse than the life of beasts, for beasts at least are guided by wholesome instinct. Traveller life is without the ennobling intellect of man or the steadying instinct of animals. This tinker 'culture' is without achievement, discipline, reason or intellectual ambition (Synon, 1996).

While this kind of diatribe is particularly shocking in the way it echoes Nazi racist propaganda, it is a manifestation of much broader anti-Traveller racism in Ireland. The colonisation of Irish Traveller identity was and is carried out by other Irish people – it cannot be blamed on external colonial forces (however, see Ní Shúinéar, chapter 13 in this volume for an argument that othering Travellers owes to the Irish having been othered by the British). Moreover the effects of this process are transparent – they are not simply 'hidden' or 'internalised' but are shockingly tangible in the unequal status of Travellers in Ireland. As Paul Noonan points out:

> Being a Traveller ... involves low life expectancy, high infant mortality and morbidity, low educational achievement, appalling living conditions and differential access to a range of state services. Clearly these outcomes cannot be viewed as a result of individual antipathies. The evidence of these obvious disparities is ipso facto evidence of discrimination, racism and institutional culpability (Noonan, 1994: 145).

The inequality experienced by Travellers can no longer be dismissed as a consequence of nomadism or by processes of pathologising Traveller culture. Indeed, the one major contribution which Irish analysis has made to wider debates around ethnicity and racism has been the dedicated work on anti-Traveller racism. This contribution has been both theoretical and practical (see McVeigh's chapter 14 in this volume). It has theorised the racialisation of a minority ethnic group that is marked by both its 'whiteness' and its nomadism but it has also developed a whole series of anti-racist projects designed to mainstream Traveller equality issues. These interventions have transformed the context in which Traveller inequality is understood. It is now difficult to argue against the thesis that Traveller disadvantage occurs because sedentary Irish society in general – and the state in Ireland in particular – discriminates against Travellers, routinely, structurally and in a racist manner. This has significant wider implications for understanding Irish racism. Most importantly, it confirms that Ireland has long had its own endogenous, organic racism, a racism that cannot be treated merely as an undesirable 'foreign' import.

If we revisit Irish antisemitism and anti-black racism in the light of this analysis of endogenous anti-Traveller racism, we find that these 'old' racisms were intimately connected to Irishness itself. They cannot simply be dismissed as 'imports': while structured by external processes, they are firmly rooted in Irishness. Thus, even before we engage in detail with the manifestations of 'new' Irish racism – against people of colour and refugees – we find that this has developed out of older Irish racisms – sometimes focused on people of colour but more particularly concerned with Travellers and Jews. Moreover, the relationship between these two 'old' and 'new' racisms is more than arbitrary – xenophobia and racism forged through antisemitism and anti-Travellerism finds convenient new targets in the people of colour and refugee communities of contemporary Ireland. Neither, however, is this to suggest a seamless transition from one to the other. There is no doubt that the 'new racism' of the late 1990s onwards reflects a new Ireland in the same period – more confident, more prosperous and situated in a new structural location *vis-à-vis* Europe and the rest of the world.

The contemporary location of Ireland – racism and subordinate privilege

We have already seen how Ireland stood in a particular relationship to the process of imperialism and colonisation and how this relationship racialised the Irish sense of self and otherness. This process is no less important in terms of contemporary Ireland. Ireland is empowered in a number of ways because of its structural location. It is empowered in terms of its whiteness; it is empowered in terms of its Europeaness; it is empowered in terms of its relationship with Irish blocs in other racialised polities like the USA, Canada, Australia and New Zealand. Over the past few years political leaders of each of these countries have been strongly identified as Irish. Moreover, many of these individuals have achieved power – to an extent at least – through the mobilisation of a distinctive Irish emigrant bloc. This empowerment extends well beyond the upper echelons of politics with identifiable Irish influence in the churches, trades unions and business. Most notably, of course, Irish America is one of the most important political blocs in the USA. Yet Irish American empowerment remains partial and still sits uncomfortably in terms of the WASP establishment.

This is emblematic of a wider *subordinate privilege* that characterises Irish identity and lends further specificity to Irish racism. Although the Republic of Ireland is placed 17th of the world's richest nations and rising, Ireland is not situated in the upper echelons of the 'new world order'. Rather Ireland finds itself in a contradictory location between the empowered and the disempowered – 'between two worlds' (O'Hearn, 1994). There is no better example of this contradictory location than with culture – Ireland exists in a situation of cultural dependency – much popular culture in Ireland is received passively from Britain and the USA. Despite the strength of contemporary Irish popular culture, at any one time approximately two-thirds of the content of Irish television is either British or American, the majority of the papers read by Irish people are British. This creates a kind of 'cultural osmosis' – Irish ideas about ethnicity and racism are crucially structured by British and American culture – yet there is no reciprocal process – Irish ideas about ethnicity and racism do not penetrate British or American consciousness. There is a racist subtext to British and American culture, which undoubtedly has its effects in Ireland. The subordination of the Irish media makes Ireland particularly vulnerable to racialisation from these sources. The racist abuse of black sports people – which has occurred in both parts of Ireland – is one obvious example (McVeigh 1996: 27). So even at the ideological level, the structural location of contemporary Ireland has obvious effects in terms of the racialisation of Irishness. This becomes even clearer when we turn to more tangible legal and political structures that continue to privilege Irish people in particular ways. Each one of these privileges encourages Irish people to adopt racialised interpretations of the world order and the benefits of the contemporary world hierarchy of 'race' and class.

One example of this is the specific position given to Irish people within successive British Nationality Acts. This gave Irish people privileged access beyond those of (mostly black) Commonwealth citizens despite the fact that (overwhelmingly white) Ireland had withdrawn from the Commonwealth.

Other privileges are most tangible in Ireland's membership of the European Union. Different measures have served to racialise the whole of the EU as 'Fortress Europe' (Refugee Forum, 1991). The Dublin Convention widened the 1985 Schengen Agreement provisions on asylum to cover all of the EU. This agreement attempted to harmonise the response to asylum-seekers in Europe to ensure that a refugee refused in one member state would be refused in all member states. It also created the Schnegen Information System (SIS) to monitor 'suspicious' persons. In combination, these EU provisions have served to integrate member states' policy in a profoundly racist way and keep 'Europe's immigrant, migrant, refugee and Black communities in thrall, unfree, more controlled and policed than ever before' (Refugee Forum, 1991: 16). On 27 November 2000 the European Commission published a paper on minimum standards for the reception of applicants for asylum in member states. Critiquing the European Commission paper, the European Council on Refugees and Exiles (ECRE, 2001) proposed that the EU approach to harmonisation should not be based on minimum standards, but should also harmonise good practice (www.ecre.org/observations/minimum). However, harmonisation seems to mean greater – albeit coordinated – restrictions on immigration and asylum, resulting, among other things, in agreements between the British and French governments on the imposition of travel documentation even when travelling inside France (Paris-Calais) in the potential direction of Britain; and in lowering the numbers of asylum-seekers allowed to board the Le Havre-Rosslare ferry to apply for asylum in Ireland, to mention but two examples.

It is emblematic of this process that with the Dublin Convention, Ireland has already lent its name of its capital to one racist EU anti-refugee agreement. In contrast to the commitment to co-ordinate racist immigration policies, the European Union has shown no rush to integrate its approach to protection from racism. In effect there is nothing in EU law on racism that even approaches the effectiveness of the law against gender discrimination. The proposal tabled by the Austrian EU presidency in 1998 called on the EU to rescind the Geneva Convention and withdraw asylum as a legal status based on right, and offer instead only temporary protection. Ireland's record on asylum is dismal ever since its refusal to admit more than 60 Jewish refugees from Nazi Europe between 1933 and 1945 (see Lentin, chapter 10 in this volume). Not surprisingly, Ireland did not figure at all in EU asylum rate tables according to which Germany granted 96,000, Sweden granted 114,500, France granted 60,000, Britain granted 41,000, and Denmark granted 12,500 people refugee status or temporary leave to remain between 1990 and 1995 (Travis, 1998: 19). According to the UN High Commission for Refugees (UNHCR), in 1999 Ireland had 3.1 per cent of all European asylum applications, compared with 23.6 per cent in the UK and 22 per cent in Germany (cited by Haughey, 1999b: 6). According to more recent media reports (indicating the extent of the continuing moral panic regarding asylum-seekers), Ireland took in fewer asylum-seekers in the first nine months of 2000 than Britain, Germany, Belgium, Sweden or France (O'Toole, 2001). Thus membership of the EU brings Ireland within the ambit of further racist structures without the compensation of further anti-racist structures. In the wake of the September 11 2001 attack on the US and the declared 'war against terror', the Council of Europe, coupling policies on terrorism and on asylum, has in its meeting in Laeken in December 2001, resolved to adopt a common policy on asylum and immigration, which, while avowedly protecting refugees in accordance with the principles of the 1951 Geneva Convention, aims to institute 'a mechanism of control of external borders' (Staunton, 2001: 10). Ireland did not beg to differ.

As Ireland rushes to place itself at the heart of Europe, it simultaneously places itself at the heart of European racism. The Republic of Ireland's racist attitude towards asylum-seekers manifested itself clearly in recent years. In 1998 4,626 asylum-seekers came to Ireland. Of these merely 82 (plus 90 following appeal) were granted refugee status, and 2,048 had their applications rejected. In 1999 7,724 people applied for asylum of whom a mere 10 were granted refugee status, and 196 were refused. In all, at the end of 1999 there were 8,725 asylum cases awaiting a hearing. In 2000 10,938 people applied for asylum, and in 2001 to the end of November there were 9,365 applications; by the end of 2001 9,339 applications were awaiting recommendations (Haughey, 1999b: 6; Office of the Refugee Application Commissioner, 2001 – personal communication). The bulk of the £4.2m spent by the government on asylum-seekers went towards the building of a 'one-stop-shop' for asylum applications. At the same time, the Irish Refugee Council depended on grants from the Department of Justice, Equality and Law Reform, although it was the only group providing asylum-seekers with independent legal advice and representation.[5] In January 2001, the government announced a new body, the Reception and Integration Agency (replacing the Directorate for Asylum Support Services and the Refugee Agency), which will offer services to asylum-seekers and cater for the integration of people granted refugee status. Like other such bodies, the new body is directed by senior civil servants; it is chaired by a Galway auctioneer and insurance agent and board members include the social partners, civil servants and one former asylum-seeker from the Democratic Republic of Congo (Haughey, 2001b).

In 1999 the Immigration (Trafficking) Bill brought forward legislation in the south to enable the Minister of Justice, Equality and Law Reform to deport non-nationals and act against carriers (including ferry companies and airlines, who, according to the act, are to be fined for each illegal entrant). After being unable to effect deportations on the wake of the Laurentiu ruling in the High Court and subsequently the Supreme Court, when the respective judges ruled that the Minister's deportation powers stemmed not from legislation enacted by the Oireachtas but rather from a ministerial order, the Minister was forced to legislate on deportation. The second part of the Immigration Bill is an amendment of the 1996 Refugee Act. While there were no deportations in 1996 and eight deportations in 1997, in 1998 the rate of deportations of rejected asylum-seekers was beginning to gather pace as close to 300 deportations were signed by the Minister for Justice towards the end of 1998. In 2000 5,852 people were refused entry to Ireland by immigration officers; almost half because they did not have 'valid' travel documents' (despite the glaring fact that asylum-seekers rarely possess 'valid' travel documents). The Refugee Act (1996) was amended in 2000 and since then, the Minister for Justice made 1,132 deportation orders and 222 people were deported between July 1999 and February 2001. The total number of people deported in 2000 was 187, including 147 whose application for refugee status was rejected. However, only one in five failed asylum-seekers against whom deportation orders were made has been actually deported, according to the Minister (Haughey, 2001c: 9).

Increased staffing in the asylum section of the Department of Justice, Equality and Law Reform (140 new staff were recruited in 1998) apparently had the sole result of increased deportation rates. Gardai escorted some of the deported to other EU states or to their countries of origin, but because most had no legal representation, there was no tracking of their circumstances following deportations (Cullen, 1998a: 9). In October 1998 the Church of Ireland synod heard predictions of mass deportations of asylum-seekers based on racist attitudes 'not worthy of any civilised nation at the end of the 20th century'. Synod spokespersons felt that by accelerating the deportation pace, the Minister was fulfilling his own prediction that 90 per cent of asylum applications were 'bogus' and would inevitably end in deportation (McGarry, 1998: 10). Various high-ranking clergy, both Catholic and Protestant, have since made similar comments. In order to facilitate the return of failed asylum-seekers to the two largest countries of origin, Romania and Nigeria, the Irish government has signed readmission agreements with the two countries (Haughey, 2001e: 4). Ironically, on his way to the World Conference Against Racism in Durban, South Africa in summer 2001, the Minister for Justice called in Nigeria to sign the agreement. In the wake of the death of eight Kurdish immigrants in a sealed furniture container off the coast of Wexford in December 2001, the government renewed its call to sanction carriers transporting undocumented migrants. While the Minister for Justice said that Ireland was the only EU state which had not introduced such legislation, a coalition of NGOs, including Amnesty International, Comhlámh, and the Irish Commission for Justice and Peace, pointed out that such sanctions 'would drive refugees into the hands of ruthless traffickers and smugglers and lead to more horrors like the Wexford tragedy' (Cullen, 2001: 2).

According to the Irish Refugee Council (1999), the Immigration Bill, despite legislating for an Appeals Tribunal and for the setting up of a Refugee Applications Commissioner and a Refugee Advisory Board, has changed nothing in the day-to-day life of asylum-seekers. The Bill gives no adequate guarantees in relation to translation and interpretation services; it makes no provisions for unaccompanied asylum-seekers who are minors, nor does it make any provisions for the right to work for asylum-seekers (Irish Refugee Council, 1999).

In July 1999 the Irish government announced that asylum-seekers living in Ireland longer than one year were eligible to seek employment. However, the government announced that employers, not asylum-seekers, must apply for work permits for which employers must pay £25 per month or £125 a year. It obliges employers to prove that they had made all efforts to recruit Irish or EEA nationals. No support mechanisms such as training or child care have been put in place, resulting in asylum-seekers finding it extremely difficult to secure employment (Irish Refugee Council, 1999; O'Halloran, 1999; Fanning *et al*, 2000). Quite apart from the racist asylum policy, legal migrants report being unequally treated in the Republic of Ireland, and workplace racial discrimination against foreigners (including unequal wages and longer working hours) has, in 2001, become a growing problem (Holland, 2001b: 10).

We have looked at a series of different processes which continue to encourage the racialisation of Irishness and which therefore mean that there is specificity to Irish racism. This specificity of Irish racism includes several discursive processes and practices. Firstly, there is the evocation of Irish cultural authenticity, and the call to preserve the right that Irish people have to the integrity of the national homeland. Anna Keogh (2000: 130) reports the fears expressed by Irish secondary school pupils in relation to Ireland losing its cultural identity with the advent of increasing in-migration. Indeed, in response to the arrival of people seeking asylum, some Irish people, such as the Immigration Control Platform (ICP), are calling upon the government to 'look after our own' first, evoking nationalist sentiments which differentiate between nationals and 'non-national' aliens (Cullen, 1998b).[6]

The second process evokes *parallels between past discourses of Irish emigration and present-day discourses of immigration into Ireland*, racialising incoming migrant and refugee 'others'. Jason King (1999) compares discourses of emigration as 'famine tide' with recent discourses of 'floods of immigrants (which) pour in and swamp the continent', and argues that viewing emigration as 'fluidity' constructs Ireland as a passive and 'porous' nation (on the link between past emigration and present day immigration see the Irish Centre for Migration Studies, www.migration.ucc.ie).

A third process is *blaming outgroups* and in-coming migrants for causing racism, despite the home truth that the Other is already and always within the gates and that racism is always caused by the 'host' community, as we argued above.

A fourth process is *projection*, which is always involved in constructing racialised stereotypes. Thus, Irish Jews can be constructed as money-oriented (as reported by MacGréil, 1996) despite recent disclosures of widespread financial corruption in Irish political life (see for instance O'Toole, 1995, for an analysis of one such fiscal corruption scandal, the 'beef tribunal'); Travellers are constructed as dirty, despite the serious litter problem Ireland faces (see Holland, 2001a:7, for a description of halting sites without refuse collection or running water, making it impossible for Travellers to compete with settled Irish people in relation to 'cleanliness'); and Black people can be depicted as hyper-sexual, despite the increasing over-sexualisation of Irish media and society, including widespread disclosures of sexual abuse in religious children's institutions (see Raftery and O'Sullivan, 1999).

Irish multiracisms – since racism is never a unitary practice – operate on individual and institutionalised levels. Thus, accusing Jewish Dáil (Parliament) members Mervyn Taylor and Alan Shatter during the 1996 divorce referendum campaign of 'not being able to understand Irish marriages' (see Lentin, chapter 10 in this volume), is, despite the public nature of the accusation, individual racism. When the Irish government refused to admit more than 60 Jewish asylum-seekers between 1933 and 1946, it is ideological and institutionalised racism. Likewise, when Traveller families are attacked by local residents, who dig trenches around their halting sites, it is individual racism. The history and ideology of settling and assimilating Travellers by successive Irish governments (see EYAR, 1997 and O'Connell in this volume) are, on the other hand, institutionalised racism.

Irish multiracisms manifest in *anti-Black* racism which owes to cultural and political imports, but also to the specifically Irish aid and missionary traditions of, for instance, supporting 'black babies' in developing countries (Aniagolu, 1997); Irish *antisemitism*, complete with unconscious phrases such as 'Jewman' to denote money lender (see MacGréil, 1996; Keogh, 1998); *anti-refugee sentiments*, whereby 'reasonable' Irish people vote in opinion poles against allowing 'more than a few' refugees, object to the dispersal of asylum-seekers by protesting or challenging planning permission for hostels for refugees (e.g., Dooley, 2000: 4; Holmquist, 2000: 2) and believe that they take Irish jobs despite the prohibition on most asylum-seekers to work and the grave shortage of labour in all areas of the Irish economy. Finally, there is the 'organic' form of Irish racism, *anti-Travellerism*, nurtured by Social Darwinism and bourgeois land-ownership fervour, understandable, perhaps, in the wake of British colonialism (see Mac Laughlin, 1995 for this interpretation of anti-Traveller racism, but see also EYAR, 1997; McVeigh, 1998; various publications by Pavee Point Traveller Centre and Ní Shúinéar in this volume). The continuing institutionalised anti-Traveller racism is exemplified, for instance, by the fact that in 2001, 24 per cent of all Travellers in the Republic of Ireland were living in unofficial sites, without electricity, refuse collection or running water. According to the Irish Traveller Movement, although local authorities were obliged by the Department of Environment and Local Government to adopt a five-year plan for Traveller accommodation, just 67 units had been completed by January 2001 (Holland, 2001a: 7). According to a survey commissioned as part of the 2001 Traveller Focus week, although Traveller respondents said they were 'satisfied with life in general' and although conditions had improved, they still faced serious discrimination: seven out of ten were discriminated against by pub owners, 40 per cent by owners of clubs, 38 per cent by gardaí, 37 per cent by shop owners, 33 by county councils and 26 per cent by the Department of Social, Community and Family Affairs (Haughey, 2001d: 11).

The roots of Irish racism lie in the specific relationship of Ireland to processes of British and other imperialisms. Contemporary Irish racism is explained by the location of Ireland inside new circuits of neo-colonialism within the 'new world order'. This analysis suggests that racism in Ireland is not about to fade away. Rather, with daily attacks on refugees and asylum-seekers and on people of colour, and with immigration and asylum restrictions which also result in stopping Irish and EU citizens of colour at points of entry, racism is likely to assume new and more virulent forms in the new millennium. We need to be increasingly vigilant of Irish racism; we need more analysis and more support for racialised ethnic communities; we also need to enact stronger and more effective equality legislation and we need more anti-racist activity.

A bibliography of racism and anti-racism in the Irish context

The attempt to pigeonhole work on racism relevant to Ireland, north and south, immediately throws up exceptions. Firstly, there are texts that are published elsewhere which have an immediate bearing on the dynamics of racism in Ireland. Here the European Parliament (1991) and Liégeois's work on Travellers (1994) are obvious examples. Noel Ignatiev's work (1995) on racism and the Irish in America has also had an impact on wider debates. Secondly, there are texts that resolutely insist on working with Ireland, north and south, as the unit of analysis for racism – albeit often with an acknowledgement of regional variations. This is true for the historiography and sociology of different minority ethnic groups, such as Louis Hyman (1972) and Dermot Keogh (1998) on the Jewish community and McCann *et al.* (1994) on the Travelling community as well as broader theorisations of Irish racism (McVeigh, 1992a, 1996; Harmony, 1990; National Youth Council of Ireland, 1995; European Year Against Racism 1998a, 1998b). Other publications look quite deliberately at north and south in comparative context (CRD, 1997). The Platform Against Racism, formed in 1997 (Platform Against Racism, 1997), has also consciously organised on an all-Ireland basis – in 1997 it seemed likely that much anti-racism activity would work within this paradigm; however it seems less likely now. The Belfast Agreement was largely silent on minority ethnic issues but it did commit both governments to establishing effective rights, safeguards and equality of opportunity to 'ethnic communities' alongside all other communities (The Agreement, 1998: 19).

It is also true that what happens in one part of Ireland cannot but impact on the dynamic of racism in the other. For example, the inclusion of Travellers in the Race Relations (Northern Ireland) Order (RRO) (1997) had significant impact in the Republic of Ireland while at the same time developments on Travellers in the Republic have an immediate ripple effect in the north. This said, it remains true that the vast majority of texts relevant to racism and anti-racism in Ireland are published in and refer to either Northern Ireland or the Republic of Ireland. Moreover, most of these texts focus fairly exclusively on only one of these regions – this is hardly surprising given the centrality of the state in the reproduction of racism and the construction of anti-racism.

Northern Ireland

Until recently there was very little systematic research on minority ethnic communities in Northern Ireland. Ephemeral and anecdotal pieces on the Traveller and Jewish communities were the nearest thing to a literature on minority ethnic groups. Northern Ireland does have one minority ethnic resource collection of world importance, however: the *L'Amie Collection* at the University of Ulster, Jordanstown (1981) is the most important resource collection of Irish Traveller materials in the world. The situation *vis-à-vis* other minority ethnic groups has changed to an extent over the past few years. This change has accompanied the growth in minority ethnic organisations – like the Chinese Welfare Association – and organisations raising debate around minority ethnic issues – like the Traveller Movement (NI) (formerly the Northern Ireland Council for Travelling People), the Race Equality subgroup of the Committee on the Administration of Justice (CAJ), the Multi-Cultural Resource Centre and the Northern Ireland Council for Ethnic Minorities (NICEM). The debate around the experience of racism has opened up around a conference on 'Racism in Northern Ireland' and an associated publication (CAJ, 1992). This was followed by a focus on the specific ways in which minority ethnic groups are affected by general issues like poverty (NIAPN, 1995; Yu, 1995) and policing (McVeigh, 1994). There was also more detailed ethnographic and quantitative work on the Traveller community (Ginnety, 1993; Noonan, 1994; Parris *et al*, 1995; Noonan, 1998; McVeigh, 1998d).

Despite this growth in research on minority ethnic communities, it is clear that many areas affecting minority ethnic communities are under-researched. The paucity of work on specific issues illustrates the degree to which minority ethnic concerns have been ignored. Research that is not focused on minority ethnic groups has almost inevitably failed to recognise that 'race' and ethnicity can be structuring factors in Northern Ireland with just as profound an impact as gender or religion.

There has, however, been an enormous increase in the literature around ethnicity and racism in the north of Ireland. In particular, four key texts published in the late 1990s have put empirical weight to the earlier, more theoretical or anecdotal accounts supporting the notion that there is a problem with racism in Northern Ireland. These texts have moved the literature away from rhetoric and anecdote and put it on a sounder empirical footing. Deepa Mann-Kler's *Out of the Shadows* provides an important qualitative assessment of the needs of minority ethnic communities focusing on the situation of young people and women (1997; see also Mann-Kler, chapter 3 in this volume). Greg Irwin's *Ethnic Minorities in Northern Ireland* does similar, if less grounded, work from a quantitative perspective (1996). In combination, these provide empirical proof, if proof were still needed, of the extent of racism in Northern Ireland. Paul Hainsworth's edited collection *Divided Society: Ethnic Minorities and Racism in Northern Ireland* (1998) provides an overview of issues around ethnicity and racism. This volume will probably be the definitive academic text on the subject for some years to come. Finally, Connolly and Keenan in *Racial Attitudes and Prejudice in Northern Ireland* (2000a) and *The Hidden Truth:*

Racist Harassment in Northern Ireland (2001) have done important new work on racism and social attitudes in the north.

There has been relatively little work on racism from the statutory sector but publications by the Central Community Relations Unit (CCRU) (1992), the Standing Advisory Commission on Human Rights (SACHR 1991, 1992, 1993), and the Advisory Committee on Travellers (ACT) (ACT, 1989, 1992; DOE, 1993, 1994) are important points of reference. Section 75 of the Northern Ireland Act (1998), which includes a specific equality duty in terms of race, is also important. This has generated a whole range of equality schemes that must pay at least passing reference to issues of ethnic equality. The Belfast Agreement also had significant wider implications for racial equality. It replaced the Commission for Racial Equality in Northern Ireland (CRENI, 1997) with a Race Equality Directorate inside the new Equality Commission. The Equality Commission, with its responsibilities for racial equality alongside sectarian, gender and disability equality, is of growing importance in terms of generating research and analysis on equal opportunities and anti-discrimination work. The British government is also moving towards introducing an integrative *Single Equality Act* to integrate existing equality legislation. This would make northern legislation much more like equality legislation in the south.

There are already a number of models of good practice in Northern Ireland. The annual reports of different minority ethnic organisations and support organisations detail the important work that has been done by this sector for many years (BTEDG, 1994). There are also a number of anti-racism training materials of variable quality (e.g. Women's Racism Awareness Group, 1997). The Northern Ireland Women's Aid Federation's *Violence on the Edge: A Training Pack for Trainers*, deals specifically with providing effective support for minority ethnic women at risk of domestic violence in Northern Ireland (NI Women's Aid Federation, 1998). Victoria Tennant's *Sanctuary in a Cell* (2000) filled a yawning gap in addressing the treatment of asylum-seekers in Northern Ireland. While numbers of asylum-seekers and refugees in the north remain tiny in comparison to the south, the imprisonment of asylum-seekers is the most shocking example of continuing abusive 'immigration' practices (McVeigh, 2001).

Several obvious gaps remain in the literature on the north. First, one of the key absences is a substantial quantitative analysis of minority ethnic groups similar to Modood *et al*'s *Ethnic Minorities in Britain: Diversity and Disadvantage* (1997) in relation to Northern Ireland. (This kind of material is also urgently needed for the Republic of Ireland.) Irwin's work began to address this gap and Connolly and Keenan (2000b) have done important work on education and training. This kind of research is absolutely vital in terms of anti-discrimination and anti-racist work. Second, there is very little work on second-generation identity. The British experience suggests that there can be very significant differences between the problems of first generation and second generation Black British people. We have little analysis of the specific concerns of this younger generation of minority ethnic people in Northern Ireland. Indeed, the question of identity is itself more complex in Northern Ireland – are people black British or black Irish or something else? (On the contradictory position of minority ethnic groups in

Northern Ireland particularly *vis á vis* Irish nationalism, see Shahidah Janjua's short piece in *MsChief*, 1997; Mann Kler, 2000; and Mann Kler, chapter 3 in this volume). Finally, there is very little critical reflection on the process of anti-racism in Northern Ireland (McVeigh, 1998a, 1998b). One of the key roles for the Equality Commission will be the encouragement of reflexive practice in addressing racism in Northern Ireland.

The Republic of Ireland

As in Northern Ireland, an earlier trickle of work on racism has begun to be supplemented by a flood of new materials. This later work has drawn on important earlier texts that are still important (Tannam 1991; Fitzgerald 1992; McVeigh, 1992a). It has not, however, made a conceptual link with earlier work on antisemitism (in particular, O'Riordan and Feeley, 1984, as well as several unpublished Masters dissertations; see also Goldstone, 1999, Goldstone, 2000, and chapter 11 in this volume). Recent work around racism borne out of the 'moral panic' over the trickle of refugees in the Republic of Ireland (see, for example, Cullen, 1997; Nozinic, 1997; Byrne, 1997; King, 1999; Cullen, 2000) has to some extent replaced an earlier concentration on Travellers as the key focus for racism in southern Irish society. There has been some solid work providing information on refugees (Storey, 2000) but this has not been fully integrated into any systematic analysis of racism in southern Irish society (Collins, 1994; Byrne, 1997). The Irish Refugee Council has published several important reports: Fanning *et al*, 2000, on the right to work; Fanning *et al*, 2001, on asylum-seeking children and social exclusion in Ireland; and Irish Refugee Council, 2001, on the fairness and sustainability of accelerated procedures for asylum determinations. These reports, as well as Faughnan and Woods's study (2000), make visible the asylum process and the lives of refugees in the Republic of Ireland.

Refugees apart, the context of racism in the Republic of Ireland is broadly comparable to that in the north. The minority ethnic profile in Northern Ireland is much closer to the Republic than to the situation in Britain (CRD, 1997), but in the absence of figures for minority ethnic groups in the Republic of Ireland as in Northern Ireland, it is difficult to contextualise racism within quantitative information. As already mentioned, the Census of Population in the Republic of Ireland does not plan to include, questions on ethnic origin; the religion question is asked only every ten years.

The situation is relatively advanced in terms of mainstreaming minority ethnic equality issues – especially in terms of Travellers (Task Force, 1995; Nexus Research Co-operative, 1994, 1997; EYAR, 1997; Murphy *et al*, 2000). The work of the Refugee Council and the Refugee Agency has also been notable for the support provided to particular minority ethnic groups, namely asylum-seekers in the case of the former and 'programme refugees' (for definitions see Nozinic, chapter 4 in this volume) in the case of the latter (Refugee Agency, 1997a, 1997b, 1997c, 1998).

The legislative framework, however, remains weaker in the south than the north. The 1989 Prohibition of Incitement to Hatred Bill is regarded as a weak piece of legislation, which leaves the onus on complainants to prove *intentionality* to incite to hatred and has therefore resulted in no litigation to date[7] (see Helleiner, 1995;

McVeigh, chapter 14 in this volume). The Employment Equality Act, 2000 and the Equal Status Act, 1998 are intended to outlaw racial discrimination alongside other discriminations. Their enactment was a significant advance for anti-racism in Ireland. Both pieces of legislation, however, are weaker than the Race Relations (Northern Ireland) Order. The Refugee Act (1996), amended by the Immigration Act (1999), is the main statutory instrument of refugee legislation in the south (for critiques of the Irish government refugee and immigration policies see the Refugee Protection Policy Group, 2000a, 2000b and 2000c; Fanning *et al*, 2000; The Irish Refugee Council, 2000). [8] On the other hand, there are significant lessons for the north in terms of integrating anti-discrimination work across different sectors (Equality Studies Centre, 1995; Dublin Travellers Education and Development Group [DTEDG] *et al*, 1993).

Much of the groundbreaking theoretical and practical work around racism in the Republic of Ireland was done by the Traveller Support Movement (DTEDG 1987, 1992, 1994a, 1994b, 1994c; DTEDG *et al*, 1993; Pavee Point 1995, 1997; Byrne, 1996; Ryan, 1995; Ryan, 1996; Pavee Point / Ryan, 1998; Fanning, 2000, links anti-Traveller and anti-asylum-seekers racism). Certainly Pavee Point (formerly DTEDG) and the Irish Traveller Movement (ITM) have undertaken work which is influential at an Irish policy level and at a European level – many British and European organisations look to the Irish Traveller support movement as a model of good practice. The efforts of these groups culminated in the work of the Irish Government's Task Force Report on Travellers (1995). This report is particularly important since it is the one example of 'mainstreaming' Travellers, or indeed any other minority ethnic issues in Ireland. While concerns remain about the implementation of the Task Force Report, there is no doubt as to the importance of the government setting out to assume such a strategic role in addressing Traveller disadvantage. In recent years there has also been specific work on gender implications for Traveller women (Crickley, 1992; Helleiner, 1997; Fay, 1999; Pavee Point, 2000; see also Helleiner, 2000).

The partnership model initiated by the Traveller Support Movement has been incorporated into the work of the National Committee of the European Year Against Racism (EYAR, 1998a, 1998b; European Parliament, 1997) and the Platform Against Racism, an independent initiative of non-governmental organisations (NGOs) working collectively to highlight and address racism in the island of Ireland. Significant work has been done in recent years on questions of ethnicity in relation to Travellers (McCann *et al*, 1994; on the debate as to whether Travellers are an ethnic group, see Ní Shuínear, and McLoughlin in McCann *et al*, 1994; Mac Laughlin, 1995; Helleiner, 2001; and in relation to Travellers and education, see Máirín Kenny's important text, 1997).

The groundbreaking nature of the work on Travellers and racism has to an extent left work on other minority ethnic groups and other racisms in the shadows. Until recently at least, other minority ethnic groups attracted much less research attention other than Mac Gréil's quantitative work on social attitudes (1978; 1996). However, work by and about minority ethnic groups and racism is beginning to be published

(Tannam, 1991; Quinn, 1994; Egan, 1997; McVeigh and Binchy, 1998; Boucher, 1998). The collection based on the the *Expanding Nation: Towards a Multi-Ethnic Ireland* conference held at Trinity College Dublin in September 1998 (Lentin, 1999b) includes several papers on minority ethnic groups and racism in the Irish and European contexts, as does the collection *Emerging Irish Identities* (Lentin, 2000). In the wake of the European Year Against Racism, several NGOs have begun working and publishing work on culturally sensitive service provision (see, for instance, Access Ireland, 1998). O'Connell and MacLachlan's volume *Cultivating Pluralism* (2000) is a collection of psychological, social and cultural perspectives on a changing Ireland. Work has also begun being published on refugees' educational and employment experiences (see, for example, Fanning *et al*, 2000; Interact Ireland, 2000). As far as social policy initiatives go, Torode, Walsh and Woods (2001) is the first resource book for social workers for working with refugees and asylum-seekers.

Work on the Irish Jewish community and on antisemitism has been undertaken by Keogh (1988, 1998), Moore (1984), Goldstone and Lentin (1997), Goldstone (1999, 2000, and chapter 13 in this volume), Ó Drisceoil (1997). There has been some work on black people in Ireland (Aniagolu, 1997) and on the construction of Irishness in terms of citizenship and racism (Lentin, 1998b, 1998c, 1999a). Significantly, in keeping with work that is gaining prominence in Britain and the USA, a body of work on gender and racism is beginning to be published (Chan, 1996; Janjua, 1997; Sinha, 1997; Joyce, 1997; Lentin, 1998a, 1998b, 1999a).

Work is beginning on the ways in which women from minority ethnic groups in Ireland are targeted by racism. In her report to the National Consultative Committee on Racism and Interculturalism (NCCRI), Lentin (1998e) lists several ways in which women from minority ethnic groups experience gender-related racism in Irish society. As mothers, women from minority ethnic groups often witness their children being humiliated by other children or by teachers. This can be subtle (putting down African culture in a class where there is an African child) or less subtle (name calling and bullying). Traveller mothers witness their children ostracised in mixed classes or put to the back of the class. They are often excluded from occasions such as 'visiting Santa' with their children. Traveller mothers are regularly followed in shops and supermarkets, which makes feeding their children difficult. Lone Irish mothers of mixed-race babies were coerced to give them up for adoption or to orphanages – there is a whole generation of 'mixed-race' Irish children who grew up in orphanages until the 1960s. Pregnant Black women (not only asylum-seekers) are routinely physically attacked when leaving Dublin maternity hospitals – the assumption is that they are getting pregnant in order to be allowed to remain in Ireland. As wives, women are targeted differently by immigration/asylum policies. When wives are not the actual asylum-seekers, they do not have the same entitlements. Women asylum-seekers are often accused of 'marriages of convenience'. Traveller women are often not allowed into pubs, even when their husbands are. Racism is often sexualised: black women are regularly sexually propositioned on Irish streets (see Janjua, 1997) and in Irish pubs. Veiled Muslim women are regularly vilified; because of the veil, they are targeted more often than Muslim men (Najjair, 2000). Irish-born women converting to Islam are accused of 'not being Irish' any more and told to 'go back to Iran' (Hughes, 1998). Women refugees, because of isolation and family responsibilities, are often excluded from language and other training programmes. Zena – Bosnian Women Accessing Education is a training initiative supported by the Refugee Agency aimed at overcoming this problem (Sultan and Zena, 1999). Despite a useful handbook on best practices in relation to women and the refugee experience (ICCL, 2000; see also UNHCR, 1999), there are no provisions or counselling and little recognition for women asylum-seekers who have experienced gendered torture (Sansani, 2001). The Irish women's movement has not yet fully faced up to the need to include women from minority ethnicities in all feminist projects, despite attempts by feminists from minority ethnic groups (e.g. Fitzgerald, 1992; Chan, 1996; Sinha, 1997 and chapter 7 in this volume) to make their gendered experiences of exclusion visible. Very few mainstream feminist projects in Ireland (as elsewhere in Europe) have met the challenge of Black and majority world women in relation to the ethnocentrism and racism of the women's movement itself (see Lentin, 1998d). However, the National Women's Council of Ireland, in an effort to reach women from racialised minority ethnic groups, published an anti-racism handbook in November 2000 (NWCI, 2000).

Christine Dibelius (2001) has contributed a useful study of the social networks of African refugee women in Ireland; indeed, one of the main issues for women from minority ethnic groups who experience racism is their isolation. The women's sub-committee of the European Year Against Racism National Committee has held several workshops during 1997 to offer a forum for women from minority ethnic groups to articulate their concerns. Creating a space for racialised women to voice their exclusion and the need to build coalitions between women from different minority ethnic groups led to establishing the Irish Association of Minority Ethnic Women in 1998. By 2001, the group has ceased its activities, yet several new organizations, such as the African Women's Network, are in various stages of formation; members of both groups attest to the difficulties women from racialised ethnic groups face in carving up culturally specific gendered spaces.

There is no doubt that the attention, in Britain and elsewhere, to other forms of racism apart from those based on colour, has helped to re-focus attention not only on anti-Irish racism (see McVeigh, chapter 9 in this volume) but also on anti-racist work in Ireland (see Tannam *et al*, 1998, and Tannam, McVeigh's chapter 14 and Lentin's chapter 15 in this volume). The ambiguity of the racism/sectarianism interface means that this will be another key issue over the coming years (Brewer, 1992; McVeigh, 1999). There has also been a great deal of new work around Romani Studies in Britain (Kenrick and Puxon, 1995; Acton, 1997; Acton and Mundy, 1997) that has implications for Irish Travellers (see McVeigh, 1997; O'Connell, 1997 and chapter 2 in this volume; Pavee Point, 1997; European Year Against Racism, 1997).

Conclusion

There are particular challenges for those who want to understand and challenge racism in Ireland in the new millennium. As we have seen, even if we focus solely on Jews and Travellers, Ireland has been a multi-ethnic country for centuries. In the last decade of the twentieth century, however, there has been a marked – and self conscious – new ethnicisation of Irishness. This has been accompanied by new formations of Irish racism. New migrants and refugees mean that Ireland is now definitely multi-ethnic, multi-faith and multi-cultural. It is also, sadly, multi-racist. It is also, more promisingly, increasingly intercultural and anti-racist. New ethnic interfaces are creating their own exciting dynamic in new varieties of Irishness. The concomitant recognition of a need for a politics of anti-racism has generated new politics of equality and human rights – a re-imagining of the politics of liberation in the Irish context. This, in turn, creates new challenges in terms of understanding racism. In particular there is a need to ensure that anti-racism is grounded in the experiences of the different minority ethnic communities. If there is one defining challenge for anti-racists in Ireland, it is the need to hand over power to the racialised. While there is a need for a continuing active partnership between white majority Irish and minority ethnic Irish who oppose racism, minority ethnic people must become the dominant rather than subordinate partners in this process.

The new dynamics around racism and anti-racism in Ireland have a wider relevance. The analysis of racism in Ireland provides an important perspective on racism in general. First, it confirms the ability of some predominantly white groups to experience racism. (It bears emphasis that this is very different from suggesting that it confirms the ability of *all* white groups to experience racism.) Travellers and white refugees have become racialised in specific ways that require analysis alongside the experiences of people of colour. In this sense racism in Ireland is an important challenge to the notion that racism is always about colour or visible somatic difference – it suggests that racism is about deeper and more complex matrices of power and signification.

Racism is not only about power in the sense that it empowers and disempowers on the grounds of ethnicity; it is also about power because it connects with and reinforces other power differentials in a specifically racialised way – across gender, class, sexuality, disability (see McDonagh, chapter 8 in this volume in this regard), as well as political formations. As we have seen, racialised identity changes in different power matrices. One thing, however, is clear – racism is a quality of these power matrices, *not of the racialised*. This is a simple point but its wider implications bear emphasis. Irish people do not cause anti-Irish racism; Africans do not cause anti-African racism; Jews do not cause antisemitism; Travellers do not cause anti-Traveller racism; refugees do not cause anti-refugee racism. We must explain racism in terms of the power matrices that racialise people, not in terms of the behaviour of the racialised.

This reality pushes us towards broader conclusions about the dynamics of racism. There must be a resistance to reified racialised continuities – whether spatial or temporal. Racism must be situated in terms of the particular polity and historical moment in which it appears. Far from being timeless or immutable, racism is characterised by its fluidity and mutability. For example, racism is hugely different in democratic South Africa from its manifestations under apartheid. Equally, however, continuities do exist and reproduce across huge spatial and temporal distances. Antisemitism, for example, reproduces across centuries and continents regardless of Jewish presence in specific societies.

Contemporary racism draws on a deep reservoir of stereotypes and projections that can be used to nurture any number of new processes of racialisation. There should be no underestimating the longevity of racialised power relationships. This is especially true since there is no simple or mechanical relationship between structural base and ideological superstructure. Racialised stereotypes can retain their ideological power long after the structural relationships that gave them meaning have been transformed. So racism is simultaneously rooted in tradition and constantly changing. Making sense of the dialectic between these realities – racism as both *continuity* and *change* – is the key to understanding the dynamics of racism in the twenty-first century.

References

Access Ireland. 1998. *Towards a Culturally Sensitive Practice: the First Steps*. Dublin: Access Ireland, Refugee Social Integration Project.

ACT (Advisory Committee on Travellers). 1989. *Final Report of the Advisory Committee on Travellers (N.I.) for the period 1 August 1986 – 31 December 1989*.

ACT. 1992. *With Not For Conference Report*. Belfast: ACT.

Acton, Thomas (ed.) 1997. *Gypsy Politics and Traveller Identity*. Hatfield: University of Hertfordshire Press.

Acton, Thomas and Gary Mundy (eds.) 1997. *Romani Culture and Gypsy Identity*. Hatfield: University of Hertfordshire Press.

Adams, Peter. 1992. *The Arts of the Third Reich*. London: Thames and Hudson.

African Refugee Network. 1999. *African Refugees: Needs Analysis*. Dublin: African Refugee Network.

Amnesty International. 2001. *Racism in Ireland: The Views of Black and Ethnic Minorities*. Dublin: Amnesty International, in association with Steven Loyal and Aogán Mulcahy, UCD.

Amos, Valerie and Pratiba Parmar. 1984. 'Challenging imperial feminism', *Feminist Review*, no. 17: 3-20.

Aniagolu, Chichi. 1997. 'Being Black in Ireland', in Ethel Crowley and Jim MacLaughlin (eds.) *Under the Belly of the Tiger: Class, Race, Identity and Culture in the Global Ireland*. Dublin: Irish Reporter Publications.

Anthias, Floya. 1992. *Ethnicity, Class, Gender and Migration: Greek-Cypriots in Britain*. Aldershot: Avebury.

Anthias, Floya. 1999. 'Institutional racism, power and accountability', *Sociological Research Online*, vol 4(1). http://www.socresonline.org.uk/socresonline/4/lawrence/anthias.html

Anthias, Floya and Nira Yuval-Davis. 1992. *Racialised Boundaries: Race, Nation, Gender, Colour and Class and the Anti-Racist Struggle*. London: Routledge.

Back, Les. 1996. *New Ethnicities and Urban Culture: Racisms and Multiculture in Young Lives*. London: UCL Press.

Back, Les and John Solomos (eds.) 2000. *Theories of Race and Racism*. London: Routledge.

Bakare-Yusuf, Bibi. 1997. 'The economy of violence: Black bodies and the unspeakable terror', in Ronit Lentin (ed.) *Gender and Catastrophe*. London: Zed Books.

Banton, Michael. 1967. *Race Relations*. New York: Basic Books.

Banton, Michael. 1977. *The Idea of Race*. London: Tavistock Publications.

Barker, Martin. 1981. *The New Racism*. London: Junction.

Bauman, Zygmunt. 1989. *Modernity and the Holocaust*. Cambridge: Polity Press.

Bhabha, Homi K. 1994. *The Location of Culture*. London: Routledge.

Bhavnani, Kum-Kum (ed.) 2001. *Feminism and 'Race'*. Oxford: Oxford University Press.
Bochain, N.M. 1990. 'The ethnic question in the 1981 census: background and issues.' *Ethnic and Racial Studies*, 13(4): 543-567.
Bonnet, Alastair. 1997. 'Constrution of Whiteness in European and American anti-racism', in Pnina Werbner and Tariq Modood (eds.) *Debating Cultural Hybridity: Multi-Cultural Identities and the Politics of Anti-Racism*. London: Zed Books.
Bonnet, Alastair. 2000. *Anti-Racism*. London: Routledge.
Boucher, Gerard W. 1998. *The Irish are Friendly, but: International Students' Experiences of Racism at Universities in Ireland, Britain and the Netherlands*. Dublin: Irish Council for International Students.
Brah, Avtar. 1993. 'Difference, diversity, differentiation', in J. Wrench and John Solomos (eds) *Racism and Migration in Western Europe*. Oxford: Berg.
Brah, Avtar. 1996. *Cartographies of Disapora: Contesting Identities*. London: Routledge.
Brewer, John D. 1992. 'Sectarianism and Racism and their Parallels and Differences.' *Ethnic and Racial Studies* vol. 15, no. 3.
BTEDG (Belfast Travellers Education and Development Group) 1994. *New Horizons for Travellers*. Belfast: BTEDG.
Bunreacht na hÉireann (Constitution of Ireland). 1937. Dublin: The Stationery Office.
Burke, Edmund. 1909 (1757). *On the Sublime and the Beautiful*. Boston: Harvard Classics.
Byrne, Ciarán. 1996. *Generating Options: A Study of Enterprise Initiatives Supported through Traveller Organizations*. Dublin: Pavee Point.
Byrne, Rosemary. 1997. 'On the Sliding Scales of Justice: The Status of Asylum-seekers and Refugees in Ireland', in Rosemary Byrne and William Duncan (eds.) *Developments in Discrimination Law in Ireland and Europe*. Dublin: Irish Centre for European Law.
Cabral, Amilcar. 1969. *Revolution in Guinea: An African People's Struggle, Selected Texts*. London: Stage 1.
CAJ (Committee on the Administration of Justice) 1992. *Racism in Northern Ireland*. Belfast: CAJ.
Carby, Hazel. 1982. 'White woman listen! Black feminism and the coundaries of sisterhood', in CCCS, *The Empire Strikes Back: race and Racism in 70s Britain*. London: Hutchinson.
Carmichael, Stokeley and C.V. Hamilton. 1967. *Black Power: The Politics of Liberation in America*. New York: Random House.
CCRU (Central Community Relations Unit) 1992. *Race Relations in Northern Ireland*. Belfast: CCRU.
Centre for Research and Documentation (CRD). 1997. *Minority Ethnic Groups and Racism*. Ireland: North/South Comparisons Series.
Cesaire, Aime. 1972. *Discourse on Colonialism*. New York and London: Monthly Review Press.
Chambers, Iain. 1990. *Border Dialogue: Journeys in Postmodernity*. New York: Routledge.
Chan, Victoria. 1996. 'Racial and sexual implications of being a minority in Ireland: a personal perspective', in Ailbhe Smyth (ed) *Feminism, Politics, Community*. Dublin: WERRC.
Cheyette, Bryan and Laura Marcus. 1998. *Modernity, Culture and 'the Jew.'* Cambridge: Polity Press.
Cohen, Phil and H.S. Bains (eds.) 1988. *Multi-Racist Britain*. London: Macmillan.
Cohen, Phil. 1988. 'The perversions of inheritance', in Phil Cohen and H.S. Bains (eds) *Multi-Racist Britain*. London: Macmillan.
Cohen, Phil. 1992. 'It's racism what dunnit': hidden narratives in theories of racism', in James Donald and Ali Rattansi (eds.) *'Race', Culture and Difference*. London: Sage.
Cohen, Phil. 1993. *Home Rules: Some Reflections on Racism and Nationalism in Everyday Life*. Dagenham: New Ethnicities Unit, University of East London.
Cohen, Phil (ed.) 1999. *New Ethnicities, Old Racisms?* London: Zed Books.
Collins, Adrienne. 1994. *Inequalities in the Treatment of Refugees and Asylum-seekers in Ireland*. Dublin: Trócaire.
Collins, Eoin. 1997. *Case Studies of Good Practice for the Prevention of Racial Discrimination and Xenophobia and the Promotion of Equal Treatment in the Workplace*. Dublin: Nexus Research Cooperative.
Connolly, Paul and Michaela Keenan. 2000a. *Racial Attitudes and Prejudice in Northern Ireland*. Belfast: NISRA.
Connolly, Paul and Michaela Keenan. 2000b. *Opportunities for All: Minority Ethnic People's Experiences of Education, Training and Employment in Northern Ireland*, Belfast: NISRA.
Connolly, P. and Keenan, M. 200.) *The Hidden Truth: Racist Harassment in Northern Ireland*. Belfast: Northern Ireland Statistics and Research Agency.
Constitution Review Group. 1996. *Report of the Constitution Review Group*. Dublin: Stationery Office.

Corcoran-Nantes, Yvonne. 1997. 'Women and slavery in Brazil', in Ronit Lentin (ed) *Gender and Catastrophe*. London: Zed Books.

CRENI (Commission for Racial Equality Northern Ireland). 1997. *What is the Commission for Racial Equality for Northern Ireland?* Belfast: CRENI.

Crickley, Anastasia. 1992. 'Feminism and Ethnicity', in *Dublin Travellers Education and Development Group, DTEDG File: Irish Travellers – New Analysis and New Initiatives*, Dublin: Pavee Point, pp. 101-8.

Crosbie, Judith. 2000. 'Bus driver guilty of racial hatred,' *The Irish Times*, 15 September 2000: 1.

Cullen, Paul. 1997. 'The 1997 border campaign: refugees, asylum-seekers and race on the borders', in Ethel Crowley and Jim MacLaughlin (eds) *Under the Belly of the Tiger: Class, Race, Identity and Culture in the Global Ireland*. Dublin: Irish Reporter Publications.

Cullen, Paul. 1998a. 'Deportations of rejected asylum-seekers begin to gather pace.' *The Irish Times*, 22 October 1998: 9.

Cullen, Paul. 1998b. 'Group concerned at level of immigration,' *The Irish Times*, 13 January, 1998.

Cullen, Paul. 2000. *Refugees and Asylum-seekers in Ireland*. Cork: Cork University Press.

Cullen, Paul. 2001. 'Unease voiced on fines for refugee carriers', *The Irish Times*, 18 December 2001: 2.

Curtis, Liz. 1984. *Nothing But the Same Old Story: The Roots of Anti-Irish Racism*. London: Information on Ireland.

De Beauvoir, Simone. 1949, 1993. *The Second Sex*. Harmondsworth: Penguin.

Dibelius, Christine. 2001. *Lone but not Alone: A Case Study of the Social Networks of African Refugee Women in Ireland*. Dublin: MPhil in Ethnic and Racial Studies, Department of Sociology, Trinity College Dublin.

DOE (Department of the Environment). 1993. *Northern Ireland Travellers Census '93*. Belfast: Department of the Environment/Advisory Committee on Travellers.

DOE. 1994. *Regional Development Strategy for the Provision of Sites for Travellers over the period 1994-2000*. Belfast: DOE.

Donald, James and Ali Rattansi (eds.) 1992. *Race, Culture, Difference*. London: Sage.

Donoghue, Miriam. 1999. 'Callely calls for tough line on asylum-seekers,' *The Irish Times*, 19 November 1999: 1.

Dooley, Chris. 2000. 'Reversal of fortune for asylum-seekers as village overcomes its "fear of the unknown"', *The Irish Times*, 15 August, 2000: 2.

DTEDG. (Dublin Travellers Education and Development Group). 1987. 'Travellers Getting Involved'. Dublin: DTEDG.

DTEDG. (Dublin Travellers Education and Development Group), ICCL (Irish Council for Civil Liberties) and ITM (Irish Traveller Movement). 1993. *Anti-racist Law and the Travellers*. Dublin: Irish Traveller Movement.

DTEDG. 1992. *DTEDG File: Irish Travellers, New Analysis and New Initiatives*. Dublin: DTEDG.

DTEDG. 1994a. *Words For Power*. Dublin: DTEDG.

DTEDG. 1994b. *Starting Out: A Resource Pack for Trainers of Traveller Women*. Dublin: DTEDG.

DTEDG. 1994c. *Reach Out*. Dublin: DTEDG.

DuBois, William E. B. 1903, 1965. *The Souls of Black Folk: Essays and Sketches*. London: Longmans.

Egan, Orla (ed.) 1997. *Minority Ethnic Groups in Higher Education*. Cork: Higher Education Equality Unit.

Equality Studies Centre. 1995. *A Framework for Equality Proofing: A Paper prepared for the National Economic and Social Forum*. Dublin: Equality Studies Centre, University College, Dublin.

Essed, Philomena. 1991. *Understanding Everyday Racism*. London: Sage.

European Council on Refugees and Exiles (ECRE). 2001. 'Comments from ECRE on the European Commission Paper on Minimum Standards for the reception of applicants for asylum in member states, 27 November 2000', (www.ecre.org/observations/minimum).

European Parliament. 1991. *Committee of Inquiry on Racism and Xenophobia*. Luxembourg: Office for Official Publications of the European Communities.

European Parliament. 1997. *Racism in Ireland: North and South (papers delivered at a conference held in Dublin Castle, October 31 1997)*. Dublin: European Parliament Office in Ireland.

European Year Against Racism. 1997. *Travellers in Ireland: An Examination of Discrimination and Racism*. Dublin: Department of Justice, Equality and Law Reform.

European Year Against Racism. 1998a. *Ireland Report*. Dublin: National Co-ordinating Committee, the Department of Justice, Equality and Law Reform.

European Year Against Racism. 1998b. *Racism in Ireland, North and South*. Dublin: Stationery Office.

Fanning, Bryan, Steven Loyal and Ciaran Staunton. 2000. *Asylum-seekers and the Right to Work in Ireland*. Dublin: Irish Refugee Council.

Fanning, Bryan. 2000. 'Asylum-seekers, Travellers and racism', *Doctrine and Life*, vol. 50, no. 6, July-August 2000.

Fanning, Bryan, Angela Veale and Dawn O'Connor. 2001. *Beyond the Pale: Asylum Seeking Children and Social Exclusion in Ireland*. Dublin: Irish Refugee Council / Combat Poverty Agency.

Fanon, Frantz. 1969. *The Wretched of the Earth*. Harmondsworth: Penguin.

Fanon, Frantz. 1970. *Black Skins, White Masks*. London: Paladin.

Farrell, Michael. 1980. *Northern Ireland: The Orange State*. London: Pluto Press.

Faughnan, Pauline and Máiríde Woods. 2000. *Lives on Hold: Seeking Asylum in Ireland*. Dublin: Social Science Research Centre, National University of Ireland, University College Dublin.

Fay, Ronnie. 1999. 'Pavee Beoirs breaking the silence: racism and violence against women,' *Community Workers Co-op*.

Fitzgerald, Gretchen. 1992. *Repulsing Racism: Reflections on Racism and the Irish*. Dublin: Attic Pres.

Gilroy, Paul. 1987. *There Ain't no Black in the Union Jack*. London: Hutchinson.

Gilroy, Paul. 1990. 'The end of anti-racism', in W. Ball and J. Solomos (eds.) *Race and Local Politics*. London: Macmillan.

Gilroy, Paul. 1998. 'Race ends here', *Ethnic and Racial Studies*, Vol. 21, number 5: 838-847.

Gilroy, Paul. 2000. *Between Camps: Nations, Cultures and the Allure of Race*. London: Allen Lane.

Ginnety, Pauline. 1993. *A Report on the Health of Travellers*. Belfast: Eastern Health and Social Services Board.

Goldberg, David T. (ed). 1990. *Anatomy of Racism*. Minneapolis: University of Minnesota Press.

Goldberg, David T. 1993. *Racist Culture*. Oxford: Blackwell.

Goldstone, Katrina and Louis Lentin. 1997. *No More Blooms: Irish Government Policy towards Jewish Refugees, 1933-1946*. Broadcast on RTE 1, 10 December 1997.

Goldstone, Katrina. 1999. 'Christianity, conversion and the tricky business of names: Images of Jews in nationalist Irish Catholic discourse', in Ronit Lentin (ed.) *The Expanding Nation: Towards a Multi-ethnic Ireland*. Dublin: Ethnic and Racial Studies, Department of Sociology, Trinity College.

Goldstone, Katrina. 2000a. 'Benevolent helpfulness? Ireland and the international reaction to Jewish refugees 1933-1939', in Michael Kennedy and Joseph M. Skelly (eds) *Irish Foreign Policy 1919-1966: From Independence to Internationalism*. Dublin: Four Courts Press.

Griffith, Arthur. 1982. 'Preface', in John Mitchell, *Jail Journal*. Dublin: University Press of Ireland.

Hainsworth, Paul (ed.) 1998. *Divided Society: Ethnic Minorities and Racism in Northern Ireland*. London: Pluto Press.

Hall, Stuart, *et al.* 1978. *Policing the Crisis: Mugging, the State and Law and Order*. London: Macmillan.

Hall, Stuart. 1980. 'Race articulation and societies structured in dominance', in UNESCO, *Sociological Theories: Race and Colonialism*. Paris: UNESCO.

Hall, Stuart. 1992a. 'The question of cultural identity', in Stuart Hall, Daviel Held and Tony McGrew (eds.) *Modernity and its Futures*. Cambridge: Polity Press.

Hall, Stuart. 1992b. 'New ethnicities', in James Donald and Ali Rattansi (eds.) *'Race', Culture and Difference*, London: Sage/Open University Press.

Hall, Stuart. 1997. 'The Spectacle of the "other"', in Stuart Hall (ed.) *Representation: Cultural Representations and Signifying Practices*. London: Sage/Open University.

Halloran, Marie. 2000. 'Son of stabbing victim decides to leave Ireland after racist taunts', *The Irish Times*, 17 August, 2000: 7.

Harmony. 1990. *Racial Discrimination in Ireland: Realities and Remedies*. Dublin: Harmony.

Haughey, Nuala. 1999a. 'Cabinet meets today to discuss asylum policies,' *The Irish Times*, 14 December 1999: 6.

Haughey, Nuala. 1999b. 'Government aims to tackle asylum-seeker crisis while reducing numbers arriving here,' *The Irish Times*, 13 December 1999: 6.

Haughey, Nuala. 2000. 'Tests on asylum-seekers deplored', *The Irish Times*, 2 February, 2000.

Haughey, Nuala. 2001a. 'Immigration officers to be part of Garda bureau', *The Irish Times*, 5 February, 2001: 4.

Haughey, Nuala. 2001b. 'Appointments to new body for asylum-seekers', *The Irish Times*, 5 February, 2001: 4.

Haughey, Nuala. 2001c. '20 per cent of failed asylum-seekers deported – O'Donoghue', *The Irish Times*, 16 February, 2001: 9.

Haughey, Nuala. 2001d. 'Education for their children is seen as a priority', *The Irish Times*, 28 February, 2001: 11.

Haughey, Nuala. 2001e. 'Groups oppose pact to speed up deportations', *The Irish Times*, 24 August, 2001: 4.

Helleiner, Jane. 1995. 'Inferioritized difference and the limits of pluralism in Ireland: the 1989 Anti-Hatred Act', *The Canadian Journal of Irish Studies*, vol. 21(2): 63-83.

Helleiner, Jane. 1997. '"Women of the itinerant class": gender and anti-Traveller racism in Ireland', *Women's Studies International Forum*, vol. 20/2: 275-288.

Helleiner, Jane. 2000. *Irish Travellers: Racism and the Politics of Culture*. Toronto: University of Toronto Press.

Hepburn, A.C. 1980. *The Conflict of Nationality in Modern Ireland*. London: Edward Arnold.

Hesse, Barnor (ed.) 2000. *Un/settled Multiculturalisms: Diasporas, Entanglements, Transruptions*. London: Zed Books.

Hickman, Mary J. 1995. *Religion, Class and Identity: The State, the Catholic Church and the Education of the Irish in Britain*. Aldershot: Avebury.

Hickman, Mary J. and Bronwen Walter. 1997. *Discrimination and the Irish Community in Britain: A report of research undertaken for the Commission for Racial Equality*. London: CRE.

Hill-Collins, Patricia. 1990. *Black Feminist Thought: Knowledge, Consciousness and the Politics of Empowerment*. London: Harper Collins.

Holland, Kitty. 2001a. 'Extreme concern at lack of progress on halting sites', *The Irish Times*, 11 January 2001: 7.

Holland, Kitty. 2001b. 'Migrant workers labour under regime of racial discrimination', *The Irish Times*, 10 November 2001: 10.

Holmquist, Kathryn. 2000. 'Influx of refugees brings mixed response', *The Irish Times*, 10 April: 2.

hooks, bell. 1981. *Ain't I a Woman: Black Women and Feminism*. Boston: South End Press.

hooks, bell. 1990. *Yearning: Race, Gender and Cultural Politics*. Boston: South End Press.

hooks, bell. 2000. '"Racism and feminism: the issue of accountability', in Les Back and John Solomos (eds.) *Theories of Race and Racism*. London: Routledge.

Hughes, Elaine. 1998. 'Irish women converting to Islam (Muslim women)', undergraduate dissertation, Department of Sociology, Trinity College Dublin.

Hulme, Peter. 1986. *Colonial Encounters: Europe and the Native Caribbean*. London: Methuen.

Huntington, Samuel P. 1997. *The Clash of Civilisations and the Remaking of World Order*. London: Simon and Schuster.

Hyman, Louis. 1972. *The Jews of Ireland*. Shannon: Irish Academic Press.

Ignatiev, Noel. 1995. *How the Irish became White*. New York: Routledge.

Interact Ireland. 2000. *Employment of Non-EU Nationals/Refugees in Ireland: Employers' and Refugees' Experiences*. Dublin: Interact Ireland for IBEC Survey Unit.

Institute of Jewish Policy Research. 1998. *Antisemitism World Report*. http://www.ort.org/community/jpr/AWR_web

Irish Council for Civil Liberties (ICCL). 2000. *Women and the Refugee Experience: Towards a Statement of Best Practice*. Dublin: ICCL Women's Committee in association with the National Consultative Committee on Racism and Interculturalism and *The Irish Times*.

Irish Refugee Council. 1997. *AGM Report*. Dublin: Irish Refugee Council.

Irish Refugee Council. 1999. 'A synopsis of the main issues surrounding the Immigration Bill, 1999', and 'Right to work for asylum-seekers', *IRC Legal Unit Information Section*.

Irish Refugee Council. 2000. *A Report on the Fairness and Sustainability of Asylum Determinations at First Instance*. Dublin: Irish Refugee Council.

Irish Refugee Council. 2000. *Manifestly Unjust: Report on the Fairness and Sustainability of Accelerated Procedures for Asylum Determinations (Project director: Siobhán Mullally, research assistant: Sheila McGovern)*. Dublin: Irish Refugee Council.

Irwin, Greg. 1996. *Ethnic Minorities in Northern Ireland: An Interim Report on Four Communities*. University of Ulster: Centre for the Study of Conflict.

James, Stanlie M., and Abena P.A. Busia (eds.) 1993. *Theorizing Black Feminisms: The Visionary Pragmatism of Black Women*. London: Routledge.

Janjua, Shahida. 1997. 'Is nationalism exclusive?' *MsChief*, no 15: 6-8.

Joyce, Catherine. 1997. 'Political discrimination and persecution', in Niamh Reilly (ed.) *Women's Rights as Human Rights: Local and Global Perspectives, Strategies and Analyses from the ICCL Working Conference on Women's Rights as Human Rights* (Dublin, March 1997). Dublin: Combat Poverty Agency and the National Committee for Development Education.

Kelly, John. 1988. 'The Constitution: law and manifesto', in Frank Litton (ed.) *The Constitution of Ireland 1937-1987*. Dublin: Institute of Public Administration.

Kendrick, Donald and Grattan Puxon. 1995. *Gypsies under the Swastika*. Hatfield: University of Hertfordshire Press.

Kennedy Patricia and Jo Murphy-Lawless. 2001. *The Maternity Care Needs of Refugee and Asylum-Seeking Women*. Dublin: Social Science Research Centre, UCD

Kenny, Máirín. 1997. *The Routes of Resistance: Travellers and Second Level Schooling*. Aldershot: Ashgate.

Keogh, Anna. 2000. 'Talking about the other: a view of how secondary school pupils construct opinions about refugees and asylum-seekers', in Malcolm MacLachlan and Michael O'Connell (eds.) *Cultivating Pluralism: Psychological, Social and Cultural Perspectives on a Changing Ireland*. Dublin: Oak Tree Press.

Keogh, Dermot. 1988. *Ireland and Europe 1919-1948*. Dublin: Gill and Macmillan.

Keogh, Dermot. 1998. *Jews in Twentieth Century Ireland: Reuigees, Anti-Semitism and the Holocaust*. Cork: Cork University Press.

King, Jason. 1999. 'Porous nation: from Ireland's "haemorrhage" to immigrant inundation', in Ronit Lentin (ed.) *The Expanding Nation: Towards a Multi-ethnic Ireland*. Dublin: Ethnic and Racial Studies, Department of Sociology, Trinity College.

King, Jason. 1999 'Porous nations: From 'Ireland's haemorrhage' to immigrant inundation – A critique of Ireland's Immigration Act, 1999' *Refuge: Canada's Periodical on Refugees* (Toronto). Vol. 18. no. 4: 19-25.

King, Jason. 2000. 'Asylum-Seekers and Irish National Sovereignty: Globalisation, International Migration, and Ireland's "Refugee Crisis"', *Review of Postgraduate Studies* (Galway), 8: 39-53.

King, Jason. 2001a. 'Between "the Face"and "the Crowd": Racism and Refugee Images in the European and Canadian Media', paper presented at the Red Stripe Anti-racism conference, Trinity College Dublin, March 3, 2001.

King, Jason. 2001b. 'Ireland abroad/broadening Ireland: From famine migrants to asylum-applicants and refugees', in Oonagh Walsh (ed.) *Ireland Abroad*. Dublin: Four Courts Press.

L'Amie, Aileen. (ed.) 1981 (but continuously updated). *The Irish Travellers: A Resource Collection*. Newtownabbey: Ulster Polytechnic.

Lentin, Alana. 2000. '"Race", racism and anti-racism: Challenging contemporary classifications', *Social Identities*, vol. 6, no. 1: 91-106.

Lentin, Louis. 1996. *Dear Daughter*. Broadcast on RTE 1, February 1996.

Lentin, Ronit. 1998a. 'Racialising (our) Dark Rosaleen: feminism, racism, antisemitism.' *UCG Centre for Women's Studies Review*, vol. 6: 1-18.

Lentin, Ronit. 1998b. '"Irishness," the 1937 Constitution and citizenship: a gender and ethnicity view.' *Irish Journal of Sociology*, vol. 8: 5-24.

Lentin, Ronit. 1998c. 'Connecting gender and racism', *Women's News*, issue 92: 10-11, Issue 93: 12-13.

Lentin, Ronit. 1998d. 'Problematising "Irish women": citizenship, ethnicity, feminism, racism.' Paper presented at the 'Emerging Voices: Irish Women Entering a New Millennium' conference, Mary Immaculate College, Limerick, April 1998.

Lentin, Ronit. 1998e. *Women Experiencing Racism in Ireland*. A report to the Roundtable Meeting for the European Monitoring Centre on Racism, the National Consultative Committee on Racism and Interculturalism, 26 November 1998.

Lentin, Ronit. 1999a. 'Constitutionally excluded: citizenship and (some) Irish women', in Nira Yuval-Davis and Pnina Werbner (eds). *Women, Citizenship and Difference*. London: Zed Books.

Lentin, Ronit (ed). 1999b. *The Expanding Nation: Towards a Multi-Ethnic Ireland*. Dublin: Ethnic and Racial Studies, Department of Sociology, Trinity College Dublin.

Lentin, Ronit (ed.) 2000. *Emerging Irish Identities*. Dublin: Ethnic and Racial Studies, Department of Sociology, Trinity College Dublin.

Liegeois, Jean Paul. 1987. *Roma, Gypsies, Travellers*. Strasbourg: Council of Europe Press.

Lorde, Audre. 2001. 'The master's tools will neer dismantle the master's house', in Kum-Kum Bhavnani (ed.) *Feminism and 'Race'*. Oxford: Oxford University Press.

Lutz, Helma, Anne Phoenix and Nira Yuval-Davis (eds.) 1995. *Crossfires: Nationalism, Racism and Gender in Europe*. London: Pluto Press.

Mac an Ghaill, Máirtín. 1999. *Contemporary Racisms and Ethnicities: Social and Cultural Transformations*. Buckingham: Open University Press.

Mac Connell. Sean. 1999. 'Pilot census form seeks answers on income and nationality', *The Irish Times*, 16 September 1999: 2.

Mac Gréil, Michéal. 1978. *Prejudice and Tolerance in Ireland: Based on a Survey of Intergroup Attitudes of Dublin Adults and Other Sources*. Maynooth: Survey Research Unit, St Patrick's College, Maynooth.

Mac Gréil, Michéal. 1996. *Prejudice in Ireland Revisited*. Maynooth: Survey and Research Unit, St Patrick College, Maynooth.

MacLachlan Malcolm and Michael O'Connell (eds.) 2000. *Cultivating Pluralism: Psychological, Social and Cultural Perspectives on a Changing Ireland*. Dublin: Oak Tree Press.

MacLaughlin, Jim. 1995. *Travellers and Ireland: Whose Country, Whose History?* Cork: Cork University Press.

Mac Síthigh, Daithí. 2000. 'Injustice by omission: The case for the introduction of 'hate crime' statute in Ireland', unpublished paper, Faculty of Law, Trinity College, Dublin.

Malik, Kenan. 1996. *The Meaning of Race*. London: Macmillan.

Mann-Kler, Deepa. 1997. *Out of the Shadows: An Action Research Report into Families, Racism and Exclusion in Northern Ireland*. Belfast: Barnardos/Save the Children Fund.

Mann-Kler, Deepa. 2000. 'Panel discussion: Beyond identity politics: Irish identity formation and anti-racism', in Ronit Lentin (ed.) *Emerging Irish Identities*. Dublin: Ethnic and Racial Studies, Department of Sociology, Trinity College, Dublin.

Marshall, Annecka. 1996. 'From sexual denigration to self-respect: resisting images of Black female sexuality', in Delia Jarrett-Macauley (ed) *Reconstructing Womanhood, Reconstructing Feminism: Writings on Black Women*. London: Routledge.

McCann, May, Seamus O'Siochain and Joseph Ruane (eds.) *Irish Travellers: Culture and Identity*. Belfast: *Institute of Irish Studies*, Queens University, Belfast.

McDonagh, Rosaleen. 2000. 'Talking back', in Anne Byrne and Ronit Lentin (eds.) *(Re)searching Women: Feminist Research Methodologies in the Social Sciences in Ireland*. Dublin: Institute of Public Administration.

McGarry, Patsy. 1998. 'Synod speaker believes treatment of asylum-seekers tarnished nation.' *The Irish Times*, 22 October 1998: 10.

McLoughlin, Dympna. 1994. 'Ethnicity and Irish Travellers: reflections on Ní Shuinéar.' In May McCann *et al, Irish Travellers: Culture and Ethnicity*. Belfast: Institute of Irish Studies.

McVeigh, Robbie and Alice Binchy. 1998. *Travellers, Refugees and Racism in Tallaght*. Tallaght: Tallaght Travellers Support Group/Tallaght Refugee Women's Group.

McVeigh, Robbie. 1992a. 'The Specificity of Irish Racism.' *Race and Class*, Vol. 33, Number 4.

McVeigh, Robbie. 1992b. 'Racism and Travelling People in Northern Ireland'; *17th Report of the Standing Advisory Commission for Human Rights*. Belfast: HMSO.

McVeigh, Robbie. 1994. *The Security Forces and Harassment in Northern Ireland*. Belfast: Committee on the Administration of Justice.

McVeigh, Robbie. 1996. *The Racialisation of Irishness: Racism and Anti-racism in Ireland*. Belfast: CRD.

McVeigh, Robbie. 1997. 'Theorising Sedentarism: The roots of anti-nomadism', in Thomas Acton (ed.) *Gypsy Politics and Traveller Identity*. University of Hertfordshire Press.

McVeigh, Robbie. 1998a. 'Racism in the north of Ireland', in European Year Against Racism, *Racism in Ireland, North and South*. Dublin: Stationery Office.

McVeigh, Robbie. 1998b. 'There's no racism because there's no Black people here': Racism and anti-racism in Northern Ireland', in Paul Hainsworth (ed). *Ethnicity in Northern Ireland*. London: Pluto Press.

McVeigh, Robbie. 1998c. 'Racism in the six counties: Theorizing the racism/sectarianism interface' in David Miller (ed). *Rethinking Northern Ireland*. London: Longman.

McVeigh, Robbie. 1998d. "Out in the Country": *The Traveller Economy in Belfast*. Belfast: West Belfast Economic Forum/Commission for Racial Equality Northern Ireland.

McVeigh, Robbie. 1999. 'Is sectarianism racism? The implications of sectarian division for multi-ethnicity in Ireland', in Ronit Lentin (ed.) *The Expanding Nation: Towards a Multi-ethnic Ireland*. Dublin: Ethnic and Racial Studies, Department of Sociology, Trinity College.

McVeigh, Robbie. 2001. *A Place of Refuge: Refugees and Asylum Seekers in Northern Ireland*. Belfast: Refugee Action Group

Memmi, Albert. 1990. *The Colonizer and the Colonized*. London: Earthscan.

Miles, Robert. 1982. *Racism and Migrant Labour*. London: George Allen and Unwin.

Miles, Robert. 1986. 'Labour migration, racism and capital accumulation in Western Europe', *Capital and Class*, 28: 49-86.

Miles, Robert. 1988. 'Racism, marxism and British politics', *Economy and Society*, 17(3) : 428-60.

Miles, Robert. 1989. *Racism*. London: Routledge.

Miles, Robert. 1993. *Racism after 'Race Relations'*. London: Routledge.

Minh-ha, Trinh. 1989. *Woman, Native, Other: Writing Postcoloniality and Feminism*. Bloomington: Indiana University Press.

Modood, Tariq, R. Berthoud *et al.* 1997. *Ethnic Minorities in Britain: Diversity and Disadvantage*. London: Policy Studies Institute.

Modood, Tariq. 1992. 'Being somebody and being oppressed: catching up with Jesse Jackson', in Tariq Modood, *Not Easy Being British: Colour, Culture and Citizenship*. Stoke on Trent: Runnymede Trust and Trentham Books.

Modood, Tariq. 1997. '"Difference," cultural racism and anti-racism', in Pnina Werbner and Tariq Modood (eds.) *Debating Cultural Hybridity: Multi-Cultural Identities and the Politics of Anti-Racism*. London: Zed Books.

Mohanty, Chandra T., Anne Russo and Lourdes Torres (eds.) 1991. *Third World Women and the Politics of Feminism*. Bloomington: Indiana University Press.

Moore, G. 1984. *Anti-Semitism in Ireland*. Unpublished Ph.D. thesis, University of Ulster.

Morrison, Toni. 1988. *Beloved*. London: Picador.

Morrison, Toni. 1992. *Playing in the Dark: Whiteness and the Literary Imagination*. Cambridge, Mass: Harvard University Press.

Mosse, George. 1985. *Towards the Final Solution: A History of European Racism*. Madison: University of Wisconsin Press.

Murphy, Frank, Cathleen McDonagh and Erica Sheehan (eds.) *Travellers, Citizens of Ireland: Our Challenge to an Intercultural Irish Society in the 21st Century*. Dublin: The Parish of the Travelling People.

Murray, Niall and Declan Varley. 1998. 'Councillor wants all Travellers tagged like cattle to monitor them.' *The Examiner*, 13 May 1998.

Myers, Kevin. 1998. 'An Irishman's Diary', *The Irish Times*, 30 January 1998.

Myrdal, Gunnar. 1962. *Challenge to Affluence*. New York: Pantheon Books.

Najjair, Rabia. 2000. 'When Irish eyes are frowning', in Ronit Lentin (ed.) *Emerging Irish Identities*. Dublin: MPhil in Ethnic and Racial Studies, Department of Sociology, Trinity College Dublin.

National Youth Council of Ireland. 1995. *Racism and Intolerance in Ireland*. Dublin: National Youth Council of Ireland, and Council of Europe.

Nexus Research Co-operative. 1994. *Preventing Racism at the Workplace*. Dublin: European Foundation for the Improvement of Living and Working Conditions.

Nexus Research Co-operative. 1997. *Developing an Anti-Racist Dimension to Government Department Customer Action Plans*. Dublin: Nexus.

Ní Shuinéar, Sinéad. 1994. 'Irish Travellers, ethnicity and the origin question', in May McCann *et al*, *Irish Travellers: Culture and Ethnicity*. Belfast: Institute of Irish Studies.

National Women's Council of Ireland. 2000. *Anti-racism Handbook*. Dublin: National Women's Council of Ireland.

NIAPN (Northern Ireland Anti-Poverty Network) 1995. *Racism and Poverty. Seminar Report*. Belfast: NIAPN in association with the Belfast Travellers Education and Development Group, the Chinese Welfare Association and the Northern Ireland Council for Travelling People.

Nic Suibhne, Maire. 1998. 'Fortress Ireland.' *The Guardian Weekend*, 3 October 1998: 32-39.

Noonan, Paul. 1994. *Travelling People in West Belfast*. Belfast: Save the Children Fund.

Noonan, Paul. 1998. 'Pathologisation and resistance: travellers, nomadism and the state', in Paul Hainsworth (ed) *Divided Society: Ethnic Minorities and Racism in Northern Ireland*. London: Pluto.

Northern Ireland Women's Aid Federation. 1998. *Violence on the Edge: A Training Pack for Trainers*. Belfast: Training for Women Network Ltd.

Nozinic, Drazen. 1997. 'Educational Needs and Possibilities for Asylum-seekers and Refugees in Ireland.' Dublin: Irish Refugee Council.

O'Connell, John. 1997. *Travellers, Gypsies, Roma*. Pavee Point Fact Sheet. Dublin: Pavee Point.

Ó Drisceoil, Donal. 1997. 'Jews and other undesirables', in Ethel Crowley and Jim MacLaughlan (eds.) *Under the Belly of the Tiger: Class, Race, Identity and Culture in the Global Ireland*. Dublin: Irish Reporter Publications.

Office of the Refugee Applications Commissioner. 2001. *Asylum-Seekers 1997-2000*. Dublin: Office of the Refugee Applications Commissioner.

O'Halloran, Marie. 1999. 'Asylum-seekers work permits cost employers £25 a month', *The Irish Times*, 13 August 1999: 5.

O'Hearn, Denis. 1994. *Free Trade or Managed Trade? Trading Between Two Worlds*. Belfast: CRD.

O'Riordan, Manus and Pat Feeley. 1984. *The Rise and Fall of Irish Antisemitism*. Dublin: Labour Workshops.

O'Toole, Fintan. 1995. *Meanwhile Back on the Ranch: The Politics of Irish Beef*. London: Vintage.

O'Toole, Michael. 2001. 'We're near top of Euro asylum list', *The Star*, 29 January 2001.

Park, Robert. 1925. 'The city: suggestions for the investigation of human behaviour in the urban environment', in Robert E. Park *et al* (eds.) *The City*. Chicago: UNC.

Park, Robert. 1950. *Race and Culture*. New York: Free Press.

Paris, Chris P., P. Maginn, and Paddy Gray. 1995. *Review of Policies Affecting Travellers*. Belfast: Department of the Environment.

Pavee Point/Lorna Ryan. 1998. *Equality Proofing, Administrative Procedures: A Review of Existing Approaches in Selected EU Member States*. Dublin: Pavee Point.

Pavee Point. 1995. *Incorporating a discrimination theme within the proposed National Anti-Poverty Strategy*. Dublin: Pavee Point.

Pavee Point. 1997. *Roma, Gypsies, Travellers East/West: Regional and Local Policies*. Report of the International Study Conference, Rome, 1991. Dublin: Pavee Point.

Pavee Point. 2000. *Pavee Beoirs Breaking the Silence: Traveller Women and Male Domestic Violence*. Dublin: Pavee Point in association with the Eastern Health Board and Women's Aid.

Platform Against Racism. 1997. *Information Pack*. Dublin: Platform Against Racism.

Quinn, P. 1995. *A Profile of the Bosnian Community in Ireland, 1995*. Dublin: Bosnian Community Development Project.

Raftery, Mary and Eoin O'Sullivan. 1999. *Suffer the Little Children: The Inside Story of Ireland's Industrial Schools*. Dublin: New Island.

Rattansi, Ali. 1992. 'Changing the subject? Racism, culture and education', in James Donald and Ali Rattansi (eds.) *Race, Culture, Difference*. London: Sage.

Refugee Agency. 1997a. *A Part of Ireland Now: Ten Refugee Stories*. Dublin: Refugee Agency.

Refugee Agency. 1997b. *Vietnamese Programme Refugees in Ireland Information Sheet*. Dublin: Refugee Agency.

Refugee Agency. 1997c. *Bosnian Programme Refugees in Ireland Information Sheet*. Dublin: Refugee Agency.

Refugee Agency. 1998. *Report of a Survey of the Vietnamese and Bosnian Refugee Communities in Ireland*. Dublin: Refugee Agency.

Refugee Forum. 1991. *The Walls of the Fortress: European Agreement against Immigrants, Migrants and Refugees*. London: Refugee Forum.

Refugee Protection Policy Group. 2000a. *The Case for Provision of Complementary Protection Status in Irish Law. Position paper no. 1, May 2000*. Dublin: Refugee Protection Policy Group. rppg@irishrefugeepolicy.org

Refugee Protection Policy Group. 2000b. *Deportation in a Human Rights Context, Position paper no 2, July 2000*. Dublin: Refugee Protection Policy Group. rppg@irishrefugeepolicy.org

Refugee Protection Policy Group. 2000c. *Statement on the Processing of Claims under Manifestly Unfounded Procedures, Position paper no 3, July 2000*. Dublin: Refugee Protection Policy Group. rppg@irishrefugeepolicy.org

Rex, John. 1970. *Race Relations in Sociological Theory*. London: Weidenfeld and Nicolson.

Rushdie, Salman. 1989. *The Satanic Verses*. London: Viking.

Ryan, Lorna. 1995. *Traveller Inclusion in the Mainstream Labour Force*. Dublin: Pavee Point.

Ryan, Lorna. 1996. *Incorporating a Discrimination Theme within the Proposed National Anti-Poverty Strategy*. Dublin: Pavee Point.

SACHR (Standing Advisory Commission on Human Rights). 1991. *Sixteenth Rights Report for 1990-91*.

SACHR. *1992. Seventeenth Report of the Standing Advisory Commission on Human Rights. Report for 1991-2*.

SACHR. 1993. *Eighteenth Report of the Standing Advisory Commission on Human Rights: Report for 1992-3*.

Sansani, Inbal. 2001. *The Provision of Services to Refugee Women who had Experienced Gendered Torture*. Dublin: MPhil in Ethnic and Racial Studies, Department of Sociology, Trinity College Dublin.

Sebag Montefiore, Simon. 1997. *The Great Hatred*. A Hard Cash documentary for Channel Four, broadcast 11 October 1997.

Sinha, Shalini. 1997. 'Is there racism in Ireland?' *MsChief*, no 15: 9

Sivanandan, A. 1983. *A Different Hunger*. London: Pluto Press.

Smith, Patrick. 1997. 'More than half of Irish see themselves as racist.' *The Irish Times*, 20 December 1997: 6.

Solomos, John and Les Back. 1996. *Racism and Society*. London: Macmillan.

Stanfield II, John H. 1985. *Philanthropy and Jim Crow in American Social Science*. Westport: Greenwood Press.

Stanfield II, John H. and R.M. Dennis (eds.) 1993. *A History of Race Relations Research: First Generation Recollections*. London: Sage.

Stanley, Liz and Sue Wise. 1993. *Breaking Out Again: Feminist Consciousness and Feminist Research*. London: Routledge.

Stanley, Liz. 1993. 'The knowing, because experiencing subject: Narratives, lives and autobiography', *Women's Studies International Forum*, 16(3): 205-215.

Staunton, Denis. 2001. 'Leaders agree to policies on terrorism, asylum', *The Irish Times*, 17 December 2001: 10.

Storey, Andy. 2000. *Farawayan: Information and Activity on Refugees and Asylum-seekers in Ireland and Abroad*. Dublin: Calypso Productions.

Sultan, Fardus and Zena. 1999. *Report of a Survey: Barriers and Needs of Bosnian Refugee Women in regard to Education, Employment and Social Inclusion*. Dublin: Zena, Bosnian Women Accessing Education.

Sweeney, John. 2000. 'Racists rule streets of Ireland,' *The Observer*, 18 June: 10.

Synon, Mary Ellen. 1996. 'Time to get tough on tinker terror "culture."' *The Sunday Independent*, 26 January.

Tannam, Marian, Suzanne Smyth and Suzie Flood. 1998. *Anti-Racism: an Irish Perspective*. Dublin: Harmony.

Tannam, Marian. 1991. *Racism in Ireland: Sources of Information*. Dublin: Harmony.

Task Force. 1995. *Report of the Task Force on the Travelling Community*. Dublin: Stationery Office.

The Agreement. 1998. *The Agreement Reached in Multi-Party Negotiations*. Belfast: HMSO.

Tennant, Victoria. 2000. *Sanctuary in a Cell: The Detention of Asylum-seekers in Northern Ireland*. Belfast: Law Centre.

Thomas, Helen. 1997. 'Female slaves and the politics of reproduction and infanticide', in Ronit Lentin (ed) *Gender and Catastrophe*. London: Zed Books.

Torode, Ruth, Trish Walsh and Marguerite Woods. 2001. *Working with Refugees and Asylum-Seekers: A Social Work Resource Book*. Dublin: Department of Social Studies, Trinity College, Dublin.

Tracy, Marshal. 2000. *Racism and immigration in Ireland*. Dublin: MPhil in Ethnic and Racial Studies, Department of Sociology, Trinity College, Dublin.

Travis, Alan. 1998. 'Fortress Europe's four circles of purgatory.' *The Guardian*, 20 October: 19.

UNESCO. 1978. *Declaration on Race and Racial Prejudice*. Adopted and proclaimed by the General Conference of the United Nations Educational, Scientific and Cultural Organization at its twentieth session, on 27 November 1978.

United Nations. 2001. *Convention on the Elimination of Racial Discrimination*. United Nations Fact Sheet 12.

United Nations High Commissioner for Refugees (UNHCR). 1999. *UNHCR Conference: Refugee Women – Victims or Survivors?* Dublin: UHNCR.

Van den Berghe, Pierre. 1978. *Race and Racism: A Comparative Perspective*. New York: Wiley.

Van Dijk, Teun. 1991. *Racism and the Press*. London: Routledge.

Van Dijk, Teun. 1993. *Elite Discourse and Racism*. London: Sage.

Ward, Tanya. 2001. *Immigration and Residency in Ireland*. Dublin: City of Dublin Vocational Education Committee.

Warm, David S. 1998. 'The Jews of Northern Ireland', in Paul Hainsworth (ed.) *Divided Society: Ethnic Minorities and Racism in Northern Ireland*. London: Pluto.

Werbner, Pnina and Tariq Modood (eds.) 1997. *Debating Cultural Hybridity: Multi-Cultural Identities and the Politics of Anti-Racism*. London: Zed Books.

Wieviorka, Michel. 1995. *The Arena of Racism*. London: Sage.

Wieviorka, Michel. 1997. 'Is it so difficult to be an anti-racist?' in Pnina Werbner and Tariq Modood (eds.) *Debating Cultural Hybridity: Multi-Cultural Identities and the Politics of Anti-Racism*. London: Zed Books.

Williams, Patricia. 1991. *The Alchemy of Race and Rights*. Cambridge, Mass: Harvard University Press.

Women's Racism Awareness Group. 1997. *An Injury to One is and injury to All: Anti-racist Training and Information Pack*. Belfast: WRAG.

Wren, Maev-Ann. 2000. 'The roller coaster decades', *The Irish Times*, 16 May 2000: 14.

Yu, Patrick. 1995. 'From Social Alienation to Social Deprivation – A Response from the Chinese Community', in NIAPN 1995.

Yuval-Davis, Nira and Floya Anthias (eds.) 1989. *Woman – Nation – State*. London: Macmillan.

Yuval-Davis, Nira. 1997. *Gender and Nation*. London: Sage.

Yuval-Davis, Nira. 1999. 'Institutional racism, cultural diversity and citizenship: some reflections on reading the Stephen Lawrence Inquiry Report', *Sociological Research Online*, vol. 4(1). http://www.socresonline.org.uk/socresonline/4/1/yuval-davis.html

Additional references not listed in the body of the text

Useful websites

ARASI (Association of Asylum-seekers and Refugees In Ireland): http://Indigo.Ie/~arasi
ARC (Anti-Racism Campaign): http://flag.blackened.net/revolt/arc.html
Bibliography of Sources on Irish Traveller Culture: http://www.pitt.edu/~alkst3/Bibliography.html
Different but the Same (Anti-racism pack for primary teachers In Ireland): http://www.tcd.ie/Education/Teachers_Pack/
Equality Commission for Northern Ireland: http://www.cre.gov.uk/about/cre_ni.html
European Commission Against Racism and Intolerance (ECRI): http://www.ecri.coe.int/
European Monitoring Centre on Racism and Xenophobia: http://www.eumc.at
European Network Against Racism (ENAR): www.enar-eu.org
Comhlamh: www.comhlamh.org
Irish Centre for Migration Studies: www.migration.ucc.ie
Irish diary on racism: http://sites.netscape.net/rarireland/racist_diary.html
Irish Refugee Council: http://www.irishrefugeecouncil.ie/press.html
Irish Traveller Movement: http://www.itmtrav.com/
MPhil in Ethnic and Racial Studies, TCD: http://www2.tcd.Ie/Sociology/mphil.html
National Consultative Committee on Racism and Interculturalism: homepage.eircom.net/~racismctee/index
Pavee Point Traveller Centre: http://www.iol.ie/~pavee/
Refugee Protection Policy Group: rppg@irishrefugeepolicy.org
Residents against Racism: residents_against_racism@ireland.com
Stop Deportations Campaign: stop.deportations:Ireland.com
The Equality Authority: www.equality.ie
The European Council on Refugees and Exiles: www.ecre.org/observations/minimum
United for International Action: www.united.non-profit.nl

2.

Travellers in Ireland: An examination of discrimination and racism[1]

John O'Connell

Introduction

Travellers are widely acknowledged as one of the most marginalised and disadvantaged groups in Irish society. Travellers fare poorly on every indicator used to measure disadvantage: unemployment, poverty, social exclusion, health status, infant mortality, life expectancy, illiteracy, education and training levels, access to decision making and political representation, gender equality, access to credit, accommodation and living conditions. It is not surprising therefore, that the Economic and Social Research Institute concluded that 'the circumstances of the Irish Travelling people are intolerable. No humane and decent society, once made aware of such circumstances, could permit them to persist' (ESRI, July 1986, Paper no. 131). The ESRI also stated that Irish Travellers are 'a uniquely disadvantaged group: impoverished, under-educated, often despised and ostracised, they live on the margins of Irish society.'

While there is a broad consensus on the low status, marginalisation and disadvantage of Travellers, there is far less agreement and much dissent when the issues of discrimination and especially racism are raised. In particular, there can be strong resistance by policy makers and others to the idea of a causal relationship between discrimination/racism and the poor living circumstances of Travellers (see, for example, McVeigh, 1996, 1997 and Ryan, 1996). This chapter sets out to provide a framework for examining issues of discrimination and racism as well as the accuracy and relevancy of applying such terms to the situation of Travellers in Ireland. It begins by tracing the development of government policies in relation to Travellers and how these have evolved, assisted by internal and external influences. The chapter will refer to the widespread tendency to deny the existence of racism despite evidence of a racialisation process in both media and political discourse. It also presents definitions and different approaches to racism, as well as examples of the specific manifestations of anti-Traveller discrimination. Finally, it will outline some possibilities and directions for tackling racism at national and European Union levels.

Development of policies at national level

The first phase of a clear and explicit government response to the Travellers in Ireland can be linked to the Report of the *Commission on Itinerancy* in 1963. The terms of reference of the Commission are revealing in the way the problem being addressed was conceptualised. The Commission set out 'to enquire into the problem arising from the presence in the country of itinerants in considerable numbers; to examine the economic, educational, health and social problems inherent in their way of life'. In order to provide a better way of life for Travellers the Commission undertook 'to promote their absorption into the general community'.

The starting point for the Commission was that itinerancy was a problem to be eliminated, and rehabilitation, settlement and assimilation were the means for achieving this. Travellers were viewed as a problem; the Commission Report comments on the social and ethical behaviour of Travellers and their tendency to keep aloof from the majority population. There was no explicit acknowledgement or examination of discrimination towards Travellers. In fact, critics of the Report saw the assimilationist policies it pursued as being discriminatory and racist. While the settlement programme could claim some success in terms of more Travellers living in houses, and more children attending schools, there were many indications of 'failure' also: twenty years later there was still the same number of Travellers living on the roadside in poor circumstances; many living in houses were not integrated and continued to experience social exclusion; some Travellers who settled left houses and returned to living in caravans.

In the subsequent two decades the Report of the Commission provided a framework for action and understanding of Traveller issues. Interventions were viewed as being 'for' rather than 'with' Travellers. Travellers were frequently referred to as being in need of charity rather than rights. In so far as there was a criticism of the majority population it was expressed in terms of failure to live out the Christian gospel (Bewley, 1974).

The second phase in government policy development with regard to Travellers is contained in the *Report of the Travelling People Review Body,* 1983. This report had the benefit of twenty years experience since the earlier report and shows a significant shift in thinking by policy makers and others involved with Travellers. The Review Body was asked to examine 'the needs of Travellers who wish to continue a nomadic way of life' and how 'barriers of mistrust between the settled and Travelling communities can be broken down and mutual respect for each others' way of life increased'. Opposition from settled and Traveller activists to the assimilationist approach contributed to a revision of the thinking. Concepts such as absorption, settlement, assimilation and rehabilitation were no longer acceptable and were rejected in the report. The term 'itinerant', which was associated with vagrancy and deviancy, was replaced with 'traveller', which was a recognition of a distinct identity.

Prejudice and hostility, misunderstanding, resistance, indifference and harassment towards Travellers were acknowledged as issues and integration was the goal.

However, there was great reluctance to name discrimination as an issue: 'The Review Body is pleased to record that there is no evidence of discrimination against Travellers in the granting of social welfare assistance and in gaining enrolment in local primary and second level schools'. The Report does refer to 'many instances of bias against Travellers in the allocation of tenancies of local authority houses'. However, the Report, in its eagerness not to be critical of official efforts, is quick to point out that '(local) authorities deserve recognition for their accomplishments, often attained in spite of considerable local opposition'.

The Review Body did consider the desirability of having special legislation to outlaw discrimination against Travellers as a minority group but concluded that '*such* legislation would be fraught with difficulties, especially in the absence of a precise legal definition of "traveller." Accordingly, the enactment of anti-discrimination laws is not sought'.

However, the naming of Travellers in legislation, without any perceived need (on the part of the government) to define 'Traveller', took place in three pieces of legislation in Ireland, subsequent to the publication of the Report and before the Task Force Report of 1995, in effect in direct contradiction of the above:

The 1988 Housing Act,
The 1989 Prohibition of Incitement to Hatred Act, and
The 1993 Unfair Dismissals (Amendment) Act.

The third phase of policy development can be associated with the publication of the Report of the *Task Force on the Travelling Community* in 1995. This document devotes a full section to the issue of discrimination, which is a reflection of the fact that the key Traveller support groups had made this a priority issue for the previous ten years. It had also become a major media issue. Discrimination and access feature right through the document in relation to Traveller/settled relations, culture, accommodation, health, education and training, youth service provision, the Traveller economy, Traveller women and disabled Travellers:

Academic debate and various international fora focus attention on the link between racism and cultural difference, particularly in scenarios of unequal power relationships. The forms of prejudice and discrimination experienced by the Traveller community equate with racism in the international context.

The Report also refers to the need to combat discrimination with legislation and education:

Over the past decade discrimination against Travellers has not diminished. Such a scenario requires new initiatives and new approaches. Public debate has increasingly focused attention on the need for legislative initiatives.

In Ireland, the 1995 Task Force Report outlines the different types of discrimination experienced by Travellers at the individual or interpersonal level and at the institutional level. According to the report, this discrimination experienced by Travellers can be direct and indirect, intentional or unintentional.

International focus on Gypsies and Travellers

The new willingness to include Travellers in legislation resulted in Traveller Support Groups, Travellers and others mobilising as advocates for Travellers' rights. It has also been facilitated to some extent by outside influences. In 1991, the European Parliament Committee of Inquiry on Racism and Xenophobia reported that, in Ireland, 'The single most discriminated against ethnic group is the Travelling People'. The Committee, referring to Ireland, recommended 'that the only Member State which has not already signed the UN Convention on the Elimination of All Forms of Racial Discrimination, do so as soon as possible'.

The UN Commission on Human Rights, in its report *Elimination of Racism and Racial Discrimination* (1994), deals with contemporary forms of racism, racial discrimination, xenophobia and related intolerance in a wide range of countries. The report states that 'Gypsies, also called Tsiganes, Rom or Romanies, are a group which is particularly targeted by rising racism and xenophobia in Europe'. With regard to Irish Travellers the report states that 'Travellers have experienced widespread discrimination in Ireland' and 'Travellers have also expressed the view that, where accommodation and services are provided, these do not always adequately reflect their needs'.

The Minority Rights Group International report published in 1995, entitled *Roma/Gypsies: A European Minority*, says:

> Policies towards Roma/Gypsies have always constituted, in one form or another, a negation of the people, their culture and their language. Past policies can be broadly grouped into three categories: exclusion, containment, and assimilation.

Denial of racism

While there is a willingness to acknowledge that there is widespread prejudice towards Travellers in Irish society and also recognition of discrimination against Travellers, there is still strong resistance among the Irish public to calling the treatment of Travellers racism. The title of an education pack *I'm No Racist, and What Is It Anyway?* (Calypso Productions, 1997) is a clever depiction of this resistance. The reasons for this denial of racism are complex and varied. First of all, Irish people are not unique in their tendency to deny the existence of racism in ourselves and in our country. Most countries have similar experiences of people seeing racism in the distance while refusing to acknowledge it at home or in themselves (Eurobarometer, 1997). Secondly, there is a tendency to see racism only in relation to skin colour. When the issue of defining the meaning of black and white arises and is combined with the task of categorising a range of other shades of skin pigmentation the issue ceases to be so simple. Usually, this involves resorting to confused usage of such concepts as 'races', 'race relations' and nationality. For instance, it is frequently said that Travellers cannot experience racism because they are white, are not 'a different race' nor a different nationality.

This denial, confusion, as well as a tendency to blame the victim is evident in the following excerpt from a written submission by an Irish MEP to the Committee of Inquiry into Racism and Xenophobia in 1990:

> Ireland is a racially homogenous country with no ethnic minority groups. As a consequence there are no racial problems of the kind experienced in countries with such groups. Neither is there a large presence of foreigners... the position could alter if the influx became sustained... there is however a minority group of travelling people giving rise to some of the problems associated with racism (cited in O'Connell, 1994).

Racialisation

The mistaken tendency to equate 'race' with colour has been refuted by many academics such as Charles Husband (1982), who refers to this quote from Charles Kingsley's correspondence about his visit to Ireland in 1860:

> I am haunted by the human chimpanzees I saw along that hundred miles of horrible country ... to see white chimpanzees is dreadful; if they were black, one would not feel it so much, but their skins, except where tanned by exposure, are as white as ours.

This quotation reflects the racialisation process whereby members of a group, in this instance the (white) Irish, are identified as belonging to a 'race' category on the basis of fixed characteristics which they are assumed to possess. Central to such race-thinking are notions of superiority and inferiority, and of purity and pollution. These notions are clearly evident in the following excerpt from a debate in the House of Commons in 1953 referring to Africans:

> Let us remember that 95 per cent of them are primitive people. One of the reasons why they are not generally accepted into hotels is because their sanitary habits are not all that could be desired ... The effect of alcohol upon an African is remarkable ... alcohol seems to bring out all the evil instincts in the African in the most astonishing way ... (Miles and Phizacklea, 1984)

Racism, as reflected in these references, is more than a prejudicial attitude. It involves a pattern of social relations, structures and an ideological discourse which reflects unequal power between groups. This understanding of racism will be examined and developed further below but as it is dependent on a racialisation process, let us first take a look at the role of the media in this process and in the reproduction of racism towards Travellers.

The media and racism

The following newspaper accounts illustrate how the negative portrayal of Irish Travellers contributes to the ideological racist discourse. Under a section on crime in *The Sunday Independent* (28th January, 1996), was the following headline: 'Time To Get Tough On Tinker Terror "Culture"'. According to the article by Mary Ellen

Synon, Gardaí believe that Travellers are responsible for over 90 per cent of attacks on the rural elderly (cf. *Pavee Point, Policy, Statement on Violence and Crime*, February 1996, unpublished). The writer states that Traveller culture:

> is a life of appetite ungoverned by intellect … It is a life worse than the life of beasts, for beasts at least are guided by wholesome instinct. Traveller life is without the ennobling intellect of man or the steadying instinct of animals. This tinker 'culture' is without achievement, discipline, reason or intellectual ambition. It is a morass. And one of the surprising things about it is that not every individual bred in this swamp turns out bad. Some individuals among the tinkers find the will not to become evil.

An article on Travellers by journalist Brendan O'Connor, also in *The Sunday Independent* (25th May, 1997) used another sensational headline: 'Patience Runs Thin When Uncivilised Travellers Spill Blood' to cover Traveller feuding. The writer gave a detailed account of the feud in a cemetery and concluded that 'It just doesn't happen in a civilised society'. He then went on to justify his use of the term 'knacker':

> Where I come from the word 'knacker' doesn't mean someone of any specific socio-economic or ethnic background. It means someone who behaves in a way that society abhors. And that's what the people who desecrated a Tuam graveyard last June were, knackers and scumbags.

The same journalist insists on using similar language in other reports, and the sub-editor used the offensive term in the headline:

> Good relations knackered: The conflict is not between settled and Traveller. It's between decent people and 'knackers' (*The Sunday Independent*, 31 August 1996).

The anti-Traveller discourse features frequently in both national and especially local newspapers and radio. Very often, as in the following, local politicians are being quoted:

> They are dirty and unclean. Travelling people have no respect for themselves and their children (County Councillor quoted in *The Irish Times*, 13th March, 1991).

> These people have been a constant headache for towns and cities throughout the country (County Councillor quoted in *The Cork Examiner*, 13th June, 1990).

> Killarney is literally infested by these people (County Councillor quoted in *The Cork Examiner,* 18th July, 1989).

> They are a constant problem, moving from one open area to another and creating problems (County Councillor quoted in *The Cork Examiner*, 13th June, 1990).

> Deasy suggests birth control to limit traveller numbers (Headline in *The Irish Times*, Friday, June 14, 1996).

In the Dáil Report column referring to remarks by Mr. Austin Deasy, T.D. Fine Gael, the deputy is reported as saying that the problem of Travellers would not be solved by providing more halting sites but by ensuring that Travellers' numbers be contained by birth control and assimilation into existing housing estates:

'Traveller tradition not a divine right.' Brendan O'Connor applauds Councillor Ann Devitt for suggesting that Traveller culture is not sacrosanct, and that the time has come for them to change their way of life (*The Sunday Independent*, June 15 1997).

The sooner the shotguns are at the ready and these travelling people are put out of our county the better. They are not our people, they aren't natives (Remarks of a Fianna Fail Councillor at a Waterford County Council meeting, *The Sunday Independent*, 14 April 1996).

These samples of media coverage of Travellers provide some indication of how Travellers are perceived and treated in Irish society. This chapter argues that such coverage and the social relations associated with it constitute a form of racism. As Helleiner demonstrates:

the powerful discourses of the press contribute to the creation of an ideological context which legitimates coercive state policies, everyday discriminatory practices, and ultimately violence against Travellers…While press reports of the 1960s and much of the 1970s were explicit in their portrayal of the Travellers and the travelling way of life as problematic, during the 1980s overtly racist discourses were increasingly replaced by more sophisticated discourses of exclusion (Helleiner, 1994).

However, the above sample of media coverage would seem to indicate that this claim of a shift from overt to more covert racism was inaccurate and it was certainly not borne out in the 1990s coverage. MacGréil in *Prejudice in Ireland Revisited* (1996), states that 'Irish Travellers are still seen and treated as a "lower caste" in society'. According to his research findings there has been a substantial deterioration in attitudes towards Travellers since 1972-3, leading him to conclude that 'Irish people's prejudice against Travellers is one of caste-like apartheid'. Máirín Kenny in her investigation into the interaction between Traveller ethnic identity and schooling, concludes that:

dominant sedentary society and its institutions remain the instigators and maintainers of institutional and interpersonal racism and exclusion, which has pressured Travellers over a long time-span into distorted performances (Kenny, 1997).

Quite clearly, a racialisation process inferring the inferiority of Travellers is the outcome of media and political discourse. Let us now return to the issue of definitions and theoretical approaches.

Approaches to racism

Racism is a specific form of discrimination usually associated with skin colour and ethnicity. It is an ideology of superiority which provides a rationalisation for oppression. It also involves an abuse of power by one group over another group. So, while racism involves negative stereotypes and assumptions it should not be reduced simply to attitudes, thereby equating it with prejudice, as pointed out earlier in this chapter. The reality of unequal power combined with prejudice enables some groups to treat others in racist ways by denying them access to opportunities, resources and decision-making processes.

The concept of racism is frequently contested among academics and others. There is the polarisation between those who argue that certain societies are inherently racist and those who claim that racism is a less serious issue related to the anti-social behaviour of some individuals. There are also a variety of approaches which can be categorised as follows: moral, biological, psychological, multi-cultural and structural.

The moral, psychological and cultural approaches tend to depoliticise the issue of racism by focusing almost exclusively on individual attitudes and behaviours dislocated from their social, political, economical, and historical contexts. Solutions based on the moral approach rightly draw attention to the reality that racism is a moral issue even though the treatment of Travellers is rarely presented in this way. If the churches, for instance, speak out on Traveller issues they tend to focus on prejudice rather than racism, thereby over-relying on attitudinal change.

The psychological approach, as Kovel argues, is by no means a sufficient tool for understanding the phenomenon of racism; it is, however, a necessary one:

> Racism, far from being the simple delusion of a bigoted and ignorant minority, is a set of beliefs whose structure arises from the deepest levels of our lives – from the fabric of assumptions we make about the world, ourselves, and others, and from the patterns of our fundamental social activities.

Kovel shows how various fantasies and personality traits can coalesce into 'race' prejudice and how this sheds light on the history of racism: 'Racist psychology is a prerequisite of racial institutions, and racist institutions engender a racist psychology' (Kovel, 1971).

The biological approach draws attention to the objective reality of certain physical differences and the specific form of racism associated with skin colour. Anti-racism does not mean a denial of these differences but does challenge the social meanings and interpretations attributed to them. UNESCO statements have debunked the so-called scientific racism based on biological determinism. However, this theory keeps recurring in the form of sociobiology, even though most geneticists and biologists acknowledge that 'the designation of the world's population into distinctive racial categories can no longer be considered a tenable scientific enterprise' (Troyna and Williams, 1986).

The multi-cultural approach is popular with many people because it is non-threatening, and can improve mutual appreciation and understanding between individuals and groups; it can also contribute to overcoming communication problems and misunderstanding, which may fuel racism. However this approach is criticised for diverting attention away from power differentials, structural oppression and for overestimating ignorance as the main factor in the creation of racism.

The structural approach provides a sociological framework for understanding racism in the context of changing historical, political, economic and social processes.

This approach provides a mechanism for going beyond symptoms and for addressing root causes. It also exposes how routine practices and procedures result in Black and minority ethnic groups having lower incomes, higher unemployment, worse health, accommodation and life chances than the majority population and less influence on the decisions which affect their lives. However, the approach has been accused of making inflated claims (see Miles, 1989) and for deterministic and doctrinaire explanations which ignore concrete situations and individual personalities (Donald and Rattansi, 1992)

Anti-Traveller discrimination and racism

In light of this examination of concepts, definitions, and approaches to racism, let us return to the concrete situation of Travellers in Ireland and how they experience discrimination. Individuals, when recognised as Travellers, are sometimes arbitrarily refused entry or access to public places or services such as shops, pubs, restaurants, laundries, and leisure facilities. Individuals often experience verbal or physical abuse because of their identity. Individual Travellers have also reported incidents of insurance companies refusing to provide them with motor insurance cover. A number of public houses consistently refuse to serve Travellers, while others do so now and then. Travellers frequently have difficulty obtaining hotels for wedding receptions. Many policies, procedures and practices reflect either a lack of acceptance or a total denial of Traveller identity. For many years Travellers experienced segregation in the provision of social welfare services. Travellers who wish to avail of supplementary welfare in Dublin have to accept a 'special' segregated service. Negative stereotypes and scapegoating of Travellers are commonplace. Traveller children in schools have also experienced segregation through 'special classes', although the current policy of the Department of Education is based on the promotion of integration. Nevertheless, some schools still refuse to accept Travellers using the pretext of being full or unsuitable. Travellers are also critical of a system which they feel undermines or largely ignores their identity in the curriculum and school ethos despite the extra capitation grants provided by the government for schools with Travellers among their pupils.

There is also a clear gender dimension to the Traveller experience of racism (Crickley, 1992). Many Traveller women are more easily identifiable than Traveller men, and are therefore more likely to experience discrimination. Sometimes evictions are carried out when Traveller men are away, leaving women to deal with the brunt of male verbal and physical abuse. But above all Traveller women, as mothers, home-makers and carers, have to make do with low incomes, in poor living circumstances, without basic facilities such as running water and sanitation.

Travellers with a disability have usually been cared for in institutions, where assimilation was the norm and where little or no consideration was given to cultural identity (McDonagh, chapter 8 in this volume; MacDonagh, 1994).

The most public and controversial area where anti-Traveller discrimination arises is in relation to the provision of accommodation. Local authorities and resident associations are accused by Travellers and Traveller support groups of turning the accommodation issue into a political football. Elected local councillors are keenly aware that their political survival depends on the support of local residents who easily outnumber Travellers. Resident associations make their opposition to Travellers living in 'their' areas very clear. Local authorities in turn have undertaken a 'boulder policy' which involves placing large rocks along the roadsides where Travellers camped or might camp illegally. This is combined with evictions of Travellers from unofficial camping sites. Gardaí and/or private security firms are sometimes involved in carrying out these evictions.

The accommodation issue highlights the underlying contradiction of the 'settlement' project, which is based on a rejection of nomadism, a carrot-and-stick approach to housing and an unwillingness by the majority population to have Travellers living near them as neighbours. Local authorities and resident associations frequently debate the idea of a Traveller quota, by discussing whether an area has taken its 'fair share of Travellers'. The term 'settled Traveller' carries moralistic connotations of the sedentarist thinking that goes with this. It suggests 'settling down' or conforming to what is considered the norm. In line with this thinking many people from the majority population believe that Travellers living in houses are 'settled', having thereby ceased to be Travellers. Nonetheless, such thinking does not mean social inclusion as equals. Ultimately, such thinking can be traced to the view that Travellers are vagrants or drop-outs in need of rehabilitation.

The deplorable living circumstances of many Travellers, because of the lack of suitable accommodation, is a crucial factor in the poor health of Travellers. The life expectancy of Travellers is far below the national average, with Traveller men and Traveller women living on average ten years and twelve years less than their sedentary peers, respectively. Traveller infant mortality is more than twice that of the majority population. These realities, combined with a failure to address them comprehensively, are seen by politicised Travellers and Traveller support groups as other manifestations of institutional racism.

In recent years some Gypsies, particularly Roma from Romania and Bosnia, have come to Ireland as refugees. The negative reaction in the media to them and to other asylum-seekers indicates the possibility of a dangerous situation arising, unless steps are taken now to confront racism and xenophobia in this context (see National Co-ordinating Committee, European Year Against Racism, Newsletter 4, June 1997).

The racism toward Travellers in Ireland is similar to racism in general insofar as it involves negative stereotyping based on notions of superiority and inferiority. Likewise it builds on fantasies related to dirt, danger, deviance, and crime. In common with some other forms of racism it invokes a pariah syndrome which is used to deny or legitimate the existence of racism. These particular features have taken on their own specific meanings in relation to the treatment of Travellers in the Irish context but perhaps what marks off this form of racism from others is the sedentarist approach to nomadism. Nomadism is viewed as an atavistic aberration which has to be eliminated by modernisation or failing that, coercion.

Anti-racist strategies

Traveller support groups have been to the fore in drawing attention to and devising strategies against the reality of racism in Ireland (McVeigh, 1997). While having a particular interest in Traveller issues, efforts have been made to develop alliances with other minority ethnic groups. This is reflected in the setting up of the Platform Against Racism, which is a coalition of non-government organisations committed to developing ways to combat racism and to promoting interculturalism. As well as providing information on Travellers and promoting greater awareness, Traveller organisations have also contributed to putting anti-racism on the agendas of other organisations and projects e.g. the Community Development Programme, area-based partnership companies, youth organisations and women's organisations.

In recent years, Traveller organisations have been able to avail of various European Commission programmes in order to develop a transnational dimension to their work. In particular, links have been developed between Traveller and Roma organisations throughout the EU as well as with other anti-racist organisations. Traveller organisations have played an active role in other organisations such as the European Anti-Poverty network (EAPN); in events like the Social Forum; in campaigns such as that led by the Starting Line Group; in the lobbying for the inclusion of a non-discrimination clause in the Treaties during the preparations for the 1997 Intra-Governmental Conference (IGC); and in committees and events during the 1997 European Year Against Racism.

Until recently, it has been almost impossible to seriously tackle the issue of racism at a political level within the EU because there was no legal basis for this in the Treaties. However, since the revision of the Treaties in Amsterdam, and the inclusion of a non-discrimination clause for the first time, a new situation exists. The potential for fighting racism at EU level has been created but requires time and further campaigning to maximise this potential. For instance, with sufficient political mobilisation it is now possible to introduce a directive or a number of directives to ensure that racism is tackled in each member state.

The designation of 1997 as European Year Against Racism has highlighted the need to take the issue of racism more seriously and to combat racism in a more concerted way throughout the European Union. The establishment of a Monitoring Centre on Racism and Xenophobia in Vienna enables member states to collect and collate data for anti-racist actions. Likewise support by the European Commission for the setting up of a European-level mechanism for co-ordinating the work of anti-racist NGOs builds on the momentum of the year.

Conclusion

The marginalisation of Travellers in Irish society is acknowledged by people of varying political positions and approaches. Past policies, while designed to overcome this marginalisation, have sometimes exacerbated the situation because of a failure to grasp the nature of the oppression experienced by Travellers. In particular, the denial of discrimination and racism, combined with a racialisation process, contributed to that marginalisation. In order to address this situation there is need for a comprehensive approach involving statutory and voluntary bodies. Legislation, information, and awareness-raising are needed to protect people and to overcome obstacles to equality. In the context of a growing acknowledgement of the dangers of racism throughout the European Union, there is an additional impetus and opportunity to face up to this challenge in Ireland, as well as throughout Europe.

Travellers: general information

Traveller population in Ireland

Estimated total 27,000.

An annual count of the number of Traveller households is the source of information on the Traveller population in Ireland. The 1994 count showed that there were 4,905 Traveller households in the country.

Age structure

The age structure of Travellers is very different from that of the general population, with relatively large numbers of children and few older people. An estimated 40 per cent of the Traveller population is aged under 10 years, and well over 50 per cent is aged under 15 years. Only 5 per cent of Travellers are aged 50 and over. This age structure is consistent with a high birth rate, a high infant death rate, and a low average life expectancy.

Education

Significant progress has been made in the provision of education for Traveller children in recent decades. This is evidenced in the increased participation in the education system. However there still remains a substantial number of Traveller children who do not attend primary school on a full-time, regular basis. This can be due to the living circumstances of the parents or to difficulty in gaining access to schools. A large number of Traveller children underachieve in school. The lack of statistical information on Traveller participation in education makes it difficult to evaluate the relative participation and outcomes for Traveller boys and girls in the education system.

It is estimated that only about 10 per cent of Travellers continue on to second level and very few of these complete the full cycle. Only a handful of Travellers go on to third level.

Employment

Traveller participation in the mainstream labour force is very low. This low participation is attributed to a number of factors: a preference for self-employment and work in the Traveller economy, discrimination, lack of skills and qualifications, low pay and poor work conditions, nomadism. The vast majority of Traveller households are dependent on social welfare.

Accommodation

In the context of statutory provision of social housing the local authorities provide standard houses for some Traveller households and in addition Traveller-specific accommodation as follows: group housing, permanent halting sites, and temporary halting sites. The 1995 Task Force Report drew attention to the deficiencies in this provision: 1,085 Traveller households living in trailers squatting on roadsides; 275 households in temporary sites; no provision for transient families; lack of facilities and/or culturally inappropriate facilities; lack of planning for the projected Traveller population increase; absence of a comprehensive government plan to accommodate Travellers.

The Task Force called for the provision of 3,100 units of additional accommodation by the year 2000, at a cost of £218 million. [The lack of progress in this regard is criticised in Irish Traveller Moment, 2001.]

Health Status

The 1982 Black Report commissioned by the UK government identified a clear link between social inequality and ill health:

> From birth to old age those at the bottom of the social scale have much poorer health and quality of life than those at the top. Gender, area of residence and ethnic origin also have a deep impact.

It is not surprising therefore to find that the health status of Travellers is much worse than it is for the general population.

Infant mortality for Travellers in 1987 was 18.1 per 1,000 births compared to the national figure of 7.4. Traveller life expectancy is at the level it was for the general population in Ireland in the 1940s (i.e. 10 to 12 years less for Traveller men and women than for men and women from the majority population).

References

Bewley, Victor. (ed.) 1976. *The Travelling People in Ireland*. Dublin: Veritas.

Calypso Productions. 1997. *I'm No racist, and What is it Anyway?* Dublin: Calypso.

Crickley, Anastasia. 1992. 'Feminism and ethnicity', in *DTEDG File*. Dublin: Pavee Point.

Donald, James and Ali Rattansi. (eds.) 1992. *'Race', Culture and Difference*. London: Sage Publications/Open University.

Dublin Traveller Education and Development Group, Irish Court for Civil Liberties, Irish Traveller Movement. 1993. *Anti-Racist Law and the Travellers*. Dublin: DTEDG.

DTEDG File. 1992. *Irish Travellers: New Analysis and New Initiatives*. Dublin: Pavee Point Publications.

DTEDG, ICCL, ITM. 1993. *Anti-Racist Law and the Travellers*. Dublin: ITM.

Eurobarometer Opinion Poll No. 47.1. 1997. *Racism and Xenophobia in Europe*. Draft final report presented at the Closing Conference of the European Year Against Racism, Luxembourg, 18 and 19 December 1997.

Helleiner, Jane and Bohdan Szuchewycz. 1994. 'Discourses of exclusion: The Irish Press and the Travelling People', in *Others in Discourse: The Rhetoric and Politics of Exclusion*. Newbury Park: Sage.

Husband, Charles. 1982. 'Race in Britain: Continuity and Change', in Charles Husband (ed.) *'Race', the Continuity of a Concept*. London: Hutchinson.

Irish Traveller Moment 2001. *A Lost Opportunity? A Critique of Local Authority Traveller Accommodation Programmes*, Dublin: ITM.

Kenny, Máirín. 1997. *The Routes of Resistance: Traveller and Second-level Schooling*. Aldershot: Ashgate.

Kovel, Joel. 1971. *White Racism: A Psychohistory*. New York: Vintage Books.

McDonagh, Rosaleen. 1994. 'Travellers with a disability: a submission to the Commission on the Status of People with Disabilities'. Dublin: Pavee Point.

Mac Gréil, Mícheál. 1996. *Prejudice in Ireland Revisited.* Maynooth: Survey and Research Unit, St. Patrick's College, Maynooth.

McVeigh, Robbie. 1996. *The Racialisation of Irishness: Racism and Anti-Racism in Ireland*. Belfast: Centre for Research and Documentation.

McVeigh, Robbie. 1997. *Minority Ethnic Groups and Racism*. CRD North/South Fact sheet Series, number 5. Belfast: Centre for Research and Documentation.

Miles, Robert. 1989. *Racism*. London: Routledge.

Miles, Robert and Annie Phizacklea. 1984. *White Man's Country: Racism in British Politics*. London: Pluto Press.

O'Connell, John. 1997. *Travellers, Gypsies, Roma*. Dublin: Pavee Point Fact Sheet.

O'Connell, John. 1994. *Reach Out*. Dublin: Pavee Point.

Roma, Gypsies, *Travellers: East/West: Regional and Local Policies*. 1997. Report of International Study Conference, Rome 1991. Dublin: Pavee Point Publications.

Ryan, Lorna. 1996. *Incorporating a Discrimination Theme within the Proposed National Anti-Poverty Strategy*. Dublin: Pavee Point.

Troyna, Barry and Jenny Williams. 1986. *Racism, Education and the State*. London: Croom Helm.

3.

Identity and racism in Northern Ireland

Deepa Mann-Kler

Introduction

This chapter is based on personal reflections. What you hear is the voice of one woman – an Indian woman living in Northern Ireland. I would like to emphasise the rich contribution made to all spheres of Northern Irish society by the thousands of women and men from 'minority ethnic' groups. We often discuss the lives of these individuals as a group, but this unfortunately dehumanises their individual experiences. Lost are the pain, joy, health, happiness, individual emotions. Lost are the thousands of life stories of people who have faced the challenges of making a successful life in another country. Why are these stories lost?

Racism: a terminology

Racism is discussed more frequently these days in Northern Ireland, but what does it actually mean? One of the many legacies of the Troubles has been the denial of the existence of racism in Northern Ireland. It is remarkable that in a society torn apart and divided by sectarianism, there is still a naïve belief held by many that prejudice stops with the issue of religion. Coupled with this is another misheld belief that racism does not exist because there are not that many minority ethnic people here yet. What this does is to lay blame for the existence of racism upon the minority ethnic person, rather than seeing it as the problem of the majority ethnic groups. On one very basic and individual level, racism is the display of personal ignorance. Racism, like other forms of prejudice, reflects people's deepest level of insecurity about themselves. Rather than confronting and dealing with this insecurity, they exercise power alongside their prejudice, to hide and run away from their insecurities. Individual racism then tends to be more overt and conscious, and its key ingredients are prejudice and power:

> a combination of prejudice and power used to inform any attitude, action or organisation which undermines a person or group because of their race, colour or ethnic difference (Crickley, 1990).

Racism can and does occur in many different forms in Northern Ireland, and is generally divided into individual and institutional racism. Institutional racism tends to be unconscious but far reaching and damaging in its impact:

wherever individuals in carrying out the routine practices of their employment or institutions, produce outcomes which in effect discriminate against members of ethnic minority populations (CCETSW, 1991).

This chapter focuses on both individual and institutional racism. Institutional racism highlights the power of institutions to exclude whole groups in Northern Ireland and has implications for policy developments and resourcing of services to minority ethnic groups:

> Institutional racism is about power, it is about who has the right to give resources to who... institutional racism happens when people go about their normal business without thinking what are the implications for other ethnic groups (Husband, 1992).

The above discussion of terminology is important in clarifying issues of racism, power and prejudice. But what about other terms we use daily, such as 'ethnic minority' or 'minority ethnic'? Why is it important to use particular words? It comes back to power and the right of individuals and groups to choose the terms by which they want to be described. How many Indian, Chinese or Pakistani people have anglicised their names? A more interesting question is why people have felt the need to do so. This experience is not unique to these communities. Many people have faced a similar oppression in wanting Irish names and it is only in recent times that there is room for the expression of these identities. Unfortunately this does not extend to many of the smaller communities here. A name is history and a future; it is identity; it is cultural value, and above all, it is power. The changing of a name is perhaps one of the most common and blatant forms of racism. A good example is how the Inuit people have renamed themselves from the previously imposed label of Eskimo.

Back to 'minority ethnic', the latest term. Traditionally the term 'ethnic minority' has and is still being used. However, it creates the impression that 'ethnic' is a term applied only to minority groups within a given society. However, all people – Black or white – belong to an ethnic group. The smaller ethnic groups are then denoted by the prefix 'minority' and the larger ethnic groups by the term 'majority' If we were to take ethnicity on global terms then the prefixes would all be reversed, with the Chinese and Indian communities forming majority ethnic groups. The subtleties of a word can change its implication from positive to negative or vice versa with 'minority' clearly having negative connotations. Another word that is regularly used is 'Black'. This is used as a politically collective term, to represent unification with other minority ethnic groups. Whilst I would use this term comfortably to describe myself, some minority ethnic people may not.

Black and minority ethnic groups in Northern Ireland must be free to choose the terminology by which they describe themselves. We should be prepared to accept the linguistic variety, which will differ from country to country. One example is the use of the term 'people of colour' in Canada – adopted to distinguish visibly different minority ethnic groups from those who called themselves 'Black'. On one level, the term 'people of colour' denotes that only visibly different minority ethnic people have colour, but we all have colour of some kind. Underpinning this is the feeling that to be white is to be neutral and to have a colour is to be different (Davies and Ohri, 1996). On the other hand, we have to be prepared to accept the right of people to describe themselves in a way they choose to.

Minority ethnic groups in Northern Ireland

Despite popularly held beliefs, at least two groups of minority ethnic women, of the Jewish and Traveller communities, have lived in Northern Ireland since before the Government of Ireland Act 1920. Migration of other communities has mainly taken place in the 1950s and 1970s. As a result we have a mixture of old and young minority ethnic communities in Northern Ireland.

Many of the women from minority ethnic backgrounds came to Northern Ireland out of economic and political necessity. Many arrived with their children in order to complete the family circle. The extent to which this has affected their position in the labour market and their position in Northern Irish society varies. The type of work available not only governs levels of income, but also determines where people settle; where their children go to school; the type of interaction that takes place with the indigenous labour force and population generally; access to services; chances of participation in civic life, and their overall status in society (Anwar, 1991). Where minority ethnic women are concentrated in a limited range of occupations, they are also concentrated in specific services and industries, which in turn has affected concentration in housing estates, towns, cities and regions.

One of the outstanding forms of segregation that is apparent in Northern Ireland today is in the labour market, where waged minority ethnic women are predominately concentrated in self-owned small businesses. These businesses include catering, restaurants, hairdressing, clothing outlets and market stalls.

Each community has its own history and within each community there are many individual stories. Travellers are indigenous to Ireland and have a history which can be traced back for centuries (Noonan, 1994). The very first Travellers were believed to be itinerant trades persons and specialists. The Traveller communities in Northern Ireland form a distinct and separate ethnic group. Furthermore, the term refers to the membership of this group and not just to the distinction between a nomadic and a settled lifestyle. Up until industrialisation in the wake of World War II, the Traveller community was an integral part of the rural economy, through tin-smithing, horse dealing, carpentry, chimney cleaning, domestic ware sales and seasonal agricultural labour. In the 1950s this economic relationship and the Travellers' way of life was changed forever, as a result of urbanisation and mechanisation, the introduction of plastic, rural depopulation and increased mobility for the rest of rural community. The direct and immediate impact was a decreased demand for the skills and services Traveller women had provided before. All this resulted in a lack of income and directly impacted on their standard of living. Resulting from this change, some Travellers today deal in scrap, carpets, caravans and tarmac.

Chinese women belong to the largest minority ethnic group in Northern Ireland. While the majority have come from Hong Kong's rural area, the New Territories, there are also a few from Malaysia, Singapore and the People's Republic of China (Marger, 1989). Unlike, the highly developed and affluent city of Hong Kong, the New Territories have remained economically, socially and educationally under-privileged. These women and their families left Hong Kong out of economic hardship and many of these fishermen and village people migrated to the United Kingdom in the 1950s. A high percentage of the Chinese female community work in self-owned catering outlets.

The first Indians to settle in Northern Ireland arrived in the 1930s. Their trade was the door-to-door sale of clothes. It was not until the 1950s that Indians began to settle in larger numbers. Initially husbands arrived first, took up a trade, and once financially established, returned to India. Their wives and families then returned with them to Northern Ireland. Today, the Indian community is involved in many different employment arenas, owning factories, grocery shops, and restaurants as well as other self-employed businesses and professional jobs.

There has been a Pakistani community living in Northern Ireland since the 1970s. Many of these families lived in the north of England before settling here. As with many other migrants, the decision to move to Northern Ireland was made for personal, social and economic reasons. Many Pakistani women have lived in Northern Ireland for 25 to 30 years. Many are market traders, specialising in clothing and bed linen.

One indicator reflecting the position of minority ethnic women in Northern Ireland is the multitude of community-based, voluntary and support organisations. Many have grown slowly out of grassroots initiatives. In the absence of statutory service provision these groups are a lifeline for many women.

The experiences of minority ethnic women in Northern Ireland

What are the daily experiences of women from the Traveller, Chinese, Indian and Pakistani communities? The evidence presented here is derived from a report published in November 1997 entitled *Out Of The Shadows* (Mann-Kler, 1997). The primary concern of this research was to give voice to the experiences of individual minority ethnic people. These individual experiences are important as they identify real difficulties encountered by people in everyday situations.

Social services

Some of the experiences of racism indicate that when women try to access health and social services they experience language and communication barriers, which often result in relying on family, friends and children. What develops are informal support structures. The development of informal support structures is repeated time and again. This is where lay health workers, who are predominantly female, have played an invaluable role in establishing links across many service sectors for minority ethnic women in Northern Ireland. In addition, many women who participated in the study's focus groups were unaware of simple rights, such as the right to choose the gender of their doctor. One daily consequence of racism is the absence of knowledge of one's rights.

Another area where racism emerges daily is in relation to primary healthcare, where Traveller people in Northern Ireland are still not given access to clean drinking water and basic sanitation. Many within the majority ethnic communities in Northern Ireland fail to recognise this as racism, especially when it comes to the issue of equity of service and Traveller provision. The assumption is that the fault derives from the fact that Traveller culture and values do not fit in with settled values.

Another area where this assumption is relevant concerns language; the belief is that if only people learned to speak English, there would not be a problem. What this fails to recognise is that even those fluent in English are being discriminated against. The 'problem' is seen to lie with the minority, as people feel that 'if they only fit in with us, everything would be alright'. Perhaps this is indicative of institutional and individual racism – where everyday practices are seen as 'normal'. Thus the definition of normal is 'what has always been done', even if this results in discrimination.

In terms of accessing the social security system, minority ethnic women face difficulties in finding out about benefits and often obtain information through informal networks. There is also much confusion around entitlement to benefits, loans and the claims process. These difficulties are further exacerbated for those who do not know how to read or write English. In consequence, many women rely on others to fill in forms. When it comes to interviews, many minority ethnic women approach health workers, whilst others rely on family and friends. This creates further difficulty around confidentiality and ensuring that information is translated properly. Once again, what is apparent is the double standard of service currently available. For too long statutory agencies had failed to take account of the specific needs of minority ethnic women.

Education and training

No provision has been made to teach minority ethnic languages in secondary schools. Ethnic diversity needs to be respected in schools by recognising religious and cultural diversity. This is not merely for the benefit of minority ethnic children, but should be part of school policy for the benefit of all children. If key elements of identity, such as culture, religion and language, are not recognised and reflected within the education system, the perception is that minority cultures and faiths have no value or place in Northern Irish society. Direct experiences of racism occur against minority ethnic pupils in schools, sometimes perpetrated by fellow pupils and sometimes by teachers. Young female Travellers leave school without having been taught to read and write. Another key area that needs urgent attention is adult education and training. There was very little awareness of the training courses available.

Accommodation

One of the areas where institutionalised racism is most evident concerns Traveller accommodation. Some families are forced to live in squalid conditions without appropriate support from statutory departments. Many Traveller sites have units without bedrooms, are built in bleak environments and make no provision for work space to enable residents to pursue income generation. Rent costs for these units are particularly high, when contrasted with what is available for a parallel rent in the private sector. Heating costs soar in the winter in the effort to keep caravans and units warm.

Racist attacks

One of the main areas of concern for minority ethnic groups is the level of racist attacks and harassment. The effects of racist attacks and harassment do not stop with the act itself, but are far deeper and often hidden. Attacks such as these affect people's self-esteem, their confidence and even their sense of place in society. Many minority ethnic women felt that crimes of this nature are not taken seriously by the police. Relations between Travellers in West Belfast and the police are equally poor.

Equity of treatment: suggested strategies

Underlying all of the above experiences are the many ways in which racism manifests itself at an institutional level and the consequences for the individual. Institutions across Northern Ireland should ask themselves whether in treating everyone the same, they are treating them equally. What action is needed to ensure equity of treatment and access to statutory services in Northern Ireland for minority ethnic groups? Some possible ideas are presented here.

There is a need to mainstream policies geared specifically to minority ethnic groups at the policy initiation stages. Alongside this there is a need to apply the Race Relations (Northern Ireland) Order 1997 and the Policy Appraisal and Fair Treatment guidelines to all existing and future policy initiatives. Promoting Social Inclusion should also be targeted at minority ethnic groups. There needs to be a democratic and inclusive consultation process with minority ethnic groups at the earliest stages of the decision making process. Regular and close consultation will ensure that needs are identified as early in the process as possible. As well as using a community development approach to identify needs, research will help statutory agencies to engage in a pro-active stance in achieving this.

Other key recommendations highlight the need to develop information and dissemination strategies to keep minority ethnic communities informed of the availability of services, where to obtain services, and who to contact for information. Integral to this is the importance of identifying key named people within statutory agencies who are responsible for minority ethnic service provision.

It is vital that policies and services targeted for minority ethnic groups are monitored for their uptake and effectiveness. This will be critical for future policy response. It will also ensure that resources are being used effectively. It is therefore essential to develop continuous monitoring strategies, which review policy, practice and service delivery initiatives on a regular basis.

It is crucial to develop ongoing training for all staff, practitioners and policy planners of service provision in anti-racism and anti-discriminatory practice. This training needs to be meaningful, and not tokenistic.

Cultural awareness and cultural fusions

Culture is an intrinsic part of one's being. It is very much in vogue these days in Northern Ireland to have 'cultural awareness training days' so that we become aware of the 'other cultures' living in Northern Ireland. Often these cultural days involve talks and displays of food, music, dance and religious background. What we get are anecdotes of people's life stories. Never in any of these cultural days has the information flow been two-way. More importantly, what do these cultural days actually achieve? Do they change the daily reality of racism and discrimination? They tokenise other cultures and comfortably delude some white people into thinking that they are actually doing something. This is no coincidence – because it can be discomforting to address one's own racism. How often do Protestant, Catholic, Irish, Northern Irish or British people sit down and think about their own culture? Are they able to describe all the aspects that go to make up their culture?

Alongside the Good Friday Agreement, one of the most important changes to occur in Northern Ireland has been the introduction of race relations legislation. The Race Relations (Northern Ireland) Order 1997 makes racial discrimination unlawful in employment, training and related matters, in education, housing, the provision of goods, facilities and services, and in the disposal and management of premises. Individuals are given a right of direct access to courts and industrial tribunals for legal remedies for unlawful discrimination. It is unlawful to discriminate against anyone on the grounds of race, colour, nationality, national or ethnic origin.

The words used to describe common identities in Northern Ireland are 'Irish', 'Northern Irish', 'loyalist', 'nationalist', 'unionist', 'republican', 'British' and so on. What room is there in these words for the identities of the Black and minority ethnic people of Northern Ireland? One of the terms I have chosen to describe myself is 'Black British'. This represents my rights of citizenship as well as my political identification with minority ethnic people across Britain. In Britain this category is widely recognised and used. The limitation of its application to Northern Ireland is self-evident.

Not only have I learnt to become sensitive to the different interpretations of British in Northern Ireland, but I am also aware of other people's interpretation of what I may mean by British. In Northern Ireland, the majority ethnic interpretations of Black British would be different from my understanding.

To give you an example: in 1998 I was training with a group of voluntary workers in West Belfast. At the end of the training session the discussion continued between myself and a man who asked, 'How would you define yourself?' I thought quickly and replied, 'Black British'. He looked disappointed and said, 'It's a shame that you've lost your culture'. In one respect he was right. Up until that point I rarely used the word Indian to describe myself. Because of the emotional baggage I had attached to it, it never even occurred to me to say I was Indian. I sought to define myself more objectively, with political intent. I later felt disgruntled at his response – I felt that he had interpreted the words that I had used to describe myself in the context of his experiences as a Catholic man in West Belfast. What I felt he had failed to do was to try and understand my experience and why I consciously used the terms I did.

Even when I use the word Black, a common reaction is, 'Well, you're not really that Black, are you?' This discussion takes place because I see Black as a political term, where others may see it purely as a descriptive term. In yet another discussion I heard recently, a speaker talked about the need to move away from 'Black and white' because it was too much 'them and us'. What we need to do instead is to talk in terms of more meaningful descriptions, such as ethnicities.

The incident in West Belfast was the start of yet another process of self-reflection, because I had been challenged. After several years of thinking and playing around with different 'labels', I find that 'Black British' in Northern Ireland is open to too many misinterpretations. In addition to all of this is the political issue of Northern Ireland. Where do I fit in this? My wish is for peace and non-violence, and for a present and future shaped by compromise. I am not unique in this.

My identity is the result of the fusion of many cultural influences – predominant amongst these are Indian and English. Whilst, I happily describe myself as Indian, I would find it uncomfortable to say I am only English. To be only English, in terms of my experiences as a child in England, was to be white. I saw little reflection or room for 'non-white' identities. At the same time however, I happily recognise and accept my social, political, legal and citizenship rights of and duties to the official state. These I fulfil and expect fully. What is missing is the positive emotional link. The absence of positive emotion is explained by my experiences of growing up in England.

As a child, I remember vividly being ashamed of not being white and embarrassed to have Indian parents. I ask myself, where did I as a young child pick up these messages? I have the answers now as an adult, but as a child all I had were confusion and sadness because I did not belong. Ironically, I grew up in England, but never felt I came from there or that I was allowed to belong. I have learnt to see strength in diversity, but I have had to learn to do this.

There are parallels between my experiences and the multitude of identities that exist in Northern Ireland. Is the inference of the word 'republican' or 'loyalist' dependent upon our experiences and political beliefs? I wonder how many different interpretations exist of words that are used daily to describe our identities? How do we reach a common understanding if we start from a misunderstanding? There is a further issue here. Are people more likely to hold a stronger opinion about something if it has been a part of their experience? Would the terms 'republican' and 'loyalist' evoke a stronger reaction than the terms 'Black' or 'minority ethnic'? Would those terms where there has been less room for experiential reflection become more likely to be accepted?

I also feel European and all of these terms combined contribute to my sense of self-identity. However, the way I choose to describe myself may change over time – depending upon my feelings, my self-understanding and the context in which I live. This journey is painful at times, but only because there is the misassumption that everyone else's identity is fixed or static. When I realised that 'non-Black' people also struggle with issues of identity, my pain lessened.

Cultural fusions are strong pools to draw inspiration from. Some of Britain's most talented people are those brought up on a multitude of cultural influences. They have learnt to harness the best of all worlds and not to feel threatened by difference. It is often the most insecure in society who are threatened by any form of difference.

Conclusion: Identity, citizenship, equality

When we discuss issues of citizenship, whose citizenship are we discussing? Is it British or Irish or Northern Irish? Is the diversity of Northern Ireland's 20,000 or so minority ethnic people recognised when we use these terms? If the new Northern Ireland is to be as inclusive as we all want it to be, then these terms must incorporate the identities of Black and minority ethnic people. What does 'incorporating' these identities mean? The direct answer lies in the issue of 'equality'. Equality is at the heart of every level of existence in Northern Ireland – equality in dignity, respect, services, goods, facilities, and most importantly the right to live free from prejudice and discrimination. Unfortunately, such equality does not yet exist. We are at the beginning, still trying to prove in our research and talks to the people who control resources that many minority ethnic people live in an iniquitous position in Northern Ireland – that Black and minority ethnic people are being discriminated against daily through institutionalised racism.

Unless we look at power and how it operates alongside prejudice, discrimination and the ideology of white superiority, very little will change. The death of Stephen Lawrence in Britain has refocused our attention on how racism should be tackled. The attention must now focus on institutional racism.

Finally, none of the above recommendations will be possible without a long term resourcing commitment in order to redress racial inequality, especially the legacy of past discrimination and neglect. Without a guaranteed funding commitment, meaningful change in the relationship between the statutory sector and minority ethnic people in Northern Ireland is unlikely.

Dealing with difference is difficult in any society, but it is an even greater challenge in Northern Ireland, which has been so identified with division. Part of creating a peaceful, democratic and inclusive Northern Ireland is the ability to recognise and celebrate ethnic differences without creating further divisions.

The search for a name for oneself has no clear-cut definitive answers. An identity is self-revealed by the process undertaken in its search. It is the process that leads to self-understanding and this journey is never complete. We live in rapidly changing times and it is all too easy to be overwhelmed. The only way we can contribute to, and feel a part of change, is to accept the responsibility of self-reflection. Black, minority, unionist, Catholic, white, ethnic, republican, Chinese, Protestant, Indian, nationalist, loyalist, Irish, British, Ulster-Scots, Traveller and all the names not mentioned are in a unique position in Northern Ireland, where they share in the search for their identity. The only difference is whether this process is taken on positively or negatively. If we all choose to stand and shout who we are – who is going to listen?

References

Anwar, M. 1991. *Race Relations Policies in Britain: Agenda for the 1990s*. Coventry: CRER.

CCETSW. 1991. *Setting The Context For Change: Anti-Racist Social Work Education*. Central Council for Education and Training in Social Work.

Crickley, Anastasia. 1990. 'Racism – the concepts, the dynamic, and the issue.' *Co-Options – Racism*, Community Workers Co-Op, March 1990.

Davies, W. and Ohri, A. 1996. *Race Equality Manual: A Practical Guide For Decision Makers*. Strathclyde Regional Council/OSDC Ltd.

Husband, Charles. 1982. *Race In Britain: Continuity and Change*. London: Hutchinson.

Mann-Kler, Deepa. 1997. *Out Of The Shadows: An Action Research Report into Families, Racism and Exclusion in Northern Ireland*. Belfast: SCF.

Marger, M.N. 1989. 'Asians in the Northern Ireland economy.' *New Community*, 15(2), pp 203-210.

Noonan, Paul. 1994. *Travelling People in West Belfast*. London: Save the Children Fund.

4.

One refugee experience in Ireland

Drazen Nozinic

'Do you know, my dear Sir, the position of a man who has nowhere to go to, and yet has to go somewhere?'

Dostoyevsky

Introduction

Asylum-seekers and refugees are undoubtedly a highly racialised group in contemporary Ireland. As recently as 1996 they were rarely spoken about and racially motivated incidents, although occurring, did not attract much media attention. The late 1990s have witnessed a huge increase in the number of such incidents, taking different forms but nevertheless identical to those manifest in other EU countries (Duncan, 1997: 43). These include unprovoked physical assaults on men and women, verbal abuse in the streets, nuisance phone calls, hate-mail and dissemination of materials that incite hatred and media hysteria, fuelling misinformation and intolerance through misleading statistics and fear-inducing headlines, harassment of children in schools and play-grounds, criminalisation of would-be asylum applicants, discrimination in housing, education, employment and in the provision of services, and racial stereotyping and abuse of power exercised by officialdom and the police.

The sudden and frequently volatile public response to our presence here is partly due to lack of acquaintance with facts regarding asylum-seekers' and refugees' legal and social conditions in the state, and partly due to the ignorance of Ireland's international obligations.

Ireland is a signatory to the 1951 UN Convention Relating to the Status of Refugees (the Geneva Convention) and its 1967 New York Protocol. Article 1 of the Convention, incorporated into domestic law, defines a refugee as:

> a person who owing to a well-founded fear of persecution for reasons of race, nationality, membership of particular social group or political opinion, is outside the country of nationality and is unable or, owing to such fear, is unwilling to return to it.

The Refugee Act 1996 includes persecution on the basis of gender, sexual orientation and membership of trade unions as a ground for claiming refugee status.

An asylum seeker is a person who fled his/her country and, in seeking asylum in another country, is claiming to be a refugee under the Geneva Convention (Collins,

1997: 94). Unlike in some other EU jurisdictions, asylum seekers in Ireland had, until July 1999, no right to work and no automatic right to State-funded English classes, education or training while awaiting decision on their cases. They receive Supplementary Welfare Allowance (SWA), the lowest social welfare payment. Asylum seekers are also entitled to other benefits: Rent Allowance, Fuel Allowance and discretionary Exceptional Needs Payments such as Clothing Allowance at the same level as Irish people receiving welfare benefits, including health care (*The Irish Times*, 23 September 1998: 4).

Asylum claims are considered by the Department of Justice, Equality and Law Reform (DOJ). According to Peter Finlay, a lawyer on the Independent Appeals Authority, which deals with asylum-seekers refused permission to stay in Ireland, most asylum-seekers make their applications without accessing the free legal advice available from the Refugee Legal Service, an off-shoot of the Legal Aid Board (although this legal aid is not directly state-funded) (Haughey, 1999a: 10).

Upon examining their case, the DOJ may grant asylum-seekers either refugee status or Temporary Leave to Remain (TLR). A Convention refugee is a person recognised as a refugee in accordance with the Geneva Convention. S/he is generally accorded the same social, economic and cultural rights as citizens, including access to employment, welfare, social housing and educational grants. S/he is entitled to a UN Convention Travel Document and to apply for family reunification. Refugees are initially granted residence in Ireland for one year, to be renewed annually. After three years, they may apply for Irish citizenship (IFS, 1998: 2-3). The IRC points out that there is an indication that people who have built up several years residency as refugees, with TLR or work visas, may now be considered for longer visas from three to five years, on the basis that they are economically self-sufficient. Since July 1999 some 2000 asylum-seekers who had been in the state for more than a year have a right to work with a work permit.

Temporary Leave to Remain – earlier called Humanitarian Permission (Leave) to Remain – is granted when a person does not qualify as a refugee under the Geneva Convention, but the DOJ decides that there are strong humanitarian reasons why s/he should not return to his/her country of origin (IFS, 1998: 2). Although codified in the Refugee Act, the Act does not specify the rights or conditions which attach to this status. Thus, 'the omission of criteria for and clearly defined conditions of TLR from statutory regulations creates a *de facto* secondary status within Irish society' (Byrne, 1997: 113). Persons granted TLR have the right to work but do not have any access to educational grants as of right. They are, however, eligible to apply for a government work scheme or a government vocational training course by virtue of the fact that they receive unemployment assistance (UA).

A Programme refugee is a person recognised as a refugee in accordance with the Geneva Convention and granted protection in Ireland under a special admission programme. Programme refugees are invited to a country as a group in time of great political turmoil and do not need to prove they are within the Convention definition. Since 1979, Ireland has offered protection to over 560 Programme refugees from Vietnam and, since 1992, over 680 from Bosnia (Collins, 1997: 94; IFS, 1998: 2) plus 833 from Kosovo in 1998-9. Unlike individual asylum applicants, Programme refugees are cared for by the Refugee Agency, a government body that was set up and is funded by the Ministry for Foreign Affairs.

Once an asylum-seeker becomes the parent of an Irish-born child or marries an Irish citizen s/he gains the right of residency. Consequent upon gaining that status s/he has the right to reside, work and be educated in Ireland. Over the last few years the DOJ officials in both Dublin and Ennis have been encouraging asylum-seekers who are parents of Irish-born children to withdraw their asylum applications. The IRC, however, has advised applicants that it is their choice, based on the merits of their Convention claim, whether or not to pursue their asylum application.

According to DOJ statistics for the period between 1992 and March 2002 39,591 persons have applied for asylum in Ireland. The Office of the Refugee Applications Commissioner (formely the DOJ Asylum section) updates its figures on the monthly basis. The figures presented in Table 1 give the number of applications made in each given year, the number of refusals, including recommendations to refuse after first interview, after second interview and recommendation that an application is Manifestly Unfounded following interview, and finally the number of applications withdrawn. As appeals are heard and representations for temporary leave to remain are made, the statistics continue to change. It is interesting to note, however, that the number of outstanding applications is continuing to fall – from 8,725 at the end of 1999, and 9,284 by the end of October 2001, to 6,889 by the end of March 2002, as the Department attempts to deal with applications faster. The small proportion of applicants granted refugee status and high number of refused applications for asylum are also noteworthy.

Table 1: Asylum-seeker statistics 1992-2002

	1992	1993	1994	1995	1996	1997	1998	1999	2000	2001	2002*	Total
Applications	39	91	362	424	1,179	3,883	4,626	7,724	10,938	10,325	2,533	39,591
Granted refugee status	7	9	43	90	171	124	82	10	211	456	240	1,443
Refused	29	30	106	113	431	1,473	1,903	196	6,183	6,501	2,142	19,107
Withdrawn	3	52	222	220	550	1,360	803	285	2,376	3,413**	na	

*up to 31st March; ** up to 31st October. In all, in April 2002 there were 6,889 outstanding cases.

Sources: Department of Justice, Equality and Law Reform, cited in Haughey, 1999b:6; and Office of the Refugee Applications Commissioner, Monthly Statistics October 31, 2001, and personal communication.

Auto/biographies and (ethnic?) identities

When I was asked to contribute a chapter to this book, I did not expect to be asked to base it on my own experiences as a former asylum-seeker in Ireland. I felt uneasy because I have never written in such a way. Writing about myself made me feel uncomfortable for one other reason – it seems unfair to over 30 million other refugees and internally displaced persons in the world, each of whom has a story that deserves to be told.

Another issue that rendered my positioning within the context of this book difficult was that of my own identity. Unlike other contributors to the book, I cannot claim to have an ethnic identity. My mother is a Croat, my father a Serb. In former Yugoslavia all of us of mixed ethnic origin are called 'half-breeds'. There are thirteen other ethnic groups in my extended family of some 500, a family that broke down because most of my relatives chose to take sides in the war – the majority of them still refusing to talk to me because I did not. This is not an unusual situation though, because there were over thirty ethnic groups living in the country, and inter-ethnic marriages occurred frequently. There were times when 'half-breeds' were seen as 'the future of the country', the guarantors of its stability, because we usually had no ethnic or religious affiliations. However, once the troubles started that outlook changed. At the outbreak of war we became outcasts, the unclean, undesirable and unreliable ones. True, one did have an option of choosing a side. However, not being of 'pure blood' s/he was to be utilised in the war if the need arose – but could never be trusted. We were openly regarded as 'disposable'. S/he could also refuse to take sides but that was usually physically punished by one of the warring factions or by social exclusion at the very best. Many of us were left with no other option but to leave.

My (cultural) habits and my mind-set have changed, giving in to the inevitable and necessary adaptation process one needs to undergo in order to endure and survive refugeeship. My language – well, I have hardly spoken it in my years in Ireland, and find it difficult to remember words or to use grammar properly.

The country I come from and used to identify with does not exist any longer. Dublin and Ireland feel more and more like home, but my feelings towards Ireland still vary, depending on the circumstances, particularly those affecting the asylum community, 'my only tribe', as I call them. This may sound like an odd statement bearing in mind that I have quite a few close Irish friends, and bearing in mind the diversity within the asylum community which originates in over 100 countries world-wide. But there is a part of me that finds difficulty in relating to a non-asylum-seeker and which, in turn, creates a strong emotional bond between those of us who have been unwillingly 'initiated' to refugeeship: that is the automatic acknowledgement of the extent of pain we carry inside, the sharing of the pain that had been inflicted on us back home, and the ever-lasting pain of being uprooted, so easily discernible in our demeanour. Only another asylum-seeker fully comprehends that it is not always in the streets where we feel most unprotected; it is in one's own bed, late at night when the lights are off. That is the time when one's mind gives in, when the memories and demons of our past lives mercilessly rise to the surface and the torment begins. Indeed, I never had nightmares when I was still in the war – because I lived one. They started here, in Dublin, over a year after I arrived. Yes, keeping asylum-seekers safe in the streets solves only half of the problem.

The unfortunate events surrounding asylum-seekers in Ireland over the last two years have brought us even closer together, as the fear of the majority population grows daily, and terms such as 'us' and 'them' have become increasingly emotionally charged. It has become difficult to cross from 'their' world to 'ours'; too many walls have been erected. The summer of 1997 was a time when I rarely went out for a drink – not that many of us did. The question in everybody's mind was: 'When does it stop; how much more do we have to put up with?' Because, for many of us, it was exactly racial, ethnic or religious conflicts that made us leave our homes in the first place and yet, here we were, exposed to the same kind of threat again. There is only so much one can take.

Céad Míle Fáilte?[1] Yeah, right!

I fled Croatia on 7 October 1991, following the announcement of general conscription to the Croatian Army broadcast that night. I went to Slovenia first, and then to Bosnia. My intention was not to leave the area. I wanted to stay close to my parents and my mentally disabled brother. I lived and worked in Bosnia until 5 May 1992. Following the outbreak of war in Bosnia a Basque friend of mine phoned me, urging me to flee to Sweden, apply for asylum there and stay with him and his family. However, once I reached Belgrade it turned out that it was impossible to cross the border with Hungary and I had to hide there, avoiding conscription to the Serb Army, until the borders re-opened in August 1992. My accent was a great give-away and as I could not look for a job, my Serb friends and colleagues looked after me. Around July 1992 I got in touch with some Irish people living in Brussels, friends of a colleague from Belgrade, people I was to meet later on that year. They offered to help me leave and provided a place for me to stay in Dublin. Crossing the border to Hungary was the only option because no flights were allowed in the Yugoslav air space and I had to take a flight from Budapest. The plane was to take me to Paris where I was supposed to take another one to Dublin – the route similar to the one many of us coming to Ireland have to take because not many countries have direct flights to Dublin.

I arrived in Dublin airport on 27 August 1992, a day before the Bosnian 'programme refugees' were brought over. I approached the passport control and said I was seeking asylum. I was immediately asked to step aside and wait, while other passengers continually stared at me, all the time observing the frantic activity behind the glass wall that my statement had caused. Twenty minutes later – that is all that took – I was given a piece of paper that read:

> This is to inform you that you are being refused leave to land because being an applicant for political asylum you are being returned to Paris where such application should have been made in accordance with the internationally recognised *principal* [sic] of first safe country and also in accordance with the *principals* [sic] contained in the Dublin Convention of June 1990. (*my emphasis*)

Needless to say, I knew nothing about the Dublin Convention. Nor I did know that the Convention was not part of domestic law; it was only on 1 September 1997 that a Treaty, called the Dublin Convention, agreed between the EU Heads of state came into operation. Nor was I aware of the 1985 letter from the DOJ to UNHCR as regards asylum procedures, stating clearly that I was entitled to apply directly to the immigration officer on arrival, and that:

> ... it was not necessary for an individual to use the term 'refugee' or 'asylum'
> in order to be an asylum-seeker...Whether or not an individual is an asylum-

seeker is a matter of fact to be decided in the light of all circumstances of the particular case as well as guidelines which may be issued from time to time by the Department. In case of doubt, the Immigration Officer shall refer to the Department of Justice...Such an individual will not be refused entry or removed until he has been given an opportunity to present his case fully, his application has been properly examined, and a decision reached on it (Points 1, 3, and 4 from the Letter).

Later on that year I was to find out that '... the invoking of the Convention was part of the same tactic used in a number of other cases, despite of the [then] recent High Court and Supreme Court judgements that found this [1985] Letter to be legally binding' (IRC in the letter to my solicitor).

As I was being escorted back to the same plane that brought me over, flanked by three men, all I could think about was what was going to happen to me if I were sent back home. And that my fate had just been decided by someone who could not even spell! I later learned that there had been questions in the Dáil regarding my deportation.

The French police were expecting me at the airport in Paris and took me in for questioning. There was no interpreter, I do not have a word of French, and that farce went on for three and a half hours. They spoke French, I spoke English and was constantly being brought some papers in French to sign. And I did because by then I was exhausted. I had had no sleep or food in 24 hours and simply did not care any more. Then I was taken to a detention centre where I was the only white inmate. There were three armed policemen watching us, the entrance and exit doors were electronically controlled, we were not allowed to close the doors of our rooms nor to open the windows and yet, a policewoman was constantly getting annoyed with me because I called the place 'prison'. As I was allowed to use the phone I phoned my contacts in Brussels who then phoned the UNHCR Offices in London and Paris and the IRC, and I was released the next day, following questioning by an official from the French Ministry for Foreign Affairs. I was given permission to stay in France for a week. But I did not want to leave the Centre just yet; it was Friday night, I did not have much money on me, I did not know Paris nor did I know a single person in France. Luckily, my friends from Brussels arranged with some French people in Paris to put me up for the weekend, after which the Irish community in Paris took over and kindly looked after me for the rest of my stay there.

On the following Monday I went to the Irish Embassy and applied for a visa. Four days later, on 3 September 1992, I received a letter from the Embassy saying:

I refer to your application for a visa and am to inform you that persons travelling on Yugoslavian passports *do not* at present require visas to enter Ireland (*my emphasis*). However, to overcome any immigration difficulties the Minister for Justice has decided that you are to be given leave to enter the State as a visitor for the period to 1 December 1992.

Some may think of me as ungrateful, but I was not impressed with the entire affair. I left for Dublin on the same day.

My first interview in the then Aliens Division was in October 1992. In the meantime, as well as afterwards, my solicitor and the IRC were exchanging letters with the DOJ which was reluctant to acknowledge that I had ever applied for asylum. The reason: I lied in my visa application saying I was coming to Ireland as a visitor. Of course I lied, everybody knew I did. So, pursuing that silly game, in the letter to my solicitor dated 25 September 1992, the Minister's private secretary simply wrote: 'I am directed by the Minister for Justice to acknowledge receipt of your recent letter on behalf of Mr Drazen Nozinic which was receiving attention'. I think I must be the only asylum-seeker in this country ever to be granted citizenship whose application had apparently never been lodged.

The reasoning behind that was to make my life as difficult as possible, so that I would leave the country. In 1992, asylum-seekers in Ireland were not receiving supplementary welfare allowance as they do today, but unemployment assistance. In order to receive unemployment assistance one needed a letter from the DOJ saying that s/he had applied for asylum. Since the letter was not coming and I was penniless, the IRC sent me to the unemployment exchange to apply for unemployment assistance anyway. In November 1992 I was, naturally, refused on several grounds, one more senseless than the next: (1) because I did not hold a work permit; (2) because I had not been granted refugee status; and (3) because I had not been among the initial group of Bosnian refugees. The letter concludes with: 'per phone call to Department of Justice'. There was nothing in that letter to make me believe that the DOJ explained to the Employment Exchange Office that an asylum-seeker was not permitted to work – hence no work permit, or that quota refugees' entitlements had been agreed with the government and were different from ours, who applied individually.

The above decision weighed heavily on my first interview. This interviewer had been responsible for my deportation. I later learned that the UNHCR were most unimpressed with him. He was, to say the least, vindictive. For over 90 minutes he was simply telling me that I had to leave for Croatia, Bosnia or Serbia – he could not care less where I went. He kept on accusing me of being an economic migrant craving for £60 worth of unemployment assistance, although I told him, repeatedly, that my parents and I used to own two flats (mine looted, that of my parents blown up), a vineyard and a house there (looted) and a house in the countryside (looted) with orchards, fields, livestock, woods and two cars and were all employed at the time the war broke out. But it was only after he accused the IRC of briefing me for the interview, to which I retorted that his attitude was 'bitchy', that he terminated the interview – and that is how I never got that letter. Luckily, a few weeks after the interview, Trinity College gave me a scholarship to do my PhD there, which provided me with an income I lived on until 1995.

My second interview, with another interviewer, took place in February 1993. It was more pleasant, but cunningly conducted. Out of the blue I was offered TLR and a work permit. At that stage, however, I already knew that TLR was not codified in any legislation and was granted at the Minister's discretion, that it could be revoked any time and did not provide me with any safeguards as regards my permanency in the country and that it was the Department of Labour which issued work permits, not the DOJ, and that the Department of Labour was refusing to issue work permits on the basis of a status that was non-existent in domestic law. So, I refused TLR deciding to take my chances with refugee status. A week later I had my third interview and this time we genuinely discussed my case. I was granted refugee status in October 1993 and Irish citizenship in March 1996.

And the saga continues...

Over the years the IRC would sometimes ask me to take part in conferences or public discussions revolving around the refugee issue. One such occasion was the 'Victim Support' conference in Malahide in April 1994. I spent 45 minutes talking about the war back home, describing the way I had been treated by officialdom here and describing the symptoms of post-traumatic stress disorder from which I had been suffering since November 1993. That was when I learnt that Irish people did not like and could not take criticism. My speech prompted one of the participants to say that I should f*** off to my own country. At the workshop later that afternoon, a few other people kept on telling me that they saw 'no reason for me being at the conference!' While I am sure that this association does good work with the bereavement of others, they showed little understanding of the suffering of a refugee.

One sunny afternoon in June 1996 I was walking back home from work. As I was passing through Bride Street a man walking towards me suddenly lurched forward, pulling my shirt, calling me a 'dirty Russian' and threatening to kill me. We had not exchanged any words prior to that outburst. After a few minutes of squabble he let go and left. I still see him sometimes, but he just passes by.

In June 1997 I participated in the 'Mary Kennedy' show on RTE. Áine Ní Chónaill, leader of the Immigration Control Platform, was there too. After the show, as I was standing talking to a Sudanese friend, she approached us and, referring to some interviews I gave to *The Irish Times* a month before, said to me: 'So, I read in the newspapers that you were threatened with the death penalty back home. Well, for me that is still not a good enough reason to have you here'. 'Well tough', I said, ' because I'm an Irish citizen now and there's nothing you can do about it'. To which she replied: 'You can't imagine how sorry I am to hear that' – and left.

During the following month I participated in the 'Davis' and 'Nationwide' programmes. That made my face somewhat familiar and people stopped me in the streets, mistaking me for a spokesperson for asylum-seekers. Every single person's opening line was: 'You know, I'm not a racist, but... those Romanians, Albanians, Africans, Muslims...' – everybody having his/her particular group to dislike. Throughout 1997 it was impossible to avoid quarrels with taxi drivers, for they all had something negative to say about us.

In December 1997 I was on the panel of the 'Prime Time' programme. After the programme, a Fianna Fáil TD, a backbencher who was not on the panel but was accompanying her fellow TD, approached me and asked: 'What are you complaining about? You are white?' Taken aback I answered: 'Yes, and so are Travellers and Jews but that has never stopped anybody, has it? Also, my Italian friend has been called "coloured" and "Black bitch" to her face by strangers in the street, and she is always asked to produce her passport at the border on her way from Belfast. So is my Bosnian friend who was attacked by two Irish men at his girlfriend's party'. The TD then went on talking about how much she had done for Travellers in her constituency – but I am still trying to figure out what was the logic behind her reasoning.

A week after that incident I was in Dublin Castle at the closing of the European Year Against Racism. A Junior Minister speaking at the ceremony calmly told us that there had been no racism in Ireland until WE started pouring in, dismissing, in that one sentence, not only the entire Traveller and Jewish experience in Ireland, but also the entire Irish experience under the British. Once again victims of racism were accused of bringing it upon themselves – by their mere existence in the country.

Anti-refugee racism in Ireland

Ronit Lentin (1997: 2) points out that Irish racism of late 1990s has focused on refugees and people of colour. Over the last year or so this has been confirmed by numerous incidents reported by many asylum-seekers, non-white Irish and other EU citizens, foreign students and legal immigrants. Lentin also argues that this specific form of Irish racism has developed out of Ireland's older anti-refugee policies that began before and during World War II, with the refusal of the Irish government to let in Jewish refugees.

Attitudes towards asylum-seekers and refugees reflect not only those myths the nation has constructed about itself – they also re-emphasise various negative stereotypes which the nation holds about the majority world, along with some cold war perceptions of Eastern Europe. Irish opinions about Travellers are remarkably similar to every prejudice I have heard on the continent regarding Roma/Gypsies. Resentment of the 'other' is not a special Irish failing, but the heinous media coverage of the issue, the number of statements given by some irresponsible candidates during the 1997 general election campaign, as well as a few unprofessional statements given by the current Minister of Justice and his officialdom, helped inculcate past fears of the 'other' into the present day anti-refugee campaign. Refugees are now seen as one faceless but uniform group threatening the very fabric of society. Sadly, certain degrading stereotypes about (Irish) women have also re-surfaced, confirming Robbie McVeigh's view (1992: 42) that racism is a means of controlling and repressing.

At times, during and after my lectures I would mention racism to my students. Typically, some of them would dismiss it by saying that Ireland has always been an insular, monocultural society, that it is not used to dealing with people of different cultural backgrounds because they have not been around before – an ethnocentric view that any archaeology or history text-book confutes. These opinions, however, point out how the perception of Ireland as homogeneous, white, sedentary, predominantly Catholic, heterosexual society, with a progressive capitalist ideology is still deeply rooted (McVeigh, 1992:34, 36, 42; Aniagolu, 1997: 45-50; Lentin, 1997: 8-9, 11).

Black people, in turn, represent the opposite end of that spectrum. They are seen as racially inferior, barbaric 'lower human beings' and in no way as people who might share the same common values with white people. Attacking them does not seem to pose any ethical dilemma to the perpetrators of the attacks. And those 'hyper-sexual Black men' should be kept away from 'Aryan women'. There is a pamphlet titled 'Blacks' that has been disseminated to Black refugees' letter-boxes throughout Dublin over the last two years. It says: '… Blacks from Africa come to Ireland trying to find unattractive, insecure women who cannot find a husband, and fall easily into the trap of an African hunting'. The infamous editorial from *The Wexford People* (August 1998) similarly talks about Roma men 'trying to impregnate young, impressionable Irish girls' because an Irish born baby provides the parent with citizenship. How very flattering for Irish women! It must be so much fun to be reduced to a body surrounding the reproductive organs.

Refugee women, on the other hand, although perceived in the same, degrading way, are even 'worse'. They are said to 'use' their reproductive organs and maternal instincts in order to abuse the system. I am not a mind-reader and can allow for the assumption that some women do get pregnant for that particular reason. However, there are some other reasons to be taken into consideration such as the human needs of a woman *vis-à-vis* the biological clock (I bear in mind the length of time it takes to get a decision from the DOJ) or her religious values which may prohibit the use of contraception. According to the Irish tabloids these 'wicked' women have been 'flooding maternity hospitals' because an Irish-born baby would allow them to stay in the country and further abuse the taxpayer. This kind of cheap scribbling resulted in several physical assaults on pregnant – not always refugee – Black women in Dublin, the consequences of which were premature labour, hospital treatment and trauma.

The above pamphlet does not forget Muslims either, which is hardly surprising bearing in mind how frequently the western media centre their coverage of Islam only around the 'fundamentalist' strains. Indeed, rarely is Islam being discussed as one of the universal monotheistic religions, highly anti-racist in its essence – more often Islam is implicitly depicted as a threat to Christianity and western values. The pamphlet 'Blacks' bristles with anti-Muslim statements and, in order to dramatise the whole issue, to strengthen their claims and emphasise the 'danger' asylum-seekers represent to Irish society, the authors of the pamphlet describe all Muslims living in Dublin as 'Black' too. Not long after the dissemination of the pamphlet the arson attack on Dublin's Sunni mosque in South Circular Road occurred (in June 1997).

The atmosphere created during the 1997 general elections showed how easy it was to manipulate the uninformed public, and to turn ordinary citizens' opinion against 'the foreigners in our midst'. In the 1997 election leaflet titled 'McGrath demands action on illegal immigrants', Fianna Fáil Councillor and general election candidate Colm McGrath skillfully avoided naming the group he was referring to and thus could not be implicated of inciting hatred towards any specific minority group. The Prohibition of Incitement to Hatred Act 1989, usually described as a 'weak piece of legislation', would require that a specific group be named before any legal action could take place. McGrath's leaflet reads:

> A ritual involving the slaughter of a lamb took place in one house with the lamb being hung on the line to 'drip-die' after having its throat slit (Tuesday, 20-05-97). Local people in Tallaght and Clondalkin are incensed at the behaviour of these alleged political refugees many of whom they suspect of being economic refugees here to milk our social welfare system...

The pattern is quite obvious here – 'strange behaviour' linked to more important key-words in the rest of the leaflet: 'illegal immigrants', 'the abuse of the system', 'various forms of anti-social behaviour', 'local residents being subjected to various forms of harassment and intimidation'. Aferim Effendi [Bravo Mr.] McGrath! And, I suppose, drunken Irish men and women urinating and vomiting in the streets on Friday nights are a good example of civilised and acceptable social behaviour one should learn from.

However, the wording in the leaflet ('the ritual slaughter of a lamb') leads one to the conclusion that the asylum-seekers involved could have been Muslims. To my knowledge regarding religious denominations within the asylum community in both Dublin and Ennis, it is only Muslims who perform such a ritual, as part of the *Greater Bairam (Idu-l-adha)* festivities. But, if the 'offenders' performed religious rituals they would probably tend to go to the mosque as well. And if they did, then they would know about a man working for the mosque, employed to perform the *halal* slaughters for all the Muslims in Dublin. As it turned out, the 'offenders' were from an Eastern European country and were not Muslims. However, even if they were, one question still remains: how can one's faith, the performing of a ritual required by one's faith, render one's asylum application unfounded? It seems to me that the entire fuss was part of a cheap political campaign of a candidate who did not have much to offer voters. On the other hand, any political party that strives to be regarded as serious, honest and trustworthy cannot in fact afford to let its members preach hatred because, by allowing them to do so, they practically sanction racism and mislead the public into believing that hostile attitude towards foreigners is an acceptable norm.

The pamphlet 'Blacks' concludes with: 'Keep Ireland green and white'. Probably unintentionally, it falls in line with another opinion I have heard mentioned on several occasions over the last few years: that only white asylum-seekers should be allowed into the country. And that is exactly why I feel white asylum-seekers may have been attacked less frequently. It is not only because we are less obvious than Black people or Muslim women wearing the *hijab* – a fair-skinned refugee is very often expected to side with the racists. Unfortunately, some Eastern European and Caucasian fellow asylum-seekers do.

There is, however, another side to that story, a leftover from the Cold War era: those of us coming from former socialist countries have been referred to as 'poor commies', which is just another expression of westerners' arrogance based on a pathetic self-illusion of superiority. The feeble-minded anti-refugee campaigners cannot get it into their heads that an asylum-seeker comes to the West looking for safety and protection, not for something an Irish or Western person might perceive as paradise. Value systems are as diverse as human kind. I came over from a country with free education and health care, from a country where religion(s) and the state were separate, where abortion had been a woman's choice since 1961, where contraception was available at the age of 14 and condoms did not need to be discussed in parliament, where homosexuality was legal etc. Bearing in mind the treatment I received from officialdom, I must say that Ireland of 1992 felt like the end of the world. Sending out New Year cards to my friends that year I wrote: 'And, as far as Ireland is concerned, I wish you all a happy 1893!'

The above points needed to be made not because my intention was to insult the host society, but to put the entire perception of us as 'lower beings' into a different perspective. Our worldviews and value systems are constantly being dismissed and looked down upon which is an attitude based on the ignorant denial of the increasingly multi-ethnic character of Irish society. Thus, we have been denied the right to exist as equal human beings here; we have been denied the right to exist within the framework of two cultures, our own and the adopted one – even before an attempt at inclusion had been made.

Up to a certain point these attitudes amount to the lack of cultural sensitivity which, I believe, while misguided, is sometimes genuinely held. Whether or not that has been the case with the DOJ interviewers is a different story altogether – my first interviewer most definitely behaved like a hotshot who had seen far too many bad American spy movies. There have been numerous other complaints about the way asylum-seekers have been interviewed, which sometimes ends up with people breaking down in tears after being practically accused of lying. My work as an interpreter in 1997 leads me to form the opinion that it is the lack of knowledge about our respective countries which causes such unnecessary misunderstandings. Questions asked by Western Europeans elicit answers which reflect our cultural, religious or political backgrounds that usually do not fit into the Western European mind-set – hence the accusations of lying. It is easier that way.

Cultural insensitivity, however, only partially explains the officials' eagerness and agility when dismissing our claims as unfounded. The climate of disbelief surrounding asylum claims and the ignorant belittling of the gravity of our situations become quite obvious when the interviews are conducted without the assistance of trained and qualified interpreters. True, section 8(2) of the Refugee Act 1996 stipulates that interviews shall be conducted with the assistance of an interpreter *where possible* (my emphasis), but I wonder how such inadequate provision can be referred to as a 'fair procedure'? When working in the Refugee Council in 1995 and 1996 I had the opportunity to read transcripts from hearings that would end with the immigration officer concluding that an asylum-seeker was telling lies because s/he had presented an incoherent story. Upon investigation it would turn out that a hastily summoned interpreter was directing a client as to what to say or the interpreter was himself/herself choosing what s/he was going to interpret. Naturally, fragmented and nonsensical stories were the most usual outcome in these cases. But there were other incidents, incidents that are simply beyond my comprehension. In 1997 the DOJ used the driver from a certain embassy to interpret for asylum-seekers from that country! Obviously nobody thought, or cared, about those asylum-seekers' families back home and the dangers this 'little lapse' might expose them to.

It is obvious that the DOJ has chosen to follow its EU partners' asylum policy. Irish policy has become more restrictive and 'miraculously' mirrors the British Home Office's policy, as one can realise from reading the summary of the UK Refugee Council's report titled *The State of Asylum*:

> During the [then] current debate over the changes to welfare provisions for asylum-seekers... a number of myths have been repeated so often that they are becoming treated as fact. Central to these are that the majority of asylum-seekers are bogus. The government cites statistics to support its arguments that action is required to stem the number of asylum-seekers arriving in the UK... This report concludes that: the high rate of refusals of asylum cannot be explained purely by economic migration. The image of asylum-seekers as bogus refugees is an invention, which conveniently falls into line with government policy. The main costs to the state of asylum seeking derive from the long waits and the growing backlog of the determination system... According to the Home Office's own research, 'the majority of asylum-seekers come with substantial work and educational qualifications, the bulk of which are under-utilised, to their chagrin and the country's general loss' ... External barriers erected by the Government [over the past ten years] deliberately hinder flight from persecution... Just like other refugees throughout history, asylum-seekers are forced to travel on false papers to escape persecution... A climate of disbelief is prevalent at the Home Office in assessing claims, which runs contrary to the spirit of international agreements. Procedures are skewed to the disadvantage of asylum-seekers... Many asylum-seekers come from countries with well-documented human rights abuses, which [the Home Office] appears reluctant to acknowledge (1996).

This quotation needs no further comment.

The Aliens Act 1935 gives the Minister for Justice enormous powers over immigration (Murphy, 1997: 96). It appears that both the current Minister as well as his predecessor have used these powers to *de facto* criminalise asylum-seekers trying to enter the state, as the right of asylum has been deliberately confused with other immigration issues. In June 1997 the former Minister for Justice Nora Owen signed an order under the Aliens Act that set up immigration control for people arriving from the UK. Under the Order, non-EU citizens entering Ireland from Britain can be sent back if their papers are found not to be in order. As it turns out, it has been non-white people who have been targeted by immigration officials at ports of entry, affecting many Irish as well as other non-white EU citizens (Summary Notes... 1998: 13). Department officials, on the other hand, were more than delighted with themselves, as is obvious from a very unfortunate statement given to *The Sunday Independent* (6/7/1997) by a Department spokesman:

The new legislation is working. We cannot be criticised for turning people down when they don't have documentation to prove that they are legitimate refugees.

Now, why didn't we think of that? Why didn't we ask our governments to provide us with 'genuine refugee documentation' prior to our departure? Or at least with labels attached to our clothes saying: 'Export. Certified Refugee. [Deportation] Best Before… ' *O sancta simplicitas!* On a more serious note however, such requirements represent a 'slight' disregard of Article 31 of the Geneva Convention, which states that contracting parties:

> … shall not impose penalties on account of illegal entry or presence of refugees… The case of the refugee constitutes an exception to the general rules regarding refusal of leave to land. This places an obligation on the state to determine the presence of a refugee and to afford that individual appropriate protection.

No one really knows how many people have been deported since the introduction of the immigration curbs, nor whether or not they have been offered interpreting services or legal advice before being shipped back to Britain or France on the grounds of the Dublin Convention. To rejoice in people's misery in this way, however, is as tasteless as it is callous. H.M. Enzensberger wrote these prophetic words in 1992:

> *The distinction between economic refugees and the politically oppressed is often impossible to draw, and a law which attempts to do so will inevitably be embarrassed* (my emphasis). After all, the war between winners and losers is carried out not only with bombs and automatic rifles. Corruption, indebtedness, flight of capital, hyper-inflation, ecological catastrophes, religious fanaticism and sheer incompetence can provide as solid ground for flight as the direct threat of prison, torture or shooting (Enzensberger, 1992: 38).

It seems to me that the Irish government's ports of entry procedures for dealing with asylum-seekers ridicule Ireland's international obligations. They make a mockery of Article 14(1) of the 1948 Universal Declaration of Human Rights, that states: 'Everyone has the right to seek and enjoy in other countries asylum from persecution'.

During and since the general elections of 1997, the DOJ has had a very strong ally in some sections of the Irish media. Indeed, the media saw to it that the DOJ was provided with plenty of scope for the introduction of restrictive measures against us. Simultaneously, the DOJ could justify these measures before the public and gave enough 'reasons' to uphold them. The media not only gave a very distorted picture of the asylum community but also did everything in their power to discredit our claims, to present us in a bad light and, consequently justify Ireland's reluctance to comply with its international obligations.

Reports in the media were linking us to rape, drug-pushing, thieving, begging and any abuse of the system imaginable. We even pushed Irish prostitutes out of business (*The Sunday Mirror*, 15/6/1997: 9)! An article from *The News of the World* (May 1997) titled 'Irish Race Riot Fears' offers the best example of such 'profound' journalism. It is accompanied with a photograph bearing the caption 'The rioting that set Brixton in London ablaze' and reads as follows:

> Ireland faces a nightmare threat of race riots because of a growing invasion of refugees from abroad. The warning comes in a secret document drawn up by the Department of Justice. It highlights a fear that refugees on the scrounge and those competing for Irish jobs could lead to race violence never seen in the country. The report also says that the tide of refugees poses a major public health-threat – the spread of diseases like AIDS and TB. A rise in crime would also be on the cards.

Gosh, one would think that if we were around at the time those freaking Vikings were invading Ireland, those guys wouldn't stand a chance – I'm tellin' ya!

This article, however, sums up the formula for the coverage of the refugee issue in most of Irish media throughout 1997, and mirrors the coverage of the same issue in Britain in 1995 (*The State of Asylum*, 1996: 3). Andy Pollak (1998) points out that, despite such accusations, no convictions were usually mentioned. Nor were the quoted sources high-ranking Garda officers. *The Irish Times* was the only newspaper that bothered to explain why asylum-seekers had to leave their countries by offering a different, more humane dimension – refugee stories. Its coverage of the issue thus far can be described as balanced and well-sourced.

Many a failure of successive Irish governments to deal with social issues has also been blamed on us. Politicians have created, and the media readily spread, a myth that our presence in deprived areas, among unemployed and working class people, causes social unrest. There is no better example than McGrath's leaflet. We are strange, we are foreign, we cause the shortage of accommodation, we steal Irish jobs while the system is generous. The reality is, alas, quite different. Refugees, just like other SWA and UA recipients, live below the poverty line – and are not complaining about it. Deprived areas offer cheaper accommodation, the only type accessible to the asylum community. The truth is that the Government has failed to respond promptly and swiftly to the housing problem (*The Irish Times*, 19 August 1997). Asylum-seekers are not, as hinted by some journalists, eligible to apply for local authority housing. The truth also is that many asylum-seekers remain in emergency accommodation for longer periods because increasingly, private landlords are refusing to accept foreign tenants (my own experience in 1992) or tenants claiming rent allowance. Asylum-seekers are in no position to compete for Irish jobs because they are not allowed to work, even though research has shown that many of them are highly educated and have certain skills and knowledge rarely found in Ireland (Nozinic, 1997). The prohibition on the right to work is usually conveniently omitted in discussions about the economic costs of asylum-seekers, thus depicting them as spongers. The Minister for Justice issued a statement to that effect, saying that giving people the right to work would raise their hopes of staying in the country (*The Evening Herald*, 16 July 1998: 8). The same lame excuse was used when refusing them entitlements to any state-funded English classes (Guidelines, 1996: 6). These arguments are, of course, a fallacy. Asylum-seekers, although dependent on state payouts, are not in a position to mar Ireland's economic achievements or its wealth. Figures from the Department of Social, Community and Family Affairs show that social welfare payments to asylum-seekers amount to only 0.5 per cent (£25 million) of the total social welfare budget (*The Irish Times*, 23 September 1998: 4). The main goal of the DOJ policy towards asylum-seekers, therefore, is to isolate them from the rest of society and to make their stay here as unpleasant as possible. Furthermore, by forcing people coming from non-welfare countries to collect money they did not work for, the government has blatantly chosen to humiliate them and to ignore the positive aspects of immigration.

It is also true that not much work has been done so far to enable Convention refugees to adjust their skills to an Irish context, nor have colleges establish a system for the recognition of foreign degrees. In fact, the Universities Act 1997 and the Education Bill 1997 do not mention ethnic minorities at all, let alone recognise the existence of particular minorities' needs as regards education. Similarly, the Irish Medical Council, for instance, has done everything in its power to prevent some 200 qualified refugee doctors from registration by imposing unreasonable administrative and financial requests the doctors cannot comply with – the consequence of which is that they are forced to sign off the dole and start signing on in the Health Board because they are not looking for work. A social welfare officer who informed me of one such case referred to it as a 'technicality'.

The psychological damage inflicted on the asylum community in Ireland is hard to grasp, the list of the government's failures to deal with the issue embarrassing. And let us not forget that the unemployed and the underpaid may have been perpetrators of racist attacks, but it is the educated – politicians and journalists – middle- and upper-class citizens, who incite hatred. Asylum-seekers have been sectioned off, demonised and then offered as scapegoats by those who do not live in one of the underprivileged and underfunded ghettos of Dublin.

Conclusion

The blame for poverty, unemployment and unfulfilled pre- and post-election promises does not lie with refugees, but with local and national politicians, just as the blame for the Irish 'refugee crisis' lies with the government's paralysis in making expeditious and fair decisions, and its failure to identify those most in need of protection within a reasonable time framework. This in turn '… has allowed those with no valid claim under the Refugee Act 1996 to remain in the state, fuelling misinformed intolerance towards the broader asylum community' (Byrne, 1997: 110-111).

The latter is a very valid point because there are opportunists or chancers among us, and they have been abusing the system. We would expect the DOJ to weed them out because they are giving us all a bad name. This, however, should be done within a proper legal framework. It is unprofessional as well as dangerous and inappropriate of the Minister to give statements in which 90 per cent of asylum applications are arbitrarily dismissed as 'bogus' (*The Irish Times*, 20/5/1998). That statement, which implies a thorough investigation into 6000 applications, sounded quite ominously to me like an invitation to an open hunting season on anybody presumed an asylum-seeker, and the Minister – deliberately or not – contributed to the already existing anti-refugee climate in the country.

Indeed, instead of dubious and fiercely criticised 'fast-track' and other ad hoc procedures, the government should fully implement the 1996 Refugee Act as the most effective means of dealing with asylum applications. Rosemary Byrne (1997: 108) points out that it is the absence of effective refugee legislation that exposes asylum-seekers and refugees to far greater risks than those resulting from the absence of equality legislation. However, I would still argue that Ireland needs anti-racist and equality legislation and ought to ratify international conventions protecting human rights. Simultaneously, education in Ireland should cover global, political, economic and social issues with particular reference to human rights and Ireland's obligations in that area (Collins, 1997: 109). The sad truth is that we and the Irish have never had time to be properly introduced to each other. Law and education combined, as well as the establishment of the Consultative Committee on Racism and Interculturalism announced in April 1998, and successful community initiatives such as 'Soccer Against Racism' can help build bridges leading to inclusion and better mutual understanding between the two communities, and facilitate the acceptance of diversity. Open-mindedness is what asylum-seekers and refugees need most at the moment. For we are fellow human beings – just a bit troubled.

References

Aliens (Amendment) (No. 3) Order. 1997. Signed by Nora Owen, Minister for Justice, Dublin, 25th of June, 1997.

Aniagolu, Chichi. 1997. 'Being Black in Ireland', in Ethel Crowley and Jim Mac Laughlin (eds.) *Under the Belly of the Tiger: Class, Race, Identity and Culture in the Global Ireland*. Dublin: Irish Reporter Publications: 43-52.

Byrne, Rosemary. 1997. 'On the sliding scales of justice: the status of asylum-seekers and refugees in Ireland', in Rosemary Byrne and William Duncan (eds.) *Development in Discrimination Law in Ireland and Europe*. Dublin: Irish Centre for European Law: 107-117.

Collins, Adrienne. 1997. 'Is Ireland meeting its international obligations towards refugees?' *Trócaire Development Review*, 1997: 93-114.

Duncan, William. 1997. 'Racism, Discrimination and Amendment of the European Community Treaty and the Treaty on European Union', in Rosemary Byrne and William Duncan (eds.) *Development in Discrimination Law in Ireland and Europe*. Dublin: Irish Centre for European Law: 43-54.

Education (No. 2) Bill. 1997. Dublin: Stationery Office.

Enzensberger, Hans Magnus. 1992. 'The Great Migration.' *Granta*, vol. 42, 16-51

Guidelines for the Reception of Asylum Applicants. Dublin: Department of Justice, June 1996.

Haughey, Nuala. 1999a. 'State's hollow response to the needs of asylum-seekers', *The Irish Times*, 4 December 1999: 10.

Haughey, Nuala. 1999b. 'Government aims to tackle asylum-seeker crisis while reducing numbers arriving here', *The Irish Times*, 13 December, 1999: 6.

IFC/UNHCR. *Ireland Fact Sheet*, July 1998.

Lentin, Ronit. 1997. 'Racialising (our) Dark Roasleen: Feminism, Racism, Antisemitism.' Paper presented at the 'Women Fighting Racism' conference, UCG Women's Studies Centre, 29 November 1997.

Letter from Irish Department of Justice regarding Asylum Procedures, December 13, 1985.

Letter from Irish Department of Justice, Equality and Law Reform to the UNHCR Representative for Britain and Ireland, 10 December, 1997.

McVeigh, Robbie. 1992. 'The specificity of Irish racism'. *Race & Class*, Volume 33, Number 4: 31-45.

McVeigh, Robbie and Alice Binchy. 1998. *Travellers, Refugees and Racism in Tallaght*. Dublin: West Tallaght Resource Centre.

Murphy, Tim. 1997. 'Immigrants and Refugees: the Irish legal context', in Ethel Crowley and Jim MacLaughlin (eds.) *Under the Belly of the Tiger: Class, Race, Identity and Culture in the Global Ireland*. Dublin: Irish Reporter Publications: 95-99.

Nozinic, Drazen. 1997. 'Educational Needs and Possibilities for Asylum-seekers and Refugees in Ireland', in Orla Egan (ed.) *Minority Ethnic Groups in Higher Education in Ireland*, Higher Education Equality Unit, Cork, 39-50.

Pollak, Andy. 1998. *Address to CLERAUN Conference*, 21 February 1998.

Refugee Act. 1996. Stationary Office, Dublin, 1996.

Summary Notes of Meeting of Joint Department of Foreign Affairs/NGO Standing Committee on Human Rights Sub-Committee on Asylum and Refugee Issues, Iveagh House, 3 June 1998.

The State of Asylum: A Critique of Asylum Policy in the UK. The Refugee Council, March 1996.

Universities Act. 1997. Stationery Office, Dublin.

5.

Racism and the Media in Ireland:
Setting the anti-immigrant agenda
Pat Guerin

Perhaps this is an obvious point, but the democratic postulate is that the media are independent and committed to discovering and reporting the truth, and that they do not merely reflect the world as powerful groups wish it to be perceived. Leaders of the media claim that their news choices rest on unbiased professional and objective criteria, and they have support for this contention in the intellectual community. If, however, the powerful are able to fix the premises of discourse, decide what the general public is allowed to see, hear, and think about, and to 'manage' public opinion by regular propaganda campaigns, the standard view of how the system works is at serious odds with reality (Herman and Chomsky, 1994: xi).

Introduction

As Irish society moves towards greater ethnic and cultural diversity, Irish media coverage of asylum, immigration and racism has been the subject of some scrutiny. The focus of this scrutiny has largely been concerned with the propensity for intemperate reporting and sensationalism on the part of some journalists and media agencies (Doyle, 1998; Valarasan-Toomey, 1998; Watt, 1997/98), coupled with an uncritical use of uncorroborated statements by Garda and Department of Justice spokespersons (Pollak, 1999). Some initial steps have also been taken in drafting a code of conduct for Irish journalists reporting on racist organisations and on racism in general (National Union of Journalists, 1998). However, for the most part this attention has concentrated on the printed media. To date, there have been no equivalent examinations of the role of Irish broadcasting media in these relatively new arenas of public discourse. And, while the negative aspects of Irish print media in this area have been subject to some level of critical analysis, the overall contribution of the Irish media in facilitating debate around these issues also needs to be explored. Sensationalism is easily identified and exposed. However, focusing exclusively on the very visible, albeit negative, aspects of the Irish media in this discourse may well be somewhat myopic. Arguably, other less visible messages deserve equal attention in any attempt to explicate the part played by the Irish media in the debate on asylum, immigration and racism. This chapter concentrates on Irish print media, although I include some reference to Irish broadcasting media as well. The arguments I put forward are therefore tentative and are aimed at broadening the discussion on racism and the media in Ireland. Firstly, I will attempt to demonstrate that the media in Ireland have been complicit, both overtly and covertly, in creating a context within which racism can flourish and where an anti-immigrant agenda is enabled. And secondly, I will argue that the debate on racism and immigration in Ireland has effectively been confined within narrow parameters that ultimately serve to reinforce and maintain the status quo.

Anti-immigrant racism in Ireland

Before I engage with the main theses of my argument it is worth exploring what might be described as the recent accelerated rise of racism in Ireland. Or, to be more exact, perhaps what we are witnessing in recent years in Ireland is best described as an increase in the manifestations of racism. Here, I am referring to the apparent increase in the open expression of antagonism towards racialised out-groups in Irish society on foot of Ireland's new position as a receiving nation for asylum-seekers and immigrants. I describe this increase as an apparent one in recognition of the possibility that recent data on antagonism directed at racialised out groups (Boucher, 1998; African Refugee Network, 1999) may have as much to do with improvements in reporting and recording such events as it does with an increase in the events themselves. This apparent increase may also indicate a greater willingness on the part of people holding such views to openly express them. If this is indeed the case, it raises the question of what has changed in Irish society to enable a freer expression of antagonism towards racialised out-groups. And, even if it is accepted that incidents of racially motivated abuse and attack have indeed increased, it remains difficult to ascertain whether this denotes the emergence of new racist attitudes and newly racialised out-groups in Irish society, or is merely a demonstration of attitudes that already existed but now find greater opportunities for expression.

It is important to emphasise that antagonism towards racialised out-groups is not an entirely new phenomenon in Irish society. The experience of Irish Travellers over an extended period of time – an experience that certainly predates recent perceptions of an upsurge in racism in Ireland – indicates the ongoing difficulty mainstream Irish society has had in accommodating difference. Incidents of anti-Jewish racism have also been well-documented (Keogh, 1998). Similarly, occasional expositions of the under-explored experience of Irish-born Black people (Aniagolu, 1997) suggest the presence of anti-black racism in Irish society long before the topic of racism became a notable feature of public discourse in Ireland. As suggested by Lentin (2000), it is perhaps more useful to think in terms of multi-racisms than in terms of a singular racism denoting a uniform set of discriminatory practices. In this way, anti-Traveller, anti-Jewish, anti-black, and anti-immigrant forms of racism in Ireland can to some extent be separately analysed. This is not to say that these forms of racism are totally separate and distinct phenomena.

McVeigh (1992) has argued that the roots of antagonism towards perceived out-groups in Ireland can be located, at least partially, in a strong sense of community in mainstream Irish society combined with a narrow definition of what constitutes that community. However, despite the probable linkages across different forms of racism in a single society, recent developments suggest that anti-immigrant racism is a new and virulent strain of racism in Irish society. Whether this represents an increase in racism or a new focus for old antagonisms remains unclear. This new strain of racism in Ireland, while primarily directed at newly arrived refugee and asylum-seeker communities, also appears to have spilled over into a more generalised anti-black racism in Irish society (Boucher, 1998).

Anti-immigrant racism and the Irish media

Recent research suggests that the Irish media have played a formative role in shaping public opinion about refugees and asylum-seekers. Curry (2000: 149) found that popular reaction to the arrival of refugees in Dublin was shaped by 'a cluster of beliefs which portray Ireland as currently experiencing a flood of bogus fortune-hunting refugees who are exploiting the social welfare system'. Similarly, Keogh (2000) found a tendency for transition year pupils to view refugees and asylum-seekers as social and economic threats. In both cases, the Irish media were found to be a primary source of information used in the construction of attitudes towards refugees and asylum-seekers. Given the nature of much of the media coverage on refugees and asylum-seekers in Ireland, it is not surprising that such views prevail. In the Irish print media the 'flood' metaphor has developed over a considerable period of time and has been extensively used in many newspapers in both tabloid and broadsheet form. Ireland's largest newspaper group, Independent Newspapers, has arguably been the greatest purveyor of the 'flood' metaphor in Irish print media and has been the subject of criticism in this regard (Doyle, 1998; Pollak, 1999). However, the use of the 'flood' metaphor in Irish print media has not entirely been the exclusive preserve of Independent Newspapers. *The Irish Times* appears to have studiously avoided direct use of the 'flood' metaphor, yet has on occasion used related terminology like the headline in August 1998: 'Legislation on way to curb immigrant flow'. In May 1997, the *Sunday Business Post* ran a story under the headline: 'Services face overload as refugee flood continues'. Similarly, *The Examiner*, a paper which was generally critical of Irish government policy on asylum and immigration, in an editorial (30/10/1999) opens with reference to 'A GROWING flood of immigrants…' (the upper case was used in the article). This sense of a deluge of asylum-seeking immigrants 'flooding' into Ireland became a feature of Irish print media from 1997 onwards following a significant increase in asylum applications (the increased level of applications was significant by Irish standards but remained relatively low by EU standards). Articles linking the rising levels of asylum applications with the housing shortage, and with increased pressures on Irish maternity hospitals contributed to the dispersal of the 'flood' metaphor. Irish broadcasting media helped purvey the general sense of alarm through news reports surrounding the temporary closure of the Refugee

Applications Centre in Dublin in November 1999. Extensive coverage was given to this closure and the inability of the Centre staff to cope with higher than average levels of asylum applicants. News reports on both RTE television channels and on TV3 were built around images of long queues of asylum-seekers at the Centre. While a certain level of criticism was directed at the Department of Justice for the 'crisis', the reports nevertheless helped reinforce the 'flood' metaphor.

As Curry (2000) found, a second element informing public attitudes to asylum-seekers in Ireland is the belief that most applications were in fact 'bogus' and aimed at defrauding the Irish welfare system. Once again, the dissemination of this view is easily traced within the print media in Ireland. As with the 'flood' metaphor, 1997 marked the beginning of a focus on refugees and asylum-seekers as expensive welfare cheats – 'Gardai move on dole fraud by day trip refugees' (*The Irish Independent*, 5/5/1997), 'Crackdown on 2,000 "sponger refugees"'; *The Irish Independent*, 7/6/1997). Some articles directly linked the attractiveness of the Irish welfare system with the 'flood' metaphor – 'Promised land draws a human flood' (*Sunday Independent*, 9/8/1998). Public outrage at the extent of this perceived fraud was also encouraged by headlines like 'Refugees put up in our top hotels' (*The Mirror*, 1/11/1999).

This process of criminalising refugees and asylum-seekers was also evident in numerous sensationalist reports on asylum-seeker involvement in criminal activity. The most notorious of these was the often-quoted 'Refugee rapists on the rampage' (*The Star*, 13/6/1997). Nigerian criminals involved in credit-card frauds and fraudulent investment schemes in 1998 also received sensationalist treatment in Irish tabloids that suggested the large-scale involvement of Nigerians resident in Ireland – 'Black Mafia' (*Sunday World*, November 1998). In this climate, even more temperate reporting of Nigerian involvement in criminal activities in Ireland was very likely to aid rather than hinder the criminalisation process – 'Nigerian criminals use credit-card numbers in large fraud operation' (*The Irish Times*, 2/4/1998), 'Nigerian fraud letters warning from gardai', (*The Irish Times*, 28/4/1998). Even though both The Irish Times articles were apparently accurate and non-sensationalist reports, no attempt was made to qualify the large-scale nature of the attempted fraud with reference to the small number of Nigerians involved in such activities in Ireland.

Although not explicitly stated, that many of those seeking asylum in Ireland were 'bogus refugees' was implicit in much of the print media coverage from 1997 onwards. Articles describing asylum-seeking immigrants as 'spongers' and 'scroungers', combined with sensationalist and non-sensationalist reports of asylum-seeker involvement in crime, inevitably contributed to creating an attitude of suspicion around these new immigrant communities. The suspicion that most claims for asylum were fraudulent was also being articulated by the Department of Justice early in 1998. In one interview Justice Minister O'Donoghue was quoted as stating that: 'International experience showed that at most 10 per cent of asylum-seekers would be found to be refugees when their claims were examined' (*The Irish Times*, 15/4/1998). Such statements were made at a time when there were in excess of 4,500 applications for asylum waiting to be processed. That such remarks might be indicative of a prejudicial view within the Department of Justice was not commented upon within the Irish media. Neither was the likely impact of such statements on Irish public opinion given any consideration. By early 1999, the Minister's prediction proved correct – 'Nearly 90 per cent of asylum-seekers are currently refused refugee status' (*The Irish Times*, 23/3/1999). Once again, no concerns were raised in the Irish media that the rejection rate should so accurately reflect the Minister's prediction of almost a year earlier. By this stage the term 'bogus refugee' had become a standard feature in the vocabulary of public debate on asylum and immigration in Ireland.

Another feature of reporting on asylum and immigration in Irish print media has more to do with the context within which the reports are written rather than the content of the reports themselves. By this I mean the sub-headings under which articles appear. For example, many of the reports in *The Irish Independent* using the terms 'flood', 'tide' and 'wave' are written by that newspapers' 'security editor'. The clear implication is that matters to do with asylum and immigration are 'security' issues. The reader is thus invited to view the issue from that perspective. When the headline reads 'A human tide sweeps in' (*Irish Independent*, 3/6/1998), there is little room for interpretation other than what we are reading is an item of national security with all the connotations that brings to bear on the subject. Similar examples are to be found elsewhere. Numerous articles dealing with immigration in *The Irish Times* were written by the 'Drugs and Crime Correspondent'. One such article – 'Eight refugees found in lorry seek asylum' (*The Irish Times*, 2/6/1998) – focuses on the trafficking aspects surrounding the arrival of these refugees and the proposed measures intended to prevent similar entries in the future. The issue of asylum is lost within a general discussion on trafficking in illegal immigrants and the criminal gangs engaged in the trade. In this way the association of asylum-seekers with criminality is emphasised, albeit inadvertently, while the conditions driving people to take such desperate measures are left unstated.

It should be noted that not all reporting in the Irish print media has been complicit in creating a negative aura around refugees and asylum-seekers in Ireland. There are numerous examples of articles denouncing the Irish government's handling of the issue and calling for a more sympathetic approach to dealing with asylum-seeking immigrants in Ireland. And, despite an apparent predilection for news stories that were more likely to inflame rather than assuage public opinion, at times newspapers from the Independent Newspapers Group did include articles of a more sympathetic and measured tone. However, as Watt (1997: 29) notes, 'the cumulative effect of many headlines can serve to neutralise the balanced and objective reporting than can sometimes appear in the same article elsewhere in the same newspaper'. The research by Curry (2000) and Keogh (2000) seems to confirm that the impact of the Irish media in general has been to designate refugees and asylum-seekers in Ireland as, at best, suspect communities and, at worst, criminal invaders who constitute a threat to Irish society. It is difficult to avoid concluding that the overriding contribution of the Irish media to the debate on asylum and immigration has been to create a climate of fear and suspicion. In these circumstances, the open expression of hostility towards immigrant communities was at the very least made easier. It may also have been encouraged.

Racism and immigration: Setting the parameters of debate

Just as the Irish media appear to have been complicit in enabling the development of anti-immigrant racism in Ireland, it also seems to have been compliant in the confinement of debate on racism and immigration within narrow parameters. On the issue of racism, the debate in the media has largely been concerned with reporting and bemoaning the rising levels of racist abuse and attack, combined with discussions around the need for education and anti-racism programmes to arrest its rise in Irish society. On occasion, reports questioned the wisdom of locating asylum-seekers in areas of social deprivation where there was already competition for scarce resources. The effect of a continued denial of the right to work in shaping public attitudes was also queried at times. Sometimes journalists were critical of delays in commencing a promised publicity programme to combat racism and in the introduction of anti-racism legislation. The Department of Justice was also subjected to some criticism for the negative reaction encountered in some rural areas during 2000 as the dispersal of asylum-seekers across Ireland got underway. This criticism, however, was primarily directed at the perceived failure of the Directorate of Asylum-Seeker Services to consult adequately with the local communities involved.

The impression created by this level of debate was that increasing racism was a consequence of a sudden influx of asylum-seekers colliding with an ill-prepared government response. Official mishandling of the 'refugee crisis', and a lack of measures to promote greater diversity in Irish society, were thus presented as the primary causes of increased racism directed at refugees and asylum-seekers. Debate in the Irish media tended to examine racism in terms of individual or group attitudes, and never, at least to my knowledge, did it explore the existence of institutional racism in Ireland. Despite ample evidence that the travel documents of Black people entering Ireland were likely to be more rigorously checked than those of white passengers, the Irish media have in the main been guarded in confronting this inherent racism in the operation of Irish immigration controls.

The Irish media have also been slow to explore other areas pertinent to the debate on asylum and immigration in Ireland. For example, there have been no media investigations into the national origins of those non-EU immigrants who were legally admitted to live and work in the state. The Department of Justice continually uses reference to this undifferentiated group as clear evidence of a realistic alternative to using claims for asylum as the immigration route into Ireland. Yet there have been no investigative forays by Irish journalists into the level of applications for work visas by people in the countries from which Ireland receives most of its asylum-seekers. It would be an interesting addition to public debate on asylum and immigration to have figures on the number of work visa applicants by Nigerian and Romanian nationals, and the rate at which they are granted or refused. Information as to whether or not Irish embassies in these countries encourage such applications might also add perspective to the debate. And, apart from occasional criticism of intemperate outbursts by individual politicians, the impact of the Irish body politic on public attitudes to asylum-seekers has not been subject to any serious media scrutiny in Ireland. Any possible links between Irish government policy on asylum and immigration on the one hand, and rising racism on the other, have not been a feature of discourse in the Irish media. Indeed, those groups within the NGO sector in Ireland who attempt to express concern at the influence of government policy on asylum and immigration in enabling racism are increasingly subject to derogatory dismissal as 'self-appointed, so-called anti-racist groups', and to the accusation that they 'are serving to poison the atmosphere' (*Sunday Business Post,* 7/5/2000). In these ways, not only is consensus established on the legitimate parameters of debate on racism, but breaking the bounds of those parameters is also discouraged.

Complicity in delimiting debate also seems very apparent in the Irish media's treatment of the immigration issue. Calls for a less rigid approach to dealing with asylum-seeking immigrants appear to have been quickly interpreted by the Irish media as a call for an open-door immigration policy in Ireland. As early as 1998, Irish people were being polled by the Irish print media on whether or not they wanted an open-door policy ('Majority say "no" to open door policy for refugees' – *Ireland on Sunday,* 8/3/1998). Given that there was no significant demand for an open-door policy, it was somewhat surprising that the question – 'Do you think Ireland should have an open door policy for all refugees and people seeking political asylum?' – should be asked in the first place. And, despite the loaded nature of the question, to which a majority of fifty-eight per cent answered no, a surprisingly large minority – thirty-seven per cent – answered yes. Almost two years later, an *The Irish Times*/MRBI poll suggested a hardening of public opinion with seventy-four per cent of respondents wanting strict limits on refugee numbers. Contradictorily, the same poll found that sixty per cent of people believed that Ireland should 'take a more generous approach' to refugees and immigrants given Ireland's history and current prosperity. The editorial interpretation of these 'results' was that there is 'no disguising the unwillingness of Irish people to allow an "open door" policy to refugees and asylum-seekers', and that this 'attitude is hardly surprising, given the sudden influx of asylum-seekers' (*The Irish Times,* 24/1/2000). Another article in the same issue interprets the poll results as indicating 'that the Minister may be closer to the public mood on immigration than previously thought by many'. Notwithstanding the spurious nature of such contradictory findings, no consideration is given to any other factors that may have influenced the formation of such 'divergent public attitudes'. In one fell swoop a hardening of public attitudes is solely attributed to the 'sudden influx of asylum-seekers', the Minister for Justice is vindicated in his hard-line stance on asylum-seekers, and an open-door policy is dismissed without debate. That statements emanating from the Department of Justice and mediated through the Irish media may have contributed to this apparent hardening of public opinion is not even considered.

During 1999 and 2000, reference to an open-door policy is increasingly used by Justice Minister O'Donoghue and other members of the government in both print and broadcasting media as a stick with which to beat their political detractors in the debate on asylum and immigration policy. In an article entitled 'FF rules out open door refugee policy' (*The Irish Times*, 4/3/2000), the Minister is reported as saying at the Fianna Fail Ardfheis (annual conference) that 'we cannot and we will not operate an open-door policy, as some of our opponents advocate'. The same article notes that delegates to the Ardfheis 'passed a motion calling for "an informed and honest national debate" on illegal immigration and the implementation of an adequately funded anti-racism campaign'. Dismissal of an open-door policy is shortly afterwards reiterated by Fianna Fail's coalition partners in government – 'Harney rules out open door to immigrants' (*The Irish Times*, 31/3/2000). The impact of this media-centred onslaught against the political detractors of asylum and immigration policy is almost immediate. In April 2000, the Labour Party is said to have 'stressed that it was not in favour of an "open door policy" on immigration' ('Labour accused of "muddled thinking" on asylum-seekers' – *Sunday Tribune*, 30/4/2000). And again early in May 2000, the leader of the Labour Party, Ruairi Quinn, wrote that Minister O'Donoghue 'has wrongly accused us of advocating an open-door policy. This is not our position and we have rebutted it' ('Deportation as sole policy response to immigrants already in State inadequate' – *The Irish Times*, 3/5/2000). Despite the calls for informed and honest debate, the cumulative effect of this episode has been to manufacture consent on the absolute necessity of maintaining immigration controls. It has also resulted in the effective closure of debate on the status of immigration controls in the world today. The Irish media has not only been a key instrument in conveying the accepted parameters of political debate on immigration controls, but has itself perpetuated this discursive closure through its unwillingness or inability to extend the boundaries of public discussion.

One example of this narrowing of the domain of debate on immigration controls has to do with the relocation of the 'immigration problem'. The deaths of fifty-eight Chinese migrants in a container on route from Holland to Dover in June 2000 coincided with the drafting of Ireland's Illegal Immigrants (Trafficking) Bill. Coverage of this dreadful event in Irish broadcasting and print media was for the most part concerned with the 'evil trade' of criminal gangs trafficking in human beings. One editorial, which could easily have been written by a 'self-appointed, so-called' anti-racist group, outlined the need for a broader debate:

> Reaction to the deaths at the EU Summit in Portugal on Monday was to bring down the shutters more firmly on illegal immigrants rather than to review existing mechanisms or to address the broader issues of world economic policy that impoverish some countries while allowing others to flourish behind protective barriers. Nobody quibbles with the need to penalise traffickers in human beings. But an alternative to paying such gangs must be provided for legitimate asylum-seekers (*The Irish Times*, 21/6/2000).

However, such calls for consideration of the 'broader issues' involved in migration were generally lost within a general media consensus, often expressed in hysterical tones, that the issue was primarily one of a war on traffickers. Thus debate on immigration is relocated away from the political and economic factors driving migration, and the 'imperative' of tighter border controls is re-affirmed.

Instead of questioning the assumptions that constrained debate on immigration in Ireland, the Irish media opted to seek out new territories of discussion inside the bordered landscapes of public discourse. One accepted terrain of discussion concerns Ireland's history of emigration, and particularly the level of governmental support for Irish illegal immigrants in the United States in the 1980s and 1990s (see Lentin, chapter 15 in this volume). Some appeals in the media for a less rigid approach to inward migration in Ireland were thus framed around calls for an honest recollection of Ireland's long history of economic migrancy ('Refugees are reminding us too eerily of ourselves' – *The Irish Times*, 7/8/1998). When faced with such inconvenient reminders of Irish double standards with regard to illegal immigration, Minister O'Donoghue quickly dismissed them as unfair comparisons between a small Irish economy and a much larger American one. These dismissals were largely made on Irish broadcasting media and the Minister managed to evade the issue by using the accusation of an unfair comparison as a standard response. As far as I am aware, the Minister was never pressed on the issue with any success by Irish journalists. Nor was he ever reminded that the issue was not about fair or unfair comparisons between different economies, but rather about a gaping inconsistency between Irish government attitudes to illegal immigration in different contexts. The success of the Minister's stance in this regard was also evident in that some journalists came to assert that 'comparisons with Irish economic migration are spurious' ('EU must have coherent policy on refugee crisis' – *Sunday Business Post*, 7/5/2000). Even within these narrow confines of debate, the Irish media largely failed to adequately present the Irish public with alternative perspectives to the official government position, effectively ensuring that the status quo is maintained by disarming and disabling debate on possible strategies for change.

Conclusion

The arguments I outlined do not pretend to be exhaustive or conclusive. Nor do I expect my views to be readily accepted, as that would be contrary to the central tenet of my case, that there is a need for a more broad-ranging and rigorous public debate on racism and immigration in Ireland than there has been to date. This debate must grapple with thorny issues like institutional racism, and the relationship between the exigencies of a government department that views most applications for asylum as fraudulent even before they are processed and the apparent increase in public antagonism towards immigrant communities in Ireland. It must also involve a thorough examination of the role played by the Irish media in facilitating or inhibiting their audience in engaging with subjects that have far-reaching consequences for the future development of Irish society. It would be a monumental crime if the media in Ireland were to drift towards a position where real investigative journalism is a rarity, and where a menu of compressed 'sound bites' merely provides a slightly distorted mirror-image of state-sponsored information management. Undoubtedly, one role of the media in a democracy is to continually critique those in influential positions of power and authority. In my view, it is also the role of the media to continually question the assumptions that underpin both public policy and private behaviour. Given the influence the media has on public opinion, it is not only necessary, but essential, that these roles are adequately performed. However, it is my contention that the Irish media have been less than assiduous in meeting these obligations with regard to debating racism and immigration in Ireland.

With regard to the issue of immigration controls, it is not my intention to imply that the media in Ireland should actively promote an open-door or no borders position. However, neither should the media unquestioningly promote the continuance of immigration controls as we know them today. It appears to me that this has effectively been the case to date in the Irish media. Debate on borders and immigration in the Irish media has only ever been framed within a context of Ireland unilaterally dismantling its own controls and welcoming all the displaced populations of the world. To the best of my knowledge, nobody has ever suggested this as a way forward. Such is the fear induced by this prospect that any debate on immigration controls is effectively strangled at birth. The issue is not the promotion of open borders, but the promotion of open debate. The result of this, I believe, has been to enable a steady transition towards ever-tighter immigration controls that have become inherently racist in some aspects, and which are responsible for untold human suffering. Controlling immigration is promoted by controlling debate. As noted by Schönbach:

> In principle there is nothing wrong with this power of television, press and radio to set the agenda for public discourse. This is what the media are for in complex societies – to help direct public opinion. But this power requires a greater consideration of the moral dilemma posed by the effect on the audience or readership that the continued use of traditional news-presentation criteria may have (1999: 57).

If there is merit in the argument that public opinion on racism and immigration in Ireland has been feeding off a less than complete menu, and that the effect of this restricted diet has been to enable anti-immigrant racism, then perhaps it is indeed time to examine the traditional methods of news-presentation used by Irish journalists.

Given Ireland's long history of emigration, Irish politicians could lead the way in campaigning against the introduction of ever-increasing draconian anti-immigrant measures both in Europe and in other wealthy industrialised nations. A first step in this direction might be an open examination of the relatively short history of immigration controls as we know them today, combined with an exploration of the social, economic, and political reasons for, and consequences of, their continued existence. In this regard there is room for a very much expanded role for the media in Ireland. By broadening the debate, we may discover that we have nothing to lose but our fears.

References

Aniagolu, Chichi. 1997. 'Being Black in Ireland', in Ethel Crowley and Jim MacLaughlin (eds.) *Under the Belly of the Tiger: Class, Race, Identity and Culture in the Global Ireland*. Dublin: Irish Reporter Publications.

African Refugee Network (ARN). 1999. *African Refugees Needs Analysis*. Dublin: ARN.

Boucher, Gerard. 1998. *The Irish are Friendly, But...* Dublin: Irish Council for Overseas Students (ICOS).

Curry, Philip. 2000. '"... she never let them in": Popular reactions to refugees arriving in Dublin', in Malcolm MacLachlan and Michael O`Connell (eds.) *Cultivating Pluralism: Psychological, Social and Cultural Perspectives on a Changing Ireland*. Dublin: Oaktree Press.

Doyle, Macdara. 1998. 'Independent means'. *Magill*, April, 56-57.

Herman, Edward. S. and Noam Chomsky. 1994. *Manufacturing Consent: The Political Economy of the Mass Media*. London: Vintage.

Keogh, Anna. 2000. 'Talking about the Other: A view of how secondary school pupils construct opinions about refugees and asylum-seekers', in Malcolm MacLachlan and Michael O`Connell (eds.) *Cultivating Pluralism : Psychological, Social and Cultural Perspectives on a Changing Ireland*. Dublin: Oaktree Press.

Keogh, Dermot. 1998. *The Jews in Twentieth Century Ireland: Refugees, Anti-Semitism and the Holocaust*. Cork: Cork University Press.

Lentin, Ronit. 2000. 'Racialising the other, racialising the "us": Emerging Irish identities as processes of racialisation', in R. Lentin (ed.) *Emerging Irish Identities*, proceedings of a seminar held in Trinity College Dublin, 27th November 1999. Dublin: MPhil in Ethnic and Racial Studies, TCD.

McVeigh, Robbie. 1992. 'The specificity of Irish racism'. *Race and Class*, 33/4: 31-45.

National Union of Journalists. 1998. *Racism in Ireland: The Media in Focus*. Report of the NUJ Conference, Dublin on February 20 1998.

Pollak, Andy. 1999. 'An invitation to racism? Irish daily newspaper coverage of the refugee issue', in Damien Kiberd (ed.) *Media in Ireland: The Search for Ethical Journalism*. Dublin: Open Air.

Schönbach, Klaus. 1999.'Agenda-setting, agenda-reinforcing, agenda-deflating? Ethical dimensions of the media's role in public opinion', in Damien Kiberd (ed.) *Media in Ireland: the Search for Ethical Journalism*. Dublin: Open Air.

Valarsan-Toomey, Mary. 1998. *The Celtic Tiger: From the Outside Looking In*. Dublin: Blackhall Publishing.

Watt, Philip. 1997/98. 'Reporting on Refugees', *Focus*, Issue No. 57/58 (Winter), pp. 29-30, Dublin: Comhlamh.

6.

The new Irish storytelling:
Media, representations and racialised identities
Elisa Joy White

Introduction

It was the autumn of the year 2000. I had recently arrived in Dublin from America for the tenure of a research grant. While jogging in place at a traffic light, two white Irish boys wearing ski masks jumped from behind a gate at a nearby housing estate and stood ten feet away. One of them pointed a toy gun at me. The other shouted, 'Hands up, nigger bitch!' While I stared with amazement, they laughed and were gone as quickly as they had appeared.

It is no mere coincidence that the boys were placing me in their racialised game and using a line that reflected any combination of Hollywood film dialogue, song lyrics and television crime drama; some of them, no doubt, even produced by people of colour. They more than likely had few other points of reference for a woman of African descent jogging in place with a headset on. Their game was no less than a micro-version of a larger societal approach to difference and part of a continuum upon which a formerly isolated society continues to construct identities for the 'other' based on remote misrepresentations. In those few seconds, it is unclear whether the boys were playing the roles of gangsters, gardai or, more than likely, a combination of both. What is clear may be that I was perceived as a potential threat of some kind. If one is a person of colour in Ireland at this point in history it is assumed that one is an immigrant and, if one is an immigrant, then one is no more than the sum of the anti-immigration rhetoric from the Department of Justice, the local papers, and the disgruntled bloke on the street. But, what is most significant about the boys' 'game' is that this convoluted composite of representations is rooted in the criminalisation of immigrants, stereotypes of Black experience derivative of equally problematic American cultural products, and a general belief that such an action is acceptable. The boys, like many an Irish adult, were relying on various media to engage my Black identity. Yet, they could not do so, because 'hands up, nigger bitch' has no referent in the life that I lead. But what may be the most frightening element, more frightening than having to determine the veracity of a child's gun, is that in this society of racialised immigration rhetoric conflated with skewed understandings of Black experience, the boys may very well believe that I *am* 'nigger bitch' and there are few representations around to dispute it.

I add my anecdotal account to the myriad others occurring daily throughout the Republic of Ireland, for it exemplifies the rampant formation of misrepresentative identities that is sweeping the nation. For, at this most nascent time, Ireland is constructing its first racial mechanisms of exclusion and the subsequent identities that will serve to peripheralise. These mechanisms of exclusion range from Department of Justice immigration policy to the mere lack of being free to walk down a street without a stranger's commentary. The mechanisms are posited as preventative, a means of saving the last shreds of Irish culture from the murky waters of difference and diversity. However, Irish culture and society will never be what it was before and it is doubtful that creating an underclass of 'others' will bring it back or, for that matter, forward.

Before any further mention of this elusive and overused concept called 'culture,' I'll offer a preferred definition: "Culture" is a construction of symbols which reflect the many life experiences of a social group (Brah 1997; Clarke, Hall Jefferson, and Roberts, 1977). It is important to keep in mind that symbols shift and by no means can 'culture' ever imply fixity.

Hence, the contours of Irish culture are no more essential than the social formations that emerge out of them. Individuals hold onto a story of culture that can never really be maintained and, more specifically, contained. Hence, the story of the developing new Irish culture is being told through various media at this crucial point in the nation's history, a period of letting go of earlier perceived essentialisms and moving towards more reflective cultural stories. Some may believe that the media perpetuates racism and xenophobia in Irish society, yet I would suggest that media have more reciprocal and reflexive relationships within the society. There is substantial evidence that various media validate racist sentiments, but it is the larger society that willingly accepts them. There is much more agency involved and it would be misdirected to blame cultural products for the culture itself. For example, when former *Sunday Independent* columnist Mary Ellen Synon stated that the spectacle of physically challenged athletes participating in the 2000 Sydney Olympics was 'perverse' and 'grotesque', the nation responded en masse with boycotts of the *Sunday Independent*, letters to the editor of numerous newspapers, and days of discussion on radio call-in programmes (Synon, 2000: *Independent Online*). Hence, even though Synon emerged out of the media, Irish society also used the media to vehemently express that her comments were offensive, unacceptable and not reflective of popular opinion.

Outside of the work of diligent anti-racism groups, there has yet to be a national response representing a broad cross-section of the Irish populace on the issue of racism and xenophobia, indicating a societal ambivalence about re-visioning Ireland as the diverse nation that it has become. So, amidst this ambivalence, the media serve as means of disseminating, constructing and defining the new language of identification and the social formations that accompany them. What occurs today, at the beginning of this new cultural narrative, will have greater implications for the years ahead and, that perhaps makes a re-invention of the form and function of current media representation all the more urgent.

A survey conducted in 2000 indicates that out of a sampling of 121 ethnic minorities in the Republic of Ireland, 64 per cent had experienced 'outright racial insults' and, more specifically, 87 per cent of Blacks (Africans and Afro-Caribbeans) surveyed stated that they had experienced 'outright racial insults' (Casey and O'Connell, 2000: 27-30). The Republic of Ireland has been thrust into the global economy and has become the beneficiary of all the technological advancement, material accoutrements, media products and flows of people that accompany this era. Hence, we see a nation that carries a legacy of anti-colonial struggle and anti-Irish racism throughout its diaspora becoming the destination for members of other diasporas, many with their own legacies of colonialism and racism. Yet, in the midst of all that is new, we see the nation relying on all that is old about 'race', ethnicity and cultural difference in an effort to assign meaning to shifts in the nation's perceived homogeneity, thus fulfilling the peculiar desire to signify phenotypical differences and perpetuate dysfunctional racialised categories, while simultaneously masking an aversion to those who are not racialised as 'white' by placing the issue in the realm of the 'immigration problem'. Hence, there is a mode of identifying differences and a more subversive way of acting upon them.

If we briefly survey a few modes in which some have attempted to apprehend the forever-problematic concepts of 'race', ethnicity and culture, we see the subtle, yet significant, modes in which the issues facing contemporary Ireland differ from circumstances across both seas. Michael Omi and Howard Winant, in their examination of race and ethnicity in America, describe a *racial formation* as 'the sociohistorical process by which racial categories are created, inhabited, transformed, and destroyed' and view it as a 'process of historically situated projects in which bodies and social structures are represented and organized' (Omi and Winant, 1994). What is interesting about the case in Ireland is that the social aspect of the 'sociohistorical' process is occurring now, but the historical aspect was constructed *vis-à-vis* a remote relationship with the now racialised groups of Ireland. An example, which I will return to later, is the role of Catholic charity in Africa and the near mythical construction of the 'Black Babies'.

Gregory Stephens, in his work on Bob Marley, Ralph Ellison, and Frederick Douglass (who was known to mention his Irish ancestry) offers a variation on Omi and Winant's 'racial formation' with variable formations that do not specifically present melanin or bloodlines as substantive racial criteria. He contends that in as 'much as we have replicated racial formations, so have we engendered *multiracial formations*' and that 'they take shape in multicultural public spheres which cannot always be mapped along colour lines' (Stephens 1999: 5, emphasis original). However, in Ireland, while 'racism' can be invoked to express a discriminatory power relationship based on nationality, such as anti-Irish bigotry in Britain may be described as 'racist', in the case of individuals racialised as Black, the predominant issue is 'Blackness' itself and any national affiliation is reduced to a code for "Black."

So, the replicated social formations of which Stephens writes have not yet found the space of the 'multiracial formation' emerging out of 'multicultural spheres'.

This is exemplified in the common use of 'Nigerian' to describe an individual of African descent in Ireland. This may have initially arisen out of the fact that Nigerians represent a majority of the African immigrant community and the ubiquitous newspaper coverage that featured Nigerians in the context of the 'immigration problem'. Yet, considering the myriad ethnic and national backgrounds of populations racialised as Black in Ireland and the world, it defies common sense to deduce that Blackness equals Nigerian nationality. So, as I will discuss later, it becomes one of several codes used to emphasise a negative association with a group without using more offensive racial language. 'Nigerian' is not used as a good-spirited attempt at properly identifying diverse members of the Irish population. It is no more than a means of expressing disinterest in the layered complexity of Black identities in Ireland. It is a way of representing a group without seeing the individual, which is what nourishes racism and xenophobia in the first place.

Stuart Hall notes that the 'great collective social identities have not disappeared' and contends:

> Their purchase and efficacy in the real world that we occupy is ever present. But, the fact is that none of them is, any longer, in either the social, historical or epistemological place where they were in our conceptualisations of the world in the recent past. They cannot any longer be thought in the same homogeneous form (Hall 1997: 45).

Hall's assertion certainly has as much resonance in contemporary Ireland as it does in Britain. However, in the case of Ireland, the 'recent past' to which Hall refers is the present and the representation of 'difference' within Irish society is a crucial aspect of the inability to envision diversity within the society.

The aforementioned modes of apprehending and explaining the contemporary experience of racialised identities and processes further highlight the fact that Ireland's history of ethnic and racial diversity, particularly in the context of individuals racialised as Black, does not fit neatly into other Western models of experience. It is almost as if the nation is experiencing a type of social whiplash as it struggles to work through processes which in any other time would take decades. Thus, we see an attempt at explaining the function of contemporary racialised social formations in the context of our more global times, a period that supposedly reflects a collective understanding of the complexity of our differences and the illogical notions we ascribe to them, yet fails miserably.

Alien invasion and the new racial tongue

Much of the popular discourse around the issues of racial and cultural difference are presented in the context of immigration, as if there is no connection between xenophobia and the oppressive, melanin-based discrimination which proceeds and accompanies the current period of globalisation. While in the American context, 'race' tends to be limited to a discussion of conflict occurring across the artificial and limiting construct of the Black/White binary, in Ireland and in the UK, where frequently 'racism' is inclusive of nation-based and ethnic-based power inequalities, we see that the terminology can at times be less specific. Hence, there may be a need to further qualify melanin-based racisms through new language in the form of immigration-based coding and to employ media to facilitate the dissemination of the grammar and vocabulary. It may be considered a polite social code, but it is as invidious as it is insidious.

A November 2000 an *Irish Times* article explains the disparity between the assumption that all immigrants are asylum-seekers and the reality:

> Many of the 48,000 immigrants into Ireland in 1999 were black and here to study and take up important positions. Fewer than one fifth of the total were asylum-seekers. Yet the public perception of almost all black and coloured people now is that they are asylum-seekers, a plenary session at the Academy of Medical Laboratory Science 2000 heard at the weekend. The small group of asylum-seekers, only 16.26 percent of immigrants, is getting 'disproportionate negative attention' the conference in Tralee heard. 'There is now generalised racism in a spontaneous manner in the streets and this is especially the case in areas where there is a preponderance of asylum-seekers', said Father Michael Begley, director of Spiritan Asylum Service Initiative. And the blacker you are the worse it is – studies have shown that racism is 'a matter of colour and degree of colour', he said (Lucey, 2000: *Irish Times Online*).

While this disparity between reality and popular assumption is related to the ubiquity of media discussion around immigrants that are seeking asylum, much like the assumption that all people of African descent are 'Nigerian', there is a larger process at work. As a means of getting to this larger issue, I'll walk through the problem of the assumption of asylum-seeker and the subsequent refugee status.

First, if the primary public concern is with asylum-seekers, why is there more 'disproportionate negative attention' paid towards Africans, even as we see that those who are considered 'blacker' are not likely to represent a higher percentage of asylum-seekers than other groups? If it is asylum-seekers to whom negative attention is directed, why do all those who are considered 'blacker' receive more attention? So, if those assumed to be seeking asylum receive the bulk of the negative attention, most people of colour are receiving the brunt of this popular assumption of asylum status, 'the blacker you are the worse it gets', and we accept that those fitting the 'blacker' category happen to be African immigrants, we can deduce that African immigrants, regardless of status, are bearing the brunt of the aforementioned 'generalized racism in a spontaneous manner'. While this indicates that there is a greater assumption that Blacks would be seeking asylum, it also presents our more insidious element. If 'blacker' individuals are considered asylum-seekers and are experiencing verbal and physical attacks because of this maligned status, while those who do not produce as much melanin, even though it is noted that they are also presumed to be seeking asylum, are not receiving the same number of attacks, this generalisation may be an indication that most individuals do not care to distinguish between levels of status when interacting with the 'blacker' populations. But, what is even more apparent is that 'asylum-seeker' and 'refugee' have not only progressed to a kind of code for people of colour, particularly Africans, but that 'asylum-seeker' and 'refugee' have become epithets, no more than state-sanctioned expressions of 'nigger'. It has become a way of vilifying and a method of noting that a person has a precarious position in society, regardless of status.

In a recent study of African asylum-seekers in Ireland, Treasa Galvin explains:

> In essence, the status of asylum is experienced as a normative order wherein the ability to meet one's own needs is withdrawn with a subsequent loss of dignity and self-esteem (Galvin, 2000: 209).

Thus, when one is called an asylum-seeker, the term carries the weight of the indignity of the experience and to extend this, refugee status becomes an extension of this distinction. An individual becomes a permanent resident but is still singled out for the reason that status was obtained and remains in a subaltern position; wearing a green 'R', if you will, and always on guard for the next person to acknowledge the sign.

I have belaboured this issue of the language of status identification because not only is it applied in the way one's social class status is expressed or one's occupation is described, but 'asylum-seeker' and 'refugee' have become racialised terminology in the same way that anti-immigration rhetoric often masks racism. One need only see that it is a matter of melanin in that immigrants racialised as 'white' are actively sought for work and immigrants racialised as 'Black' or 'darker' are recruited as an afterthought, if at all. This is apparent when we consider which nations are excluded from active recruitment to work in Ireland. As one article states, in an effort to prevent the growing worker shortage in a nation expecting 350,000 new jobs within the next five years, since its 1999 launch, the Jobs Ireland Campaign has 'travelled to the UK, mainland Europe, North America and South Africa. This year it will travel to Russia, USA and Australia' (Walshe, 2000: *The Irish Independent Online*). There is a curious avoidance of nations with high populations of colour. If we note that the only African nation targeted for recruitment is South Africa, a nation that would present numerous white applicants, it becomes clear that the Irish recruiters are opting for locations where the majority of applicants will potentially be white. In addition, it does not seem much of a stretch, considering the popular assumption that most Blacks are seeking asylum, that the prohibition of asylum-seekers from working is a means of ensuring that Blacks are not seeking work in Ireland. We see this in the histrionics of Áine Ní Chonaill's Immigration Control Platform:

> There should be a qualifier as to whether immigrants are economically necessary. Immigrants are socially unwelcome and I think there should be controlled immigration. The government should introduce laws so that employers pay massive fines if they employ illegals (Hanley, 2000: *News of the World Online*).

Ní Chonaill and her supporters are well represented in the media as the voices of the anti-immigration movement, though it is the state that *enables* their rhetoric. Immigrants, as the above quote indicates, are presented as a last option to be avoided if at all possible, unwelcome impositions and in need of control, which leads to their dehumanisation *vis-à-vis* an identity based on the lack of the much coveted work permit.

Quite clearly, these imposed identities are solidified by the repetition of their use in inflammatory and sensational contexts in various media. Even in what some would consider more innocuous contexts, the label 'refugee' printed in bold text confirms and essentialises the identities of individuals. An example of such a situation appeared on the front page of an October 2000 issue of *The Sunday Times*. Under the headline 'Refugee camp to be built at Dublin airport', there is a photo of a young boy of African descent holding a sign which reads, 'Refugees are welcome here' and the caption below states, 'Crisis: an asylum protest' (McHugh and Sheehan, 2000: 1). The article discusses Minister for Justice John O'Donoghue's plans to open 'compounds' for those seeking asylum and while they note that civil liberties groups were 'alarmed' by the Minister's plans, the article did not mention the anti-racism protest to which they seemingly were referring in the photo caption. The photo was placed out of context and it could be argued that the photo of a child may inspire some to oppose the project, which is clearly akin to a prison camp (even if it includes sports facilities). But, the problem is that the juxtaposition of 'refugee' in the headline above the photo of the boy and 'refugee' on the sign in his hands reinforces the refugee identity and constructs a type of poster child, rooted in earlier Irish obsessions with saving 'Black babies'. Of course, I am by no means presenting an argument for article 19 of the Refugee Act of 1996, which prohibited the identification of asylum-seekers in the media without the permission of the individual and the Minister for Justice. This merely served to strip those seeking asylum of an identity and voice, which could only be reclaimed if Justice Minister O'Donoghue deemed one's expression of self-appropriate. At the time of writing, after much cry of censorship, particularly from the National Union of Journalists, Article 19 is facing repeal.

Arjun Appadurai contends that we live in a world of 'scapes' which include what he describes as 'mediascapes', referring to the distribution of various electronic and print media, as well as the representations of the world that emerge from the media (Appadurai, 1997). The most important aspect of mediascapes, he argues, is that 'they provide ... large and complex repertoires of images, narratives, and ethnoscapes to viewers throughout the world, in which the world of communities and the world of news and politics are profoundly mixed' (Appadurai 1997: 35). However, he adds that there is a blurring of the 'lines between the realistic and the fictional landscapes ... so that the farther away these audiences are from the direct experiences of metropolitan life, the more likely they are to construct imagined worlds that are chimerical, aesthetic, even fantastic objects, particularly if assessed by the criteria of some other perspective, some other imagined world' (Appadurai 1997: 35).

So, it is not inconceivable that fictional narratives of the lives of people of colour in Dublin, or 'ethnoscapes', precede their arrival and whatever identities have been formed are not only projected upon the immigrant, but also justify the placement of the immigrant within a specific societal context. This becomes a particular concern when the narrative of asylum-seekers becomes a story of invasion, even to the point of expressing a fear that they would be carrying illnesses, an invasion of micro-organisms and their human hosts. The aliens are coming and, for once, it is the receiving community that is green. Besides the science fiction quality of it all, it is also no surprise that the rhetoric is similar to that of the discussion around the border crossing of animals with foot and mouth disease in the late Winter of 2001, as it is becoming more difficult to determine whether individuals such as Áine Ní Chonaill are talking about human beings or sheep.

But, one cannot construct the tale of invasion without the media. There must be a medium in which remote communities can, to extend Appadurai's explanation, make up the story of the world they do not know with whatever pieces of that world they believe are real. But, as Appadurai speaks of a rural context, we may even argue that all of Ireland, until recently, was outside of the metropolis of which he speaks. Nevertheless, during the current period of globalisation, Ireland's rural areas seem even further removed from the metropolis when one considers the growth of Dublin and the nation's smaller cities (McDonald, 2001: *The Irish Times Online*).

We see a chapter of the rural dimensions of this narrative and get a glimpse of the bits used to construct the whole in a May 2000 *Sunday Independent* article with the headline 'Villages "cannot veto immigrant influx"'. The first sentence reads:

> The head of the Directorate of Asylum Support Service has warned that rural communities will not be allowed to veto the arrival of immigrants among them or negotiate the number to be accommodated (Grennan, 2000: *Sunday Independent Online*).

The message was sent beyond the metropolis to rural communities and framed as a problem with which they would have to contend. But, if that was not sufficient, the same issue includes an article titled 'Mishandling of refugee issue may cost more than money' (O'Malley, 2000). So, not only is there an invasion involved, but if one's life is more costly than money, then that is what the headline implies. But, the article, written by political correspondent Joseph O'Malley, actually refers to political careers being lost due to rural outrage at the government 'dispersal' discussed in the prior article. O'Malley writes:

> Certainly, it could strain social cohesion as tensions rise among local communities directly affected by the government's new 'dispersal' policy in the placement of asylum-seekers, and who are also outraged by the failure to consult adequately in advance. Indeed, some of last week's reactions illustrate the potential for trouble that lies ahead (O'Malley, 2000: *Sunday Independent Online*).

O'Malley goes on to mention a fire in a Tipperary hotel intended for asylum-seekers and 'populist scare mongering from South Kerry Independent TD, Jackie Healy Rae', who, he writes, 'claimed there were 80,000 asylum-seekers in the country, about seven times greater than official figures suggest, and warned of "civil rumpus" unless tougher policies are introduced' (O'Malley, 2000). In one paragraph, O'Malley has foreshadowed the script of a television movie, which I will examine next. But, first it should be pointed out that in this article O'Malley also shed light on another potential problem. He writes:

A failure to pursue a tolerant and liberal approach to asylum-seekers might not just be a breach of our international obligation. It would also reduce our ability to attract the skilled immigrants we need to fill job vacancies (O'Malley, 2000).

Beyond the presumption that asylum-seekers are not necessarily skilled labour, O'Malley has turned the gaze of difference upon Irish society, who may end up being represented as something other than human.

Remote racial renderings

As the print media grapple with the issues of 'race' and culture and negotiate that somewhat reflexive place it holds in a community, the television film 'Black Day at Blackrock' takes advantage of the impressionable capacity of media representations and holds a looking glass to the society to which O'Malley refers. Gerry Stembridge's film aired on 29 January 2001 on RTE and told the tales of the previous summer via a comedic story in a fictional setting. While it was not as acidic and pointed as it potentially could have been, it certainly offered a less than flattering view of the fictional composite of the communities touched by the 'dispersal' plan and questioned the assumptions rooted in notions of racial purity, cultural sanctity, sexual mythologies and the all-consuming aversion to difference. As one *Irish Times* review noted, 'Although there were many home truths here, Stembridge didn't hold up a mirror to rural (or rural/suburban) Ireland. Instead he poked fun at it' (Fottrell 2000: 10). However, I would argue that even though the film lacks the edge that inspires ideological transformation, it does offer a layering of details that expose the contradictions at the core of anti-immigrant rhetoric. He holds a mirror up to the contradictions that are intricately woven into the mundane details of the village life and, for that matter, all Irish life. In the space of one scene Stembridge offers us a montage of products that imply that the everyday lives of these Irish villagers are linked to the 'blackness' which they appear to abhor. In the midst of anti-asylum discourse, we see customers searching and reaching for Uncle Ben's and Aunt Jemima products. After an older villager asserts, 'Any them blackies come near me, I'll give 'em a work-up', without skipping a beat, she asks for 'El Paso' corn crisps. Of course, it is a superficial relationship that the villagers have with these products, as this is only about 'Blackness' for consumption and pleasure when it suits them; much like a Motown tune on the radio or a group of white Irish youths dancing to the latest R&B hit in a Dublin club. What further problematises the villagers' consumption of these products is that these representations of 'Blackness' are rooted in some of the most painful issues of territoriality and invasion, as they have emerged out of equally complex and undoubtedly invidious responses to difference.

'Uncle Ben' and 'Aunt Jemima' are icons rooted in the bondage of African people in the antebellum American south, a world in which all identity was constructed through the gaze of an all-controlling master – another example of life without dignity. These products are representations of roles imposed upon them, a role that became their identity and was disseminated throughout the culture as reality. The real Uncle Bens and Aunt Jemimas of America's plantations may have smiled on the packages, but they would have been less than happy. The 'El Paso' Tex-Mex snack says less about spiciness and more about American imperialism, as the south-western city of El Paso, Texas sits on the United States side of the Mexico-United States border. It is a border created through a brutal conquest to make American spaces out of formerly Mexican spaces. Thus, the product tells a story of an American society that enjoys Mexican-style cuisine, but would prefer that the Mexicans stay and not come north of the border. In these products, we see the story of many an immigrant in Ireland.

Stembridge also highlights the degree to which the immigration issue has become a type of 'white man's burden' by presenting less than spirited civil servants. They are not particularly keen on the presence of asylum-seekers but, as one civil servant says, 'It's part of being in the EU and we're stuck with it'. His partner concurs, 'That's the EU for you'. Thus, we see that if it were not for European Union membership, not to mention the United Nations Human Rights Commission, Ireland would not have to worry about immigration. Of course, the reality is that without such membership, immigration would be the very least of the nation's worries.

Some of the most vehement protest in 'Blackrock' comes from a character called Terry, who is, perhaps, modelled on the aforementioned TD Jackie Healy Rae. At one point, Terry expresses concern that village residents will be 'bumping into big lips' at every turn. This is noteworthy if we are to extend the argument that 'asylum-seeker' is a racialised category and that she or he embodies an identity that is used as a racial epithet and, in cases of exclusion, racist endeavour. We see that, at its most basic level, Terry's concern is about a body part: lips. Now if we consider Terry's concern and take into account that concerns about difference are often conflated with economic discussions around immigrants taking work from Irish workers, we realize that it is never really about jobs in the first place; for, unless one is a supermodel, it is a rare thing to have a mere protrusion of lips take a job away from you. It is about fear and mockery of difference.

Yet, the immigration issue is much too layered to be specifically about dislike of all members of a racialised group, for there are clearly variations and levels of aversion, as we saw with the consumption of 'Black' products. From the most superficial to the most resonant level, Irish people have a relationship with 'Blackness' that may explain the confusion, contradiction, and equivocation that materialises in discussions and media about immigrants and immigration. Stembridge's project, by including characters who admit they like Denzel Washington and other famous Blacks, implicates the selectivity that accompanies racialised interactions and acceptance.

If we look at other media, we see that RTE airs the Oprah Winfrey Show no less than twice daily. TV3 runs *Any Day Now*, an American television drama which focuses on the lives of two women, one white and one Black, who grew up as best friends in the 1950s civil rights era south and regularly features flashbacks of their lives. On one particular Saturday, TV3 not only broadcast an episode of *Any Day Now* in which the African-American character is involved in a tribute to her late Civil Rights leader father, but also aired the film, *Mississippi Burning*, the Alan Parker ode to heroism, albeit dubious, on the part of the Federal Bureau of Investigation (FBI) in the African-American civil rights movement.

It is difficult to imagine mass public outcry in Ireland about the transmission of Oprah Winfrey into lounges throughout the nation, for she is famous, receives that gaze we reserve for famous people and, if she gets out of line, the channel can be changed. In actuality, if she were here in person, it is conceivable that she would be quite welcome, Blackness and all. But, the TV3 broadcasts of *Any Day Now* and *Mississippi Burning*, surely created cognitive dissonance in the viewer. If we consider that the dialogue in these Civil Rights dramas focuses on human rights, anti-racism and the accompanying discrimination aimed at those racialised as Black Americans, it is not difficult to imagine that Irish viewers use distance, time and the medium employed to separate themselves from these representations of Black experience which echo their more immediate reality. But there is a more significant explanation revealed here. While it can be argued that on some level Irish viewers identify with the oppressed, I would suggest there is another element at the core of this interest in the African-American civil rights era struggle for equality and justice which is the crux of much of the anti-asylum or, more specifically, anti-Black rhetoric and representations: 'Black babies'.

Robbie McVeigh, in *The Racialisation of Irishness*, asserts that while Protestantism had a more direct relationship with British imperialism and its racist ideology, Catholicism 'was certainly implicated in a specifically Catholic western religious imperialism' (McVeigh, 1996: 32). He explains:

> If Catholicism carried an inherent anti-Semitic racism, it also manifested elements of anti-Black racism in a specifically religious phenomenon. This is illustrated by the collections for 'Black Babies' which were until recently a ubiquitous feature of Irish Church propaganda. The 'Black Babies' phenomenon conditioned Irish Catholic people to regard Black people in a particular way – as passive victims who could only be saved by the good offices of the Catholic Church (McVeigh 1996: 31-32).

The legacy of charitable association with Africa and the perception that Black individuals are no more than the collective embodiment of the malnourished child on a parish poster presents a contemporary problem: what happens when Africans deviate from their perceived role as 'Black babies' waiting to be filled by those running a step ahead of their sins? What happens when remoteness is replaced with proximity accompanied by an assertion of a contrary representation of self?

It becomes abruptly apparent that while it may be all right to save Africans from starvation or, in the case of the anti-apartheid movement in Ireland, oppressive socio-political systems, such a relationship only exists as long as Africans remain beyond the contours of the Irish border. Hence, when Africans arrive on Irish soil, a fantasy is disrupted and a mechanism of guilt assuagement is invalidated. The African immigrant or perceived asylum-seeker becomes not only an object of derision, but becomes the object of suspicion, as she will never fully live *down* to the representations which preceded her. Though it is a prickly consideration, we may wonder if perhaps there is still some comfort from the sad fact that there continue to be starving babies in Africa and if one turns on the telly there is at least the opportunity to view the old familiar representations of Africa and to offer kindness remotely, rather than at home, where all the 'Black babies' have mobile phones.

Towards a bright green future

When *The Sunday Tribune* presented '100 foreigners who wield enormous power over Irish life', a side bar stated: "Whether Irish people realise it or not, many foreigners, most of whom have never even set foot in the country, have power at most and influence at least, over the way Irish people live their lives' (Cooper et. al., 2000: 14). The list included four individuals of African descent: former South African President Nelson Mandela, former ANC official turned Belfast agreement weapons inspector, Cyril Ramaphosa, British disc jockey, Trevor Nelson and American golfer, Tiger Woods. While four individuals may not be a particularly large group, we see that Blacks are not always relegated to the victim space in Ireland, but can actually dominate or 'wield enormous power'. Of course, it could be argued that Mandela and Ramaphosa are merely 'Black babies' that the Irish public permitted to grow up. But, the latter two may be more related to what the upbeat sidebar describes as 'the wider availability of foreign media' which means that 'many of the popular obsessions of other countries are shared by Irish people of all ages' (Cooper et. al., 2000: 14). So, maybe heroes are exempt from the more problematic consequences of the Irish gaze upon the 'blacker'.

This gaze upon the Black hero can be seen in the success of footballer Paul McGrath, the late rocker Phil Lynott, the band 'Relish', which includes twins of African and Irish descent, and pop star Samantha Mumba – all considered Irish, all racialised as Black. But, the Black heroism of the not-so-famous reveals the society's racialised presumptions and the difficulty of reconciling heroism with a potential pariah. This is seen in the case of a Dublin actress who was saved from a mugging by an unknown man of African descent. *The Evening Herald* front page reads, 'Hero: Dubliners look on as an African man helps Jeananne Crowley' and in larger titles, 'Dublin actress seeks her saviour' (Power, 2001: 1). The first paragraph states:

> Actress Jeananne Crowley today publicly thanked the black man who came to her rescue as she was being mugged on a Dublin street during evening rush hour (Power, 2001: 1).

Crowley tells *The Evening Herald*, 'I think the man who came to my rescue was African' and that 'maybe he is an immigrant or a refugee. I really would like to thank him properly for having had the decency to come to the aid of a woman in jeopardy. And if he needs a friend in Dublin, and refugees often do, he has one in me' (Power 2001: 4).

While this is probably not meant to be a harmful story, it is interesting how Africans are seen as separate from Dubliners, refugees are separate from immigrants, and there is a more than descriptive emphasis on the fact that the hero is African. This is not new that racial descriptives are saved for those who do not fit into the normalised category of 'white'. But, three days later, the mystery man was located and a photo appeared on the front page of *The Evening Herald* with the headline: 'Uncaring City: Londoner is amazed Dubliners did nothing to stop attacker'. The rescuer turns out to be a 'British-born businessman, whose parents come from Nigeria' (O'Keefe, 2000: 6). When he is no longer the generic African, immigrant, or refugee, and is firmly taken out of the Irish context, he becomes a man of a place and of a city, a *Londoner* rather than an 'African' suspended between nation and nowhere. The Dubliners at the mugging were looking on as a Londoner saved the day. This hero story, in the end, lauds a foreign Black hero and becomes a condemnation of Dublin cowardice, his Blackness and Britishness adding insult to injury.

Identifying 'Blackness' with the nation is a slow process at this time. Yet, there are more subtle representations emerging. In Gerry Stembridge's well-received feature film *About Adam*, he places the new Dublin on the screen and though none of the principal characters are of colour, there are Black 'extras' in many of the street and bar scenes. This is not necessarily the achievement to end all, but it certainly challenges the prior representations of an all-white Ireland that are usually manifest in productions that predate the current period. Also, if one walks up O'Connell Street in Dublin, one can see 'Black' mannequins and even dreadlocked 'white' mannequins expressing a kind of sartorial bliss. There are also counter-representations that emerge out of the immigrant community. *MetroEireann*, a free paper with the motto 'Many voices, one Ireland', focuses on multicultural issues facing the nation. There is also a website called 'African's Magazine' which was developed as a source of information for and about the African communities.

It is a wonderful thing to be Irish at this point in history, a time when the nation is faced with the choice of growing stronger and reflecting the larger world to which it is already inextricably linked or isolating itself from the world and only partaking of its bits and pieces *vis-à-vis* a scattering of representations and remote acts of kindness. A choice will have to be made and one hopes that history, too, will be as kind.

References

Appadurai, Arjun. 1997. *Modernity at Large: Cultural Dimensions of Globalization*. Minneapolis: University of Minnesota Press.

Brah, Avtar. 1996. *Cartographies of Diaspora: Contesting Identities*. London and New York: Routledge.

Casey, Sinead and Michael O'Connell. 2000. 'Pain and prejudice: Assessing the experience of racism in Ireland', in Malcolm MacLachlan and Michael O'Connell (eds.) *Cultivating Pluralism: Psychological, Social and Cultural Perspectives on a Changing Ireland*. Dublin: Oak Tree Press.

Clarke, John, Stuart Hall, Tony Jefferson, and Brian Roberts. 1997. 'Subcultures, cultures and class', in Stuart Hall and Tony Jefferson (eds.) *Resistance Through Rituals*. London: Hutchinson.

Cooper, Matt, Shane Coleman, Matthew Magee and David Cronin. 2000. 'Our world in their hands: 100 foreigners who wield enormous power over Irish life', *The Sunday Tribune*, 22 October 2000: 14-16.

Fottrell, Quentin. 2001. 'The grey reality beneath the Technicolor glare', *The Irish Times*, 3 February 2001: 10.

Galvin, Treasa. 2000. 'Refugee status in exile: The case of African asylum-seekers in Ireland', in Malcolm MacLachlan and Michael O'Connell (eds.) *Cultivating Pluralism: Psychological, Social and Cultural Perspectives on a Changing Ireland*. Dublin: Oak Tree Press.

Grennan, Sinead. 2000. 'Villages "cannot veto immigrant influx",' *The Sunday Independent Online*, 7 May 2000.

Hall, Stuart. 1997. 'Old and new identities, old and new ethnicities', in Anthony King (ed.) *Culture, Globalization and the World-System: Contemporary Conditions for the Representation of Identity*. Minneapolis: University of Minnesota Press.

Hanley, Valerie. 2001. 'Firms face rap over migrants', *News of the World Online*, 7 January 2001.

Lucey, Anne. 2000. 'Attitudes to blacks criticised', *The Irish Times Online*, 13 November 2000.

McDonald, Frank. 2001. 'Dublin sprawl may "colonise most of Leinster",' *The Irish Times Online*, 6 March 2001.

McHugh, Fiona and Maeve Sheehan. 2000. 'Refugee camp to be built at Dublin airport', *The Sunday Times*, 1 October 2000: 1.

McVeigh, Robbie. 1996. *The Racialisation of Irishness: Racism and Anti-Racism in Ireland*. Belfast: Centre for Research and Documentation.

O'Keefe, Alan. 2001. 'I rescued mugged actress', *Evening Herald*, 12 January 2001: 1.

O'Malley, Joseph. 2000. 'Mishandling of refugee issue may cost more than money', *The Sunday Independent Online*, 7 May 2000.

Omi, Michael and Howard Winant. 1994. *Racial Formations in the United States: From the 1960s to the 1990s*. London and New York: Routledge.

Power, Bairbre. 2001. 'Mugged actress seeks her saviour', *Evening Herald*, 9 January 2001: 1.

Stephens, Gregory. 1998. *On Racial Frontiers: The New Culture of Frederick Douglass, Ralph Ellison, and Bob Marley*. Cambridge: Cambridge University Press.

Synon, Mary Ellen. 2000. *The Sunday Independent Online*, 22 October 2000.

Walshe, John. 2001. '350,000 workers needed to sustain economy', *The Irish Independent Online*, 19 January 2001.

7.

Generating awareness for the experiences of women of colour in Ireland

Shalini Sinha

Introduction: the burden of anti-racism

In this chapter I will seek to generate awareness for the particular experience of racism facing women of Colour. As our experiences across this group are varied, I will do this by raising issues which I see to be common and relevant to many of us. Given the very nature of racism, however, discussing our experience is not simple. It is essential that we take the power to share our experience on our own terms, despite the many forces which would have it otherwise. Thus, in the spirit of awareness building, I will begin by outlining one common misunderstanding about anti-racism which attempts to dislodge this power.

In reality, an effective challenge to racism will only come when those who are subjected to the oppression ('us' – in Ireland we are Travellers, people of Colour, Jewish and Muslim people and others from ethnic minorities) and those who are dominant within it ('you' – in Ireland you are the white, settled, Christian population) are able to work together equally. Understanding how racism works to undermine our power, then, will open the doors to such constructive, allied work against racism.

I am an Indian woman, born in Canada and immigrant to Ireland where I am now a permanent and active member of Irish society. As a trainer and teacher in this area, I am continually talking to people about racism in Ireland. Repeatedly, I encounter a certain attitude among the dominant group – that is, the way to challenge racism is to learn about the experiences of the oppressed groups ('us').

There are two important assumptions underlying this view. First, there is the belief that we are the ones affected by racism, so anti-racist action must essentially focus on us. Second, from this perspective, the focus of anti-racist actions becomes 'protecting' us from racism and 'helping' us to cope with it. Of course, these two assumptions are both incorrect and offensive.

In reality, racism is an everyday experience. It is something we deal with on a daily basis. Clearly, then, it deserves recognition that – over the days, years, decades, generations – we have developed strong and suitable strategies for coping with racism. We *are* in fact the best skilled and equipped to deal with it. We don't need help. On the contrary, in the course of a day it is likely we will have confronted numerous inappropriate behaviours and attitudes and moved passed them, perhaps without even applying conscious effort, and certainly before you notice them. Our experience of racism has taught us to move on. Yours has taught you not to notice. Thus, there is a great deal of arrogance involved in this 'helping' or 'protecting' attitude which, by its very nature, does not recognise our intelligence.

Second, this way of thinking comes directly from racism. Within the attitude of racism is the belief in one's superiority over others. This attitude exposes the belief that 'you' think you are better able to deal with this than 'we' are, and thus we require your assistance. It is an insult to our intelligence. In fact, it is not our ability to cope which is the pressing issue. As all humans, we are well able to survive and live our lives despite being subjected to racism. It is not our *ability to cope*, but what we are coping with, that should concern you.

We are not victims. We are people, and every bit as intelligent, creative, flexible and capable as any other human being. We do not need 'you' to protect us, or make victims out of us by focusing on the struggles we face as a result of having our basic human rights denied (at the very least, our rights to safety, dignity and to being totally valued). The last thing we need is for our struggles to be used to reinforce the false ideas of our inferior abilities to live our lives, use our intelligence and build useful achievements. Fixating on our experience only allows the system of unearned 'race' privilege to remain invisible.

The other question I must ask is, who are you trying to protect us from? Is it not members of your own group? Is it not, then, yourselves? It is that critical question, 'Am I racist?' that is currently plaguing most of you today. We must begin to make a commitment to the reality of our society; there is racism in Ireland, and that racism is systematic and institutionalised. The only way I can see to challenge this is to keep all of our attentions focused on the system – thus, not on how we cope, but the role we each play in allowing racism to continue.

Thus, it is not our experience that should preoccupy you. We each must look at our own participation in this abominable system and challenge that. Any paralytic feelings that make us not want to look at the system at hand must be disempowered. For example, there is guilt on your side. I believe 'guilt' is often used by you to try to let us know that you've recognised something is wrong and you feel bad about it. In this way, guilt is used ironically to make you feel better for having noticed, but also allows you to feel overwhelmed and thus immobilised. In this way, guilt is a barrier, an excuse, that stops you from accessing your personal power and taking responsibility.

And then there is anger on our side. Make no mistake, I am angry. I remind you, however, that my anger is not an open door for you to run through, dismissing my insight, expertise and the content of my message. My anger is actually helpful to you. As Audre Lorde (1984: 127) reminds us, 'Focused with precision it [anger] can become a powerful source of energy serving progress and change'. In this chapter, I will focus my anger so that you may see those areas of injustice which you have long since been taught not to recognise. I want you to know my anger, not so that you shrivel up in guilt, but in the hope that you will find the strength to become enraged along with me and that we can work constructively against this together.

This is where you come to realise that racism does not just affect 'us'. If we are subjected to it, you – as a member of the majority – are participating in it. This participation may not be obvious, but I would like to remind you that even unaware acceptance of privileges – or unearned, unquestioned membership into the dominant group, or even unawareness of others' exclusion from this group – all allow the system of racism to continue. And so, the focus of anti-racism becomes the questioning of your *participation* in what it is we are coping with.

Being faced with racism on a daily basis, we have more access to knowledge and awareness about the injustice than you do. While we have both been conditioned not to pay attention to it, our experiences are harder for us to ignore. Given appropriate spaces and support, we have more opportunities to identify the oppression in operation.

This is our contribution to the process: to write or speak about our experience despite our frustration. It is important that through this, you learn to see our humanity. Instead of making it the focus of enquiry, our experience can help to identify, by contrast, areas where unearned and unacceptable privilege and superiority run uninterrupted, and we are systematically excluded by the racist system. Your part of the process is to recover your sense of rage about this injustice and focus that on constructive efforts to break down this system of privileges. When you remember not to focus on our ability (or your perception of our inability) to cope, and focus on gaining awareness of all the injustices of this system, then we are beginning to work together. In this spirit, I will now raise key issues outlining our experiences as women of Colour in Ireland.

Women of Colour: diversity and stereotyping

First of all, 'women of Colour' make up a very diverse group, including Black Irish, migrants, women of various and sometimes overlapping ethnicities, working and middle class, disabled women, heterosexuals and lesbians, the list goes on. As we are diverse, so too are our experiences. The only thing we may have in common is that we experience racism, and for many very legitimate reasons, this is difficult to look at.

Such diversity presents a problem in naming this group in Ireland. As we are still isolated from each other, we have not yet organised and claimed terms to identify ourselves. For this chapter, I have used the term 'of Colour' which comes from North America and is meant to be all encompassing. This, however, does not make it an appropriate term for Ireland, let alone one that women here identify with. Another umbrella term, 'Black', comes from Britain and carries with it a history specific to Britain. It too is used here (perhaps more commonly), and it too may not be appropriate. Even in Britain, not all groups placed in this category identify with 'Black'. For example, after several years of getting used to identifying myself with the term, I have recently learned I would more commonly be referred to as 'Asian' in Britain. Use of the terms 'Black and Asian' does give us a sense of this diversity, but it too may not be inclusive enough.

Because this question has not yet been resolved in Ireland, I would like to have the option of using any one of these terms at different times throughout this chapter. Unfortunately, self-identification is rarely that flexible, and habit returns me to using 'women of Colour'. Even without concrete terminology, however, I do not think there is any confusion about who I am writing about.

Grasping our diversity can lead to challenging the ways in which we are stereotyped. Most women I know are aware of the ways they are stereotyped and, consciously or habitually, work to avoid them. Some of the stereotypes women of Colour are subjected to include considering Black women to be sexually available, or Asian women to be extremely submissive.

Considering all non-Western cultures, and thus women from those cultures, to be more oppressed than those in the West is also very common. I have even had it said to me that my commitment to feminism must have come from living in the West, thus having the opportunity to see just how oppressed Indian women really are. The implication here is that women from non-Western cultures and countries are not only extremely oppressed, but also unaware of their own oppression. Belief in false stereotypes has allowed histories of women's awareness and resistance in non-Western countries to be ignored.

Acting on stereotypes has led to the harassment of Black women in Ireland when they walk down the street, by people assuming that they are prostitutes. It has also led to exclusion from social supports which others take for granted. For example, one woman I spoke with was a student and having some financial difficulties. She told me that although she was sorting out her difficulties, they had added extra pressure to her studies. She didn't, however, feel comfortable about accessing support from others in her class or those co-ordinating the course because of their attitudes towards her. There is a common stereotype that women of Colour come from developing countries, and thus are poor and lacking information to help themselves. She was very aware that when she spoke of any difficulties, people thought she was poor and pitied her. As a result, she did not feel she could access emotional support and still maintain credibility.

In another case, a woman I interviewed spoke of how she was denied career guidance in her school (in the eighties) because of stereotypes based on the colour of her skin. She said:

> I went to the career guidance teacher who informed me that all I would ever become in my life was a prostitute. That was my lot in life, the type of person that I was going to be. 'What else should I be?' it was put, even in his ignorance. It was kind of, because of the colour of my skin, I couldn't really make it at anything else except a street person.

I do not believe I need to outline the implications such treatment would have on an individual's experience of herself and her future. Such a dismissal of a person's capabilities and potential contribution to society, at the very least, increases one's risk of poverty. This illustrates the serious consequences involved with the stereotypes currently operating in Ireland.

Stereotypes are often justified when behaviours can be seen to support them. However, no one of us should be seen to represent 'our people', particularly when our experience of oppression has left us in such bad shape that we turn to behaviours for which our group is stereotyped. You must not confuse our humanity with those behaviours and reinforce a narrow (not fully human) view of us. Those of us who are having a very difficult time, especially, must be supported and not dismissed.

It must be clear that our experience of racism is not the *sum total* of our experience. As women of Colour, we have strong identities. What's more, we have the right to take pride in and express those identities. We have many, varied experiences and do not wish we were a member for the dominant group. While racism is pervasive, it does not define our experience, and our lives. Racism contributes a certain dynamic, but certainly is not the most significant aspect of our experience. However, the fight to claim our identities is not easy, particularly if you are a woman of Colour and Irish.

In reaction to her experience of being denied career guidance, the woman above went on to say:

> That was where I decided I had to fight back. From here on in, whether you like it or not, I am Irish and that's it. I'm Irish and you'll have to look at me with a straight face and understand that. I may have been a mistake in some people's eyes, but I'm here. I wasn't meant to be knocked off this earth.

This fight to claim one's Irish identity is a feature of being Irish for Black women. As another woman said:

> You're born here, you're Irish and that's it. That doesn't mean that you don't have to fight to be comfortable with and own that. You do. I think that's what's different, essentially, about being born White here and being born Black here.

Understanding that racism is not the sum total of our experience also involves distinguishing between our experience of racism and our experience of our 'race'[1] Racism is an oppression. There is nothing positive about it (except, of course, for the strength, wisdom and character gained through overcoming it). However, there are a great number of positive things about being a woman of Colour. As Afshar and Maynard have commented:

> We question the assumption that 'race' is necessarily and always experienced in a negative way, for it can also provide a context for celebration. Although racism is a highly significant and under-researched issue, in feminism and elsewhere, we contend that there is more to an understanding of black peoples' experiences than can be portrayed by focusing on racism alone (Afshar and Maynard, 1994:1-2).

While it is necessary to distinguish between 'race' and racism, I believe, we must take the discussion further. To understand a woman's overall experience, we must frame her experience of racism within the greater context of her experience of her *self*.[2] Thus I must ask, what is the impact of racist oppression on one's identity?

Everyday racism: Isolation and identity

Women of Colour are isolated. We are excluded from identifying as members of Irish society. Our experience involves physically seeing very few of us, and certainly not seeing our identities positively reflected in a significant way in Irish society. We rarely see images of ourselves or our experience in the Irish media or school curricula. We grow up with few role models, if any. We are used to being the only woman of Colour in a group, and dealing with people's awkward interactions with us. Thus, our isolation includes not seeing each other, not talking to people who share our experiences, not having those experiences reflected, not being allowed to fully identify as members of Irish society, and continuously interacting with people's awkwardness around us.

A good example of this isolation came via a joke at the meeting of the first discussion group I ever organised of women of Colour in Ireland (four women participated). I was asked how many women I had been in contact with. At that time, I knew 17 women who were interested in participating. To this, the response was, 'There's seventeen Black women in Ireland!' With that, the whole room laughed. Although this was a light-hearted remark, to me it spoke volumes about the isolation we accept as normal.

Thus, women of Colour in Ireland experience many levels of isolation – from each other as well as from the rest of society. As we are geographically scattered and always in the minority, it is very difficult for us to gain social support and validation of our experience. Even if we were not so removed from each other, it we would still be psychologically isolated. In the US, it has been noted that isolation within Black communities can prevent people from effectively organising against oppression (Combahee River Collective, 1982). When a group experiences such isolation *within*, it cannot educate, support and organise itself, leaving racism to go unchallenged.

It is important to recognise the dynamics of such isolation. Women of Colour are often left without the supports needed to counter the daily experience of racism. As a general policy for liberation, I believe it is essential that we each go out of our way to make genuine contact with and support anyone who is systematically isolated in our society.

The denial of racism in Ireland also forces those of us who discuss our experience to have to prove it. One example of this came from a forum I was involved in organising on behalf of the Platform Against Racism.[3] Many people from throughout Ireland came to speak about their experiences of racism and work to identify areas of common concern and issues to address. During the early part of the session, I noticed each experience presented consisted of incidents of physical violence, usually in the streets. It wasn't until after several people had given such accounts that the discussion turned to the less obvious, more common, *everyday* aspects of racism.

Here, we see the apparent need of people of Colour to justify their experience of racism by providing 'authentic examples'. Such a situation is set up by a massive denial of racism in Ireland, and has two clear implications. First, this leads to misunderstanding the nature of racism. There is a common misconception that racism consists of what McIntosh has called 'individual acts of meanness' (McIntosh,

1993:37). This, however, is incorrect. While specific 'acts of meanness' do occur, racist oppression goes beyond them to being systematic and institutional. It is in this context that racism must be understood and recognised as an everyday experience. Still, my experience is that most people in Ireland do not realise this. As understanding these aspects of racism is key to becoming aware of our experience, I will briefly outline them here.

Racism is *systematic*. This means it pervades all our attitudes and activities. Thus, it is more than violent attacks that may be reported in the media, name calling, or being refused service in a pub or shop. It goes much further with a much more harmful effect. It is about receiving an overall message of being unacceptably different. Furthermore, this is a system of thinking and acting that everyone is born into – although some experience privilege by it while others are disadvantaged. Thus, it is something that we all have to deal with, regardless of whether we intend participating in it or not.

Racism is *institutionalised*. This means it goes beyond the actions of individuals, to racist attitudes operating in our institutions (e.g. education, media, law, state). Therefore, racism is not about one person's attitudes and behaviours towards another, but a whole group's attitudes and behaviours towards other groups, where that dominant group also controls the institutions. In this way, racism operates in one direction. (This is also true for sexism and any other oppression a woman of Colour may find herself on the wrong side of). Women of Colour in Ireland, then, find they are at a disadvantage in society's institutions. As we all must deal with these institutions on a daily basis and our interactions with them influence our future opportunities, this has overarching effects on a woman's life.

Finally, it has been expressed to me over and over again that racism is an *everyday* experience. Essed notes that everyday racism 'involves only systematic, recurrent, familiar practices' (Essed, 1991:3). As a result, the experience of racism becomes 'normal'. We learn to cope with it without even thinking, and learn to forget that what we experience is an injustice. One woman I know described everyday racism as 'mental abuse'. I find this to be both a strong and accurate description of the experience. In her own words:

> You come out every day and it's a battle. You walk down the streets and you're afraid. I am always afraid. I'm terrified of being abused. I'm terrified of being insulted. I'm terrified of people even saying 'hello' to me. It is a tension. People don't realise what that does to you mentally. We always talk about racism in terms of what it does to you physically. It's a mental abuse, and it begins to make you not even achieve. You begin to go through the back door even when the front door is open. You begin to fear approaching people in any sort of normal way.

In this way, racism must indeed be outlined as a health issue. Again, there are particular concerns here for women of Colour. As a result of our experience of sexism and socialisation as women, we are generally more likely to have poor mental health. Furthermore, as it has also been widely shown that racialized groups are at greater risk of poor mental health, research into the specific status of mental health among women of Colour in Ireland is needed.

As was indicated by the women quoted above, our experience of racism affects our behaviour. First, our continual exclusion amplifies the need to fit in and be accepted. Part of our experience is constantly receiving the message that we are unacceptably different, that we are not part of what is considered 'normal'. The impact of this feeling is pervasive. Gretchen Fitzgerald describes her experience:

> My middle-class, black femaleness was perceived as 'exotic', 'exciting', 'dangerous'. I was stared at, often to the point of rudeness, particularly when walking through the college canteen, a torture I soon gave up. I also stopped attending some lectures, for the same reason. My social relations with other students became limited and distorted... for the most part, I retreated into solitary loneliness. My feelings of inferiority and unacceptable 'difference' did not disappear when I began to work in Ireland, or later when I married an Irishman... (Fitzgerald, 1992: 9).

This experience is common to women of Colour in Ireland. In reaction to this, many of our strategies for coping include learning not to draw attention to ourselves. We aim to counter the messages of 'being so different' by presenting an image of having no struggles. Given how habitually we deal with racism and how we are taught to see it as normal, this may not take effort. As women, it is common – in the interaction between sexism and racism – for our 'differences' to be glorified. Fitzgerald noted this above when she used the terms 'exotic' and 'exciting'. Even under this guise, such terms still give the distinct message that we are much removed from what is 'normal'. In this way, our glorified 'differences', sometimes presented as 'curiously attractive', are still used to undermine us. This fact prompted the Combahee River Collective to say, 'We reject pedestals, queenhood, and walking ten paces behind. To be recognized as human, levelly human, is enough' (CRC, 1982:16).

Racism also affects both our abilities to achieve and our needs to achieve. First, as the woman above describing everyday racism as mental abuse put it, racism, 'begins to make you not even achieve. You begin to go through the back door even when the front door is open.' The overwhelming daily experience coupled with poor support and massive isolation tends to cloud one's potential. As another woman I interviewed explained:

> To me that was the first instance that somebody was pointing out to the world, 'You're different. You look different. You will always be different. This is your role in life'. Now I was only a young girl of fifteen, but I felt this is what I was being told. At that stage I had become so difficult in school. I didn't want to go to school. I didn't want to be there because I knew this is what I had to meet every day.

Second, with our thinking constantly undermined through sexism and racism, women of Colour have to fight much harder to prove what others assume to be human. Women in general must work harder and be much more effective to gain the same credit men will be easily given. This is even more so for women of Colour who are repeatedly undermined due to their position in more than one oppression. In response to our experiences of being unjustly held back, we sometimes learn to become more aggressive in order to be heard and taken seriously.

A woman of Colour's experience of racism is particular because, in addition to heritage and/or culture, it is her physical features – such as skin, hair, eyes, lips – which are targeted. These clear, visible markers distinguish a person of Colour's experience from that of other people's experience of racism. The manner in which women are objectified for their physical features adds a particular dimension to a woman of Colour's experience of racism and of herself. Our most apparent form of self is our body – an aspect not acquired, but granted. When your body is targeted by an oppression, it can draw your whole self into question. Having one's physical features targeted brings with it a huge visibility (albeit disempowered). A woman's 'differences' are stereotyped and targeted before she even interacts with others.

As a result, part of our experience is constantly being exposed. With this comes an unrelenting fear of physical violence. While this is common to women (and Black men) in general, it takes on a particular dimension for women of Colour. As one woman noted:

> I have always felt physically threatened just walking down the street. I have always felt that I'm visible. I'm a target for just any joker or any drunk or anybody, whether it's getting on a bus, or going to an area I don't know – a place where I'm not known. My social life is curtailed, because I am very aware of going into places where people stare. They don't do anything, but they stare. And it makes me feel embarrassed or uncomfortable.

Thus, because our physical features are targeted, a lot of our public experience can be uncomfortable. As a result, we are ceaselessly on guard.

All of these fears are based on real experiences, on things that have happened directly to us or to someone else. One woman, when describing how she was recently bombarded with phone calls informing her of racist attacks said, 'It is so depressing. It could be me, just the other person happens to be there. It's just another person in your place.' It is impossible to ignore the fact that one person was attacked for having the same features that you possess. Thus, it does not have to happen to us specifically for us to understand the implications for ourselves.

Another element of this experience involves not having significant aspects of our identity (e.g. physical features or ethnicity) reflected in the society in which we live. This reinforces the message that we do not belong and are unacceptably different. This has particular implications for Irish women of Colour. All the women I interviewed who were born and raised in Ireland commented on how others did not accept them as Irish, even when they made it clear that they identified themselves as such. Furthermore, they saw the categories of 'ethnic minority' and 'Irish' as mutually exclusive. Those who identified with another ethnicity as well as 'Irish' felt they had to choose between them.

Finally, one of our strategies is just to get on with our lives. Particularly as women, we learn to move ourselves into the system and become as successful as we can despite our experiences of multiple oppressions. Society, on the other hand, either leaves us on our own or focuses on us in a disempowering way. As a result, we rarely stop to think about our experiences. Furthermore, as part of our practice is not to draw attention to ourselves, we are less likely to vocalise this experience.

There are ways in which racism affects us specifically as women. First, we are not seen to be as threatening to society as Black men. Thus, the forms of racism we deal with are often more difficult to identify. Similarly, our opportunities to overcome our oppression take different forms. Second, dealing with sexism as well as racism, our thinking is often undermined. The combination of racism and sexism makes the politics of inter-cultural, inter-'racial', heterosexual relationships more complicated.

There are, of course, positive outcomes from these experiences. I myself have gained great strength, determination and grounding. In order to survive without going mad, I have learned to take on my life. Knowing that racism will always be a feature, I have learned to set my life up in a way that will be helpful to me. Hence, the awareness, skills and strengths I have developed allow me to lead a very challenging and fulfilling life despite the isolation.

Anger and privilege: Creating spaces to organise against racism

Because isolation and silence help keep racism in place, it is extremely important that we who are subjected to it get together and discuss our experience. We need to generate and pass on clear information and awareness as to how this oppression works. We must also remember that experiencing racism does not by itself generate this understanding.

As a result of the denial of racism in Ireland and our isolation, however, we have few spaces to reflect on our experience. Still, creating such spaces is necessary in order to generate what Essed (1991:77) calls 'general knowledge' of racism, an understanding and analysis of the oppression and experience by those who experience it, which is passed on to the general community. This is necessary for challenging racism. As general knowledge of racism is missing in Ireland, our challenges to racism here must include presenting counter information to the denial and creating spaces for reflection and organisation for us who experience it.

Before we can organise ourselves, we will have to decide consciously to examine the impact of racism on our lives. This is difficult, particularly when limited support is available. In the process, many emotions will surface and we must not get lost in them. Lorde wrote of how her response to racism was anger (Lorde, 1984). Accessing and expressing that anger, however, poses particular difficulties for people subjected to oppression, and especially for women subjected to multiple oppressions.

Many attempts have been made to condition women of Colour out of our anger. We have been taught not to draw attention to ourselves and to present ourselves as non-threatening (as if we were a threat in the first place). This conditioning must be overcome in order to be comfortable with and skilled at expressing our anger. Without our anger, we cannot expect to challenge racism or any other oppression we experience. In contrast, if we all harness our anger, we would easily find solidarity and collectively oppose systematic injustice.

To further complicate the issue, anger is commonly (and falsely) confused with hatred and violence. As a result, many people are afraid to acknowledge, express or encourage anger for fear of being seen to promote hatred or violence. Clarification is needed as these are three distinct concepts. Anger is a natural, healthy and necessary emotion in response to injustice. Focused anger gives us a chance to feel hope and compels us to demand change. Hatred occurs when we destructively pin our anger onto others in an attempt to set blame. Violence is the result of acting out this blame without taking responsibility. When we take responsibility for our anger, there can be no resulting hatred or violence.

I can particularly understand the confusion between anger and violence since so much of what is presented in our society is a total lack of responsibility. As a result, we are witness to extensive violence, oppression, injustice and drug addiction. Recognising the distinction between anger and violence, however, will give us space to examine our anger and focus it in the spirit that Lorde had envisioned.

I have shared with you some of 'our' experience. The purpose of this, you will remember, was to give you the opportunity to identify, by contrast, areas where unearned and unacceptable privileges run uninterrupted. I will now take the liberty of mentioning some of the injustices I have noted in your experience of privilege.

Privilege, too, is an everyday experience, considered 'normal' rather than unfair and dehumanising. While providing systematic advantage, privilege also lessens and cheapens your lives. It dehumanises you by asking you to be more than human and less than human at the same time. The experience of privilege also brings with it isolation, fear and naivety as to what the world is like for the majority of people. Intolerance for privilege is, perhaps, the only credible motive you can have for pursuing anti-racism.

For those with privilege, the unconscious messages of our 'difference' prevents you from fully identifying with us, and so keeps a distance between you and us. This can happen even within inter-racial relationships; it is unrealistic to pretend that because one partner experiences racism, the other will automatically have either an awareness or an understanding of that experience. Challenging privilege means challenging anything that keeps you from fully identifying with those of us who are isolated and stereotyped by racism.

In analysing privilege, there is a particular place for white women. When examining oppression, white women's focus has commonly been on your subjection to sexism. Analysing your privilege in racism, however, will add an important dimension to understanding oppressions as a whole, and thus further your liberation. As Frye has noted, white women can get caught up in neglecting their privilege from one oppression as a way of gaining a false sense of overcoming their experience of sexism:

> A white woman's whiteliness is deeply involved in her oppression as a woman and works against her as a woman… White women are deceived, deceive ourselves and will deceive others about ourselves, if we believe that by being whitely we can escape the fate of being the woman of the white men (Frye, 1992:160).

In a similar way, it is particularly useful for white Irish people to analyse your privilege. As a group which has been both oppressed and racialized, challenging current privileges will allow greater success in overcoming the legacies of the past. Because of Ireland's position between 'two worlds' (McVeigh, 1996), we have a unique opportunity of analysing privilege. Such analyses have the potential to influence global understandings of oppression and liberation.

It is important for those of you with privilege to organise yourselves and explore that privilege together. While it is inappropriate to ask people of Colour to do this for you, there are ways we can work towards gaining an understanding together. Common to both Irish white people and people of Colour, whether born and raised in Ireland or coming from elsewhere, is a shared experience of colonisation. As this is a distinct aspect of our heritage, we can support each other in overcoming it. First, however, the connection must be made. It is also useful to remember that a history of colonisation, which we have in common, is one of the defining aspects of the Irish national identity.

In conclusion, having laid out aspects of our experience, I remind you that your task is not to become fixated on them. We are fully capable of dealing with these, and do so on a daily basis. We do a good job of living with your privileges – sometimes too good to remember those privileges are unacceptable. What we all need is change, the change of a system which denies each of us our proper humanity.

References

Afshar, Haleh and Mary Maynard. 1994. 'Introduction: The Dynamics of "Race" and "Gender", in Haleh Afshar and Mary Maynard (eds.) *The Dynamics of 'Race' and Gender: Some Feminist Interventions.* London: Taylor and Francis.

Combahee River Collective (CRC). 1982. 'A Black Feminist Statement', in Gloria T. Hull, Patricia Bell Scott and Barbara Smith (eds.) *All the Women are White, All the Blacks are Men, But some of us are Brave.* Black Women's Studies. New York: Feminist Press.

Essed, Philomena. 1991. *Understanding Everyday Racism: An Interdisciplinary Theory.* Newbury Park: Sage Publications.

Fitzgerland, Gretchen. 1992. *Repulsing Racism.* Dublin: Attic Press.

Frye, Marilyn. 1992. 'White Woman Feminist 1983-1992', in *Wilful Virgin: Essays in Feminism 1976-1992.* California: The Crossing Press.

Lorde, Audre. 1984. 'Uses of Anger: Women Responding to Racism', in Audre Lorde, *Sister Outsider: Essays and Speeches by Audre Lorde.* Freedom: The Crossing Press.

McIntosh, Peggy. 1993. 'White privilege and male privilege: a personal account of coming to see correspondences through work in Women's Studies', in Anne Minas (ed.) *Gender Basics: Feminist Perspectives on Women and Men*. Belmont: Wadsworth Publishing Co.

Acknowledgements

Thanks to all the women I have talked to and worked with in this area, and thanks most of all to Willie Sweeney without whose loving support, I could not overcome the hurts of my own experience to be useful in writing on this subject.

8.

The web of self identity: Racism, sexism and disablism

Rosaleen McDonagh

Introduction

In the area of cultural and anthropological studies, there has been much emphasis placed on gender differences. This has illuminated the different experiences of racism concerning men and women. These studies relating to gender difference have also exposed structures within indigenous or ethnic minority groups. Studies or issues concerning disabled people within these particular minority groups are quite often sidelined or ignored in the context of a particular study. Health issues and age-related studies have touched on some issues that confront people with disabilities within ethnic minorities but the emphasis has always focused on a medical model of rehabilitation rather than on seeing the status of a disabled person as being fully human, in no need of mending or fixing.

This chapter deals with the complexity of multiple identity. The intersection of racism and sexism is interlocked in attitudes towards women from minority ethnicities by the dominant culture and Western values. However, like women, disabled people from ethnic minorities experience a double sense of isolation. In the dominant culture, disabled people are not valued in the social, political and economic contexts nor are they afforded the status of fully autonomous humans. Within ethnic minorities, such as the Travelling community, disabled people experience a sense of shame and are located in an infantile position both within the family circle and the extended family and culture. In the dominant culture disabled Travellers are seen as the product of intermarriage and this sets up a type of moral judgmental negative contract of racism towards vulnerable individuals and their families. In order to unravel the layers and nuances of this complex multiple identity, this chapter will link ethnicity and disability. The dynamics of sexism and racism are the benchmarks for this debate. The chapter will evolve in two strands. Firstly, it is based on personal narrative, which becomes a blueprint for the personal to become political. The second strand is in the context of racism. In dealing with such a complex issue it is important to set parameters to work within. Sexism for disabled people is turned upside down. Disabled women are often referred to in a way that defies gender, so issues of contemporary feminism such as childcare, equal pay or the abortion question are not on top of our agenda. This does not suggest that disabled people do not have a role to play in these discussions, particularly in relation to the abortion debate. The struggle for us as disabled people is different: the issues are basic, such as the right to live, the right to be seen as fully autonomous humans and the right to be seen as individuals with different genders and histories.

The chapter focuses on the indigenous population of Travellers. It is written in an Irish context where there is no anti-discrimination legislation. Much work and much discussion have taken place over the last thirty years as to whether Irish Travellers are an ethnic group or not. These discussions have not so much helped the status and reputation of Travellers, but have encouraged Travellers to respond and participate not just on a discussion level but on a community and policy level.

Experience

Being an adult now I have difficulty trying to describe my childhood. I am very conscious that as a feminist I am politicised to the extreme in terms of my Traveller identity. The danger for me is that I live in an environment where the structures are still very anti Traveller. Involving myself with disability and Traveller rights politics has given me an acute awareness around racism. The reality is I have been conditioned to think that discrimination towards my disability was easier to understand than racism around my ethnic identity. On the political level racism is quite easy for me to talk about. I have internalised so much anti-Traveller prejudice that discussing the litany of personal attacks seems pointless.

As a disabled person, the moment I was sent to residential care I was encouraged not to be a Traveller, not to look like a Traveller and especially, not to think like a Traveller. I grew up in the seventies. My family had a house in Donegal but moved to Dublin in order for me to attend a special school. My memory around how and why I went into care is not very clear. As an adult, I have had conversations with my mother and first she was saying that as Travellers they felt they could not give me a good start. However, as these conversations developed, it became apparent that my parents were put under tremendous pressure to give me over to a settled medicalised care environment. Now my mother would frequently tell me that she was made feel an unfit mother and that somehow the health officials were constantly wanting to know whether or not my parents were cousins. At the time, when my mother first started to talk about these highly emotional experiences, neither of us knew what racism was. Things are different now. Racism and discrimination are words that my mother's generation safely uses to describe past and present experiences.

Being away from home was not just about being away from my family, it was also being away from my culture. This means things that were familiar to me were taken away. My way of talking, my way of dressing, eating and learning were all stopped and as a child I was being prepared to live in a settled identity. Like I said earlier, even as a teenager, I did not know the word racism or what it meant. In school I knew I was being treated differently. This did not matter because other children with significant disabilities were treated badly as well. When I speak about being treated badly, I refer to the fact that a lot of us never got the opportunity to attend secondary school. At the time most of us thought we were not good enough or we were too disabled, but now I know that it was because I was a Traveller. Being a Traveller in a settled environment where there was an already low expectation in terms of academic or other achievements around disabled people, became more deeply rooted when it came to disabled Travellers. For me and my family this was the biggest hurt of all. They thought when I was eighteen I would be educated.

My experience is not that different compared with other Irish disabled people of my generation. Lots of us never got a decent education. Our talents, whether they would be in art or sport, were never encouraged. These residential schools are meant to build your self-esteem and encourage you to think in an independent way. Instead, for my generation it broke our confidence, took away our gender and individual personal histories. More importantly, these residential schools encouraged families to take a secondary role. Numerous families who were interested in fostering were encouraged to meet me. These fostering attempts never worked out. This was done in order to break any contact with my blood Traveller family. Again it was racism at its most explicit and legitimate format but I did not understand why they were trying to break up the relationship between me and my family. Some of the families were very nice but my own family would make regular visits to see me and take me home so for me it was clear from whom and where I got the most love. On these visits there was a visiting room that most parents were brought to. Mine were always left in the corridor, and regardless of how far they had travelled, they were not encouraged to stay very long. I am not sure whether or not these incidents were racist. I have to constantly check my memories with my family. Some of my friends who came from working class or poor backgrounds have similar memories and they tell me that racism was an affirmed practice of the day.

Another strong memory I have was that the care workers or nurses in charge went out of their way to ensure Travellers did not play together. We were always separated. I still do not understand why this was so important. There was a small number of Travellers in this particular special school. Some were from a generation before me. So targeting disabled Travellers by making them settled was well established by the time I was a teenager. As children, we can only resist so much. In a settled environment, being singled out as a 'knacker' was strange. I was exposed to settled people's values twenty four hours a day. Any time issues around Travellers came up on television or the media, I felt alone and unsure about whether or not I was actually a Traveller.

Context – Travellers

In order to understand my situation when I talk about feeling isolated and being constantly forced to adapt to an almost foreign environment, it is important to point out how racism worked at a policy and institutional level in the context of the general attitude to Travellers in the seventies. Firstly, assimilation and rehabilitation were considered a way of forcing Travellers to integrate into mainstream settled culture. We were called itinerants and different reports (Commission on Itinerancy, 1963; Report on the Travelling People Review Body, 1983) recommended different forms of assimilation. Generally in schools there was no recognition of our separate culture and identity. Traditional places to camp were becoming less and less available. Accommodation issues were building up a momentum of serious hatred and hostility between Travellers and settled people. Growing up in a settled environment in this type of atmosphere gave me a very distorted image of who I really was. There seems to be a hierarchy about Travellers who settled. These idiosyncrasies about what makes a good Traveller were done within the rehabilitative model. The more Travellers emulated settled people's values and lifestyle the more they were considered 'decent' Travellers. I found myself being caught in this trap. Any achievement in terms of education was considered bettering myself not just around acquiring knowledge, skills and information but also getting away from my Traveller identity.

The way Travellers were treated and the way disabled people were treated were based on similar methods of altering identity. This was done with physical alterations in the form of operations and exhaustive methods of therapy that would involve emulating and taking on a non-disabled persona. This would mean a constant reinforcement of the imperative to improve oneself by way of being physically independent regardless of the amount of time and effort it took to do a simple task such as tie a shoelace. Tying the shoelace was considered an important part of being independent. Very little emphasis was put on self-organisation and self-development. I never did achieve the task of tying a shoelace for myself and my friends who now use personal assistants have realised, like me, that this particular rehabilitative exercise was completely pointless.

Bearing all this rehabilitative process in mind it was hard to encourage service providers to see or understand difference relating to disabled people not just in terms of ethnicity but also in terms of gender. It's hard to cope with this as an adult. Although my own politicisation is assertive and empowering, in the service industry, and particularly in sheltered or residential accommodation for adults with disability, there is an entrenched long standing culture of maintaining a system where disabled people have as little power as possible in terms of basic decision making. Although my lifestyle involves living with and around settled people, it's a choice that I constantly have to re-evaluate. Racism and discrimination are not just about not being served in pubs or hotels. Racism is also about constant harassment and bullying.

In my early twenties I was involved in a residents' group where disabled people lived. After many years, the residents who were significantly disabled wanted to have single rooms. These men and women ranged in ages from twenty to sixty. When we approached management with a proposal, I was told that as a Traveller, I should be grateful that I was allowed there. It is hard to describe or understand racism in the context of corrective discrimination. Bullying and harassment can be done in very subtle ways. Occasionally at conferences or other public events when disabled people talk about residential accommodation, when we return home, the punishment can be done in ways such as being left on the toilet for two and a half hours. The excuse is always lack of resources.

Looking at the experience of Travellers with a disability, it is important and relevant to put experiences of racism and discrimination into different categories. Examples of this would be gender, age and whether a particular condition is genetic or the result of an accident or a disease. These categories have different types of discrimination attached to them, both within and outside the culture. When looking at ethnicity and disability we must also be aware that on the one hand it is quite difficult and sometimes dangerous to explore the negative aspects of one's culture concerning disabled people when society at large paints an already distorted picture of Traveller culture. It is appropriate to understand ethnicity and disability in the perimeter of the social model of disability. This model focuses on the structures within society and the ideology of strength, ableness and perfection as being questionable. It also refuses to get into a discussion of particular medical conditions and strongly opposes the notion of rehabilitation for disabled people.

Despite the developing consciousness of Traveller rights, the struggle to be recognised as an ethnic nomadic group is still not widely accepted. On a personal level I welcome debate and dialogue but I resent journalists and other public figures being allowed the space in the public domain to be racist. The Task Force on the Travelling Community (1995) highlighted the growing consciousness of Travellers and our right as Travellers to self-determination and self-identity. While carrying out research for both the Task Force and the Commission on the Status of People with Disabilities, it would appear that Travellers with a disability were ignored or lost in the area of service provision. When questions were raised around intercultural education or relevant materials in the classroom to affirm Travelling children's experience and identity, these were answered with 'all our children are the same' and 'disabled Travellers can't expect preferential treatment'.

The Task Force report on the Travelling Community (1995) recommended that health boards and the Department of Health, as appropriate, should support and resource care service providers to develop in-service training on intercultural work practices in co-operation with Traveller groups. This is largely ignored on both practice and policy level.

The Commission only refers to disabled Travellers twice, under the heading of Vulnerable People (p. 265) and Education and Training Needs:

> The Commission also identified other groups as having particular concerns and needs over and beyond those of the general population with disabilities. These include young people with disabilities, people who are deaf/blind, elderly people, Travellers with disabilities, gays and lesbians with disabilities. All these groups would be helped by targeted awareness programmes aimed at professional working in disability fields as well as at the general public (*A Strategy for Equality: Report of the Commission on the Status of People with Disabilities*, 1996).

The Commission ignores the real issues concerning the vulnerability of Travellers. It fails to acknowledge our separate ethnic nomadic culture. If this document is for the use of service providers, it endorses racist models which are taken as the norm in terms of ethical and administrative practice.

Context – people with disabilities

The concept of a social model of disability is not upheld on any concrete basis within Irish society. This has many disadvantages not just in terms of alienation, discrimination and oppression or the fact that disabled people have no legal redress in terms of status and recognition of personhood and self-determination. The real problem with the concept of a social model of disability within an Irish context is that there is a pretence that practices and policies are all built upon a notional or aspirational understanding of the social model of disability rather than an actual focus on equality. This lack of knowledge has many reasons, mainly because the social model of disability comes from an American and English environment. In an Irish context information for disability awareness or equality training is given to non-disabled people. This is then filtered very sporadically towards disabled people who very often do not have the resources to seek information or form contact with other activists who are developing theories and practices around the empowerment of people with disabilities.

As a result, the notion of examining the issues of ethnicity and disability within an Irish setting is often dismissed. The old argument of Irish society as homogenous is not longer given credit. There is some recognition that Travellers do have their own identity and culture. The problem for disabled Travellers is not being given recognition of their culture and identity; in Ireland most disabled people are never given a history, a gender or an identity. This web that is spun by policy makers and service providers makes the process of constructing self-identity difficult.

A good example of xenophobia and racism in relation to disabled people is the Commission Report on the Status of People with Disabilities (1996). This report did not recognise cultural diversity within the Irish disabled community. Although it did refer to Travellers, and did stress people with disabilities who live in residential care, the report did not endorse the recommendations of the Task Force Report on Travellers (1995) which included intercultural education, monitoring and supporting Traveller groups in programmes around ethnicity and disability. There is still no progress in moving towards the recommendations.

In relation to disabled Travellers, the issues are much more complicated. They involve long-term expectations and care needs. Obviously the settled dominant cultural network focuses on physical difference in a negative way. Travellers are no different by way of parenting and the emotional psychological aspirations around children's needs are very much part of the fabric of our culture. There is an intrinsic desire to do what is best in relation to the individual's needs, however, this, like other parenting skills, is always caught up in a sense of overprotection for a child with special needs. Like in the dominant culture, Traveller families and extended families operate differently by way of negotiating parenting skills. With different impairments, different skills are required. Within the Travelling culture, there is a tendency to locate the person with a disability regardless of age into a childlike position. This is not uncommon in the dominant culture too. However Traveller parents are faced with a bigger dilemma in looking for support for their disabled child. In seeking adequate facilities, we as disabled Travellers are automatically thrown into a structure which focuses purely on settled people's needs. Because of this, some Traveller families choose not to seek help for their offspring. While this decision is respected within our own community, there are ambiguous questions around the individual's needs and quality of life. There has to be some acknowledgement that while negotiating service provision for disabled Travellers there is no respect afforded to Traveller ethnicity or nomadic lifestyle. There is an unspoken assumption that we as disabled Travellers are more vulnerable and at the same time there is a tendency to blame Travellers because of the endogamous arrangements within the Traveller culture. I have on occasion heard disabled Travellers being blamed by service providers for their own condition, calling us the products of inbreeding. Bearing all this in mind, disabled Travellers are seen as prime targets by service providers for assimilation practices.

Conclusion

This chapter examined the complexity of a multiple identity. The history of discrimination towards Travellers in assimilatory and rehabilitative practices is not unlike the treatment of disabled people by government policy directives. There is a superficial picture being portrayed of Irish disabled people as being pro-active members of society. However, like the situation for Travellers, the reality is that without specific anti-discrimination legislation, debates around racism often erase and ignore the experiences of disabled people from ethnic minorities.

References

Commission on Itinerancy. 1963. Dublin: Stationery Office.
Commission on the Status of People with Disabilities. 1996. *A Strategy for Equality: a Report of the Commission on the Status of People with Disabilities.* Dublin: Stationery Office.
Department of the Environment. 1983. *Report of the Travelling People Review Body.* Dublin: Stationery Office.
Task Force on the Travelling Community. 1995. *Report of the Task Force on the Travelling Community.* Dublin: Stationery Office.

9.

Nick, Nack, Paddywhack: Anti-Irish racism and the racialisation of Irishness

Robbie McVeigh

Paddy is a moron – spud thick mick,
Breeds like a rabbit – thinks with his prick,
Anything floors him if he can't fight or drink it,
Round 'em up in Ulster, tow it out and sink it...
And if the victim ain't a soldier, why should we care?
Irish bodies don't count, life's cheaper over there.
Green wogs, green wogs, your face don't fit,
Green wogs, green wogs, you ain't no Brit.

(Stiff Little Fingers, 'White Noise')

Y ou don't have to look very far to find evidence of the embedded nature of anti-Irish racism in British culture. The English language is replete with anti-Irishisms – from the ubiquity of 'taking the mick' or 'taking the michael' and 'throwing a paddy' or 'in a bit of a paddy' to the slight more arcane references to 'paddywagons' (police trucks), 'donnybrooks' (violent melees) and so on. In the traditional order, the Irish are, as everyone knows, 'beyond the pale'. As Liz Curtis has illustrated, stereotypes first developed by Geraldus Cambrensis in his *History and Topography of Ireland* which was written 'within the pale' during the English colonisation of Ireland in the twelfth century, continue to influence contemporary historiography (1984: 9-11). Even English children's rhymes extend the invitation to 'whack paddy'. British popular culture continues this tradition from the ridiculous 'leprechauns' who hosted the BBC children's programme 'Live and Kicking' with the worst 'oirish' accents ever heard. British soaps have made their own particular contribution to anti-Irish stereotyping. They have featured wife-beating and psychosis (*Coronation Street*), wife-beating and incest and rape (*Brookside*) and a week-long sojourn in a dysfunctional Irish community (*Eastenders*).

This kind of stereotyping draws on a long tradition – so long-established is the anti-Irish 'stage Irishman' that several books have been written on the subject (Bartley, 1954; Brown, 1919; Truniger, 1976; Waters, 1984). The core identity of this anti-Irish construction is fairly constant. Firstly, Paddy is almost exclusively male. (Only in the

USA does 'Bridget', his female alter-ego, make any sustained appearance). Paddy is the subject of ridicule: stupid, drunken, violent, incomprehensible. He has few redeeming features, although writers like Matthew Arnold allow a kind of Celtic spirituality – incapable of self-government of course, but sometimes capable of aesthetic inspiration. Writers like Sommerville and Ross allow a quaint charm countering the fair but slightly foppish English administrator in Ireland. So we can see the subject of anti-Irish racism even before engaging with British colonial policy in Ireland or the nativist movement in the USA in the nineteenth century or the contemporary demography of the Irish in Britain. Anti-Irishness is a core part of British culture.

As with other theorisations of racism, the notion of anti-Irish racism was born of struggle. It was not 'discovered' by diligent academic research but rather named by Irish communities who had lived with its destructive consequences. While the racial stereotyping of Irish people had received earlier attention in Ireland, Britain and elsewhere (Curtis, 1971, 1986; Truniger, 1976), the definitive moment for anti-Irish racism came with the radicalisation and ethnicisation of politics in Britain in the early 1980s. For the Irish in Britain this combined with the politicisation around the hunger strikes and the rise of organisations like the IBRG (Irish in Britain Representation Group) which focused on anti-Irish racism as one of its key organizing principles.

The new theorisation of anti-Irish racism found expression in Liz Curtis' 1984 classic *Nothing But the Same Old Story: The Roots of Anti-Irish Racism* which was published by the GLC (Greater London Council) and carried a foreword by GLC leader Ken Livingstone. Anti-Irish racism was being named and addressed for the first time as part of a new, radical, anti-racist Left politics centred on London and the GLC.

I arrived into this political ferment in 1984 as a 22 year old Protestant from Omagh. I was going to study for a Masters at the London School of Economics. I was ambivalent about my own cultural and political identity. I was a kind of socialist unionist; my major cultural influence was British punk music; the political traditions I identified were those of the British Left (Hyndman, 1997: 298-304). I was certainly anti-Republican. I left London three years later a convinced republican, much more assured of my own Irishness. To paraphrase the arch-imperialist Kipling, 'What do they know of Ireland who only Ireland know?'!

There was a lot happening politically in London when I arrived. The hunger strikes were still reverberating around the Irish community as Sinn Féin began to build its political base in the Six Counties and started engaging with the British Left. The Left was still in control of the metropolitan councils and the GLC. The miners' strike was approaching. Uprisings in Brixton and Broadwater Farm were just around the corner. Councils were starting to develop 'positive images for gays and lesbians'. It is easier to see in retrospect what a remarkable time it was.

While the appalling banality of Blairism appears to have hammered the last nail into the coffin of the British Left, at that time there was a widespread belief in the possibility of socialist transformation. It was also just good fun – there were a whole host of new, interesting ethnic encounters. Nobody can convince me that the uprisings in British cities in 1981 were unconnected to the widespread media coverage to opposition to the state in Ireland during the hunger strikes. Certainly, most of what I learned about racism I learned from African Caribbean and Asian friends. It seemed as though everybody was talking about racism and anti-racism and everyone was doing radical intercultural stuff. My Black British friends were taking me to Hugh Masakela and Bangra while I was getting them into Moving Hearts and Planxty.

One of my first experiences of anti-Irish racism was being called an 'Irish bastard' and thrown out of a party with four other Irish students. Even that was a collectivizing experience – certainly the racism was unpleasant but the collective experience was confirming my Irishness whether I liked it or not. After a year I left the genteel racism of academia for the more earthy and honest racism of the building sites of north London. Here again the experience was contradictory. Every racialized encounter with a white English worker confirmed that I was not the same as them – I was beginning to like this. In addition, there were a lot of us about – the English couldn't get too smart because they were surrounded by big men from Kerry and Antrim and everywhere in between. I don't want to make it sound as if the experience of anti-Irish racism was therefore a 'positive' thing – it wasn't. But it was a defining experience and it gave me a politics and an identity with which I continue to be happy for all their contradictions. It also forced me to adopt a broader approach to racism – if I was going to challenge anti-Irish racism, I couldn't ignore Irish racism (McVeigh, 1992).

Later I would have a less affirming experience of the isolation that other racism can bring. Coming home through Stranraer, a policeman was alerted to my possible links to Irish subversion by the fact that I carried with me a copy of the record 'Free Nelson Mandela' – it was this fact which first drew his attention to me. This led to an hour-long dissection of my belongings, my address book and my politics. The humiliation of the Prevention of Terrorism Act (PTA), experienced by so many Irish people, was the downside – there was nothing affirming or liberatory about it – it was simply frightening. I got on the boat to Larne believing that I would be lifted on the other side. I destroyed everything in my possession which might seem 'suspicious'. Even my Starry Plough badge went overboard. Even now it is hard to explain how debasing the experience was but the crucial thing was that *they made me forget that I had done nothing wrong*.

In a curious way, three years in Britain and the associated anti-Irish racism made me what I am – much more secure in my Irish identity, much more aware of the need to challenge anti-Irish racism, much more committed to solidarity around anti-racist projects. It also took me home. I had become more and more involved in Irish politics in Britain. I had started doing anti-racist work. However, I was also aware of the contradictions of my new-found Irish consciousness.

There were two key points here. First, I was tired of meeting Irish people who were going home next week. I knew I was reaching the point where I would have to go home or else admit that I was going to settle in Britain. Second, I knew that it would be harder for me to reconcile my Protestantness and Irishness back in the Six Counties. Always one for a creative dialectic, I headed back to Belfast to study the relationship between sectarianism and anti-Irish racism. By 1987, the political landscape I was leaving behind was pretty bleak. The Tories had defeated the miners, they had dismantled the GLC, they had ratecapped radical local councils. The Irish solidarity movement was also in tatters, riven with internal splits and recriminations. So I said slán to the Haringey and Camden Irish Centres, to the Green Ink and Four Provinces bookshops, to the pubs on the Holloway Road and in Kilburn and the Mean Fiddler, and to the Labour Party Irish Sections and I did that most difficult thing for the children of the Irish Diaspora – I came home.

What is anti-Irish racism?

While anti-Irish racism was named relatively recently in Britain in the early 1980s, this drew on much older analyses of anti-Irish sentiment in Ireland, Britain and the USA. Certainly, there had been a long tradition of anti-Irish racism in Ireland before independence – indeed, anti-Irish racism was almost the definitive imprimatur of colonialism. Certainly, the nineteenth century USA threw up a 'stereotype of the Irish which conforms to conventional definitions of "racism"' (Knobel, 1986). And the Northern Ireland statelet had, from its inception, been associated with a particular and obsessive anti-Irishness (Farrell, 1980).

Liz Curtis drew on these histories in her ground-breaking *Nothing But The Same Old Story : The Roots of Anti-Irish Racism*. She argued:

> Anti-Irish prejudice, from which anti-Irish humour springs, is a very old theme in English culture. It is one of the oldest manifestations of the pervasive delusion that the English are a culturally and physically uniform people – white, Anglo-Saxon and Protestant – who are 'superior' to every other kind of person. The renewal of the conflict in the North of Ireland in 1969 brought with it an upsurge in anti-Irish prejudice in England. Politicians and media commentators have refused to recognise Britain's responsibility for the 'troubles', and instead have portrayed Britain as a disinterested third party, and the Irish as irrational and innately prone to violence. Newspaper cartoonists have taken up the theme depicting the Irish as bestial or sub-human, while anti-Irish jokes have spread the message that the Irish are 'stupid'... The widespread association of the Irish with stupidity has for years caused concern, anger and distress in Britain's several million strong Irish community. Some have been tempted to deny their Irish identity... Many Irish people, however, have recognised that anti-Irish prejudice, now as in the past, says nothing about their own level of intelligence, but is rather a symptom of English ignorance and self-deception – not only about Ireland and Irish people, but about England's history and the British government's role in Ireland today (1984: 5-6).

As Curtis suggests, anti-Irish cartoons were a key source of evidence of anti-Irishness. Indeed, a defining feature of this paradigm was the dominance of this specific form of discourse analysis – deconstructing racist cartoons – in the analysis of anti-Irish racism. The work of first Lewis Perry Curtis and then Liz Curtis made certain that this was a key way in which people would come to understand anti-Irish racism. Almost every subsequent analysis makes at least reference to these anti-Irish cartoons.

It also defined key American texts on anti-Irishness (Knobel, 1986; Ignatiev, 1995). There was nothing wrong with this – similar analysis could be done on racist cartoons of Black people (Curtis, 1984: 92) – but it was unusual. No doubt in part it was particularly important in terms of Irish people precisely because it illustrated so clearly the racialisation of Irish people – they, like Black people, were specifically simianised and sub-human. The ubiquity of the anti-Irish cartoon in the analysis of anti-Irish racism is explained, at least in part, by its use of visual images which clearly racialize. The simianisation – which is often taken for granted in the analysis of anti-African racism – is equally explicit for the Irish – they are made to look like apes. The racism is easy to see in these cartoons and it cannot simply be dismissed as xenophobia or religious prejudice. The invisibility of the white Irish becomes visible – in these cartoons *anti-Irishness becomes a racism.*

Hazel Waters develops the idea of the rootedness of anti-Irish racism in British colonial history. She identifies An Gorta Mór as the defining moment: 'Nowhere has the trajectory of official anti-Irish racism been more starkly defined than in the final responses of the English government to the Great Famine of the mid-nineteenth century' (Waters, 1995: 95). Waters goes on to usefully examine the interplay between religion, ethnicity and class in the dynamics of anti-Irish racism:

> The Great Famine and its reverberations traumatised Irish society for generations. Through the way it was apprehended and dealt with, anti-Irish prejudice became crystallised into racist hostility, often with overtones of class and religion, with one or other of these factors becoming dominant at different times and in different circumstances. When Ireland as a troublesome colonial entity came to the fore, 'race' would sound the dominant strain, with a descant on religion. When the Irish as part of the threatening 'dangerous class' were the problem, then the note of class would be struck most loudly (Waters 1995: 106-7).

The analysis of contemporary anti-Irish racism – particularly the issues of the *possibility* and the *specificity* of anti-Irish racism – was developed in the intellectual and political context of 1980s Britain. Some writers were keen to include Irish people in the analysis of racialised groups. For example, Sivanandan – in the process of critiquing the concept of 'ethnicity' and wanting to include the Irish within anti-racist struggle – identifies the Irish as 'politically Black':

> Ethnicity was a tool to blunt the edge of black struggle, return 'black' to its constituent parts of African Caribbean, Asian, African, Irish (Sivanandan, 1983: 4).

Others argued that a distinction must be made between racism (which is experienced by Black people) and the qualitatively different prejudice and discrimination experienced by Irish people (and other non-Black minority ethnic groups). In this analysis, colour – or visible difference – became the definitive interface within racism. As Connor pointed out, this kind of approach precludes the possibility of anti-Irish racism:

[D]iscussion on the white/black power dichotomy negated the existence of an anti-Irish racism. It was based on a premise which was given expression in the equation 'racism = power + prejudice'. Inserting the proposition that all white people have power over black people meant, by definition, that all white people were seen to be in control of power structures... The end result is a position where the reductionist argument of white over black does not accommodate an anti-Irish racism. Conversely, ethnicity, although useful in distinguishing the Irish and other ethnic groups in terms of disadvantage and need, does shift power relations to the personal and away from the white power structures of the British ruling class (Connor,1987: 23).

While this debate is by no means exhausted, by the 1990s the notion of anti-Irish racism had achieved new levels of acceptability. Mary Hickman did important theoretical exploration of the sectarianism/ethnicity nexus in her groundbreaking *Religion, Class and Identity* (1995). Hickman and Walter developed this work with important new primary research on the Irish community and, in 1997, the British Commission for Racial Equality (CRE) published their *Discrimination and the Irish Community in Britain*, which provided the first comprehensive empirical study on the effects of anti-Irish discrimination in Britain. In response to this report the CRE began to acknowledge the Irish as 'Britain's largest ethnic minority group' (CRE, 1997: 1). The CRE had finally recognised Irish people's experience of 'inequality, discrimination and prejudice'.

This was remarkable given that anti-Irish racism had been attacked as a construction of the 'loony-left' less than twenty years earlier (Curtis, 1980). Although the CRE remained coy about actually naming this experience as 'anti-Irish racism', this marked the point at which the concept achieved 'respectability' within the British establishment. The CRE also takes substantial numbers of cases on behalf of Irish people (CRE, 1997: 3-4). Anti-Irish racism – or anti-Irish discrimination at least – is now part of the broad British 'race relations' agenda.

While anti-Irish racism in Britain has finally been named and acknowledged, it is still not particularly well-theorised. In particular, the whiteness of most Irish people and the reality of Irish racism are rarely addressed. The ubiquitous 'No Blacks, No Irish, No Dogs' has been used liberally as evidence to illustrate the connectedness of Irish and Black experiences but this also serves to disguise the tensions between Irish and Black people – not least the tensions caused by Irish racism. There has been little attention to the specificity of anti-Irish racism; little concern for the contradictory racialized location of Irish people – both racist and racialized; little attempt to make sense of the differences between anti-Irish and other racisms. The concept has not been particularly well-developed in the years since it was first named. As we have seen, the concept of anti-Irish racism has become eminently respectable. However, the normalisation of anti-Irish racism in the British context raises important conceptual questions about the very possibility of anti-Irish racism in Ireland and beyond.

If anti-Irish racism has achieved 'respectability', it remains under-theorised and under-researched. There has been very little attention to nuances within anti-Irish racism beyond tentative explorations of the connection between anti-Irish racism and religion, ethnicity, class and gender. If anti-Irish racism is to be more appropriately theorised, each of these elements will need to be developed.

More specifically, *sectarianism* has been under-theorised as an explanatory concept – despite the fact that the term is used to explain a whole series of acts and events in Ireland (McVeigh, 1995). As a consequence the relationship between anti-Irish racism and sectarianism is profoundly undertheorised (McVeigh, 1998). It is clear that there is an ever-present overlap between anti-Catholicism and anti-Irishness. But it is also clear that these are not the same things – anti-Irish racism can be directed towards Irish Protestants and anti-Catholicism in Britain and the USA, while it was often ethnically focused on the Irish as the dominant Catholic group, had a much wider ethnic reference at times. I have argued elsewhere (McVeigh, 1998) that the anti-Irish racism/sectarianism debate should not be seen in terms of either/or. Rather they should be seen as parallel discourses which often mutually reinforce each other (as do, say, sexism and racism.)

Ethnicity has been central to the development of analyses of anti-Irish racism – but only because identifying the Irish as an ethnic group was part of the overall process of deconstructing whiteness and mobilising against anti-Irish discrimination. There has been little attempt to develop any more sophisticated analysis of the interface between anti-Irish racism and ethnicity. For example, minority ethnic Irish people – Jews, Travellers, Black Irish – are just as likely to experience anti-Irish racism as white Irish people. Moreover, this is often combined with other racisms. Yet their experiences have never been the subject of analysis. It is often assumed that anti-Irish racism only happens to white people.

Class has rarely entered the analysis of anti-Irish racism. Connor and Waters made tentative steps towards an integration of class into the analysis of anti-Irishness, but there is a need for much further work in this area. For example, the dilution of anti-Irish racism in the USA can be very closely associated with the embourgeoisment of elements of the Irish community. Economic and political power made it more difficult to stereotype in an anti-Irish way and made Irish people more capable of resisting that stereotyping and concomitant discrimination.

Gender, with a couple of honorable exceptions, has rarely featured in the analysis of anti-Irish racism. In Britain the stereotype Irish person was almost inevitably male – Irish women are strangely absent from anti-Irish discourse in Britain although they – very unusually among emigrant groups – formed the majority of the Irish emigrant community (London Irish Women's Conference, 1984). There is clearly a particular challenge to explain what Hickman and Walter call this 'gendered invisibility'. As they point out, Irish women are invisible within British constructions of Irishness (1995: 12-13). Their explanations are, however, not entirely convincing.

Each of these dynamics – religion, ethnicity, class and gender - needs to be central to any useful theorisation of anti-Irish racism. I want to use the rest of this chapter to begin to explore the connection between anti-Irish racism and each of these four under-theorised dynamics. I want to do this explicitly in comparative context and look at these elements as they connect with anti-Irish racism across different social formations. As we have seen, the analysis of anti-Irish racism has mostly focused on Britain. While there is a particular potency and relevance to British racism towards Irish people, however, it also took root in countries with British colonial hegemony or significant Irish migration. Notable among these were the USA and Canada and Australia and New Zealand. In each of these situations anti-Irish racism correlates closely with the *racialisation* of Irishness in that context.

The way in which Irishness constructs and is constructed by the host society plays a defining role in the dynamics of anti-Irishness. For example, the empowerment of Irish blocs in areas of settlement like the USA and Australasia has seen a concomitant decline in expressions of anti-Irish racism, yet even in these situations vestigial manifestations remain. The anti-Irish joke is still popular in Australia and New Zealand and the USA still routinely produces waspish stereotypes of Irishness - particularly Irish Catholicism. Alongside these histories of anti-Irish racism in British colonial formations is the parallel problematic of whether anti-Irish racism is significant - or, indeed, even *possible* - within Ireland itself. In the south of Ireland, at least, Irishness appears hegemonic and there is an immediate question around whether this precludes any manifestation of anti-Irish racism.

Anti-Irish racism - the defining role of the state

It is clear, even from this cursory overview, that there are substantial differences between the character of anti-Irish racism within particular social formations. This makes anti-Irish racism specifically interesting as a case study since it contrasts with other racisms - like antisemitism or anti-African racism which are often regarded as 'universal'. Anti-Irish racism and anti-Irish prejudice is significantly different in different contexts. In particular, anti-Irish racism is defined by the state formations within which it appears: Britain, Scotland, Northern Ireland, Republic of Ireland, the USA and Canada, Australia and New Zealand. The increase in migration from Ireland to continental Europe may also see new formations of anti-Irishness in places like Germany and the Netherlands. For example, a Dutch-speaking Irish friend of mine was recently offered a job over the phone in Amsterdam but warned that he would have to work with Irish people.

There are similarities and dissimilarities across these formations - for example the anti-Irish racism/sectarianism interface is most pronounced in Scotland and Northern Ireland. The empowerment of Irishness - and consequent challenges to anti-Irish racism - is most apparent in the Republic of Ireland and the USA. These comparisons across state formations are useful in themselves but they also make a broader point about the nature of racism. More specifically they make important points about the articulation of racism with the processes of religion, ethnicity, class and gender.

Britain

Britain, as we have already seen, is characterised by significant anti-Irish racism both in terms of the normalcy of anti-Irish stereotypes in popular culture and the systematic inequality consequent upon this racism which is increasingly recognised in broader quantitative work. Britain proved to be a particularly cold climate for Irish emigrants across the last two centuries (Swift and Gilley, 1985; Hillyard, 1993). For Marx, these experiences were more than an addendum to the history of Britain - they were central to the construction of the English working class:

> Every industrial and commercial centre in England now possesses a working-class divided into two hostile camps, English proletarians and Irish proletarians. The ordinary English worker hates the Irish worker as a competitor who lowers his standard of life. In relation to the Irish worker he feels himself to be a member of the ruling nation and so turns himself into a tool of the aristocrats and capitalists of his country against Ireland, thus strengthening their domination over himself. He cherishes religious, social and national prejudices against the Irish worker... The Irishman pays him back with interest in his own money. He sees in the English worker at once the accomplice and the stupid tool of English rule in Ireland. This antagonism is artificially kept alive by the press, the pulpit, the comic papers, in short by all the means at the disposal of the ruling classes. This antagonism is the secret of the impotence of the English working class (Marx and Engels, 1983: 407-408).

It is striking how this antagonism has been mediated over the past 150 years (Neal, 1988; Phillips, 1982; Waller, 1981). The negative experience of anti-Irish racism forced people into assimilation and self-denial. For example, the British Labour party has been led by Healys and Callaghans. The present Northern Ireland Office includes a Murphy (from an English constituency) and a McFall (from a Scottish constituency). These individuals clearly came from Irish emigrant stock and yet this is almost meaningless in terms of their politics and identity. (Contrast this with the bizarrely torturous attempts to find an Irish connection for Presidents Reagan and Clinton). If these British Labour politicians were conscious of their own Irishness at all, they certainly made no issue of it, it was denied rather than mobilised.

This history of repression and assimilation meant that there could be no easy reconciliation of Britishness and Irishness - there could be no construction of Irish Britishness in parallel with the project of Black Britishness - despite the existing model of Irish Americans/American Irish (Ullah, 1985). Irishness and Britishness were too contradictory to allow this kind of synthesis - Britishness had been explicitly about denying Irishness for too long. What did occur was a specific development of regional identities - Liverpool Irish, Manchester Irish, Birmingham Irish, London Irish. Alongside this, there was a positive identification of being Irish in Britain - from the Pogues to the IBRG - which created a space in which anti-Irish racism could be named.

The British experience throws particular light on the racism/sectarianism interface. Hickman's definitive analysis of anti-Irish racism clearly regards anti-Irish racism and anti-Catholicism in Britain as different, if constantly overlapping, discourses (1995: 19-53). Thus, in the British context, sectarianism and anti-Irish racism are not the same thing. Furthermore, some of the highest profile CRE cases of anti-Irish discrimination have involved northern Irish Protestants whose own sense of identity was ethnically 'Protestant' and politically unionist - so, in Britain at least, anti-Irish racism involves discrimination against Irishness abstracted from religious, political and national identity (Hickman and Walter, 1997: 11).

As we shall see, anti-Irishness has been mediated in other contexts. In Britain, however, anti-Irish racism retains all its venom. The Irish in Britain remain what Hillyard described as a 'suspect community' policed by the 'institutionalised racism' of the PTA (1993: 33, 258). While earlier analysis usefully depicted the ideology of anti-Irish racism, more recently commentators have begun to trace the social consequences of anti-Irish racism - in terms of violence against Irish people, mental health problems, unemployment and so on (CARA, 1991; Connor, 1987; Greenslade *et al.*, 1992; Hickman and Walter, 1997; O'Flynn *et al.*, 1993; Taylor, 1992). Hickman and Walter conclude their empirical work with an overview of this reality:

> The main findings of this research are that there is an extremely strong resistance to recognition of the distinctiveness of Irish experience in Britain which results in a lack of acknowledgment of Irish needs and rights, but that at the same time there is a widespread, and almost completely unquestioned, acceptance of anti-Irish racism in British society... There is clear evidence that events connected with Northern Ireland have heightened expressions of anti-Irishness at particular times. However, what also emerges is the extent to which deep-seated anti-Irish stereotypes form part of a more general response to Irish people. This affected many areas of interviewees' lives, including workplaces, access to housing, treatment at benefits offices and interactions with neighbours and the police (Hickman and Walter, 1997: 240).

Because of this work, the negative consequences of anti-Irish racism are easy to see. Britain will remain a focus in terms of both the manifestation of anti-Irish racism and the analysis of its consequences.

Scotland

Scotland produced its own specific variation on this wider British/English theme (Handley, 1947; Hickman and Walter, 1997: 138-148; Miles, 1983). There is no doubt also a more specific Welsh dynamic to anti-Irish racism but there is almost no research on the experience of the Irish in Wales despite long-term and concentrated migration to Wales.

The contradictions of Irish identity in Scotland are captured in different contexts from the 'tattie hokers' or migrant Irish rural labourers to Hibernian supporting, republican ballad-singing Edinburgh Irish of Trainspotting to the predominance of Irish in the Scottish Catholic Church. 'Irish in Scotland, Scots everywhere else' is a dominating theme in the identity of the Irish in Scotland (Devine, 1991). Nowhere, outside of the Six Counties, is anti-Irish racism more closely tied to sectarianism (Gallagher, 1987; Miles, 1982; Miles and Dunlop, 1987; Murray, 1984). Though republican and anti-unionist in the context of Ireland, the Scots Irish are simultaneously unionist and Labour supporting in the Scottish context because of fears about the traditional anti-Catholicism and Orangeism of Scottish nationalism.

Hickman and Walter identify the sectarianism/racism interface as the key question in terms of anti-Irish racism in Scotland:

> The differentiation of religious discrimination from racism is a critical part of the discourses in Scotland about ethnic cleavages in Scottish society. This emerged strongly from our interviews. Either the interviewees held that view themselves, or if not, they informed us it was a dominant view and gave reasons why they viewed it as problematic. The differentiation of sectarianism from racism depends on an understanding of racism as a phenomenon solely concerned with visible difference. However, recognition of the existence of cultural racisms means that any group which has been located in ethnic terms can be subjected to 'racism' as a form of exclusion... Given that anti-Catholicism can be generated quite autonomously from any ethnic identification, the point at issue becomes the relationship between anti-Irishness and anti-Catholicism in Scotland (Hickman and Walter, 1997: 144).

In practice, anti-Irishness and anti-Catholicism are constantly overlapping discourses in Scotland. Thus, physical or verbal attacks on Catholics are simultaneously attacks on the Irish in Scotland and vice versa. Scotland provides a crucial example of the need to both unpack and theorise the racism/sectarianism interface outside of the north of Ireland context (McVeigh, 1998).

Miles's work on the racialisation of the Irish in Scotland also has much wider implications (Miles, 1982; 1993; Miles and Dunlop, 1987). He used the example of the Irish to challenge biologically rooted notions of 'race' and develop his own notion of 'racialisation'. This has been important in terms of understanding the racialisation of Irishness. It has been equally important, however, in illustrating the ways in which notions of 'race' and racism can attach to predominantly white groups, particularly when they are racialized by migration.

North America

The Irish presented a key challenge to North American society as the first white minority ethnic group (after German Jews). They arrived in increasing numbers from the start of the nineteenth century to a society profoundly divided on racial lines - white, African American and Native American. The Catholic Irish arrived from the start of the nineteenth century into a society which had already been moulded by other Irish settlers - the 'Scots-Irish' and immediately generated a whole 'nativist' response to their presence. This was both anti-Catholic and anti-Irish but the anti-Catholicism was clearly focused on the Irish population as the principle source of Catholic immigration. For example, Knobel's *Paddy and the Republic* records a whole genre of 'nativist' anti-Irish and anti-Catholic sentiment in the USA:

> Undoubtedly the sense of ethnic difference implicit in the late antebellum verbal stereotype of the Irish conforms to conventional definitions of 'racism' in important respects... By mid-century language had built into American folk culture a sense that 'American' and 'Irish' were innately and permanently -

physically - different from one another and that intelligence, morality, religious inclination, political affiliation, social conduct, and economic behaviour were all derivatives of 'race'. Anglo-Americans unquestionably got into the habit of nationalizing themselves and denationalizing the American Irish by the routine use of a verbal stereotype which made the Irish seem 'racially' distinct (Knobel, 1986: 100)

Knobel suggests, therefore, that this American anti-Irishness was a racism. As Ignatiev has suggested, the story of the Irish in America is the story of 'how the Irish became white' and escaped this racialisation:

> What did it mean to the Irish to become white in America? It did not mean that they all became rich, or even 'middle class' ... to this day there are plenty of poor Irish... even the marriage of Grace Kelly to the Prince of Monaco and the election of John F. Kennedy as President did not eliminate all barriers to Irish entry into certain exclusive circles. To Irish laborers, to become white meant at first that they could sell themselves piecemeal instead of being sold for life, and later that they could compete for jobs in all spheres instead of being confined to certain work; to Irish entrepreneurs, it meant that they could function outside of a segregated market. To both of these groups it meant that they were citizens of a democratic republic, with the right to elect and be elected, to be tried by a jury of their peers, to live wherever they could afford, and to spend, without racially imposed restriction, whatever money they managed to acquire. In becoming white the Irish ceased to be Green (Ignatiev, 1995: 2-3).

Alongside Ignatiev's definitive work, there has been a growing body of writing on the specific experience of the Irish as an ethnic group in the USA (Gordon, 1993; Miller, 1985). This should provide a stimulus to further interrogation of the specificities of the racialisation of Irishness and anti-Irish racism in the North American context.

Australasia

In Australia and New Zealand, as in the USA, an Irish emigrant bloc was central to the wider definition of white settler identity. There was a specific dynamic to this around the large number of Irish felons who were transported to Australia - both ordinary felons and political prisoners. In this sense the Irish were defined from the first as a 'criminal' community. From Ned Kelly and the hero of 'Waltzing Matilda' to Peter Lalor (brother of Fintan Lalor and leader of the Southern Cross rebellion at Eureka stockade) and Charles Gavan Duffy, Irish emigrants and felons played a key role in the construction of Australian identity around 'mateship' and anti-Englishness.

Alongside this, British colonial government constructed the Irish in Australia as a specifically dangerous community (rightly so, in terms of their own perspective, given the role that Lalor and others played in Australian anti-colonialism). This history left a legacy of establishment British anti-Irish stereotypes. Here also anti-Catholicism added a specific dynamic to anti-Irishness. Later this legacy was overlaid with a more internal dynamic based on the formation of Irish Australian and Irish New Zealand communities and social/political blocs. For example, the opposition of Archbishop Mannix to conscription in the first world war generated a host of anti-Irish and anti-Catholic sentiment. In the 1950s the Australian Labour Party split along left/right lines that were simultaneously demarcations for secularist and Irish/Catholic factions within the party.

Ireland - north

While anti-Irish racism is perhaps more visible in the north of Ireland than anywhere else - loyalist walls are routinely daubed with slogans like 'KAI' ('Kill All Irish') and 'Irish Out' - the concept has rarely been used to make sense of conflict there. Its use has usually been limited to explanations of British actors in the north. For example, the ubiquity of anti-Irish racism used by British soldiers against nationalists in the north means that it will be named in this context (McVeigh, 1994: 103-13). It is less likely, however, to be used to make sense of the dynamic between unionists and nationalists - 'sectarianism' remains the preferred option in this context.

This is not, however, entirely satisfactory. As I have argued elsewhere, the boundary between anti-Irish racism and sectarianism appears increasingly blurred (McVeigh, 1998). This does not imply, however, that the two categories should necessarily be collapsed. The reality is that there are two different - if constantly overlapping - dynamics at work in the north. Anti-Irish racism by British people against Irish people and sectarianism between Protestant and Catholic Irish people.

The comparative analysis of racism and sectarianism in the north of Ireland has much to offer in terms of unpacking the religion/ 'race'/ ethnicity nexus in Ireland and beyond. There is a 'resonance' between racism and sectarianism which means that comparing them offers unique insights into the nature of both. Whether or not sectarianism is racism, however, depends on the definition of racism adopted. From the perspective of the British Race Relations Act (1976), sectarian identity is indistinguishable from ethnicity and sectarianism is a 'race relations' situation. From the perspective of sociological notions of ethnicity, sectarianism involves different ethnic groups to racism and there is a point in maintaining the integrity of sectarianism as an explanatory concept - particularly in the context of social conflict in Ireland.

In terms of broad distinctions: sectarianism involves the relationship between Irish Protestants and Catholics; anti-Irish racism involves the relationship between British people and Irish people; and racism in Ireland involves relationships between majority and minority ethnic groups either constituted as 'white people' and 'people of colour' or 'settled people' and Travellers. Whether or not sectarianism is seen as the same thing as racism, it should not be regarded as a 'religious' phenomenon. In so far as the two can be disaggregated, 'sectarianism' is about ethnicity much more than it is about religion. In this sense, sectarianism is much the same as racism - religion plays a part, but only a part, in the construction of both.

The developing debate about the anti-Irish racism/sectarianism interface will be forced into focus by legal and political developments in the north of Ireland - not least because sectarianism and anti-Irish racism are now legally recognised but still regarded as 'different' phenomena. This will have significant wider implications for the theorization of anti-Irish racism.

Ireland - south

The south of Ireland bore the brunt of both the racialized stereotyping and racist practices associated with British colonial rule in Ireland. Despite this, however, the existence of anti-Irish racism has received little theoretical attention in Ireland. It is not insignificant that anti-Irish racism has been theorised in the context of situations involving Irish people *outside* of Ireland. The question of the existence of anti-Irish racism in the contemporary south of Ireland is perhaps the most problematic of all. Since Irishness appears hegemonic in the Republic of Ireland state it seems questionable to begin to identify continuing anti-Irish racism. Clearly, however, it did exist historically. The colonial nexus generated centuries of anti-Irish sentiment and practice. The interesting question is whether this stopped abruptly in 1922. (We might ask a similar, if more obviously rhetorical, question about racism in South Africa - did it cease to exist with liberation?)

The concept of anti-Irish racism has rarely been utilised in the south of Ireland despite the increasing acceptance of the term in Britain. This is curious since the manifestation of phenomena that would be named as anti-Irish racism in Britain is commonplace in Ireland. Some Irish people actively reproduce anti-Irish prejudice despite the fact that it is clearly derogatory about themselves. Such racism appears regularly as a cultural artifact in the forms of anti-Irish 'humour'. Irish tourist shops are littered with 'Letter from an Irish mother' tea clothes, anti-Irish joke books, 'genuine Irish mugs' (with handles on the inside) and so on. This is at least tolerated by most Irish people despite its racist message.

Historically this kind of anti-Irishness was often characterised as 'West Britonism' and associated with the cultural and political denigration of Irishness and the attendant championing of Britishness as a superior identity available to people on the island of Ireland. A specific variant of these kinds of ideas became a crucial element in the construction of unionist/loyalist identity in Ireland.

This category of anti-Irish discourse is couched in terms of the backwardness of things Irish and the civilised nature of things British. In this sense it goes well beyond the critiquing of aspects of Irishness and Irish society that are genuinely problematic. It not only suggests that there are problems with phenomena like 'gombeenism' or, indeed, Irish racism, it also suggests that these problems are innate to Irishness. This kind of anti-Irish discourse is explicitly racialized - Irish society is imperfect not because the country has been underdeveloped or because of the evolution of a particular political culture but because it is Irish.

The expression of something akin to anti-Irish racism in Ireland by both Catholics and Protestants is important in terms of the definition and reproduction of cultural and political identities. It raises core questions about contemporary Irish identity including the internalisation of racist stereotypes, the articulation of racism and sectarianism and the persistence of the phenomenon of 'West Britonism'. There is no question that a sustained analysis of anti-Irish racism in Irish society would produce interesting results. The notion of anti-Irish racism is one of the key missing explanatory concepts in contemporary understandings of Irish society.

Conclusion

The analysis of anti-Irish racism provides an important perspective on racism in general. First, it confirms the ability of some predominantly white groups to experience racism. In this sense it is an important challenge to the notion that racism is always about colour or visible difference; it suggests that racism is about deeper and more complex matrices of power and signification. Attention to anti-Irish racism also highlights the crucial importance of state formations in the construction of racism. Anti-Irish racism cannot be abstracted from state power; in this sense it has little to do with the qualities of the racialized - the same person can be racialised in completely different ways in different contexts. Again, there are important wider implications here.

The comparison of anti-Irish racism across social formations also makes a broader point about the nature of racism. Racism is not only about power in the sense that it empowers and disempowers on the grounds of ethnicity; it is also about power because it connects with and reinforces other power differentials in a specifically racialised way. As we have seen, racialized identity changes in different power matrices. The same Irish person can move between the north and south of Ireland and England and Scotland and Germany and the USA and Australia and be empowered and disempowered by her or his Irishness in very different ways in each location. Anti-Irish racism changes its character in each power matrix. Racism is not static precisely because it is about power - it changes constantly over both time and place. This is one of the reasons why racism is so difficult to define and to challenge. One thing, however, is clear - racism is a quality of these power matrices not of the racialized. If ethnic individuals or ethnic groups caused the racism they experience, we would expect a broadly similar reaction in different contexts. Instead, the same individual can be empowered by his or her Irishness in one place and disempowered by it in another.

The analysis of anti-Irish racism therefore encourages us towards broader conclusions about the dynamics of racism. There must be a resistance to reified racialized continuities - whether spatial or temporal - racism must be situated in terms of the particular polity and historical moment in which it appears. The reality of anti-Irish racism was very different pre- and post- the 1921 settlement. As we have seen, Geraldus Cambrensis continues to cast a shadow over the historiography of Ireland - even after 800 years. Contemporary racism draws on a deep reservoir of stereotypes and projections which can be used to nurture any number of new processes of racialisation. There should be no underestimating the longevity of racialized power relationships. As the American Irish experience continues to demonstrate, racialized stereotypes can retain their ideological power long after the structural relationships which gave them meaning have been transformed. Anti-Irish racism is simultaneously both rooted in tradition and constantly changing. This dialectic between continuity and change is the key to understanding the dynamics of anti-Irish racism.

References

Bartley, J.O. 1954. *Teague, Shenkin and Sawney*. Cork: University Press.
Brown, S.J. 1919. *Ireland in Fiction*. Dublin: University Press.
CARA. 1991. *Irish Homelessness: the Hidden Dimension*. London: CARA, Irish Homeless Project.
Commission for Racial Equality. 1997. *The Irish in Britain*. London: CRE.
Connor, Tom. 1987. *The London Irish*. London: London Strategic Policy Unit.
Curtis, Liz. 1984. *Nothing But the Same Old Story: The Roots of Anti-Irish Racism*. London: Information on Ireland.
Curtis, Lewis Perry. 1971. *Apes and Angels: the Irishman in Victorian Caricature*. Washington: Smithsonian Institute Press.
Curtis, Lewis Perry. 1986. *Anglo Saxons and Celts: A Study of Anti-Irish Prejudices in Victorian England*. Conference on British Studies, University of Bridgeport, Connecticut.
Devine, Tom M. 1991 (ed.) *Irish Immigrants and Scottish Society in the Nineteenth and Twentieth Centuries*. Edinburgh: John Donald.
Farrell, Michael. 1980. *The Orange State*. London: Pluto.
Finnegan, F. 1985. *Poverty and Prejudice: Irish Immigrants in York 1840-1875*. Cork University Press.
Gallagher, Tom. 1987. *Glasgow, the uneasy peace: Religious tension in modern Scotland*. Manchester University Press.
Greenslade Liam, Maggie Pearson and Moss Madden. 1992. *Generations of an invisible minority: the health and well being of the Irish in Britain*. Liverpool. Institute of Irish Studies.
Gordon, Michael A. 1993. *The Orange Riots: Irish Political Violence in New York City, 1870 and 1871*. Cornell University Press.
Greater London Council. 1984. *Policy Report on the Irish Community*. London: GLC.
Hickman, Mary J. 1995. *Religion, Class and Identity*. Hampshire: Avebury.
Hickman, Mary J. and Bronwen Walter. 1995. 'Deconstructing Whiteness', *Feminist Review* no. 50.
Hickman, Mary J. and Bronwen Walter. 1997. *Discrimination and the Irish Community in Britain*. London: CRE.
Hillyard, Paddy. 1993. *Suspect Community: People's Experience of the Prevention of Terrorism Act*. London: Pluto.
Hyndman, Marilyn. (ed.) 1996. *Further Afield: Journeys from a Protestant Past*. Belfast: Beyond the Pale.
Knobel, D.T. 1986. *Paddy and the Republic: Ethnicity and nationality in Antebellum America*. Connecticut: Wesleyan University Press
Ignatiev, Noel. 1995. *How the Irish Became White*. New York: Routledge.
London Irish Women's Conference. 1984. *Irish Women: Our Experience of Emigration*. London: Women in Print.
McVeigh, Robbie. 1994. *Harassment - It's Part of Life Here: The Security Forces and Harassment in Northern Ireland*. Belfast: Committee on the Administration of Justice.
McVeigh, Robbie. 1995. 'Cherishing the Children of the Nation Unequally: Sectarianism in Ireland' in Patrick Clancy, Sheila Drudy, Kathleen Lynch, and Liam O'Dowd (eds.) *Irish Society: Sociological Perspectives*. Dublin: IPA.
McVeigh, Robbie.1998. 'Racism in the Six Counties?: Theorizing the racism/sectarianism interface' in David Miller. *Rethinking Northern Ireland*. London: Longman.
Marx, Karl and Frederick Engels. 1983. *Ireland and the Irish Question*. London: Lawrence and Wishart.
Miles, Robert. 1982. *Racism and Migrant Labour*. London: Routledge and Kegan Paul.
Miles, Robert. 1993. *Racism after 'Race Relations'*. London: Routledge.
Miles, Robert and A. Dunlop. 1987. 'Racism in Britain: The Scottish Dimension' in P. Jackson (ed.) *Race and Racism: Essays in Social Geography*. London: Allen and Unwin.
Miller, Kerby. 1985. *Emigrants and exiles: Ireland and the Irish Exodus to North America*. New York: Oxford University Press.
Murray, B. 1984. *The Old Firm: Sectarianism, sport and society in Scotland*. Edinburgh: Donald.
Neal, F. 1988. *Sectarian Violence, the Liverpool Experience 1819-1914: An Aspect of Anglo-Irish history*. Manchester University Press.

O'Flynn, Joan, D. Murphy and M. Tucker. 1993. *Racial Attacks and Harassment of Irish People*. London: Action Group for Irish Youth.

Phillips, P.T. 1982. *The Sectarian Spirit: Sectarianism, society and politics in Victorian Cotton Towns*. London: Toronto University Press.

Sivanandan, A. 1983. 'Challenging Racism'. *Race and Class*, 25(2).

Stiff Little Fingers 1978. *'White Noise', Inflammable Material*. Rigid Digits: Rough Trade.

Swift, R. and S. Gilley (eds.) 1985. *The Irish in the Victorian City*. Beckenham: Croom Helm.

Taylor, Seamas. 1992. 'The Irish in Britain: A Profile of Discrimination and Prejudice'. *Report of the Race Equalities Unit*. London: Borough of Haringey.

Truniger, A. 1976. *Paddy and the Paycock: a Study of the Stage Irishman from Shakespeare to O'Casey*. Basle: Cooper monographs.

Ullah, P. 1985. 'Second-generation Irish Youth: identity and ethnicity', *New Community* 12(2).

Waller, P.J. 1981. *Democracy and Sectarianism; a Political and Social History of Liverpool*. 1868-1939. Liverpool: Liverpool University Press.

Waters, Hazel. 1995. 'The Great Famine and the rise of anti-Irish racism', *Race and Class* 37(1).

Waters, Maureen. 1984. *The Comic Irishman*. Albany: The State University of New York Press.

10.

'Who ever heard of an Irish Jew?' Racialising the intersection of 'Irishness' and 'Jewishness'

Ronit Lentin

At first thought it may seem strange that the anti-Semite's outlook should be related to that of the Negrophobe. It was my philosophy professor, a native of the Antilles, who recalled the fact to me one day: 'Whenever you hear anyone abuse the Jews, pay attention, because he is talking about you'. And I found that he was universally right - by which I meant that I was answerable in my body and my heart for what was done to my brother. Later, I realized that he meant, quite simply, an anti-Semite is inevitably anti-Negro (Frantz Fanon, cited by Gilroy, 2000: 1).

Introduction

Ireland, they say, has the honour of being the only country which never persecuted the jews... And do you know why? ...
Because she never let them in, Mr Deasy said solemnly... (Joyce, 1960: 44).

And I belong to a race too, says Bloom, that is hated and persecuted. Also now. This very moment. This very instant... Robbed, says he. Plundered. Insulted. Persecuted. Taking what belongs to us by right...
Are you talking about the new Jerusalem? says the Citizen.
I'm talking about injustice, says Bloom (Joyce, 1960: 431-2).

When Joe Cohen, newly arrived from Cork, looks for a job with the London Jewish Sabbath Observers Employment Bureau, the receptionist asks him if he is sure he is Jewish, saying they had never met an Irish Jew before. He gets a job at Levin Brothers Ltd where, at 200, the Jewish employees number more Jews under one roof than the whole community he had lived in all his life. His Jewish workmates nickname him 'Seamus' and tease him about Irish Jews going to *shul* (synagogue) on St Patrick's Day. At Levin Brothers he also meets the Black packer Gary, who, when told Joe is Irish, giggles to high heaven: '"Man," he sang, his words dancing with incredulous laughter, "who ever heard of an Irish Jew?"' (Marcus, 1990: 13). Like *Ulysses*, which portrayed the racialisation of Irish Jews at the turn of the century, David Marcus's interracial encounter, which confronts Joe with his multi-layered positionings as Irish, Jewish and 'white', expresses masterfully the complex cycles of racialisation, 'othering' and emigration of Irish Jews in Catholic Ireland.

This chapter, written from the embodied position of an Israeli-born Jewish woman living in Ireland since 1969, examines the specificities of Irish antisemitism and the racialised intersection of 'Jewishness' and 'Irishness'. Analysing *antisemitism*, rather than *anti-Semitism* implies more than dropping the hyphen: it means taking antisemitism seriously as a thesis without an antithesis, for there is no *Semitism* (Fein, 1987: IX). Following Tony Kushner's (1998) analysis which places antisemitism as central to understanding British racism, I argue that Irish antisemitism is not simply the work of extreme fascist groups (although those have existed and do exist), but is woven into the construction(s) of Irishness in several ways. Kushner argues in relation to Britain that 'the work of the so-called "new school" in British Jewish studies, as well as those in cultural studies working on "race," such as Paul Gilroy, have shifted the emphasis to the intolerance *within* the liberal tradition in Britain and elsewhere' (Kushner, 1998: 226). He cites Zygmunt Bauman who argues that it is precisely when 'ethnic-religious-cultural strangers' seem close to embracing the liberal vision of group emancipation, that 'a dagger of racism is flung from beneath the liberal cloak' (Bauman, 1991: 71).

The ethnically narrow definitions of 'Irishness' point to an antisemitic exclusion beyond overt manifestations of racist violence. Antisemitism, together with anti-Traveller racism, has been the most prevalent form of racism in 20th century Ireland until quite recently, yet it is omitted from understandings of racism as recently as during the European Year Against Racism (although sociologists Mícheál Mac Gréil [1996] and Robbie McVeigh [1996], do include antisemitism as one form of ethnic prejudice/racism in Irish society). This omission is due to the trivialisation of and the refusal to acknowledge the seminal influence of the treatment of the Jewish minority, and Jewish refugees, on race relations (c.f. Kushner, 1998: 235). The very use of the term racism in contemporary social sciences is linked to Nazi antisemitism and refers to 'ideas which defined some racial or ethnic groups as superior and others as inferior' (Solomos and Back, 1995:4) and to the determination that never again would the ideology of 'race' be used to inferioritise a group of people.

In view of daily attacks on refugees and asylum-seekers and of anti-Traveller racism in contemporary Ireland, and of the small number of overt antisemitic incidents in recent years, is it fair to speak of active antisemitism in Ireland? Or should we speak instead of what Bauman (1998: 143) calls 'allosemitism': 'the practice of setting Jews apart as people radically different from all others, needing separate concepts to describe and comprehend them'?

Although racism in Ireland is primarily anti-refugees, anti-Travellers and anti-Black, I would argue that Irish Jews are the archetypal 'Others' of Irish Catholic nationalism. Jews are seen as unassimilable, as a people apart, and are racialized by society and state which, at the same time, deny the existence of racism. Meanwhile, our everyday existence, despite the prominence of many Irish Jews in business, the professions, politics and the arts, is largely obscured from view.

The continued existence of a tiny Jewish community in Ireland, in the face of adversity and in view of our declining numbers, has attracted disproportionate attention. There have been several histories of Ireland's Jews (e.g. Shillman, 1945; Hyman, 1972; O'Riordan and Feeley, 1984; Ó Drisceoil, 1997; Keogh, 1998; Goldstone, 1998 and chapter 11 in this volume) and several media producers have given us their attention (most recently in television programmes by Sebag Montefiore, 1997; Goldstone and Lentin, 1997; Price, 1998). Irish Jews themselves have written family histories (e.g. Solomon, 1956; Zlotover, 1966), fiction (e.g. Marcus, 1986, 1990; Lentin, 1985, 1996), plays (e.g. Kostick, 1993) and essays (e.g. Leventhal, 1945; L. Lentin, 1996). There have also been numerous newspaper articles (e.g. Donovan, 1998: 13; *The Irish Times* supplement, July 1998).

How to explain this disproportionate attention to Ireland's smallest ethnic minority? One explanation is the very 'peculiarity' of its persistent existence in the face of persecution, immigration restrictions during World War II (see Fisk, 1985; Keogh, 1988; Goldstone and Lentin, 1997; Goldstone, 1998, 2000; Keogh, 1998) and increasing youth emigration even during the current economic boom. Another way of explaining this attention is the fact that the archetypal literary Jew of all times, Leopold Bloom, was created by the Irish writer James Joyce. Bloom personifies 'otherness' and hybridity vis-a-vis the construction(s) of 'Irishness', as illustrated by the opening quotes; he is indeed, as argued by Reizbaum (1999), 'James Joyce's Judaic other'. Ultimately, however, the ongoing attention to matters Jewish must be explained by the 'normality' and acceptability of antisemitism in Irish society, particularly, but not exclusively, before World War II.

As in other European countries, the specificities of Irish racism have included Christian traditions of hatred towards Jews. Since, like Britain, Ireland was not under Nazi occupation, 'scientific racism' as practised by the Nazis did not become a central formative experience in the construction of the nation. Irish Jews, whose contribution to Irish society is unquestionable, have not only played a central role as 'others' in relation to Irish Catholicism, they have also been crucial as scapegoats towards whom intra-community tensions are projected, as was apparent in the 1904 Limerick pogrom.

This chapter begins with an account of some of my personal experiences of antisemitism and goes on to situate the specificities of Irish antisemitism within a framework of Irish racism.

Auto/biographies and ethnic identities

My autobiography, like those of former slaves, migrants, emigrés, exiles, refugees and assorted ethnic minorities, intersects acutely with (multiple) ethnic identities: Jewish, Israeli (born in Palestine under the British Mandate), of Romanian descent, Irish citizen. I regard my involvement in anti-racism not merely as a human rights task or duty. For me, campaigning for an Irish welcome for refugees and asylum-seekers and for greater ethnic equality stems from the not-too-distant refugee history of my own family. In 1940 my grandparents, my mother and uncle, forced to flee war-torn Romania, left their family home and business, carrying only one suitcase per person and a hamper with the family linen. They spent long months on the road, waiting for a transit visa to Palestine for which they had entry certificates bought with grandfather's hard-earned money. They were the lucky ones; they left on time, but most of their relatives and friends were either incarcerated by the Nazis in the Czernowitz ghetto, deported to Transnistria, the Romanian-Nazi concentration camp in Southern Ukraine where some of them perished, or sent to Soviet labour camps. Eventually most of them reached Palestine, where I was born. Refugeeship and persecution is a central part of my personal history in another way too. Since 1967 I have been involved, together with other Israelis, in campaigning for Palestinian self-determination and for a just peace in Israel/Palestine (Abdo and Lentin, 2002).

Being persecuted for your ethnic belonging as part of 20th century European history is also my story; refugeeship is not something which happens to 'other people'. However, in what follows, I won't begin from the beginning, with the 'ethnic cleansing' that was the Shoah (Holocaust) which more than halved Europe's Jewish population. Nor will I begin with the Israeli-Palestinian conflict. Instead I will start in the middle, with my arrival in Ireland, 'post-nuptially' naturalised, in the year of 1969 (together with those other 'troubles').

Dublin, 1970. I am a researcher in the RTE current affairs programme *Seven Days*. One evening a young Irish woman, when she hears I am an Israeli Jew, asks me why I crucified her Lord. Young, and lost for words, I am relieved when RTE's director of religious programmes gives the young woman her first lesson in comparative religion.

Some weeks later I receive anonymous phone calls, from within RTE, telling me to go back to where I came from; I was not wanted here, a foreigner. When I tell colleagues, they play a hoax, repeating the calls from the neighbouring room, observing my response. I fail to get the joke.

Dublin, 1982. After a scuffle outside Stratford College, the Jewish school in Rathgar, a boy calls my seven-years old son a 'dirty Jew'. My son asks me, 'Why does everyone hate the Jews?' I recall my father telling me, years earlier in post-Shoah Israel, 'Unlike us, you will never experience antisemitism…' Little did he know.

Dublin, mid-1980s. I am invited, as a Jewish feminist, to a television discussion on: 'Woman: Madonna or Eve?' Alice Glenn TD, another panellist, asks me earnestly, 'What have the Jews *done* that everyone hates them?'

From time to time, after a public appearance, an article or a television production we are involved in, my husband and I receive antisemitic letters and phone calls. The Rathfarnham-born Jewish TD Alan Shatter, who is often told in the Dáil to 'go back to where he came from', told me of his bulging 'death file'.

Dublin, circa 1996. At a dinner party at a friend's house, a leading Fine Gael politician, one of the guests spouts abuse at Travellers. When I say that as a member of an ethnic minority, I find the conversation racist, my hostess and her guests reassure me: 'It's not about you, Ronit, you are one of *us*…'

October 1997. In the Channel Four programme *A Great Hatred* (Sebag Montefiore, 1997) the Irish writer Francis Stuart, who, as member of *Aosdána*, and *Saoi*, has the highest award accorded by the Irish cultural establishment, is asked about his wartime broadcasts for Nazi Germany. He quotes his own writing that 'the Jew is the worm that got into the rose and sickened it…' and says that no, he does not regret his pro-Nazi past. I watch and weep and feel erased. A motion on 26 November 1997, by poet Máire Mhac an tSaoi to *Aosdána*, calling for his resignation, is defeated by a large majority (Moroney, 1997: 7). The ensuing public debate concluded that Stuart could not be considered antisemitic.

Dublin, 14 February 2000. After writing an article opposing a proposed visit by the Shoah-denying 'historian' David Irving, I receive a very special (anonymous) St Valentine's card telling me, in bad German, to beware, because 'Our day will come'. The two nice local gardai do not really understand why this middle-class, middle-aged woman is so frightened by the possibility that a nationalist neo-Nazi group might be watching her every step.

Throughout my career as journalist, writer and academic, I have come to realise that my 'in-betweenie' status pertains most of all to my contested hybrid ethnicity as a Jewish woman in Irish society.

Racism and antisemitism: Jews as Ireland's archetypal Others

In this section I will draw links between racism and antisemitism and argue that 'Irishness' as constructed by the 1937 Constitution is exclusively Roman Catholic and ethnically homogeneous (see Lentin, 1999). A young Irish-Jewish woman told me recently: 'I am fourth generation Irish-born. How can I be more Irish other than being Catholic?' I would further argue that although racism in late 1990s Ireland is primarily anti-Traveller, anti-black and anti-refugees, Jews are the archetypal Others of Ireland's national Catholicism. Or, as Edward Lipsett, Dublin Jew turned convert, journalist, novelist and contemporary of James Joyce put it, Jews are in a 'peculiarly peculiar' position in Ireland (Lipsett, 1906, cited in Hyman, 1972). Jews are seen by Irish people variably as the killers of Christ (one sixth of the respondents in Mac Gréil's 1978 survey on prejudice in Ireland believed Jews were to blame for the crucifixion)[1], displaying dual loyalty (to Ireland and to Israel, or to international Jewry, a claim put forward forcibly in the 1930s by Irish antisemites such as Holy Ghost priest Denis Fahey and Jesuit Edward Cahill; Keogh, 1988: 92-7), or simply as a people apart, and 'not really Irish'.

Irish Jews are also seen by Irish people as wielding disproportionate financial power, (although there are no Irish Jews among Ireland's richest people). In 1978 Mac Gréil found that 42 per cent of his respondents disagreed that 'it would be good for the country to have many Jews in positions of responsibility in business'; 25 per cent agreed that 'Jewish power and control in money matters are far out of proportion to the number of Jews' and 57 per cent thought that 'Jews were behind the money lending rackets in Dublin' (Mac Gréil, 1978: 333). A subsequent survey published in 1996 recorded a relatively high level of prejudice against Jews in rural areas. 20 per cent still regarded Jews responsible for the crucifixion, although prejudice related to money matters has declined since the earlier survey (Mac Gréil, 1996: 223).

These perceptions are in stark contrast to the way most contemporary Irish Jews see themselves, as being fully integrated into Irish society. David Marcus, whose *A Land not Theirs* (1990) depicts the complex links between Irish nationalism and the close-knit 1920s Cork Jewish community, believes that 'by and large the Jewish experience in Ireland has been a happy one' and cannot recall ever encountering antisemitism apart from 'rowdy boys in the streets of Cork'. However, he acknowledges that 'most of the boys did medicine and were not really able to build up a practice in Ireland' because 'Catholics preferred to go to Catholics' (McGarry, 1997: 2). David Warm's interviews with Jews from Northern Ireland indicated little complaint of antisemitism. While Northern Ireland's Jews manage to keep a distance from the sectarian divide, and despite emphasising the 'importance of loyalty to the host society', some of Warm's interviewees did admit 'the Troubles' were a key factor in the numerical decline of the community (Warm, 1998: 234-7).

Indeed, privately some of us admit to feeling 'the odd person out', and having to act as 'Jews at home and Irish people outside'. When we choose to be publicly Jewish, we must face the consequences. These may be 'only' jokes, anonymous letters and telephone calls or inappropriate comments such as Francis Stuart's. Or they can be more public verbal attacks such as the accusation by Muintir na hÉireann against TDs Mervyn Taylor and Alan Shatter during the 1995 divorce referendum campaign that the two Jewish TDs, despite their recognised legal and legislative expertise in Irish family law, did not have 'a full understanding of Christian marriages' and were therefore unfit to lead the pro-divorce campaign (*Antisemitism World Report*, 1996: 151).

However, the most serious consequence is the continuing decline in the numbers of Ireland's Jews. Jewish population patterns vary greatly from general population trends in the Republic of Ireland. Between 1881 and 1911, the high period of Jewish immigration into Ireland, the average annual rise in the number of Jews was 8 per cent. Between 1926 and 1946 the community continued to increase at a rate of 0.3 per cent per annum despite a fall in the general population. Since then, there has been a steady decline: 1.2 per cent per annum between 1946 and 1961 and 3 per cent per annum between 1981 and 1991 (the date of the last census in which the religion question was asked) (Sexton and O'Leary, 1997). In all between 1946 and 1996, the Jewish community in the Republic declined by more than 70 per cent, from 3,900 in 1946 to some 1,000 in 1996. Warm (1998: 227) reports a similar pattern in Northern Ireland. The Northern Irish Jewish community grew steadily in the first 100 years of its existence to reach a peak in the late 1960s with 1,500 people. From then on the numbers dwindled so that, by 1997, the Northern Ireland Jewish community had been reduced to 230 individuals of all ages. 1999 was a historic crossroads as the 107-year-old Orthodox synagogue at Adelaide Road, Dublin closed due to small attendances and the congregation amalgamated with the Terenure synagogue congregation. The Cork synagogue, where it is near impossible to assemble a ten-man prayer quorum, is also threatened with closure.

The census portrays a rapidly ageing community: there has been a steep decline both in the Republic of Ireland and in the North of Ireland in the number of Irish Jews under 14 years, a steady decline of 15-34 years old Jews, but a huge increase of Jews over 65. In 1999 60-75 per cent of the Republic's Jews were over the age of 50. While both Protestant and Catholic emigration from the Republic has declined in the current economic boom (in 1997 alone 44,000 immigrants came to the Republic of Ireland, a net migration of 15,000; see Central Statistics Office, 1998), the emigration of our young generation continues even during the current economic boom: more than half of my children's 20-30 year old Jewish friends have emigrated or are preparing to emigrate.

The use of the term 'antisemitism' as a specific hostility towards Jews, is justified in light of Christian culture which peaked with the Nazi 'Final Solution' that killed six million Jews. Antisemitism has received little sustained social science attention. An exception is sociologist Helen Fein who defines antisemitism as:

> a persisting structure of hostile beliefs towards *Jews as a collectivity* manifested in individuals as attitudes, and in *culture* as myth, ideology, foloklore, and imagery, and in *actions* - social or legal discrimination, political mobilization against the Jews, and collective or state violence - which results in and/or is designed to distance, displace, or destroy Jews as Jews (Fein, 1987: 67).

Her definition differs from scholarly distinctions of antisemitism as an historically-specific ideology, restricting the term to the social movement labelled 'antisemitism' by Wilhelm Marr in 1879; and from distinctions between 'racial', 'Christian' and 'socialist' antisemitism, or between antisemitism and anti-Judaism. Langmuir (1987) distinguishes between realistic, xenophobic and chimeric assertions about Jews and restricts antisemitism to chimeric assertions which have no base in reality. Analysing seminal antisemitic texts, Fein points to stereotypes of the Jew as betrayer (Judas), exploiter or usurer (Shylock), revolutionary ('the red Jew'), non-human or diabolic murderer or sexual aggressor (Fein, 1987: 72), all of which shift the blame for antisemitism onto the Jewish outgroup.

While Langmuir (1987) and Banton (1992) claim that antisemitism and racism are two different concepts, Solomos and Back (1996: 50) and Miles (1989) position the history of contemporary racism within the influence of the experience under fascism and Nazism. I contend that analyses of antisemitism must fall within broader understandings of 'cultural racism' beyond colour-based 'racial' distinctions (cf Modood, 1992).

It is therefore appropriate to analyse Irish antisemitism within the specificities of Irish racism, one aspect of which, according to McVeigh (1992, 1996) is the importation, by returning Irish emigrants, of the racism they learnt abroad. One such returning emigrant was Father John Creagh, who, though born in Limerick, was influenced by a right-wing continental Catholic tradition (as were Fathers Fahey and Cahill in the 1930s). In 1904, as director of the Limerick Redemptorist arch-confraternity, he incited arch-confraternity members against 'blood sucking' Jewish moneylenders and travelling pedlars. In his sermons, Creagh depicted the Jews as

Christ crucifiers and great enemies of the Catholic Church, particularly in France, where, he claimed, Jews and Freemasons 'succeeded in turning out of their country all the nuns and religious orders. The Redemptorist Fathers to the number of two hundred had been turned out of France, and that is what the Jews would do in our country if they were allowed into power' *(Limerick Journal* 1940, cited by Keogh, 1998: 30). There is indeed little doubt that French antisemitism inspired Creagh: a 1900 antisemitic illustration from Edouard Drumont's *La Libre Parole* (*Grand Journal Antijuif*) showing a classical hooked-nosed mean looking Jew, was found in the arch-confraternity's records (Keogh, 1998: 40).

Creagh's sermons brought about a two-year trade boycott of Jewish businesses, which was accompanied by intimidation, abuse, harassment, burnings and beatings, and resulted in the almost total departure of the 150-strong Limerick Jewish community (O'Riordan and Feeley, 1984; Keogh, 1998).

However, the support Creagh's sermons received from Arthur Griffith's nationalist *United Irishman* runs contrary to the argument that antisemitism is a foreign import:

> No thoughtful Irishman or woman can view without apprehension the continuous influx of Jews into Ireland and the continuous efflux of the native population. The stalwart men and bright-eyed women of our race pass from our land in a never-ending stream, and in their place we are getting strange people, alien to us in thought, alien to us in sympathy, from Russia, Poland, Germany and Austria - people who come to live amongst us, but who never become of us... (*United Irishman*, 23 April 1904, cited by Keogh, 1998: 42).

At its highest point, in 1946, the Irish Jewish community numbered, according to the census, 3,907 men, women and children, hardly an influx, just as asylum-seekers in present-day Ireland cannot be considered an influx. Yet Griffith's antisemitic, anti-immigration rhetoric is not dissimilar to contemporary anti-immigration discourses voiced, for instance, by the Immigration Control Platform.

Kalman Lentin, my grandfather-in-law, who probably came to Ireland alone in 1884 as a fourteen-year old boy escaping conscription in Lithuania, and who built a commercial career in Limerick as a pedlar and scrap merchant, was one of the few Jews who remained in Limerick.

The issue of the Limerick pogrom has resurfaced three times in the past thirty years, when various individuals sought to justify it. In 1965 there was correspondence following an RTE television programme on the incident. In 1970 there was further controversy when the then Lord Mayor of Limerick, Stephen Coughlan, declared his support for Father Creagh's 'defending the impoverished Limerick population against the exploitative Jews'. The issue flared up again in 1984, with the Jews being defended mainly by the former Jewish Lord Mayor of Cork Gerald Goldberg and by left-wing politicians such as the late Jim Kemmy. Only in 1990 did Limerick make amends to its Jews by restoring the city's Jewish cemetery (*Antisemitism World Review*, 1996: 150).

Before and during the war, neutral Ireland refused to admit more than a handful of Jewish refugees fleeing Nazism. One excuse, given by antisemitic civil servants, was that Jews have dual loyalty to international Jewry, and couldn't be trusted to be one hundred percent Irish (Eunan O'Halpin, cited in Goldstone and Lentin, 1997). The other excuse, that allowing Jews in would *cause* antisemitism, was manifested in Minister for Justice Gerry Boland's response to the request to allow Jewish orphans into Ireland in 1946: 'It has always been the policy of the Minister for Justice to restrict the admission of Jewish aliens, for the reason that any substantial increase in our Jewish population might give rise to antisemitic problem' (cited in Goldstone and Lentin, 1997). This is amazingly similar to contemporary arguments, that allowing refugees into Ireland would cause ghettoising and racism - see, for instance, Kevin Myers writing in *The Irish Times* in July 1998: 'We can listen and we can learn from the experiences of others. We must have controls over immigration... And we should certainly not expect the least advantaged and least educated communities in Dublin and elsewhere to be the sole unassisted hosts of ghettos and newcomers. Down that road lies certain disaster' (Myers, 1998: 15).

Such responses shift the blame onto racialized minorities, rather than dominant majorities. Indeed, Kushner argues in relation to Britain that not allowing in more than a few Jewish refugees into Britain[2] as well as limiting the immigration of Black people, was underpinned by the assumption that 'the British people would be hostile to their entry and that racism would be caused by their presence. In both cases it was taken for granted that it was something about the nature of the minority that created the racism of which they were the victims, and that therefore nothing could be done to counter hostility within Britain other than to keep out the cause of the "problem"' (Kushner, 1998: 234).

There is no evidence that Taoiseach Eamonn De Valera expressed any condemnation of Nazi atrocities. In 1939, in a recorded discussion with Eduard Hempel, the German Minister in Dublin, a Nazi party member, De Valera agreed that Nazi procedures against the Jews 'must primarily be explained by the behaviour of the Jews after the First World War' (*Antisemitism World Report*, 1996: 150). In Hempel's 1938 reports to Berlin, the envoy recorded an 'unease' of the Irish public and the government about immigration of 'Jewish elements' into Ireland (Keogh, 1998: 146).

Antisemitic disturbances in Dublin in the 1930s were infrequent, despite radical anti-Jewish articles carried by Catholic publications such as *The Irish Catholic*, *The Catholic Bulletin*, *The Irish Mind*, *The Irish Rosary* and *The Cross* (Keogh, 1998: 92). However, towards the war radical nationalist groups, such as the *1916 Veterans Association* and the *Irish-Ireland Research Society*, expressed antisemitic ideas and called on the government to stop Jewish immigration into Ireland (Keogh, 1998: 147-8). Again, this presumed large numbers to have arrived, when, in fact, only a trickle was admitted. In February 1939 the words BOYCOTT JEWS appeared on walls around Dublin (not unlike anti-Black graffiti in contemporary Dublin) and several Dublin Jews received warnings to 'clear out of the country or they would meet the same fate here as the Jews in Germany' (Keogh, 1998: 149).

Keogh also records the existence of several prominent Fascists and Nazis in Dublin including Helmut Clissman, an associate of Francis Stuart in Berlin, who although he spied for the Nazis, was allowed to return to Ireland in 1948 (Keogh,

1998: 151-2) and ironically, was the founder of the Irish branch of Amnesty International. Until the late 1980s, the National Socialist Irish Workers' Party distributed neo-Nazi literature printed in Sweden as well as its own publications with Shoah-denial, neo-Nazi, antisemitic and anti-Traveller slogans. The NSIWP may have been responsible for a series of attacks on a Jewish butcher's shot in Dublin in 1986 (*Antisemitism World Report*, 1997: 184).

On the eve of the war, the Irish Jewish community was fearful of a Nazi invasion. In 1991 Conor Cruise O'Brien claimed that Ireland's '4,000 Jews would have been handed over to the Nazis had Germany won the war' (*Antisemitism World Report*, 1996: 150).

Only 60 Jewish refugees were allowed into Ireland between 1933 and 1946. While some Irish diplomats were trying to be as helpful as they could, others, such as Charles Bewley, the Irish envoy in Berlin, a well known supporter of Nazism, actively obstructed Jewish immigration to Ireland (Keogh, 1998: 129-136). Bewley's reports to the Department of Foreign Affairs reflect stereotypes of Jewish dual loyalty and financial dominance:

> ...governments... have been led by their experience to the conviction that Jews, even when settled in a particular country for centuries, do not become assimilated to the people of that country, but, when the interest of the country of their birth come into conflict with their own personal or racial interests, invariably sacrifice the interests of the country of their birth to Jewish interests ... The Jews had acquired so dominating a position in the financial world that they were in a position to control public policy... they monopolised the learned professions and held important positions in the universities out of all proportion to their numbers... (Bewley to Walsh, 9 December 1938, cited by Keogh, 1998: 132-3).

In 1943, at the height of the Shoah, TD Oliver Flanagan chose to make his notorious outburst in Dáil Éireann:

> There is one thing that Germany did and that was to rout the Jews out of their country. Until we rout the Jews out of this country it does not matter a hare's breath what orders you make. Where the bees are there is honey and where the Jews are there is the money (Flanagan, cited in Lentin and Goldstone, 1997).

Dáil members made no comment.

Despite neutral Ireland's pro-Allied stance, De Valera visited the German legation in Dublin on 2 May 1945 to express condolences on the death of Adolf Hitler.

Irish restrictive immigration policy continued after the war. There were long deliberations in relation to post-Shoah Jewish refugees in the Departments of Justice, External Affairs and Industry and Commerce. Despite De Valera's supposed readiness to admit 'at least 10,000 aliens' (Keogh, 1998: 6), the immigration of what Irish civil servants borrowed Nazi terminology in calling 'non-Aryans' remained extremely restrictive. In 1946 some 700 non-Jewish German children were brought to Ireland by the Red Cross in 'Operation Shamrock'; many remained in Ireland. On the other hand, permission for 100 Jewish Polish orphans to be settled in Clonyn Castle, County Westmeath, purchased by a London Jewish society, was given for two years only, on condition 'that they would be removed to some other country as soon as arrangements could be made, and that the Chief Rabbi's Religious Emergency Council would take full responsibility for the proper care and maintenance of the children while they remained in this country' (Department of Justice memorandum, April 1948, cited by Keogh, 1998: 211).

All these, and other exclusions are trivialised, dismissed and omitted from public consciousness. Jews, and antisemitism, are simply irrelevant. After all, some of their, your, best friends are Jews. I cope through political and academic work on racism and anti-racism. Only recently have I begun speaking and writing publicly about antisemitism.

Fear paralyses.

Conclusion

Can there be nationalism without racism? Nationalist projects always involve inclusions and exclusions. According to Nira Yuval-Davis (1997), the conflation of 'nation' and 'state' and the hegemony of one group over both state and society are at the basis of the link between nationalism and racism. Irish nationalism has meant the hegemony of a Catholic, 'white', sedentary collectivity over both state and society, without reference to the truly multi-ethnic nature of Irish society.

On the night of her victory President Mary McAleese spoke of being the president of 'the whole Irish nation', not the president of the Irish state and its citizens. During her visit to the Adelaide Road synagogue in February 1998, the President addressed the congregation as 'my fellow Irish men, women and children', yet spoke of 'your ambassador' when referring to the Israeli ambassador to Ireland. The subtext was, yet again, Jewish dual loyalty. Furthermore, the amendment to Article 2 of the Constitution speaks of two tiers of 'Irishness', those born on this island who are now part of 'the nation', and those residing in Ireland who are (mere) citizens. Once again I feel erased in the state whose passport I have carried since 1969.

The position of the Jewish community in contemporary Ireland is one of quiet co-existence with majority Irish society, despite occasional antisemitic media discourses. On 31 July 1993, during Israel's bombardment of Hizbullah strongholds in southern Lebanon, a cartoon by Martyn Turner of *The Irish Times* depicted a dinosaur wearing a helmet with a Star of David, preying on fleeing people. The caption, referring to the film *Jurassic Park*, read: 'Jewrassic Park - aka South Lebanon: 60,000 years in the making... one week in the destroying'. The equation of Zionism with Judaism is politically justified, since Israel defines itself as the state of the 'Jewish nation', but the antisemitic overtones (denied by Turner) are unmissable. Despite a large number of protest letters to the editor, the paper refused to apologise and the editor closed the correspondence in the middle of August (*Antisemitism World Report*, 1994: 47-8).

Few Irish Jews admit to the existence of antisemitism: better let sleeping demons rest. The autumn 1994 issue of *The Jewish Voice: Dublin's Alternative Jewish Press* published a survey of opinions which demonstrated contradictory Jewish attitudes. While only 14 per cent of respondents thought 'racism was a problem in Dublin', 24 per cent thought 'antisemitism was on the rise in Ireland'. While only 10 per cent were 'affected by antisemitism in the past five years', 48 per cent did not think that 'the police do enough in these circumstances' or that 'Irish law protects Jews from racism' (*Antisemitism World Report*, 1995: 151). Some Irish Jews speak of the ghost of dual Jewish loyalty: the painter Gerald Davis writes that he is often asked whether he had been 'back' to Israel. 'Back to Israel? I was from Kimmage... I am, for better or worse, a product of Ireland, my mentality and mores conditioned by a mixture of Anglo-Saxon, European and Celtic cultures, albeit with an overlay of traditional Judaism' (Davis, 1998: 3).

Others are more vocal. Gerald Goldberg has spoken of his sadness about the demise of the Cork Jewish community which 60 years ago numbered 400 Jews: 'In a heartfelt way I am sad to say that for the local community this seems to be the end'. He blames Irish government policy during the war for the precipitous decline and says that the scenario today would be different for Ireland's Jews if European Jewish refugees had been allowed into this country (McGarry, 1998: 2).

I end with another reflection on those 'peculiarly peculiar' Irish Jews. Louis Lentin, commenting on Joyce's Mr Deasy's antisemitic remark about Ireland never letting in the Jews, writes:

> ... the vitally important word being in - fully in - not half in, or with a foot in the door. My English dictionary defines the word *in* as, among other things, belonging to, being a member of, having a share or part in. So maybe Mr Deasy is right after all... it is worth asking if there really is any difference between the attitudes and opinions Joyce provides for his acutely observed cast of Dubliners in 1904 and those expressed to me both openly and anonymously more than sixty years later. Do we Jews of the Diaspora, like Leopold Bloom, still exist only in a limbo of alienation? (Lentin, 1996: 63).

References

Abdo, Nahla and Ronit Lentin. 2002. *Women and the Politics of Military Confrontation: Palestinian and Israeli Narratives of Dislocation*. Oxford and New York: Berghahn Books.

Antisemitism World Report. 1993, 1994, 1995. London: Institute of Jewish Affairs.

Antisemitism World Report. 1996, 1997. London: Institute for Jewish Policy Research and American Jewish Committee.

Banton, Michael. 1992. 'The relationship between racism and antisemitism.' *Patterns of Prejudice*, vol 26, nos 1&2: 17-27.

Bauman, Zygmunt. 1991. *Modernity and Ambivalence*. Cambridge: Polity Press.

Bauman, Zygmunt. 1998. 'Allosemitism: premodern, modern, postmodern', in Bryan Cheyette and Laura Marcus (eds.) *Modernity, Culture and 'the Jew.'* Cambridge: Polity Press.

Central Statistics Office. 1998. 'Population and migration estimates.' Press release, April 1998. Dublin: CSO.

Davis, Gerald. 1998. 'A Jew from Kimmage', in *Israel and Ireland: an International Supplement on Israel's 50th Anniversary. The Irish Times*, 23 June 1998.

Donovan, Katie. 1998. 'Ireland's young blooms', *The Irish Times*, 7 January 1998: 13.

Fein, Helen. 1987. 'Introduction', in Helen Fein (ed.) *The Persisting Question: Sociological Perspectives and Social Contexts of Modern Antisemitism*. Berlin and New York: Walter de Gruyter.

Fein, Helen. 1987. 'Dimensions of antisemitism: attitudes, collective accusations, and actions', in Helen Fein (ed.) *The Persisting Question: Sociological Perspectives and Social Contexts of Modern Antisemitism*. Berlin and New York: Walter de Gruyter.

Fisk, Robert. 1985. *In Time of War: Ireland, Ulster and the Price of Neutrality 1939-1945*. London: Paladin.

Gilroy, Paul. 2000. *Between Camps: Nations, Cultures and the Allure of Race*. London: Allan Lane, the Penguin Press.

Goldstone, Katrina and Louis Lentin. 1997. *No more Blooms: Ireland's attitude to the Jewish refugee problem 1933-46*. A Crescendo Concepts documentary for RTE, broadcast 10 December 1997.

Goldstone, Katrina. 1998. 'Irish government policies towards Jewish refugees and the ideological roots of restrictive immigration.' Paper presented to the MPhil in Ethnic and Racial Studies seminar series, Department of Sociology, Trinity College Dublin, 16 January 1998.

Goldstone, Katrina. 2000. 'Benevolent helpfulness? Ireland and the international reaction to Jewish refugees 1933-1939', in Michael Kennedy and Joseph M. Skelly (eds). *Irish Foreign Policy 1919-1966: From Independence to Internationalism*. Dublin: Four Courts Press.

Hyman, Louis. 1972. *The Jews of Ireland from Earlier Times to the Year 1910*. Shannon: Irish University Press.

Joyce, James. 1960. *Ulysses*. London: Bodley Head.

Karpf, Anne. 1997. *The War After*. London: Minerva.

Keogh, Dermot. 1988. *Ireland and Europe 1919-1948*. Dublin: Gill and MacMillan.

Keogh, Dermot. 1998. *Jews in Twentieth Century Ireland: Refugees, Anti-Semitism and the Holocaust*. Cork: Cork University Press.

Kostick, Gavin. *The Ash Fire*. Play produced by Pig's Bank Theatre Company.

Kushner, Tony. 1998. 'Remembering to forget: Racism and anti-semitism in postwar Britain', in Bryan Cheyette and Laura Marcus (eds.) *Modernity, Culture and 'the Jew.'* Cambridge: Polity Press.

Langmuir, Gavin. 1987. 'Towards a definition of antisemitism', in Helen Fein (ed.) *The Persisting Question: Sociological Perspectives and Social Contexts of Modern Antisemitism*. Berlin and New York: Walter de Gruyter.

Lentin, Louis. 1996. 'I don't understand. I fail to say. I dearsee you too', in Morris Beja and David Norris (eds.) *Joyce in the Hibernian Metropolis: Essays*. Columbus: Ohio State University Press.

Lentin, Ronit. 1985. 'Tea with Mrs Klein', in Ronit Lentin, James Liddy and Tomas O Murchadha,*Triad: Modern Irish Fiction*. Dublin: Wolfhound Press.

Lentin, Ronit. 1996. *Songs on the Death of Children*. Dublin: Poolbeg Press.

Lentin, Ronit. 1999. '"Irishness," the 1937 Constitution and citizenship: a gender and ethnicity view. *Irish Journal of Sociology*, Vol 7, no 2.

Leventhal, A.J. 1945. 'What it means to be a Jew.' *The Bell*, vol x no 3: 207-216.

Lipsett, Edward Raphael. 1906. In *Jewish Chronicle*, 21 December, 1906.

Mac Gréil, Mícheál. 1978. *Prejudice and Tolerance in Ireland: Based on a Survey of Intergroup Attitudes of Dublin Adults and Other Sources*. Maynooth: Survey and Research Unit, St Patrick's College, Maynooth.

Mac Gréil, Mícheál. 1996. *Prejudice in Ireland Revisited*. Maynooth: Survey and Research Unit, St Patrick College, Maynooth.

Marcus, David. 1986. *A Land Not Theirs*. London: Bantam Press.

Marcus, David. 1990. *Who Ever Heard of an Irish Jew?* London: Corgi Books.

McGarry, Patsy. 1998. 'Ireland's dwindling Jewish community', in *Israel and Ireland: an International Supplement on Israel's 50th Anniversary*. The Irish Times, 23 June 1998.

McVeigh, Robbie. 1992. 'The specificity of Irish racism.' *Race and Class*, vol 33, no 4: 31-45.

McVeigh, Robbie. 1996. *The Racialisation of Irishness: Racism and Anti-racism in Irish Society*. Belfast: Centre for Research and Documentation.

Miles, Robert. 1989. *Racism*. London: Routledge.

Modood, Tariq. 1992. *Not Easy Being British: Colour, Culture and Citizenship*. Stoke on Trent: Runneymede Trust and Trentham Books.

Moroney, Mic. 1997. 'Stormy Aosdana assembly votes against call for Stuart resignation.' *The Irish Times*, 27.11.97: 7.

Myers, Kevin. 1998. 'An Irishman's diary.' *The Irish Times*, 30 July 1998, p. 15.

Ó Drisceoil, Donall. 1997. 'Jews and other undesirables: anti-Semitism in neutral Ireland during the Second World War', in Jim Mac Laughlin and Ethel Crowley (eds.) *Under the Belly of the Tiger: Class, Race, Identity and Culture in the Global Ireland*. Dublin: Irish Reporter Publications.

O'Riordan, Manus and Pat Feeley. 1984. *The Rise and Fall of Irish Antisemitism*. Labour History Workshop: stenciled.

Price, Stanley. 1998. *Somewhere to hang your hat*. A documentary for RTE, transmitted in the 'True Lives' series, 2 February 1998.

Reizbaum, Marylin. 1999. *James Joyce's Judaic Other*. Stanford, CA: Stanford University Press.

Sebag Montefiore, Simon. 1997. *The great hatred*. A Hard Cash documentary for Channel Four, broadcast 11 October 1997.

Sexton, J.J. and Richard O'Leary. 1997. 'Factors affecting population decline in minority religious communities in the Republic of Ireland', in *Forum for Peace and Reconciliation, Building Trust in Ireland*, Belfast: The Blackstaff Press.

Shillman, Bernard. 1945. *A Short History of the Jews in Ireland*. Dublin: Easons and Son.

Solomon, Bethel. 1956. *One Doctor and His Time*. Dublin: Easons and Son.

Solomos, John and Les Back. 1996. *Racism and Society*. London: MacMillan.

Warm, David D. 1998. 'The Jews of Northern Ireland', in Paul Hainsworth (ed) *Divided Society: Ethnic Minorities and Racism in Northern Ireland*. London: Pluto.

Wasserstein, Bernard. 1997. *Vanishing Diaspora: The Jews in Europe Since 1945*. Harmondsworth: Penguin Books.

Yuval-Davis, Nira. 1997. *Gender and Nation*. London: Sage.

Zlotover, Melisande. 1966. *Zlotover Story: A Dublin Story with a Difference*. Dublin: Melisande Zlotover.

11.

Christianity, conversion and the tricky business of names: Images of Jews and Blacks in the nationalist Irish Catholic discourse

Katrina Goldstone

Then it dawned on we with certain suddenness that I was different from the all others; or like mayhap, in heart and life and longing, but shut out of their world by a vast veil (W.E.B. Dubois quoted in Holt, 1995: 1).

If the problem of marking reveals itself, as Frantz Fanon describes it, 'in a thousand details, anecdotes, stories', or as Dubois suggests in jokes, songs… then one appropriate response would seem to be to re-write the stories (Holt, 1995: 18).

We're all tempted to turn our backs on some parts of our history: the 'we' being non-Jewish historians (Richmond, 1994: 9).

These quotes are emblems of some of the themes I want to look at in relation to difference and what Thomas Holt has referred to as marking. As he explains, 'I use marking here in a double sense as the act of representation that is the marking of race and as the act of inscription that is the marking of history' (Holt, 1995). I want to look at some of the ways difference has been marked in the past and is being marked in the present in the Irish context and to think about the implications of designating difference, both for those who experience it and those who mark it out. It is important to be prepared to explore thoroughly how difference has been marked through illiberal nationalist discourse and triumphal Catholicism before we race headlong towards some utopian vision of a multi-ethnic nation. For it seems to me that this vision will remain largely unfulfilled until we confront and resist the barriers in both the past and the present that prevent not just imagining a multi-ethnic nation but actually living it. These barriers include the legacy of triumphal Catholicism and the aspects of Irish nationalism of discourse that focus on the alien. In triumphal Catholicism I include the culture of conversion which influenced Christian attitudes to Jews (Richmond, 1994). Needless to say, the conversionary ethos of Christianity also carries with it immense historical implications in regards to missionary work in Africa and the construction of images of Africans as a people who need to be converted. I want us to consider the longevity of 'old racisms' in Irish society and to look at the various ways these hostilities could be expressed.

I write from the odd perspective of a Jew-not-a-Jew, born and brought up in Northern Ireland. I am often perceived as a Jew because of my name. I am not regarded as a Jew by many Jews because my mother was not Jewish. In both my academic and activist work to date I have been very preoccupied with images and perceptions. At the core of what I do is a fascination with the hows, whys and wherefores of demonisation: why certain groups are set apart and the discreet and not so discreet ways of marking someone out as 'different'. For the last few years I have been studying the images of Jews, both official and popular, in a historical context. I am also part of a refugee solidarity and lobbying group and much of our time is spent monitoring the media, trying to combat the many untruths, innuendoes and lies about refugees being presented in some media and public discourses.

I suppose this horrified fascination partly dates back to my childhood when I realised that people would treat me differently depending on what they perceived me to be. As the child of a Jewish father and a Catholic mother in Northern Ireland I was brought up in what might now be termed a multi-denominational home, with each parent trying to be even-handed about the other's religious heritage. My father wanted me to go to a multi-denominational school but there were no places, so I was enrolled in a convent school. My father apparently asked the nuns at the interview were they going to teach me that the Jews killed Christ. I was brought up as a Catholic whilst also attending Friday night, Jewish High Holy-days and attending an endless round of weddings and barmitzvahs. In my green school uniform I was marked for a Catholic and when times were bad in North Belfast in the 70s, the uniform turned you into a target. I was bemused that when I went across town to play with Jewish cousins who socialised mostly with Protestants, I was 'safe' as long as they didn't 'discover' I was 'really' a Catholic. My recollection is that neither my cousins nor I ever disabused our Protestant playmates of their assumption that I was really a Catholic. Maybe we were all trying to 'pass' in one way or another.

Marking difference

When I first started to research the history of Irish government policy towards Jewish refugees in the 1930s, I didn't realise how central images and perceptions would be in the evolution of a restrictive policy. Nor did I realise how much I would have to confront the spectre of antisemitism and Christian culpability (Goldstone, 1995). The more I study this kind of history, the sort not much taught in Irish schools, the more I come to believe that it is imperative to look coldly at aspects of the past, to examine the old racisms of Irish society, like anti-Traveller feeling and antisemitism, and to recognise how these have helped to provide a bedrock for new prejudices to thrive. It is vital to be aware that the language and images of yesteryear provide templates for the articulations of new fears, about a new group of Others/Strangers/'Aliens'. In some cases indeed whilst the targets of opprobrium have changed, the fears remain the same. Fears of engulfment, social or sexual, fear of loss of identity - these themes occur and re-occur.

Ireland in the years 1881-1901 witnessed an extraordinary increase in the Jewish population, going from 394 in 1881 to 3,006 in 1901 (Hyman, 1972: 160) This heralded a new dawn for a Jewish community that had seemed on the verge of extinction in the 1870s. Nonetheless, at various times in the 1880-1920 period the increase in numbers sparked unfavourable notice (Garvin. 1988: 70-72; 122; 124). Nationalist polemicists like Arthur Griffith and D.P. Moran used antisemitic imagery in *The United Irishman* and *The Leader*. But fears of a 'Jewish invasion' could also be voiced in religious publications and provincial newspapers, and they continued to occur even after the initial key period of migration in the 1880-1919 period. Take this editorial from *The Tuam Herald*:

> We have coming in on every boat, persons of every nationality and every religion and no religion - the greatest to an alarming extent, the Jews. Now personally, these formally chosen people may be very pleasant and very nice to meet, and one would not be inclined to object to the advent of a few of that creed and class, but when they come in thousands, as they are every year, and when settling here and displacing natives, it is a matter of public concern and serious importance (reprinted in *The Irish Rosary*, April 1927).

That was written in April 1927, but it could have appeared yesterday, and one has only to change the word Jews to 'Romanians' or 'refugees' and one has something entirely contemporary. Language is one of the main frontiers of battle in the struggle for equality not just of rights but equality of representation. And in an increasingly popular or dumbed-down culture, how we use imagery to describe difference is crucial. Whether it be in the cold, banal tones of the civil service document which justifies exclusion as those written about Jews in the 30s and 40s, we have to be aware of those 'thousands of details, anecdotes, stories', all the myriad ways of marking difference. Otherwise it will be difficult to challenge it.

In August 1998, a Wexford alderman expressed fears that Romanian men might attract and run off with impressionable Irish girls (McDonald, *The Observer*, 30 August 1998). The threat of foreigners attracting Irish girls seems more important than the fact Irish girls are routinely abused by figures of authority and indeed in some cases, members of their own family. Racist literature circulated at the same time as this outburst crudely expressed fear about African men and Irish women (Magee, *The Sunday Tribune*, 9 August 1998). Protests like this, but as regards Jewish men and Christian girls, occurred as a sub-text in the discourse of Irish antisemitism in the 1920s and 1930s. One extremist journal went so far as to issue a stern warning worded thus:

> To our Christian girls Fourteen Days notice is hereby given that names and addresses will be published of Christian girls travelling with Jews (*Aontas Gaedheal*, June 21, 1935).

Indeed with regard to the potentially sectarian murder of two Jewish men in 1923, amongst the possible motivations, it was suggested by one neighbour that it was as punishment for walking out with Christian girls (interview with David Cristol, 1994). Jewish lubriciousness or degeneracy was a sub-theme in antisemitism from the middle ages right down to the mid-twentieth century (Garb, 1995: 21; 26-7; Gilman, 1991) One priest, Father Denis Fahey, who wrote a number of antisemitic texts in the 1930s, referred to this in a book published and approved of by the Irish hierarchy. The targets change but the charges against the Other remain stubbornly the same. These are examples of populist fears and how they are used to mark the Other as 'different'. But bureaucratic language can also be employed in the marking of difference.

I shall not forget the shock of reading for the first time the Justice Department memo that set out why the entry of Jews to Ireland had been limited:

> In the administration of the alien laws it has always been recognised in the departments of Justice, Industry & Commerce and External Affairs that the question of the admission of aliens of Jewish blood present a special problem and the alien laws have been administered less liberally in their case. Although the Jewish community in Ireland is only 3,907 persons according to the 1946 census, there is a fairly strong anti-Semitic feeling throughout the country based perhaps on historical reasons, the fact that Jews have remained a separate community and have not permitted themselves to be assimilated and that of their numbers they appear to have disproportionate wealth (Department of the Taoiseach, S11007A28, February 1953).

The document is referring to 3,000 odd people in a population of over 3 million. In my research I could not find Jews at the time who ran newspapers, banks or held high office or in fact had what one might call real power and I have been unable to establish what 'disproportionate wealth' means. Many Jews were beginning to become middle-class, if you like, in the 1930s and 1940s. The census statistics which collate religion and occupation show that within the Jewish community a proportionally high number of Jews were engaged in small businesses. However as a proportion of the overall population, the figure is 687 Jews out or 82,746 Catholics engaged in the commercial, finance and insurance sectors. Yet these were used as legitimate justification for exclusion, though it sounds like stereotyping to me. (That is an obvious example of making difference.)

In both illiberal nationalist and triumphal Catholic discourse there has consistently been place for setting apart 'Others', the not-Irish, the not-Catholic or not-Christian. But as well as the blindingly obvious ways of marking difference, there are subtler, more discreet manifestations.

Let's take, for instance, the tricky business of names. Let's leave aside that casual yet distinct way of marking that refers to a first name as a Christian name. Instead let's look briefly at how surnames and stereotypically Jewish names were used to indicate difference and at times, to highlight reprehensible or shady behaviour. This was a theme in a number of extreme antisemitic journals, none of which had a long life (*Aontas Ghaedheal* 1-4, 1935; *Penapa*, 1940). But it also occurred in the pages of *The Irish Worker* as early as 1911 (Keogh, 1998:55). It was also used in the Dáil in debates about what was called the alien penetration of industry - a telling phrase in itself. In the 1930s a debate about alien penetration of industry formed a subtext to nationalist debates that tried to clarify just what Irishness meant in the newly independent state.

> Alien penetration in Eire, the acquisition of property by aliens… and the ease with which aliens could assume Irish names and trade under them were discussed at the 37th annual meeting of NAIDA. F.M. Summerfield said that it was too easy for an alien to come into the country and change surname by deed-poll. Non-nationals were getting their hands on the life-blood of the country in ever increasing numbers (*The Irish Times*, 10 February 1942).

The reference to changing names or assuming Irish names could occur in business journals or in Dáil debates. In some debates in the Dáil, deliberately Jewish names were picked out to indicate foreignness and also in some cases to typify shady business behaviour (*Dáil Debates*, vol. 1, 15 November 1933-2, March 1934, 22 November, cols 346-8; *ibid*, col. 891; *Dáil Debates*, 29 November 1933, cols 696-8).

In a debate on the Alien Bill (later to become the 1935 Aliens Act) Deputy Patrick McGilligan referred to the business of changing names:

> Say you have a gentleman called Wassenfeldt or some name of that kind, that he decided to Irishise his name, and that he becomes O'Maguire on a particular date. If it is later he may find that there are too many O'Maguires in the country and he can change his name to something else (*Dáil Debates*, vol. liv, 14 November-21 February 1935; 14 February, col. 2034).

Even Taoiseach Eamon De Valera could not escape suspicion. In March 1934, in order to scotch the continuing and persistent rumours that he was Jewish, he referred to what he called 'this dirty innuendo' in the course of a Dáil debate:

> There is not as far as I know a single drop of Jewish blood in my veins. I am not one of those who try to attack the Jews or want to make nay use of the popular dislike of them. I know that they were originally God's people; that they turned against him and that the punishment which their turning against God brought upon them made even Christ himself weep (*Dáil Debates*, vol. L, 2 March 1934, col. 2514).

De Valera also referred to the other occasions when the issue of Jewishness had come up, notably when he went for a job as a maths teacher (*ibid*, 2 March 1934, col. 2515).

This rumour, plus the fact that the Fianna Fail party boasted the only Jewish TD, meant that the accusation that Fianna Fail was too thick with the Jews could be, and was, thrown up in the cut and thrust of political debate (Dunphy, 1995: 161). The business about names is interesting; what is or is not a real Irish name and who has the right to change or assume an Irish name is part of the panoply of difference that has been created about certain groups in Irish society. It may seem a harmless sort of distinction to some, but I think it well fits the criteria of the thousands of ways difference can be marked.

And before we set out to create a truly multi-ethnic notion we must recognise both the tenacity and subtlety of the myths about who is really Irish.

The tricky business of names

Let's think too about what makes people change their names and what makes people conscious of their name. I can honestly say I have never been so aware of my name as I am in Ireland; to a certain extent, I feel I have been 'Jewified' here. I have lived in Northern Ireland, France, Spain, England and the Republic of Ireland. More comment has been passed on my stereotypically Jewish surname here than anywhere else, though the most threatening use of it was in Northern Ireland when a policemen stopped me on a lonely road, and when he looked at my driving licence, sneered, 'Goldstone, sounds like a Jew to me'.

This business of names could even be applied to first names. Playwright Arthur Miller recalled various agonies of embarrassment about his father's name when he went to apply for a library card:

> Now the lady asked my father's name. I had not expected any of this, thinking I was simply going into this place to happily claim my rightful card... Looking up into her blue eyes, I could not bring myself to voice my father's so Jewish name, Isidore. I was paralysed, could only shake my head... (Miller, 1990: 24).

Miller was six at the time and vows he could not even have heard an antisemitic remark. What makes people change their name? I am talking now about a deliberate, not an accidental, alteration. Not the process that took place at ports and immigration centres in New York, Hull, Liverpool, everywhere where Jews were received in the 19th and 20th centuries. No, I mean the change by deed poll, such as those that appeared in Iris Oifigiuil in the 1940s: Schatz to Shorts, Cohen to Collins.

Why do you change your name? Is it a purely practical move so the people can pronounce your obviously foreign name? Is it an attempt to belong or hide what you are? Or is it, as is most likely, a mixture of the two? My Romanian grandmother changed her first name, Gittel, to Kate, and gave all her children very English first names but refused to change her married surname even though in the Manchester of 1930s it must have been difficult to have that obviously Jewish surname. My father was taught to box 'to defend himself'. The way he tells it is he was a target because he had a big nose.

In the imagery of Jews in past nationalist discourses distinctions are made between the good and bad Jew and this phenomenon was not unique to Ireland (Dinnerstein, 1994: 53-4; Alderman, 1992: 256; Cesarani, 1993: 12). Thus the Jews who are acceptable to Irish society are those who have shown themselves to be both loyal citizens and ardent nationalists. Thus the Briscoes, Michael Boyk and families like the Solomons and Wines can be presented as the ideal Jew who has both served his country, and excelled in the professional sphere. This is very much a legacy from the era of emancipation when in order to justify being granted full civil rights in the 1850s and 60s, Jews in Europe swapped official laws that proscribed their behaviour for unofficial demands that they be worthy of citizenship. As Tamar Garb has written:

> the secularising and universalising dream of emancipation, whilst purporting to be inclusive and democratising, resembled the proselytising ethos of the

Christian missionaries in a fundamental way. It was premised on the eradication of difference that was by no means reciprocal. There was no negotiation of a new shared culture of Christians and Jews, involving give and take, a symbiosis of mutual respect. Rather, Jews were expected to discard their own cultural specificity for a more 'rational', 'modern', 'universal' identity... This involved the relinquishing of language, dress and religious and cultural expression in favour of the dominant cultural modes (Garb, 1995: 24).

Perhaps one of the most powerful images of dislocation was presented to me by a distant relative, an artist. She spoke of a strange photograph she had found of her grandparents' family who originally came from Aleppo in Syria and were Sephardic Jews. They had immigrated to Canada and in the tradition of immigrants made good, had arranged for a family portrait to be taken. These types of photos have a powerful resonance for all class of immigrants. 'Look how well we've done', they boast and in later years, if the family fell on hard times, they were an uncomfortable reminder of the precarious position of the outsider with only a toe-hold in society. My relative felt uncomfortable about the photograph, the family all decked out in the best of Victorian finery, high lace collars for the women, the men with suits and top-hats. But the faces dark, swarthy and Oriental somehow looked at odds with the propriety of the assumed dress which seemed to her more like theatrical costume than everyday wear.

We still hear echoes of this type of bargain today, that demands that immigrants relinquish their identity, garb and culture. The immigrant or refugee is supposed to 'contribute' to society, to become 'integrated' and is even expected to have standards of moral behaviour far above those used to judge the 'native population'. This barometer of what constitutes moral probity is highly selective. Funnily enough when one of our ex-Taoiseachs was investigated by a tribunal for fraud and other offences, we didn't see editorial after editorial about the thieving propensities of all the Irish. But when one member of any ethnic minority does anything, we are all guilty.

'Race making'

When I came to think about how subtly difference is demarcated as well as the larger, more lethal differences, I kept coming back to Thomas Holt's essay on race-making, his thesis about the importance of the everyday and his particularisation of it with the example of the American minstrel show and its perpetation of a popular image of American Blacks as both subservient but happy to be subservient. What images have we imbibed in the past in this society that have had for the most part to feed on image exclusively as regards both Jew and Black? During the 1930s the main conduits of antisemitism were both Catholic religious texts and popular religious publications. Thinking about these as a means of promoting distorted imagery, it occurred to me that in the past some of the few images of Africans coming to Irish people were through missionary and religious magazines. Even in my own childhood we regularly received mission publications as well as collected tinfoil and milk bottle tops for the black babies. Even a superficial perusal of missionary journals of the 1920s, 30s and

40s shows the condescending attitude of the missionary. An early editorial in *Missionary Annals* spells out the message:

> Conversely, not being a Christian is, despite other attainments of intellect or will, to possess a sorry type of existence. It is missing the whole point of existence ... Such unfortunately is the state of poor forlorn Africa. Africa is a sad spectacle in many ways, sad in being intellectually feeble, in being morally ailing but above all in being spiritually corpse-like. Is there any hope for the poor, unfortunate children of the Dark Continent? Thank God, there is, because missionaries are going out to them. They are going to drag those abandoned creatures from the jaws of hell, to make of them by Baptism children of God, and heirs to his Kingdom (*Missionary Annals*, Vol. 11, no, 12, December 1929).

This is one of the ways perceptions of blacks had been transmitted in the past. It occurs to me that because the Irish have been, or have been perceived to have been predominantly white and Christian, the knowledge people garnered about different religions or ethnicities was second-hand and frequently distorted through the prism of Christianity. Those images of Blacks in Irish missionary journals play up the superiority of the white priest and his Christian beliefs and also create disempowered images of black people always laughing and happy. They couldn't possibly be experiencing the ravages of colonialism or loss of their spiritual and cultural heritage, could they? And ironically, although today the bulk of African refugees are Christian, that does not prevent them from being attacked and vilified on our streets.

It seems to me to be stating the obvious to say that you do not go out to convert a group of people whose beliefs you genuinely respect. By looking from another angle at the history of Christianity and indeed its role in colonialism, one is forced to confront the unpleasant aspects about Christianity's role in fomenting and sustaining prejudice, by creating a culture of superiority and disdain. This is not a criticism of individuals who are Christians but a criticism of the abuse of parts of Christian theology which have underpinned persecution. The emphasis on 'Christian' values as being superior to all others carries within it the seeds of contempt. Again the simple use of terms like 'unchristian' to denote opprobrium quickly establishes norms of behaviour that are 'acceptable'. Ironically there are more than vestiges of this today. Alderman Paudge Reck who expressed fears about Romanian men seducing Irish girls prefaced his prejudiced remarks with the statement, 'I'm not racist or unchristian...' (McDonald, *The Observer*, 30 August 1998).

Again we must face these unpleasant aspects of the past before we can embark on plans for the future. We must examine the role of Christianity in education today and question whether a truly multi-ethnic nation can be envisaged in tandem with the monopoly of one religion of the educational establishment. And we must be vigilant to hear the echoes and distortions of the past as they are re-applied to other groups of 'strangers' to these shores. The images of the past may have been created to serve circumstances and social contexts which have changed long ago. Nonetheless the fears about the Other still remain:

It is nothing new to say that history is the version of events told by the conqueror, the dominator. Even the dominators acknowledge this ... without our own history we are unable to imagine a future because we are deprived of the precious resource of knowing where we come from: the valour and the waverings, the visions and defeats of those who went before us (Rich, 1994: 141).

Conclusion

I have been looking at the significance of images, the interplay between the past and the present and the act of marking difference. The act of marking always diminishes. It sets apart one person from another and at times it can feel like being kept apart from 'their' world by that vast veil Dubois described. In studying history, a history unknown to me, the history of ghettos, pogroms and the Holocaust, the history of Irish ambivalence towards Jews, I have been pushed forward, been 'Jewified' and have indeed, to a certain extent 'Jewified' myself. I lobby for refugees and asylum rights as best I can because I am so acutely aware that the pleas of Jewish refugees for sanctuary fell on deaf ears. Yet as well as the immense sorrow of learning of Jewish suffering, there is also another story of struggles and strategies and creativity. History and personal history intersect. I understand more about the idiosyncracies of my family, their 'minority anxiety' and their deep-rooted mistrust of people. I can no longer interrogate them about their past. Those I want to ask questions of are dead. But I can make more educated guesses about how their lives were shaped and by what factors. To untangle the great mess of distortions, belittling assumptions and downright lies which are told about 'the Other', be they Travellers, Jews, Blacks or refugees, we must understand the insidious versatility of 'difference' before we can dismantle it altogether.

References

Alderman, Geoffrey. 1992. *Modern British Jewry*. Oxford: Clarendon Press

Aontas Gael. 1935. National Library

Carmody, Fiona and Margaret Daly. 1984. 'Irish Jews and Anti-semitism in the early 20th Century.' *Retrospect*, new series, no. 4, pp. 46-50.

Cesarani, David. 1987. 'Anti-Alienism in England after the First World War', *Immigrants and Minorities*, vol. vi, no. 1, pp. 5-29

Cesarani, David. 1993. *Reporting Anti-Semitism: 'The Jewish Chronicle' 1987-1979*. Southampton: University of Southampton.

Cesarani, David. (ed.) 1990. *The Making of Modern Anglo-Jewry*. Oxford: Basil Blackwell.

Cesarani, David and Tony Kushner. 1993. 'An Alien Concept? The Continuity of Anti-Alienism in British society before 1940', in David Cesarani and Tony Kushner (eds.) *The Internment of Aliens in 20th Century Britain*. London: Frank Cass.

Dinnerstein, Leonard. 1994. *Anti-Semitism in America*. Oxford: Oxford University Press.

Duffy, Mark J. 1985. 'A socio-economic analysis of Dublin's Jewish community, 1880-1911.' Unpublished M.A. thesis, University College Dublin.

Dunphy, Richard. 1995. *The Making of Fianna Fail Power in Ireland 1923-48*. Oxford: Clarendon Press.

Fahey, Denis. 1939. *The Rulers of Russia*. Dublin: Brown and Nolan, 3rd edition reprint.

Falk, Gerhard. 1992. *The Jew in Christian Theology: Martin Luther's Anti Jewish 'Vom Shem Hamphoras'.* Jefferson, N.C: McFarland.

Garb, Tamar. 1995. 'Modernity, Identity, Textuality' in Tamar Garb and Linda Nochlin (eds.) *The Jew in the Text: Modernity and the Construction of Identity.* London: Thames and Hudson.

Garvin, Tom. 1987. *Nationalist Revolutionaries in Ireland 1858-1928.* Oxford: Clarendon Press

Gilman, Sander. 1991. *The Jew's Body.* New York and London: Routledge

Holt, Thomas. 1995. 'Marking: Race, Race Making and the Writing of History.' *American Historical Review,* no. 100, February, pp.1-17.

Hyman, Louis. 1972. *The Jews of Ireland from Earliest Times to the Year 1910.* Shannon: Irish University Press.

Goldstone, Katrina. 1995. 'Jewish Refugees of World War II: Irish Government Policy and Public Opinion: 1933-45'. Unpublished M.A..Thesis, St. Patrick's College, Maynooth.

Goldstone, Katrina. 1998. 'Listening to other voices', *The Sunday Tribune,* 5 April 1998.

Keogh, Dermot. 1983. 'De Valera, the Catholic Church and "the Red Scare"', in J.P. O'Carroll and John A. Murphy (eds.) *De Valera and his Times.* Cork: Cork University Press.

Keogh, Dermot. 1988. 'Herzog, De Valera and Irish Policy towards Jewish Refugees in the 1930s and 1940s', in *Remembering for the Future,* vol. 1. Oxford: Pergamon Press.

Keogh, Dermot.1998. *Jews in Twentieth Century Ireland: Refugees, Anti-Semitism and the Holocaust.* Cork: Cork University Press.

Kushner, Tony. 1989. *The Persistence of Prejudice.* Manchester: Manchester University Press.

Kushner, Tony. 1990. 'The Impact of British Anti-Semitism 1918-1945', in David Cesarani (ed.) *The Making of Modern Anglo-Jewry.* Oxford: Basil Blackwell.

Livshin, Rosalyn. 1990. 'The Acculturation of Immigrant Jews in Manchester 1980-1930', in David Cesarani (ed.) *The Making of Modern Anglo-Jewry.* Oxford: Basil Blackwell.

London, Louise. 1990. 'Jewish Refugees, Anglo-Jewry and British Government Policy 1930-1940', in David Cesarani (ed.) *The Making of Modern Anglo-Jewry.* Oxford: Basil Blackwell.

Miller, Arthur. 1990. *Timebends.* London: Minerva.

Moore, Gerry. 1981. 'Socio-Economic Aspects of Anti-Semitism in Ireland 1880-1905', *Economic and Social Review,* vol. xii, no. 3.

Moore, Gerry.   1984. 'Anti-Semitism in Ireland 1880-1905.' Unpublished Doctoral thesis, Ulster Polytechnic.

Penapa. 1940-1. National Library of Ireland.

Rich, Adrienne. 1994. 'Split at the Root' and 'Resisting Amnesia', in *Adrienne Rich, Bread, Blood and Poetry.* London: Virago.

Richmond, Colin. 1994. '`Medieval Jewry: Postmodernism and Marginality', *Patterns of Prejudice.* vol. 28 nos. 3-4, pp 5-17.

12.

Othering the Irish (Travellers)

Sinéad ni Shuinéar

Introduction

Othering - denying equal legitimacy to individuals and cultures that do not conform to one's own arbitrary, ever-shifting criteria of normality - is a two-sided coin. On the one hand it creates a clearly defined, undifferentiated 'them' embodying every sort of negativity - including excess of essentially positive traits. On the other, it forges a bond of solidarity between those who reject these aberrations: the fictive homogeneity of a constantly evoked but never defined 'us'. Robbie McVeigh (1996: 33) insulates Traveller/mainstream Irish relations, claiming that 'The colonization of Irish Traveller identity was and is carried out by other Irish people - it cannot be blamed on external, colonial forces'. I disagree. Given a shared history of eight centuries of pervasive colonial experience, no aspect of Irish culture - least of all self-loathing and scapegoating - can claim such insulation. The purpose of this chapter is to demonstrate how popular images of Irish Travellers are merely the most extreme manifestation of an ancient Anglo-Saxon tradition of othering the Irish in general. Forged in England within specific political and historical circumstances, these images, purposefully constructed in the service of hegemony, have come to be accepted as timeless, objective truths, including - selectively - by the Irish themselves, with all the tragic consequences that invariably arise when one group has the power to act out its convictions that another is less legitimate 'Other' than itself.

Culture Shock - A Guide to Customs and Etiquette is a series of British travel guides explaining local realities in some forty-three different countries. It is worth noting that ten of these are EU member states; Canada and Australia are also covered, and the US merits three regional volumes. The fact that there is a market for such explanations within the English-speaking continuum itself challenges smug notions of homogeneity even among peoples sharing a single language, let alone the existence of a 'European' or 'Western' 'us'. Be that as it may, let us turn to the volume on Ireland, which endeared itself to me by opening with a synopsis of an episode of 'Star Trek':

> The USS Enterprise encounters a colony of people who have been abandoned on a far-flung planet for generations. They now need rescuing and are brought aboard as a temporary safety measure. They all have stage Irish accents, wear peasant clothes, sleep alongside their animals, distil their own alcohol and play folk music

on violins. The male members of the community leave all the work to the women, being more concerned with getting inebriated. They have little knowledge of even twentieth century culture, let alone the twenty-fourth, and almost set the ship ablaze by kindling a fire out of sticks on one of the cargo decks. The leading woman is a fiery redhead who berates all men and is characteristically presented with her sleeves rolled up and on her knees washing the floor (Levy 1996: 10).

The author lists the all-too-familiar stock images: the idle, drunken Irish man, the Irish woman as virago, the simple peasant with the gift of the gab, the fighting Mick for whom unprovoked, indiscriminate brawling is a gleeful contact sport. What she doesn't note is the crude evolutionism of the episode title, Up the Long Ladder, a journey upon which these beings at the bottom have yet - four centuries from now! - to embark.

'Star Trek', a series tirelessly promoting cultural relativism in an idealised future, unproblematically portrays the Irish as more alien than Klingons simply by evoking stereotypes forged a millennium before the era of the episode in question. Their formulation was anything but accidental: you cannot invade, massacre, subjugate, exploit and oppress people who have just as much right to live their lives as you do. There has to be a reason for it, you have to be justified, and 'wanting to steal their resources' isn't nearly good enough. Defining them as an active threat, by contrast, makes your actions self-defence, and defining them as benighted savages who are a threat to themselves makes your willingness to pull them up to your own lofty standards downright noble: the White Man's Burden.[1] This is a universal of imperialist ideology, evoked from the genocide of the indigenous peoples of the Americas and Australia to the direct rule of Africa and India; Edward Said's detailed analysis of one of its milder forms, *Orientalism* (1978), came as a sincere shock to an English readership.

English othering of the Irish

The natives are other. They are different from 'us' in every conceivable way, though the emphasis shifts along with historical circumstance: they differ in religion, race, language, age, gender, class, time, and that package deal of behaviour and character traits we call 'culture'. Let us begin by examining English othering of the Irish, bearing in mind how successful the process has been: as Liz Curtis (1984: 45) notes, 'The very word Irish is enough to provoke roars of laughter from television studio audiences, and is used in everyday conversation to describe behaviour that is confusing or illogical'. A paddywaggon transports criminals, especially rioters, into custody; to throw a paddy is to display irrational anger; to take the mickey is to mock; to be beyond the pale is to be outside of civilised norms - 'the Pale' being the area around Dublin under direct English rule (Curtis 1984: 56,10). The first Irish jokebook, *Teagueland Jests and Bog Witticisms*, came out in 1749 (Curtis 1984: 10); two centuries on, Futura sold half a million copies of three 'Official Irish Joke Books' over 1977-79 (Curtis 1984: 8) - a particularly fraught period in Anglo-Irish relations.

The 12th century Anglo-Norman conquest of Ireland was a religious mission undertaken with the blessing of the Pope (Curtis 1984:8), an extra which the 16th century Tudor reconquest and the 17th century Cromwellian genocide, also conceived in terms of religious mission, did without. Protestants see their rejection of Catholicism in terms of philosophical enlightenment and, unsurprisingly, those who fail to see the light as literally backward, their faith mere superstition; the contrast with Ireland, where statues move and the natives go in for sectarian murder, is all the greater now that England is an effectively secular society.

Like any colonists, these new arrivals had a practical interest in local laws, customs and religion - which Edmund Spenser (1596) dubbed Ireland's three 'evils' - and a spate of commentators addressed the demand.[2] Famously, Geraldus Cambrensis (Gerald of Wales) justified the conquest as a civilising venture: 'They live on beasts only, and live like beasts. They have not progressed at all from the habits of pastoral living' (cited in Curtis 1984: 10). A 1589 publication describes a three-tiered native social organisation comprising an aristocracy, professional warriors, and 'the third sort' - obviously the bulk of the population - are 'a very idle people not unlike our English beggars, yet for the most part of pure complexion and good constitution of body' (cited in Harrington 1991: 53). Ireland's pastoralist economy, strongly contrasted to the tillage and burgeoning urbanism of England, is typically portrayed as barbarism with racial overtones:

> ... much like the Tartar hordes, being a number of people some more or less, men, women and children under a chief or head of the name or family, who range about the country with their flocks or herds and all the goods they have in the world, without any settled habitation, building huts wherever they find pasture for their cattle and removing as they find occasion.[3]

From the very beginning, then, backwardness, nomadism and beggary are portrayed as general Irish characteristics, compounded by superstition (later Popery), anarchy, and a penchant for violence. As we have seen, most of these stereotypes still apply on board the starship *Enterprise*; together they form the core of conventional wisdom regarding Irish Travellers today. This timelessness - the 'denial of coevalness' - is in fact the base line of all 'othering': 'they', unlike 'us', exist outside of history.[4]

Allow me to skip over Anglo-Irish relations through the centuries, to the eve of the 19th. In 1799, the year before the Act of Union dissolving the Irish parliament and annexing the nation into the United Kingdom, another English visitor had this to say: 'They are more approximate to the degraded state of a horde of Hottentots... miserably destitute of fear, reason, and often of humanity'.[5] There was nothing new about portraying the Irish as racially other, but the context had changed: unlike the mythically distant Tartars, Irish and Hottentot[6] alike were part of the white man's burden now being manfully shouldered by Britannia, which endeavour in turn gave rise to a cohesive ideology translating English technical and military superiority into natural (and thus both inevitable and divinely sanctioned) phenomena.

Scientific racism

The notion that the human book can be read by its cover - the proverbial weak chin, for example - had been around since Aristotle, but in the wake of Darwin it was systematised and extended to explain every aspect of human existence. The 19th century concept of race was a far more precise tool than the crude skin colour indexing to which it has been reduced today, and was, in fact, two notions: one, that biological inheritance - race - rather than environment or learning determined human behaviour and two, that the physical indicators of this inheritance could be objectively measured and quantified - and as we all know, anything which can be expressed in numbers must be true.[7] By the end of the century the explanatory role of 'race' had been expanded from shared physical and mental traits to 'that force or agency which had shaped the destiny of mankind' (Curtis 1968: 20). Measurement was not limited to slope of brow and length of upper lip: for example Bleddoe, a founder member of the Ethnological Society and later President of the Anthropological Institute, devised an 'index of Negrescence' by which he measured an invisible but decisive factor, 'residual melanin' - the highest concentrations of which were, unsurprisingly, found to be amongst the Irish (Curtis 1968: 19-20). Outside the sober confines of the ivory tower, these notions found less restrained expression, fuelled from the mid-1840s by a tidal wave of desperate immigrants fleeing famine in Ireland and the need to formulate an acceptable explanation for their condition; when violent agitation for land reform in Ireland swelled over the following decades, this irrational truculence - the classic explanation for native resistance - was incorporated into the picture.

Coincidentally with these developments on the scientific and socio-political scene at home, English explorations in darkest Africa were leading to major discoveries regarding the 'primitive' life-forms - primates, human and otherwise - there. The gorilla was identified at the end of the same decade, and by 1860 London Zoo had its first live specimen. This was a long time before Sigourney Weaver got us all misty over them: explorers' accounts of encounters with 'killer gorillas' were best-sellers in Victorian times (Curtis 1997: 121), and the fantasy of 'ape rape' lingered right through to King Kong (Curtis 1997: 171-2). It is no coincidence that London's first gorilla was christened Paddy (Curtis 1997: 101); nor that the caricatures of the day simianised the Irish. Cambridge historian Charles Kingsley, visiting Ireland in 1860, agonised, 'But I am haunted by the human chimpanzees I saw along that hundred miles of horrible country. I don't believe they are our fault, I believe there are not only many more of them than of old, but that they are happier, better and more comfortably fed and lodged under our rule than they ever were. But to see white chimpanzees is dreadful; if they were black, one would not feel it so much, but their skins, except where tanned by exposure, are as white as ours' (cited in Curtis 1968: 84). Two years later a *Punch* article on 'The Missing Link' put it more light-heartedly:

> A gulf certainly does appear to yawn between the gorilla and the Negro. The woods and wilds of Africa do not exhibit an example of any intermediate animal. But... a creature manifestly between the gorilla and the negro is to be met with in some of the lowest districts of London and Liverpool... It comes from Ireland, whence it has contrived to migrate; it belongs, in fact, to a tribe of Irish savages, the lowest species of the Irish Yahoo. When conversing with its kind it talks a sort of gibberish. The somewhat superior ability of the Irish

Yahoo to utter articulate sounds may suffice to prove that it is a development and not, as some imagine, a degeneration of the gorilla.

Under scientific racism, every physical attribute, including age and gender, combined to determine one's place on the evolutionary ladder.[8] Children, even of superior races, were quite literally savages, an earlier stage of development. Boys grew out of this but girls never did. Women were simply inferior men, the weaker sex in need of guidance and protection, not least from their own irrational impulses. Gender-specific characteristics were also attributed to 'races': 'they' are feminine (weak, irrational, driven by emotion) and 'we' are masculine. This makes the 'other' half of each population an awkward anomaly: just as the English woman is a racially superior but nonetheless inferior being, the Irish man is a beast from whom 'we' must gallantly protect the quintessentially female, childlike Irish. In Victorian cartoons it is only the adult male Irish who display apelike features; Hibernia herself is a comely maiden seeking the protection of a stronger - sometimes sisterly, sometimes lecherously male - England.[9]

Irish heterogeneity

The colonial experience is that ALL 'natives' (whatever their pre-colonial status) are disenfranchised. Colonial Irish society was polarised, with class and ethnicity synonymous: an English and Anglo-Irish Ascendancy versus an indigenous Catholic, Irish-speaking peasantry dubbed the 'Wilde Irish', 'mere Irish' or simply 'the common enemy'.[10] The native Irish were peasants and labourers, because there were laws explicitly barring them from power, property and intermarriage; there was no indigenous middle class until the repeal of the Penal Laws[11] in the 19th century, and the Anglo-Irish elite retained a near-monopoly on both the land and the professions until well into the 20th century. Visions of essentially homogeneous Irishness played a crucial role in the struggle for independence, and post-colonially the myth of internal Irish classlessness is still being used to paper over the chasm between the interests of the wealthy and those of the bulk of the population.

But this shared myth of Irish homogeneity does not stand up to scrutiny. There is, for starters, the linguistic divide: on the eve of the Famine, Irish ('a sort of gibberish') was spoken by some four million Irish people; within a decade, death and emigration had reduced this to one quarter of the population (Ó Tuathaigh 1990: 157). Irish is itself subdivided into quite separate dialects, as is the Hiberno-English, now spoken by most of the population: the notion of 'an Irish accent' (aka 'the brogue'), while taken for granted outside of Ireland, is as much an absurdity in Ireland itself as that of a - singular - English or American accent would be to those who make this assertion. We shall return to this theme: that Irish people are more gifted (or cunning) in their use of language than the English is the one stereotype on which the two agree.

Other obvious divides within Irish society are urban/rural, waged/self-employed, class divisions within the colonising Protestant population, and often minutely regional specificities.[12] All of these were invisible to the English eye, just as the English ear does not perceive the various accents of Hiberno-English. Given that the entire population comprised 'horrible' 'human chimpanzees' who had not 'progressed' from nomadism, 'idle, dissolute, violent, intemperate, dirty, garrulous and emotionally unstable',[13] commentators literally could not see the trees for the wood. Irish history has been written in the English language in the service of English policy, by the English themselves or, worse again, by the Ascendancy - bearing in mind that 'The first article in an ascendancy's creed is, and always has been, that the natives are a lesser breed and that anything that is theirs (except their land and their gold) is of little value' (Corkery 1924: 9). It is hardly surprising that we search this history in vain for unambiguous reference to an indigenous nomadic minority with distinctive speech.

'Gypsies' and 'Tinkers'

The patent inferiority of other races did not preclude their being useful objects of study, and in the 19th century anthropology, ethnography and philology became popular fields for gentleman scholars. The first issue of *England's Journal of the Gypsy Lore Society*, July 1888, features a major overview of the 'Early Annals of the Gypsies in England', stating that, though 'The date of the first appearance of Gypsies in England is unknown':

> From the fact of their formerly common occupation as tinkers, it has been conjectured by some that they have inhabited these islands from prehistoric ages. 'Tinkler' and 'Tinker' as proper names can be traced to the thirteenth century at least; but in those days there seem to have been two classes of tinkers, the one sedentary and perhaps equivalent to our modern ironmongers, and the other styled 'wandering tinkers', who were 'the itinerant menders of our pots and pans' (Crofton 1888: 5-6).

I want to draw your attention to the fact that at this point - 1888 - the word 'tinker' clearly means itinerant whitesmith, but conveys 'indigenous British Isles' with no Celtic, and certainly no Irish, overtones, with a very fuzzy demarcation between 'tinker' and 'Gypsy': that same year, for example, the *JGLS* reproduced a hedgehog recipe collected from 'a Gypsy tinker' in Bettws-y-Coed, indicating that Wales had not yet been designated the bastion of Romani purity. The term was also applied outside the British Isles: the *JGLS* published articles on Belgian, Italian and Swiss tinkers,[14] and soon posed the question whether 'tribes of wandering oriental tinkers were not the ancestors of modern Gypsies' (MacRitchie 1890:63) - the Indian origins paradigm had not been established either, nor had the notion of racially exotic Gypsies diametrically opposed to cheap, inferior domestic copies. It took just over a decade for a polarised vision of Travelling People to take shape: by the early 20th century the now-familiar dichotomy of 'genuine Romanies', different in every possible way, racial, linguistic, and cultural Indians, geographically displaced in a time warp, versus Travellers, racially, linguistically and culturally indigenous, albeit with a time warp, was firmly entrenched.[15]

JGLS coverage of 'Irish Tinkers and their Language' began in 1889: 'Although the caste of 'Tinkers' cannot be regarded as identical to that of the Gypsies, yet it is undeniable that the two are closely associated, and that a great number of Gypsies are tinkers... These remarks are necessary as an introduction to a study of the Gypsies of Ireland... the tinker caste in Ireland is certainly Gypsy to some extent' (MacRitchie

1889: 350-1). The bulk of this article consists of sensational allegations of wife-swapping, but offers precious insights into contemporary thinking on Irish Travellers' recently discovered language: 'undoubtedly a form of Gaelic, it is not confined to those districts where Gaelic is still spoken, but is employed by tinkers and tramps throughout the British Islands; of whom it is to be presumed that a great number have never been outside the borders of *England*' (MacRitchie 1889: 354, my italics). MacRitchie also notes that 'until comparatively recent times the Gaelic of Scotland was known to the English-speaking people of Scotland as "Irish"... This detail is noted here in order to emphasise the fact that the "Irish Tinkers" under notice are not confined to Ireland, but belong equally to the "Irish" districts of Scotland - (not to mention other parts of the British Islands where Irish is not a local form of speech)' (MacRitchie 1889: 355 fn).

Within a year all this had changed: now *JGLS* coverage of Irish Tinkers is justified not because of overlap but on the grounds of coincidences 'which link the Celtic to the Romani vagrant... in Ireland, at least, as distinct a caste as our English Gypsies' (Sampson 1890: 204). Suddenly Gypsies are English and Romani in equal measure while Tinkers are not only Celtic, but particularly Irish,[16] with all that this implies in the England of 1890. John Sampson spoils one for choice of illustrative quotes, but the following has to be my favourite.

Often they quarrel among themselves over ill-gotten spoil. Then... they retire to a ruined castle or lonely hillside, and while the men do battle, the women shriek untranslatable defiance at each other... Soon the fray becomes general, in which young and old engage with equal fury, to end not infrequently in the arrest of the whole party, and the restoration of the cause of dispute to its rightful owner' (Sampson 1890:205-6). This quote has everything: ruined castle on lonely hillside as a site for free-for-all brawling over ill-gotten spoils in shrieks of untranslatable gibberish, and the timely intervention of English peacekeepers. How Irish can you get? What's more, the language is no longer a pan-British phenomenon: its mainland version, 'English Shelta', is dismissed as 'Babelonish, model-lodging-house jargon... Scarcely a tithe of the words in daily use by the Irish tinker are intelligible to his English half-breed cousin' (Sampson 1890: 208).[17]

Academic coverage of Traveller language, which crystallised in the last decade of the 19th century, has not moved on since.[18] Given prevailing English opinion on white chimpanzees, 'Shelta' as a scrambled version of their 'gibberish' was instantly adopted as conventional wisdom, despite the fact that those confirming it had no first-hand knowledge of the Irish language. In 1891, however, the great Celtic scholar Kuno Meyer turned his attentions to it. Building on rather than testing the 'scrambled Irish' hypothesis, Meyer claimed that 'Shelta' was very ancient indeed, even devoting some serious consideration to pre-Celtic ('Pictish') origins (Meyer 1891: 246). He has had only one major successor, the archaeologist R. A. Macalister (1937) who anthologised existing material - he collected none and, despite living in Dublin, never heard the language spoken - arguing the case of very recent origins based on the bizarre claim that Shelta comprises entirely random modifications based on how words are spelled rather than how they sound. It is interesting to note that Macalister, much prone to theorising on specialist topics he knew nothing about, and dismissed by Celtic scholars even within his lifetime, remains Holy Writ in Gypsilorist circles, while Meyer, the one qualified Celtic philologist of the lot, is treated as the odd man out. It is also worth noting that Traveller language, like Travellers themselves, has yet to be investigated on its own terms rather than as a 'perversion' (Sampson 1890: 209) of somebody else's.

Academic othering: Irish peasants

We have traced the process whereby the pan-British Tinker was transformed into the outcaste of an outcaste race, denied even the noble savage status of the genuine - English - Romani. Once this was established, Gypsilorist interest waned, and *JGLS* coverage was sparse thereafter. The mainstream Irish were, meanwhile, deemed worthy of study by a small number of ethnographers willing to work in Europe, or rather, to seek out their own past by studying our retarded present. The 20th century saw four seminal studies (three American, one English) of Ireland, all of them undertaken in rural communities on the Western seaboard selected for their isolation and perceived stasis. It is worth noting that all but one of these communities were also Irish-speaking, though the researchers were not; communication in the local language was merely the first of the cardinal rules of ethnographic research to be overlooked in these cases. The first (Arensberg and Kimball 1968), carried out in the 1930s, described Irish country life as stable, satisfying, 'traditional'; in effect it created an idyllic straw man repeatedly trashed by its successors. '[T]he theme of the dying peasant culture of the remote West came to dominate anthropological research', caricaturing 'Ireland as a dying society, a culture in demise, a social system characterised by pathogenic tendencies' (Curtin, Donnan and Wilson 1993: 9). In contrast to the holistic functionalism of the original study, these later authors are monomaniacs: one (Messenger 1983) interprets the whole of Irish culture in terms of sexual repression, another (Brody 1973) as self-loathing and a longing to escape to the more normal lifestyle of England, and the third, under the inspired title of *Saints, Scholars and Schizophrenics* (Scheper-Hughes 1982), sees the Irish as - literally - insane.

This last is worth looking at, not only because it is the most recent but also because it struck such a chord in its Anglo-Saxon audience that it won the prestigious Margaret Mead award for anthropological excellence. I think we should be wary when a writer introduces her work with the claim that ethnography 'should not leave the native reader cold and perplexed. *Angry and hurt*, perhaps, but not confused and perplexed' (Scheper-Hughes 1982: viii, my italics), and when the preface to the second edition triumphantly lists manifestations of Irish anger and hurt at the first edition as proof that she has struck some nerve of truth. Getting this truth was, we are told, no simple task: 'Yes,' she tells us, 'the Irish lie, and lie they do with admirable touches of wit and ingenuity' (Scheper-Hughes 1982: 11) - a line echoed years later by Isabel Fonseca as 'Gypsies lie. They lie a lot - more often and more inventively than other people' (Fonseca 1995:15). This is not plagiarism; it is simple Othering. They say the same things because they view their subjects with identical contempt. In essence, both are saying, 'I do not understand these people, so my incomprehension must be due to their malice rather than my ineptitude'.

As for lying: Scheper-Hughes, who unblushingly admits her complete lack of training in psychiatry (1982: 74) and her inability to communicate with her subjects in their own language (1982: 60), does not hesitate to formulate sweeping analyses at the deepest level, in which the concept of *dutcas* ('breeding'), illustrated with many disturbing direct quotes, is identified as crucial (Scheper-Hughes 1982: 168-70). For example, a mother explains her children's unruliness as 'They're too full of their father's dutcas'; the author adds that 'whole family trees often become characterised by a single dutcas'. There's just one little problem. There is no such word as dutcas in any dialect of the Irish language, so the author cannot have heard it or any of the alleged quotations in which it figures: the word is *dúchas*. The only possible explanation is that she found it in a dictionary and, being unfamiliar with the Irish alphabet, mis-transcribed it and used it as the basis for an elaborate theory backed by imaginary folk usages.[19]

This particular example hinges on demonstrable lying rather than - as is more common - merely biased representation. Yet Scheper-Hughes herself, in her introduction, calls the Irish supremely literate; she knew very well that her book would be widely read within the broad community it purports to describe. The Irish, who speak and are able to read Scheper-Hughes' language, were indeed acutely aware of her work, and expressed their outrage through the full range of academic and mass media channels; their protests were dismissed (or even perversely flaunted as proof she'd hit a nerve) and she got the Margaret Mead prize. What, then, of peoples who do not speak the ethnographer's language or cannot read what has been written about them, and who lack academic, diplomatic and mass media channels of their own? What is to prevent the ethnographer from indulging their wildest fantasies in portrayal of the exotic other?

Academic othering: Irish tinkers

The first ethnographic portrait of Irish Travellers to reach an international readership did just this. Written in 1975 by an American, Bettina Barnes, who endeavours to camouflage her complete lack of training by the (mis)use of anthropological jargon. For example, 'my father's brother' - a blood relationship - is described as 'affinal' (Barnes 1975: 237), and surnames become 'patronyms' (Barnes 1975: 238). Her assertions are reminiscent of Sampson's exoticising sensationalism: she reports 'a ritual consisting of mock rape where every female down to the age of five years was roughed up by a male and pretended to scream' (Barnes 1975: 245). Not to worry, 'children born out of wedlock, or as products of incestuous unions (of which there is some evidence) are given equal footing' (Barnes 1975: 242).[20] In fact there are simply no words to convey how repugnant the notion of sex outside of marriage is to Irish Travellers, and these fantasies go beyond distortion to calculated insult.

George Gmelch's *The Irish Tinkers. The Urbanization of an Itinerant People* (1985), written a few years later, combines the 'dying rural tradition' model with the established image of the Untermensch 'tinker' in a political context of fervent assimilationism.[21] Gmelch's non-Traveller contacts (whom he calls 'middle-class Irish' - Gmelch 1985: 190 - to avoid any hint of ethnic division) were the leading lights of the settlement movement (his list of personal thanks - Gmelch 1985: xi - is a who's who and includes Patricia McCarthy and Bettina Barnes, both cited here), which had been under way for a decade and a half and evolved a coherent view of 'the problem' and how to solve 'it'.[22]

Fundamental to this view was the notion that, while 'itinerants' had once had a viable rural lifestyle, modernisation made their skills redundant, and they must now (with our help) make major adjustments. Just as the most truly representative non-Traveller Irish were deemed to dwell in isolated rural communities on the Western seaboard, the most truly representative Travellers were demoralised urban shanty-dwellers. I want to point out that the settlement movement, and under its tuition Gmelch, disclaimed any connection between economically successful Travellers (dubbed 'mobile traders') and tinkers or itinerants; only pathetic incompetents qualified. Gmelch therefore sought out and found the 1970s equivalents of Leland's 'eccentric and miserable fellows',[23] and, sitting 'on urine-soaked mattresses trying my best to seem indifferent to the odor of unwashed bodies and the filth of the surroundings' (Gmelch 1985: 184),[24] he observed a miserable other he repeatedly compares to a range of Untermenschen in his own homeland, including 'Appalachian mountaineers' (1985: 88), 'Kentucky hillbillies' (1985: 89), 'lower-class [Black] ghetto families' (1985: 122), 'migrant labor camps' (1985: 100) and 'North American Indians' (1985: 88, 104, 121),[25] but never, of course, to 'real' Gypsies.[26] Theirs, he tells us, is an 'atomistic' society (Gmelch 1985: 91) where 'strong social contacts are absent' (Gmelch 1985: 99) and 'one half of most families' income [is] ' spent on alcohol' (Gmelch 1985: 104).[27] Quoting the same Sampson text I cited earlier as proof of a tradition of wife-swapping, Gmelch asserts that Travellers 'often want more children in order to increase their [social welfare] benefits' (Gmelch 1985: 81) and dump them as soon as this function ceases: 'The fact that adolescents over sixteen do not qualify as dependants for the purpose of state welfare benefits contributes to parents' desire to have them marry' (Gmelch 1985: 99). Gmelch's descriptions of Traveller marriage include that of 'a forty-two-year-old widower to his fourteen-year-old daughter' (Gmelch 1985: 131) - a total impossibility as father-daughter marriage is explicitly prohibited by both church and state, and is inexpressibly abhorrent to Travellers themselves. In fact, the incest taboo is the one human universal; that no one challenged Barnes's or Gmelch's assertions that Travellers do not observe it is eloquent proof that they are indeed defined as supremely and absolutely 'other'.[28]

Irish othering of Irish Travellers

I conclude this chapter by illustrating exactly how English 'othering' of the Irish has never been confronted or refuted by the Irish themselves, but simply transferred to the Traveller population. This brings us back to familiar themes of race, culture, gender and all the rest, albeit in contemporary guise. The inherited insistence on Traveller non-Romaniness defines them as utterly Irish, but leaves the Irish themselves to grapple with the question of why, if they are of us, are they not identical to us?[29] The conventional answer is that Travellers are the descendants of those victims of colonial policy - famine, evictions, land clearances - who (unlike 'us') stayed down when they were pushed down, and ceased to experience history.[30] Travellers are essentially Irish peasants in a timewarp, a concept lyrically expressed by Patricia McCarthy in her seminal 1971 thesis:[31] 'It appeared in many ways as if the folkways of the travellers had been frozen at some point around the end of the last century... Most of the folkways of the present-day travellers can be found in accounts of the rural Irish... with certain pragmatic adaptations to suit the travelling life and its extreme poverty... The donkey, the pony and cart, the barefoot children, the dress of the women, the squalid living conditions, all have a negative value now for Irish people because of their association with poverty' (McCarthy 1971: 13). She goes on to tackle 'confusion between travellers and gypsies': 'The latter, according to the available evidence, constitute a separate ethnic group with a separate 'secret' culture... In the case of the gypsies, nomadism is an essential part of a total culture and should not be interpreted merely in terms of comparison with the settled life...' (McCarthy 1971: 12-13). By contrast: 'It is a basic assumption of this study that Irish travellers are not gypsies and do not constitute a separate ethnic group... Poverty is considered to be basic to the problem of itinerancy...' (McCarthy 1971: 6). The problematic - intolerable - nature of 'itinerancy' is the pragmatic reason why the line between legitimate Romanies and peasants in a timewarp must never be blurred: 'The danger of a highly romanticised view of the itinerant life is that it may well lead to a justification for doing nothing' (McCarthy 1971: 13). They cannot be Gypsies, because if they were, they would have a right to be different; this way, we have not only the right but the duty to intervene.

Back to *Culture Shock: Ireland*, where coverage of Travellers (Levy 1996: 206-9) is accompanied by a photograph of a new trailer with the caption, 'Have satellite dish, will travel'. This is supposed to be an amusing, ironic or even absurd juxtaposition of an archaic lifestyle with contemporary trimmings that ill become it. The accompanying text is the usual regurgitation of Gmelch plus settlement propaganda, including disavowal of any connection with 'Romany Gypsies' - the first item on every agenda.

Age and gender othering are very much on the agenda, too. Not only are Travellers essentially children requiring remedial socialisation - a 1981 report recommended 'a community care worker or dedicated volunteer per family who could call very regularly and help with budgeting, planning of menus, cooking lessons, child care, basic hygiene and practical advice' (ATTP 25:3) - but, since the adults are basically lost causes, effort is channelled into 'educating' Traveller children. This led one Dublin social worker (Phibbs 1986) to write a paper entitled 'The Adult Traveller - An Unknown Species' (significant word choice) and Canadian anthropologist Jane Helleiner to write on 'The discourse and politics of Traveller childhood in Ireland' (1998).

The net has since broadened to include Traveller women, now seen alongside children as victims of Traveller men. As a 1979 report puts it:

The father's role has been diminishing over the past twenty-five years. As late as the middle 1950s the travelling man could still do a bit of work, tinsmithing, harvesting etc. as his father had done before him. That work decreased and finally disappeared... The wife and mother has the responsibility for the maintenance of the family... if they cry during the night she must attend to them... at the same time receiving abuse from her spouse at her ineptitude as a mother. It is ineptitude he feels that has caused the baby to be fretful, nothing else... as they live in a society where physical force is often used to get one's way or settle differences, it will be the physically strong spouse who will be dominant (ATTP 21: 15).

Or, more succinctly a couple of years later, 'Men are not useful as family builders and are very often a bad influence on their children' (ATTP 23: 5). In other words, men are a write-off. The Traveller Women's Forum, a nationwide organisation, has no male-oriented equivalent. Moreover, the supposedly gender-neutral local Traveller support groups are essentially female, not only in their personnel but also in their activities: assertiveness, healthcare and crafts training for women, homework and youth clubs for children, neither training nor recreation for adult men. Domestic violence - Traveller men's abuse of Traveller women - and childcare (without which Traveller women cannot attend courses) are recurrent themes in the work of Pavee Point, also supposedly gender neutral.

The Catholic Irish see no incongruity in looking down on Catholic Irish Travellers' religious barbarity, as in this quote from an Irish priest: 'I get the impression that Mass, though a sacred duty, has nothing like the meaning for them it has for even the more deprived settled people... Being emotional and impetuous they will, in the event of serious illness, dash to some priest or nun or holy well...' (ATTP 17: 18-19). Note that although Travellers in search of healing go to (Catholic!) priests and nuns, not witchdoctors, this practice has fallen out of favour with the mainstream population and so is condemned - a neat combination of religious and chronological othering.

The one exception to popular denial of internal Irish class divisions is in relation to Travellers. Never themselves labelled in class terms, Travellers are nonetheless routinely contrasted to 'the middle class', which appears to embrace the whole of the non-Traveller population and is a de facto ethnic label: teachers, for example, are often reminded that Traveller children's needs differ from those of 'middle-class' children.[32] This is, of course, ironic, since Travellers cluster, and attend school, in deprived areas, not affluent ones.[33]

Nearly forty years have passed since Ireland adopted assimilationist policies towards Travellers, yet there are more today - on the roadsides and elsewhere - than ever before. This persistence of difference requires explanation. The 'race' model says that physical and psychological characteristics go together; they are inborn and cannot be changed. The cultural model says that physical and psychological characteristics are separate, and that psychological difference is due to environmental factors - change the factors and eradicate the difference. When people who 'should' change do not, this can only be explained in terms of wilful perversity - or a return to the race model. The latter is in fact what is happening on the ground, as we can see from a glance at 'hard science' studies of Irish Travellers. The first of these, in 1974, measured 'Retarded Brain Growth in Irish Itinerants' (Carroll *et al*, 1974), concluding that Traveller babies' skulls, and the brains inside them, would be bigger if they were better nourished (change the factors and eradicate the difference). Twenty years of unsuccessful assimilationism on, however, the focus had shifted to 'Congenital Anomalies in the Irish Traveller Population' (Barry *et al* 1997) - in other words, they're born that way. Genetics, the late 20th century version of scientific racism, has become an obsession in relation to Irish Travellers, their metabolic disorders due to 'in-breeding' the subject of parliamentary debate as far back as 1993. A propaganda video (Forde 1996) graphically illustrating the alleged dangers of consanguineous marriage is required viewing on compulsory 'marriage preparation courses' for Traveller couples. Everyone - including the Catholic Church, normally opposed to such practices - urges Travellers to seek genetic counselling before marriage.[34] More generally, there is a deep-rooted popular belief that Travellers, like 'Abos' and 'Red Indians', 'go mad' when they have alcohol taken (this also explains much-highlighted Traveller violence as independent of social and political factors). Travellers are thus physiologically othered within the parameters of 'pure Irish' racial status.

As for Traveller culture, those 'frozen folkways' the rest of us have left behind, the checklist is a familiar one: 'idle, dissolute, violent, intemperate, dirty... and emotionally unstable' (Curtis 1968: 23) and, in continuation of that most Irish of othernesses, nomadic. In fact there's just one exception to the wholesale transferral of English stereotypes from the Irish in general to Irish Travellers, and that is in relation to language; while distinctively Traveller language, as was once the Irish it is purportedly scrambled from, is dismissed as gibberish, the mainstream Irish refuse to concede that Travellers have any linguistic skills whatever. Speech therapy remains high on the agenda in Traveller 'education' (Boyce 1995), the first national coordinator for which repeatedly asserted that Traveller parents do not teach their children to talk.[35]

Perennial notions of otherness lie just below the surface. Anti-Irish racism has been tempered in the media. Irish Travellers are a different story and, as in Victorian times, academic expression, outlined above, is mild indeed compared to more popular channels. Anybody can say anything they like about Irish Travellers, including that they shit in people's doorways, with absolute impunity.[36] The assertion that Traveller life is characterised by 'damage without compensation, assault without arrest, theft without prosecution, and murder without remorse. It is a life worse than the life of beasts, for beasts at least are guided by wholesome instinct. Traveller life is without the ennobling intellect of man or the steadying instinct of animals', under the rallying-cry, 'Time to get tough on tinker terror 'culture'' (*Sunday Independent* 28/1/96) was found to be so unremarkable that the civil rights group attempting to have the journalist responsible prosecuted for incitement to hatred was told that it had no case. Two years later, a politician advocating that all Travellers be electronically tagged became the first person in the country to be tried for incitement - and acquitted (all national dailies, 2/3/99).[37]

Conclusion

At this point, I hope I have demonstrated how this came to pass. The process continues. Let us examine the representation of two well-known contemporary young men. The first is Brad Pitt, 'the sexiest man on earth', in the recent film *Snatch* in the role of 'an Irish gypsy boxer'. According to Pearce (1999: 4), it took three hours to get the prosthetics onto his nose and forehead to give him an appropriately simian look - that's longer than it takes to transform Michael Dorn into Worf, everybody's favourite Klingon. When we compare the simianized Brad Pitt to earlier cartoon characterizations of Irishness, we note the continuity. We also note the stark contrast with Francie Barrett, who proudly carried the Irish flag in the opening ceremony at the Atlanta Olympics - a flesh and blood 'Irish gypsy boxer' (see *Ireland* 1998).

The othering of the Irish, forged by the English, should have been confronted and refuted by its victims. Instead we took the lazy way out - transferred the entire package onto Irish Travellers: 'Yes, the stereotypes are all true - but not about us! About *them*!!' There is nothing accidental about 'othering'. It is a sociopolitical manoeuvre forged in historic circumstance. It defines 'us' in terms of who we are not, and creates a sense of fundamental unity overriding internal difference. But we have a choice as to who and what we define ourselves against, and whether we interpret difference as threat, challenge, simple alternative or enrichment. And it's high time we stopped colluding in the perpetuation of these eight-hundred-year-old myths.

References

Acton, Thomas. 1974. *Gypsy Politics and Social Change*. London: Routledge and Kegan Paul.

Arensberg, Conrad M. and Solon T. Kimball. 1968. *Family and Community in Ireland*. Cambridge: Harvard University Press 1968 (first edition 1940).

ATTP (Association of Teachers of Travelling People) *Newsletter*, subsequently renamed Glocklaí, various issues, here listed in order of citation:

ATTP *Newsletter*, no. 38, October 1987, p. 9.

ATTP *Newsletter*, no. 11, July 1975, p. 13.

ATTP *Newsletter*, no. 17, October 1977, pp. 18-19.

ATTP *Newsletter*, no. 21, May 1979, p. 15.

ATTP *Newsletter*, no. 23, January 1981, p. 5.

Barnes, Bettina. 1975. 'Irish Travelling People,' in F. Rehfisch (ed.) *Gypsies, Tinkers and Other Travellers*. London: Academic Press, pp. 231-55.

Barry, J. and P. Kirke. 1997. 'Congenital Anomalies in the Irish Traveller Population' *Irish Medical Journal*, vol. 90, no.. 6, October 1997. Abstract taken from http://www.imj.ie.issue05/papercongenital.htm

Boyce, Sara. 1995. 'Speech and Language Therapy and Traveller Children: Barriers to Service Delivery', *Glocklaí*, no. 3/4, 1995, pp. 26-7.

Brody, Hugh. 1973. *Inishkillane: Change and Decline in the West of Ireland*. London: Pelican.

Carroll, L., T. Coll, D. Underhill and B. McNicholl. 1974. 'Retarded Brain Growth in Irish Itinerants'. *Journal of the Irish Medical Association*, 67 (2), 1974.

Corkery, Daniel. 1977. *The Hidden Ireland. A Study of Gaelic Munster in the Eighteenth Century*. Dublin: Gill and Macmillan (first edition 1924).

Crofton, H. T., 1888. 'Early Annals of the Gypsies in England', *Journal of the Gypsy Lore Society*, Vol. I No, 1 July 1888, pp 5-24.

Curtin, Chris, Hastings Donnan and Thomas M. Wilson (eds.) 1993. *Irish Urban Cultures*. Belfast: Institute of Irish Studies.

Curtis, L. Perry Jr. 1968. *Anglo-Saxons and Celts. A Study of Anti-Irish Prejudice in Victorian England*. Connecticut : University of Bridgeport.

Curtis, L. Perry Jr. 1997. *Apes and Angels. The Irishman in Victorian Caricature*. Washington and London: Smithsonian Institute Press.

Curtis, Liz. 1984. *Nothing But the Same Old Story: The Roots of Anti-Irish Racism*. London: Information on Ireland.

Dineen, Rev. Patrick S. 1927. *Foclóir Gaedhilge agus Béarla*. Dublin: The Educational Company of Ireland.

Dwyer, Sr. Colette. 1975. 'Report on Educational Provision for and Needs of Travelling Children', submitted by the National Coordinator for the Education of Travelling People, Sister Colette Dwyer', reproduced in ATTP *Newsletter*, no. 11, pp 11-17.

Evans, E. Estyn. 1957. *Irish Folk Ways*. London: Routledge and Kegan Paul.

Fabian, Johannes. 1983. *Time and the Other. How Anthropology Makes its Object*. New York: Colombia University Press.

Fonseca, Isabel. 1995. *Bury Me Standing: The Gypsies and their Journey*. New York: Vintage Books.

Forde, Mary 1996. *Partnerships for Health*, Health Promotion Unit, Department of Health, and the Dioceses of Clonfert, Galway, Tuam and Elphin and Travellers' Health Research, Galway County Council.

Glocklaí. 1995. No. 3/4 November 1995, p. 8.

Gmelch, George. 1985 [1977]. *The Irish Tinkers. The Urbanization of an Itinerant People*. Prospect Heights: Waveland Press.

Gould, Stephen J. 1981. *Mismeasure of Man*. London: WW Norton and Co.

Griffin, Dr. Christopher. 1999. 'Pollution Concepts and Purity Practices Among Irish Travellers: The Outcasts of Ireland and Britain'. Unpublished paper presented to the 86th Indian Science Congress, Chennai, January 1999.

Hancock, Ian. 1998. 'The Struggle for the Control of Identity', *RPP Reporter*, Vol. 1, No. 1, May 1998; taken from the website of the Open Society Institute, Budapest: <http://www.osi.hu/rpp/perspectives1f.htm>

Harrington, John P. 1991. *The English Traveller in Ireland: Accounts of Ireland and the Irish through five centuries*. Dublin: Wolfhound Press.

Helleiner, Jane 1998. 'Contested Childhood: The discourse and politics of Traveller childhood in Ireland' in: *Childhood*, Vol. 5 No. 3: 303-32.

Ireland 1998. 'Francis Barrett, Boxing Clever', December 1998/January 1999. Issue 60. Dublin: Film Base

JGLS (Journal of the Gypsy Lore Society), *Liverpool - various issues 1888-1907*.

Lalor, Brian. 1997. *The Laugh of Lost Men: An Irish Journey*. London: Mainstream Publishing.

Leland, Charles Godfrey. 1881. *The Gypsies, Boston* (this section republished *JGLS* vol. 1 series 2, vol. 2, October 1907, pp. 168-80 under the title 'Tinkers and their Talk').

Levy, Patricia. 1996. *Culture Shock - A Guide to Customs and Etiquett. Ireland*. London: Kuperard.

Mac Laughlin, Jim. 1995. *Travellers and Ireland: Whose Country? Whose History?* Cork: Cork University Press.

Macalister, R.A. Stewart. 1937. *The Secret Languages of Ireland*. (Partly based upon the Collections and Manuscripts of the late John Sampson). Cambridge University Press, facsimile edition Armagh, Craobh Rua Books, 1996.

MacRitchie, David. 1889. 'Irish Tinkers and their Language' *JGLS*, vol. II, no. 6, October 1889, pp. 350-7.

MacRitchie, David. 1890. 'Notes and Queries', *JGLS*, Vol. II, No. 1, January 1890, p .7.

McCann, May, Seamus O'Siochain and Joseph Ruane (eds.) 1994. *Irish Travellers: Culture and Ethnicity*. Belfast: Institute of Irish Studies.

McCarthy, Patricia. 1971. 'Itinerancy and Poverty: A Study in the Sub-culture of Poverty'. Unpublished Master's Thesis, Dublin 1971.

McCarthy, Patricia. 1994. 'The Subculture of Poverty Reconsidered' in McCann *et al*, (eds.) 1994. *Irish Travellers: Culture and Ethnicity*. Belfast: Institute of Irish Studies, pp. 121-29.

McVeigh, Robbie. 1996. *The Racialization of Irishness*. Belfast: Centre for Research and Documentation.

Messenger, John. 1983. *Inis Beag, Island of Ireland*. Holt Rinehart and Winston (first edition 1969).

Meyer, Kuno. 1891. 'On the Irish Origin and Age of Shelta', *JGLS*, vol. II, no. 5, January 1891, pp. 241-46.

ní Shuinéar, Sinéad 1994. 'Irish Travellers, Ethnicity and the Origins Question', in McCann *et al* (eds.) 1994. *Irish Travellers: Culture and Ethnicity*, Belfast: Institute of Irish Studies. pp. 54-77.

ní Shuinéar, Sinéad. 1997. 'Why do Gaujos hate Gypsies so much anyway?' in T. Acton (ed.) *Gypsy Politics and Traveller Identity*. University of Hertfordshire Press, pp. 26-53.

ní Shuinéar, Sinéad. 1999. 'Solving itinerancy: Thirty-five years of Irish government commissions', *Europaea, Journal of the Europeanists* 1999 V-1. http://www.unica.it/europaea/1999v1.html.

ní Shuinéar, Sinéad. (forthcoming) 'The Curious Case of Shelta' in Ó Baoill, Donal, and J. Kirk (eds.) *Anthology on Irish Traveller Language*. Belfast: Institute of Irish Studies.

Now: The Voice of Women in Britain, (weekly magazine). 1 December 1999, pp. 4-5.

Ó Tuathaigh, Gearóid. 1990 [1972]. *Ireland before the Famine 1798-1848*. Dublin: Gill and Macmillan.

Parish of the Travelling People, Dublin. 1993. 'Discussion document on Travellers and consanguineous marriage submitted to the Bishops' Conference meeting in October'.

Pearce, Garth. 1999. 'Brad becomes an EastEnder'. *Now: The Smarter Women's Weekly*. London 1/12/99: 4-5.

Phibbs, Anto. 1986. 'The Adult Traveller - An Unknown Species'. Privately circulated.

Government of Ireland. 1963. *Report of the Commission on Itinerancy*. Dublin: The Stationery Office.

Said, Edward W. 1978. *Orientalism*. New York: Random House.

Sampson, John. 1890. 'Tinkers and Their Talk'. *Journal of the Gypsy Lore Society*, vol. II, no. 4 October 1890, pp. 204-21.

Scheper-Hughes, Nancy. 1982. *Saints, Scholars and Schizophrenics*. London: University of California Press.

13.

Questioning Irish anti-racism

Marian Tannam

Introduction

There has been very little empirical research or theorisation of anti-racism within the Irish context. This contrasts with the growing literature on Irish racism at individual, institutional, cultural and theoretical levels (Boucher, 1998; Fitzgerald, 1992; Hainsworth, 1998; Harmony, 1990; Lentin, 1998, 1999, 2000; McVeigh, 1996, 1998; Mac Gréil, 1980; Tannam, 1999, 1992). The analysis of racism in Ireland has leaned towards a differentialist approach. The dichotomy of 'black-white' that has sometimes occurred in Britain and the USA (Mac an Ghaill, 1999) has been avoided in Ireland principally through the central role that Traveller-led organisations have played in Irish anti-racism. This had the consequence of widening the understanding of racism beyond an analysis based on phenotype to encompass ethnicity and situating the 'new politics of cultural difference' in the debate. Emerging anti-racism initially also responded in a differentialist way.

Despite the emergence of a huge variety of anti-racist groups, partnerships and government initiatives over the past five years, however, the main thrust of anti-racism has been from an essentialist and reductionist model, especially in terms of recognition of, and engagement with emerging anti-racist and solidarity groups. The first part of my analysis provides an historical perspective of the emergence of anti-racisms in Ireland. The second part explores the question of whether there is a space for the merging of these anti-racisms. This questions whether this space - assuming it exists at all - can provide representation, recognition, respect, solidarity and equality for the multiplicity and plurality of activists, initiatives, groups and individuals who are contributing or have the potential to contribute to the larger framework of anti-racism.

Irish anti-racism (and racism) is in a period of transition; in many ways the building blocks of anti-racism are being laid. It is important that the foundation is a landscape that allows both rootedness and shifting (Yuval Davis, 1997: 130). We can learn from the experience of other countries and perhaps avoid the 'crisis' in anti-racism that has taken place in other situations. As well as engaging in debates as to which is the most strategic anti-racism to implement (universalism versus differentialism; recognition versus redistribution, or a combination of all of these), we need to ensure that all anti-racism movements and initiatives are built on egalitarian principles which give political voice to those most affected by racism. One of the challenges for Irish anti-racism will be to ensure that its alliances do not unconsciously mirror the structures and conditions which (re)produce inequalities in society. It must recognise and address the fact that its participants are at differing levels of ability and resources:

> For anti-racism to be taken to a new level that recognises the need for the empowerment of minority ethnic groups but does not create a separatist politics, new forms of agency must be conceptualised that operate horizontally as well as vertically, amongst agents as well as between agents and institutions (Lentin, A 1997: 12).

My involvement in and knowledge of anti-racism comes from a number of perspectives: being part of an intercultural family in Ireland for over twenty years; being a founder member of 'Harmony' and subsequently being a member of various anti-racist committees and initiatives; my studies and research in communications and equality studies which have concentrated on anti-racism and in more recent years my work as an anti-racism trainer. As such my involvement includes the familial, activist, academic, researcher and trainer. However, it has been my experience of parenting a child of dual cultural heritage in Ireland that has led me to question and challenge racism at personal and societal levels and to try and link theory and practice in effecting change. In this chapter I use the terms 'Black' and 'White' throughout in the political construct sense and not in any way denying the multiple and shifting identities found in each of these categories.

My personal and political experience connects with a changing context for anti-racism in Ireland. There is a range of activity and activism around international events like the European Week against Racism and the International Day Against Racism. Moreover, for the first time there is substantial state funding and support for this kind of activity, north and south. At this level it is clear that anti-racism has arrived in Ireland. On one level this is no more than recognition of the widespread problem of racism. It confirms the need to question Irish racism. But there is also a need to interrogate the efficacy of the different initiatives against racism in Ireland - especially since these have begun to shift from their base in the community sector to a new position within the state. There is no more apposite time for questioning anti-racism.

The emergence of anti-racism in Ireland

Anti-racism initially emerged within the voluntary/community sector in Ireland.[1] The concept of ethnic mobilisation within this sector against racism is an integral aspect of anti-racism.[2] Harmony, founded in 1986, was the first specifically anti-racist organisation in Ireland. Prior to this a number of individuals had identified the need for a legislative framework through which to challenge racism. In 1971, Sean McBride commented that the failure to act and to become involved in the world struggle against racism 'puts in question our sincerity when we profess loudly our attachment to the ideals of human liberty' (Kirby, 1981).

Michéal Mac Gréil (1980) called for a 'Minorities Rights Act' and said his research findings showed evidence of 'the existence of a moderate degree of anti-Semitic prejudice in Dublin' and 'the relatively severe degree of (latent) racial prejudice'. He went on to point out that:

> There seems to be a small but significant percentage of 'hard core' racialists among the respondents. The willingness to discriminate against racial minorities in respect of living accommodation and immigration/migration by more than a quarter of the respondents is sufficient warning to merit legislative protection for a potential future racial minority and for those of Black or Coloured appearance already resident in Ireland (Mac Gréil, 1980).

In 1980 Kadar Asmal (then of the Irish Anti-Apartheid Movement, now a government minister in South Africa) stated:

> One significant way in which illegitimate racist practices can be controlled or restricted is by legislation. This can be done by translating into national legislation some of the most impressive treaties adopted by the international community in recent years (Asmal in Tannam, 1991: 23).

Ireland had signed the UN International Convention on the Elimination of All Forms of Racial Discrimination in 1968, yet it took thirty years for the necessary domestic legislation needed to ratify this convention to be enacted. McVeigh points to the need for legislation: 'Anti-racism must be supported by strong and effective legislation. While legislation is never a panacea, it makes it clear that racism is no longer sanctioned by the state' (McVeigh, 1996: 44).

As the Irish state prevaricated on the need for any effective anti-racist infrastructure, the community sector began to develop its own notion of anti-racism in Ireland. Representatives of Comhlamh, APSO, NCDE (National Committee for Development Education), Harmony and some development aid organisations came together in the mid-eighties in the Anti-Racism Coalition and this was the first alliance of this nature. Individuals and groups active in early anti-racism operated mainly in isolation and without a legislative framework. Today partnerships and alliances provide the potential for solidarity in anti-racism work and the long awaited and campaigned for legislative framework is in place. Comhlamh has continued to provide grassroots support and solidarity to refugees and asylum-seekers and in 2000 set up the Le Chéile - Artists Against Racism - project.

Motivation for the majority of the people who became involved in anti-racism came from broader-based human rights activity and community development work. The late John O'Connell spoke of how Pavee Point (formerly the Dublin Travellers Education and Development Group) began:

> We started in '83/'84 and began to meet a group of individuals, some of whom had involvement with Travellers. I had involvement in justice and peace issues and human rights issues and came in contact with some people who had worked directly with Travellers and we began to talk to Travellers. We were critical of the prevailing approach of voluntary organisations as well as statutory in

responding to Travellers and we were coming from a different perspective, that perspective did contain within it an explicit anti-racist dimension.

The founding of Harmony was less theorized - it was a direct result of the personal experiences of members of intercultural families who came together both for mutual support and in order to campaign for the introduction of comprehensive anti-racist legislation. Harmony's management committee was always a partnership of members of minority and majority ethnic groups. This reflected the more personal partnerships of many of its members who were in inter-cultural marriages and relationships. Harmony provided a forum for people who had experienced racism themselves, or whose family members had experienced racism, to meet and support each other. One of Harmony's strengths was the informal network of support that has built up between members over the years. Harmony was dissolved in early 1999. The dissolution of Harmony could be attributed to a number of factors - burnout on behalf of committee members; never having made the transition to an organisation with employed staff - this was partly due to a lack of recognition in the early years of the need for an intercultural or anti-racist organisation of this nature; lack of funding; lack of organisational development; too ambitious a range of activities - from multi-cultural to anti-racist. It has not been replaced by any obvious successor providing a space for intercultural families in Ireland and the increasing number of bi-racial Irish people. For all its limitations, Harmony was a key player in putting racism/anti-racism on the Irish agenda and provided support, solidarity and built up a degree of expertise and knowledge in this area.

Harmony was followed by a number of other organisations working on racism outside the Traveller community. (There was, of course, a huge amount of Traveller-specific anti-racist work taking place in parallel). These groups and developments, particularly in the past few years, widened the base of anti-racism work and provided a framework of support. These developments included:

The coming together of development education, aid organisations and anti-racist groups in the mid-1980s as the Anti-Racist Coalition, which focused particularly on policy and practice and the stereotypical images used in development aid campaigns. This group is no longer in existence but is of importance both in its work and in the fact that it was the first structured bringing together of organisations working in anti-racism.

The All Different/All Equal Youth Campaign against Racism, Xenophobia, Antisemitism and Intolerance launched in 1994 and part of a European campaign which was facilitated by the National Youth Council of Ireland in conjunction with DEFY (Development Education for Youth Project).

The establishment of the Platform Against Racism in 1996. The Platform Against Racism is an independent initiative of non-governmental organisations working collectively to highlight and address the issue of racism in the island of Ireland. Founding members were the African Cultural Project; Cities Anti-Racism Project; European Union Migrants Forum; Harmony; Irish Council for the Welfare of Immigrants; Irish Refugee Council; Irish Traveller Movement; Pavee Point;

National Traveller Women's Forum; Northern Ireland Council for Ethnic Minorities. Its aims are:

To enhance our capacity to work collectively to highlight and address racism.

To further develop the commitment and efforts of our individual organisations to eliminate all forms of racism.

To promote the commitment and efforts of our individual organisations to create an intercultural society that values and resources cultural difference and ethnic diversity (Platform Against Racism Pack).

The designation of 1997 as the European Year Against Racism and the establishment of the National Coordinating Committee of the EYAR. The EYAR Framework Programme identified two key aims for the Year in Ireland:

Establishing the profile and purpose of the year with key decision making bodies and the general public.

The development of sustainable policies and strategies to address racism particularly at public policy level.

The establishment of the National Consultative Committee on Racism and Interculturalism (NCCRI). The framework programme of this committee says it will advise the government with regard to racism, develop responses to racism and undertake initiatives, research and reports as appropriate.

The enactment of the Employment Equality Act (1998) and the Equal Status Act (2000) provided a legislative framework and enabled the UN Convention on the Elimination of All Forms of Racism to be ratified.

The establishment of the Equality Authority further enhanced this framework.

At European level a number of developments have strengthened and supported anti-racism work both in Ireland and Europe. These include:

The 1985 Evrigenis and 1991 Ford Reports.

The 1995 Report of the EU Consultative Commission on Racism and Xenophobia (Kahn Commission)

The designation of 1997 as the European Year Against Racism.

The insertion of an anti-discrimination clause (Article 13) in the Amsterdam Treaty.

The establishment of a European Monitoring Centre on Racism and Xenophobia and its development of a European Information Network on Racism and Xenophobia (RAXEN).

The 1998 Commission 'Action Plan Against Racism'.

The establishment of a European Network Against Racism.

It can be seen from the above that the voluntary/community sector has played a central role in anti-racism in Ireland. Alliances and partnerships have been formed over the years. The European Year Against Racism was in many ways a catalyst for anti-racism in Ireland. With the establishment of a National Committee of the EYAR which was a partnership of government, statutory and voluntary representatives, anti-racism was for the first time moved out of the voluntary and community arena.

Minority ethnic mobilisation

Drury defines ethnic mobilisation as:

> a process in which members of an ethnic group, in specific and relevant situations: first, develop heightened levels of group consciousness *vis-à-vis* other groups; second, employ cultural criteria or other symbols of their unity (including religion and phenotype) to sharpen the boundaries between themselves and others; third, prepare, organise and consolidate their resources in order to take action and fourth, take action, usually of a political kind, in order to defend, promote and/or create collective as opposed to individual goals (Drury 1994: 15).

Taking the first point of heightened levels of group consciousness, we see that Travellers have been identified and identified themselves as a distinct ethnic group. (Travellers also appear to have filled the criteria of points two, three and four more than other minority ethnic groups in Ireland). Not surprisingly therefore, Travellers generated some of the most focused work around discrimination and racism. The earliest example of an autonomous, rights-based minority ethnic group was that of *Minceir Misli*, an all-Traveller group that operated for a few years in the 1980s.

> They adopted the tactics of direct action. They fasted publicly, they invaded the County Council office, they organised marches, they pursued alliances with Third World groups and they achieved a high media profile (Crowley, n.d.: 8).

The long-established Irish Jewish community also has a *group consciousness* of itself that encompasses both Jewishness and Irishness. A number of young Jewish people spoke to Katie Donovan (1998) about being Irish and Jewish:

> 'I belong here. My family has been here for over 100 years', David Woolfson (30) is speaking about his sense of Irishness. 'I don't belong to a mainstream identity but there is an other, different identity that is Irish too'... 'We're Irish but even more so, we're Irish Jews', is how Judy Davis (28) puts it (Donovan, 1998: 13).[3]

Perhaps because there have not been large numbers of members of specific minority ethnic groups present in Ireland until the 1990s, this heightened awareness of group consciousness has arguably only begun to develop over the past few years. It could be suggested that there is a minority ethnic *group consciousness* of itself as 'other' which has come about as result of the negative reaction to their presence in Irish society. The establishment of groups such as the Association of Asylum-seekers and Refugees in Ireland (ARASI), the Pan African Organisation and the African Refugee Network are examples of ethnic mobilisation (albeit encompassing members from many ethnic groups) initiated from within minority ethnic groups themselves. Drury refers to this heightened level of consciousness of itself as a 'group' *vis-à-vis* other groups - in this case the majority ethnic group.

Smith and Mutwarasibo (2000: 8) point to the 'absence of specifically African directed services' in Ireland as the motivating factor for a variety of solidarity and support groups which have emerged and attempted to fill the gaps and facilitate efforts at communal living among Africans from individual countries or Africans in general. Some of these include the Sudanese and Congolese solidarity groups. The Zena Project for Bosnian Women, now defunct, was another example. Smith and Mutwarasibo also found that many of these groups 'find it difficult to sustain themselves beyond the initial crisis or situation that prompted their emergence'.

The establishment of an Islamic centre and mosque shows group consciousness around being Muslim, which spans a number of cultures and ethnicities including Irish. This demonstrates Drury's second point regarding the employment of cultural criteria (including religion) to sharpen the boundaries between themselves and others. Although there has been a consolidation of resources within the Muslim community and the creation of collective as opposed to individual goals, there has not been any great level of political action.

Speaking about the Irish Black and Migrant Women Group, Camilla Dorcey says (personal communication):

> It's a women-only group, we set it up for women only because often the men have other ways of getting things done and women have different problems...We are saying that we are black migrant women. You see the issues that we will be dealing will be to do with Black people who have experienced them.

Dorcey (personal communication) did indicate that white Irish women who are in marriages or relationships with Black men or who have children from such relationships were welcome to become members of IBMW. She went on to give one of the reasons for excluding White Irish women (not in such relationships) and discuss barriers to campaigning and political action:

> We would prefer to have people who are in it because they have first hand experiences. But also some members are working for White Irish families, say a White Irish mistress who is keeping their passport, so we can't be talking about those people who have no right to keep their passports. You see what I mean? We can't have those here. A lot of our members come from different backgrounds where a lot of them wouldn't have campaigned. Some people were at a very high level, like people who had been running their own companies and there were people who had never been to a formal meeting. So it took a long time until some people were at the campaigning level and other people were even afraid to campaign because of what that might bring on themselves or the repercussions that it might bring on their families back where they came from.

Although still in existence, the IBMW group has not been very visible and does not appear to be linked into any anti-racism alliances.[4]

Difficulty in sustaining groups through lack of resourcing and recognition has curtailed the organising, preparing and consolidating resources for action. Political action has been mainly where individual members of minority ethnic groups have joined already established organisations and networks usually set up by committed members of the majority ethnic group. There is some evidence of political action being taken in terms of lobbying government and campaigning, but again this tends to be linked into already established networks. A recent example is the joint hosting of a conference by the Pan African Organisation and the Irish Council for Civil Liberties (27 January 2001). There are a number of groups such as the Indian-Irish society but these are mainly centred around cultural activities and do not have an anti-racism focus. The continuing emergence of groups from within minority ethnic communities has the potential for anti-racism activity. It remains to see what position such groups will adopt in terms of existing anti-racism alliances.

The Irish Association for Minority Ethnic Women, whose membership initially was open only to women who were members of minority ethnic groups but who had strong links with allies from majority ethnic women is an example of a coalition-based group which was very active both at a political and a cultural level. However, within two years, questions around process, timing and constituency plus the pressures of running an under-resourced organisation led to the organisation fragmenting. Rather than viewing this as an entirely negative development, it could be seen as an interesting test case in that attention was being paid to process, an element often missing in anti-racism developments.

There are several reasons why minority ethnic groups (other than Travellers) have not mobilised to a greater extent. Unlike other European countries where there are already established support networks of second-generation minority ethnic groups, migrants to Ireland often experience isolation and exclusion. Coming to terms with living in a new country, in some cases learning a new language, coping with racism or in the case of refugees and asylum-seekers the trauma of their experiences and the uncertainty of their status, migrants often find coping with living difficult enough without having to get organised to join anti-racism campaigns. For others there is a fear of speaking out in case it should bring repercussions either in terms of physical or verbal abuse or in terms of their legal status:

> The things I am saying now, I couldn't have said ten years ago. I wasn't in myself free enough. I remember meeting a lot of black students on the road and saying, 'How are you, how are you getting on, is there any racism?' They said, 'Where have you been, what bush have you been hiding under'. They would tell me that they were too frightened to talk. The fact that people are too frightened to talk, that in itself shows... they were afraid if they talked they would get into trouble. Fear of being deported, fear of losing their residency, fear of losing their flats (Interviewee in Tannam, 1996).

In a society such as Ireland where members of the majority ethnic group rarely see anti-racism as their responsibility and where numbers of minority ethnic group members are small and so far activity in anti-racism from amongst these groups low, the onus of representation tends to fall repeatedly on the same few people. This can result in overexposure, an unrelenting burden of responsibility and a higher public profile than many individuals would wish for.

Majority ethnic mobilisation

Majority ethnic mobilisation may have either an anti-racist or racist perspective. Rex points to policies of assimilationism and exclusion as likely to foster racist mobilisation in the indigenous population (Rex, 1994: 164). Policies of assimilation and exclusion have been applied to Travellers and have proven unacceptable to Travellers and have indeed fostered racist mobilisation in the majority ethnic population. It could be argued that the lack of appropriate policies in relation to refugees and the lack of protection for members of minority ethnic groups in Ireland has fostered racist mobilisation in the indigenous majority settled population.

Debates on refugees have originated from 'moral panic' and 'refugees as a problem' perspectives. This is indicative of the xenophobic attitudes of a people who on the one hand want to keep Ireland for the Irish and on the other expect special treatment for the thousands of Irish who emigrate to the US and other parts of the world. Whilst racism is central to the experience of most asylum-seekers and refugees, this constant juxtaposing of 'racism' and 'refugees' detracts from the nature of racism in Ireland and gives Irish society an excuse not to examine and challenge its racism in the wider and historical contexts. Mac an Ghiall (1999: 113) quotes Hickman as saying that one effect of the dominant anti-racist black-white dualistic model is that it converges with the British state's construction of the problem of immigrants and racism as narrowly constituted and of recent origin. So far anti-racism in Ireland has avoided this dualistic model mainly due to the grounding of anti-racism in Traveller issues that broaden out the analysis to ethnicity and the politics of difference. However, both media and government racist and anti-racist discourses tend to focus on refugees and asylum-seekers. It is crucial that any anti-racism initiatives encompass aspects of racism in Ireland that are historical and acknowledge the experiences of all members of minority ethnic groups in Ireland, whether they are Irish-born, immigrants, resident workers, tourists, business people, asylum-seekers, refugees or Travellers. Secondly anti-racism initiatives must acknowledge that the responsibility for racism in Ireland lies with the majority ethnic population. Majority ethnic Irish people are situated in a privileged position *vis-à-vis* minority ethnic people and they remain in control of the decision-making processes and resulting policies and practices. The National Consultative Committee on Racism and Interculturalism has recommended this approach in its framework for the long-awaited National Anti-racism/Interculturalism Public Awareness Programme (see Lentin, chapter 15 in this volume).

January 1998 saw the epitome of Irish xenophobia as Áine Ní Chonáill launched the Immigration Control Platform. This is an example of the 'racist mobilisation' that John Rex refers to. In her press release (7/1/1998) Ní Chonáill expressed concern about the 'increasing immigration from the EU, particularly Germany and Britain to rural Ireland and ... the influx of asylum-seekers, refugees and illegal immigrants to Ireland'. People of opposing opinion were concerned at the amount of airtime she received. For example, she was interviewed on RTE's 'Late Late Show' - a popular evening entertainment and talk show. The presenter indicated at the start of her interview that the Anti-Nazi League had declined to appear on the show. However there were a number of other anti-racist groups who would have been willing to appear and enter into debate with Ní Chonáill. Whilst a number of individuals and representatives of organisations were invited to be part of the audience, none of them received the uninterrupted airtime that Áine Ní Chonáill was given. The media have a role and responsibility in ensuring that they contribute to balanced coverage (see Guerin, chapter 5 in this volume for a discussion of racism and the Irish media).

With regard to anti-racist mobilisation in the majority ethnic group, the late 1990s saw a myriad of anti-racist initiatives mainly as a direct response to the treatment of asylum-seekers and refugees and the mainly negative press coverage of these issues. Many of these groups have brought a radical as opposed to a reformist perspective to anti-racism - groups such as the Anti-Racist Campaign, the Socialist Workers Party, Anti-Fascist Action and Residents Against Racism have all been vocal in their criticism of government policy and have used strategies of protest and anti-deportation campaigns. These groups have not been linked into the existing anti-racism alliances (spear-headed by the NCCRI) to any degree.

Other initiatives have arisen from a development education or community development perspective. One example of a model of good practice is the Anti-Racism Education Group, which each year runs a course for teachers. From the initial planning of the course to its delivery, members of minority ethnic groups are involved. The course covers racism, interculturalism and anti-racism from a wide based analysis. In 2001 this group was in consultation with the Irish National Teachers Organisation (INTO) with a view to expanding the availability of such courses. The work of this group is funded by the National Committee for Development Education (NCDE), which has been funding grassroots projects and organisations for many years. In response to increased applications for funding of development education with an anti-racist perspective NCDE commissioned a piece of research to assess groups' understanding of what racism and institutionalised racism are in order to ensure that projects are effective in challenging racism. One of the difficulties in the area of development education is that there tends to be a narrow focus on refugees and asylum-seekers and the reasons why they have come to Ireland and a failure to go beyond this to examine racism in the Irish context at institutional and individual levels. This can lead to the misperception that racism is *caused* by refugees and asylum-seekers. I would also suggest that the criteria of the local/global link often fails to recognise that the global is now local. Another example of good practice is the 'whole organisation' approach of the Mahon Community Development Project in Cork which is involving staff, volunteers and management committee in its anti-racism strategies, policy development and training. The National Women's Council of Ireland has been looking at the role of majority ethnic women in combating racism and promoting interculturalism. This is an important initiative that addresses the criticism often justifiably levelled at majority ethnic women of not acknowledging and challenging their own racism.

Another significant initiative has been the establishment of the Gardaí Racial and Intercultural Office at the Gardaí Community Relations section to 'deal with the issues raised by Interculturalism' (Walsh, 2000: 173). As this initiative is in its very early days it remains to be seen if it will experience any constraints through its direct linkage with the Department of Justice, Equality and Law Reform.

Comhlamh continues to be a strong NGO voice and grassroots organisation in solidarity with asylum-seekers and refugees and in challenging racism. The Le Chéile: Together - Artists Against Racism Project, based in the Comhlamh organisation, has brought a new dimension to anti-racism. Robert Ballagh (2001: 22) identifies Le Chéile's two aims - to raise consciousness and raise capital to fund an educational programme to combat racism. Ballagh tells how he and producer Moya Doherty used *Riverdance* as a vehicle to launch the Le Chéile project and raise consciousness and funds. Additionally, throughout the country local initiatives and support groups for asylum-seekers have emerged as a result of the dispersal policy. Many of these groups now form part of the Integrating Ireland Network of support and solidarity groups for asylum-seekers, refugees and immigrants. This nationwide initiative originated with Comhlamh and the Irish Refugee Council. The launch of Comhlamh's *Focus* magazine special issue on challenging racism is a further example of the development education sector engaging with anti-racism.

In the context of this increasing volume of work around racism and anti-racism, anti-racism training has become a buzzword, with many organisations and government departments developing anti-racism sessions. However, this is an area that has not yet been critiqued to any significant extent in the Irish context. It is widely recognised that it is specific in nature and if not carried out by competent people it may actually reinforce stereotypes and discriminatory practices. For any real effectiveness it must take place within a whole organisational framework that supports training with appropriate policies and practices. Questioning the efficacy of anti-racism training is a key part of the process of questioning Irish anti-racism.

Conflict of interests

The establishment of the National Committee on Racism and Interculturalism was an important development that produced wide-ranging policy documents both in an advisory capacity to government and as resource material for mainstreaming anti-racism. The NCCRI also carried out research on the best model for the National Anti-racism/Interculturalism Public Awareness Programme and other projects. This continued the partnership approach of the National Committee of the EYAR. However, the fact that the NCCRI is under the aegis of the Department of Justice, Equality and Law Reform, which is now the main funder of anti-racism, poses some concerns and threatens potential constraints. It could be argued that linking the Department of Equality with the Department of Justice is itself a conflict of interests that put constraints on anti-racism work. It may prove difficult to criticise a government department that is funding core areas of work, which at the same time is implementing what many see as racist policies and practices, especially in the areas of immigration and asylum.

The fact that successive Ministers for Justice failed to prioritise the ratification of the UN Convention on the Elimination of Racism has undermined the experiences of every member of minority ethnic groups who are members of Irish society - including those who were present here before 1968 - when Ireland signed the Convention. It also undermines the commitment attached to the signing of such conventions and indicates an analysis of racism that operates from the numbers mindset and the linking of racism to the presence of members of minority ethnic groups rather than locating it and challenging it within the majority society itself.

Whilst there is a major role for such a body as the NCCRI, it is crucial that it can operate within a framework of good practice and that principles of transparency, accountability, representation, engagement and participation inform all of its developments and work. There is an indication of a need for a stronger 'voluntary' sector voice. There is also an argument for individual groups to maintain their autonomy. Whilst recognising the value of working in partnership with other organisations and agencies, Pavee Point emphasise the need to retain identity and autonomy as a voluntary non-government organisation when entering into a partnership with state agencies (Pavee Point, 1995: 11).

(Re)searching anti-racism

Debates and analysis around theories of anti-racism in the Irish context are starting to emerge. There is often a criticism that research is both removed from the everyday lived experiences of anti-racists and often carried out in a discriminatory way. Research should be done from an equality perspective. Speaking about the ethos of the Equality Studies Centre, Kathleen Lynch (1999: 3) says it works within an epistemological tradition that supposes that the purpose of academic discourse is not only to describe and explain the world, but also to change it. Any institution has the potential for both (re)producing racism and challenging it. Our academic world is intrinsically linked to the one we inhabit. We do not operate in a vacuum. Lynch (1999: 6) sees one of the severe limitations of mainstream positivism as not defining people in a holistic way and that 'understanding of their subjectivity and their relational conditions of structured inequality often become invisible'. Moves towards more reflexive and constructivist research are to be encouraged. Alana Lentin supports Ben-Tovim *et al*'s (1986) argument for recognising the importance of combining a traditional researcher's approach with that of 'other groups of workers and volunteers including professionals, individual trade unionists and activists working in the community'. Lentin says that the distance between 'action' and 'research' has hindered a deeper understanding of the politics of anti-racism and quotes Ben-Tovim *et al*:

> On the one hand universities and other academic institutions control a range of useful resources which, if directly harnessed to anti-racist struggle, could provide a valuable influx of skills and resources. On the other hand, the bad

reputation of 'research', together with misconceptions about its potential, has meant that political activists and organizations have frequently failed to build a research function into their operation (Ben-Tovim *et al.*, 1986, cited by Lentin, 1997: 7).

Relational learning where there is not a presumption of common ground but rather a search for mutual respect and engagement and the commonality that can consequently result is an alternative: 'A common beginning in such relational pedagogies is exploration of the learner's own sources of ideas, values and commitments' (Schneider, 1998: 16). In an ever-changing society students need to be prepared for diversity.

Anti-racist alliances

Anti-racism has to be grounded in the agendas of minority ethnic Irish people. If anti-racism in Ireland is not responsive to the specific needs of the people who are disadvantaged by racism, it will either achieve nothing or actually do further damage (McVeigh, 1996: 44).

Membership of anti-racism alliances and how they operate are important issues if such alliances are to be as inclusive as possible. Ways of enabling participation of minority ethnic groups and allowing them to set the agenda must be found. To date anti-racism in Ireland has been led by majority ethnic group and Traveller organisations. McVeigh (1996) argues that the anti-racist alliance, which sees the Traveller support movement work alongside other ethnic groups, must be both valued and strengthened. The anti-racism movement in Ireland is firmly grounded in ethnicity and is inclusive of Travellers in a way not found in other European countries. As more minority ethnic groups become proactive in anti-racism there is danger anti-racism in Ireland experiencing some of the problems identified in anti-racism abroad. Alana Lentin argues that:

One of the central problems confounding inter-ethnic dialogue is the attempt by each group to claim to be more 'oppressed' or discriminated against than the other... prioritisation of certain struggles and the hierarchies of oppression that confound anti-racist politics have led to disunity, a lack of public support and to calls for the construction of a more plural anti-racism (Lentin, 1997: 3).

There must be a commitment from all concerned 'to refuse to participate unconsciously in the reproduction of the existing power relations' (Yuval-Davis, 1997: 130). As stated in the introduction, one of the challenges for Irish anti-racism will be to ensure that its alliances do not unconsciously mirror the structures and conditions which (re)produce inequalities in society. 'Failure to link anti-racist mobilisations with minority communities' histories of protest' (Lloyd, quoted in Mac an Ghiall, 1999: 116) will seriously undermine Irish anti-racism. 'To what extent the various partnerships are really empowering for those who are most marginalized is the subject of continual debate' (Lynch *et al* 2001:17). Another challenge to those of us who have been involved in the anti-racism movement from the beginning is to be prepared to 'shift' and engage with new groups who may operate differently from 'the way it has always been'. This in no way meant to undermine the work that many of us have contributed to anti-racism in Ireland; we need to do so in order to avoid further down the road 'having to take a hard and perhaps painful look at the terms under which [Irish] anti-racism has operated so far' (Bonnett, 2000: 144).

I support Taylor's (1997: 67) view of engagement as a preferential terminology to that of inclusion, which he sees as implying a sense of passivity on behalf of those from minority ethnic groups. He views engagement as processes which are used or developed by those from minority groups as well as processes which result from the actions of majority groups.

Some anti-racist activists in Ireland have expressed the need for a separatist space in which to explore issues relevant to them. However this expression was usually framed within a context of the need of minority ethnic 'space' for a limited time or to address particular issues but with the clear understanding that participation and active involvement with other partnerships and networks would be ongoing. The use of separatist spaces can enable groups to identify their own needs and strategies and give them a stronger voice when it comes to setting the anti-racism agenda. Ann Phillips (2000) says, 'Oppressed or subordinated groups have to be able to find their own voice, to speak for themselves, to be recognised as active participants ... people are seeking ... a place at the conference table, a chance to articulate their own, possibly different, perspectives and priorities, and a guarantee that they too will be acknowledged as equal'. Lack of recognition can be a barrier to people actually getting to the conference table. Lynch *et al* (2001: 20-21) discuss the 'politics of recognition' and say that 'inequalities of recognition or social status are often rooted in inequalities of access, participation and outcome' and point to the usefulness of distinguishing respect and recognition as a specific dimension of equality. Phillips (2000: 3, 8) says that 'the issues thrown up in a politics of recognition or, sometimes, the "politics of difference" have always included questions about the distribution of resources'. In the Irish context this is of significance for new groups emerging that do not have access to resources in the same way that longer established groups will have. Phillips (2000: 10, 11) sees much of the struggle for recognition as a struggle for political voice - a struggle for recognition of the members of a particular group as political actors in their own right.

Recognition can lead to representation and participation, although very often recognition only goes as far as consultation. There are issues around representation both for differing groups and for anti-racism alliances. Mac an Ghiall (1999: 104) poses two questions that need to be addressed in relation to issues of representation. 'How our identities are represented in and through the culture and assigned particular categories?' 'Who or what politically represents us, speaks and acts on our behalf?' There is a need for active participation of minority ethnic groups in all decision-making procedures. According to Young (1990), 'specific representation for oppressed groups ... promotes justice ... It assures procedural fairness in setting the public agenda'. She further says:

Social and economic privilege means, among other things, that the groups who have it behave as though they have a right to speak and be heard, that others treat them as though they have that right and they have the material, personal and organisational resources that enable them to speak and be heard. As a result, policy issues are often defined by the assumptions and priorities of the privileged. Specific representation for oppressed groups interrupts this process, because it gives voice to the assumptions and priorities of other groups (Young, 1990: 184-5).

Whilst there are issues around representation and the invisibility of inequalities within groups, especially in relation to women, disabled and gay people, the question of whether there is space at the table needs to be asked.

Looking at this question in a more global context, we see that increasingly women and others who are marginalised and not listened to, seek separatist spaces from which to challenge the dominant and patriarchal discursive practices. A growing feeling of alienation and injustice felt by many individuals and groups provides ties to each other that cross boundaries of borders, gender, class, race and age. This has created a 'space' where difference is the basis of empowerment and the master narratives that silenced and marginalised 'others' are challenged and deconstructed. A new cultural politics has emerged which 'has developed struggles to turn sites of oppression and discrimination into spaces of resistance' (Keith and Pile, 1993: 1). The essence of this margin as a site of radical possibility and resistance is captured by bell hooks in her essay 'Choosing the Margin'. hooks sees this space as 'a central location for the production of a counter-hegemonic discourse' (hooks, 1990: 149). Seeing the margin as a place of mere despair allows a 'deep nihilism' to permeate one's being. Whilst the margin is not a safe place, as the site of a 'community of resistance' it is central to the struggle of the oppressed and dominated. Nor is this margin a stepping-stone to the centre, rather, as hooks says 'a site one stays in, clings to even, because it nourishes one's capacity to resist' (1990: 150). The result of ideologies which sought to legitimate and justify the control which the dominant group claimed as their 'right' has been that those who were marginalised have had no space to challenge what was accepted as the norm.

Nira Yuval-Davis (1997) says it is vital in any form of coalition and solidarity politics to keep one's own perspective on things while empathising and respecting others. She advocates a transversal perspective and discusses the dialogue developed by Italian feminists (from the movement Women in Black):

> The Italian women used as key words 'rooting' and 'shifting'. The idea is that each participant in the dialogue brings with her the rooting in her own membership and identity, but at the same time tries to shift in order to put herself in a situation of exchange with women who have different membership and identity. They called this form of dialogue 'transversalism' - to differentiate from 'universalism' which, by assuming a homogeneous point of departure, ends up being exclusive instead of inclusive, and 'relativism' which assumes that, because of the differential points of departure, no common understanding and genuine dialogue are possible at all (Yuval-Davis, 1997: 130).

This model of dialogue would enhance inter-ethnic (including majority/minority ethnic groups) anti-racism work and promote solidarity and equality within alliances.

Amongst his criteria for strengthening Irish anti-racism, McVeigh points to the need for a connection to be made between opposing anti-Irish racism (which most Irish people support) and opposing racism in general (which most Irish people remain equivocal on). He also says that:

> It is not enough to simply create a space for 'ethnic politics'. Challenging racism means centring anti-racism in every other liberation struggle - anti-imperialist, socialist, feminist, Lesbian and Gay, Trade union and so on. (McVeigh, 1996: 44).

Conclusion

Until the late 1990s, anti-racism in Ireland has very much been marginalised and located in the voluntary/community sector. In recent years links between anti-racist groups within Ireland and throughout Europe have been strengthened. The designation of 1997 as the European Year Against Racism and the subsequent setting up of the National Co-ordinating Committee, which comprised of a partnership between representatives of the voluntary and statutory sectors contributed greatly to widening the base of anti-racism. In the late 1990s there was evidence of strong solidarity within anti-racist alliances; however whether new and emerging groups feel part of these alliances is questionable. Ways of maximising this solidarity must be continuously explored and re-evaluated as membership of alliances increases and new groups emerge. A framework of strong and effective legislation must support anti-racism work. There is a need for anti-racist networks not to reflect the power imbalance in society and for their agendas to be set by all minority ethnic groups; anti-racism must be informed by a 'bottom up' approach with engagement at its core. A partnership approach, if grounded in equality, recognition, representation and engagement, can provide a good working model for anti-racism at all levels. If partnerships and alliances are not grounded in models of good practice, the tensions between minority/majority anti-racism and state/non-state anti-racism will grow. This is not the time to be territorial. We are in a period of transition regarding anti-racism in Ireland, and if the foundations are not grounded in the agendas of members of minority ethnic groups, the profusion of building blocks will prove less than effective. Ways of harnessing the commitment, experiences, knowledge and expertise of the wide range of anti-racist organisations in Ireland must be found. This includes a whole continuum of different organistions and approaches: old and new, minority ethnic and majority ethnic, NGO and state. Emerging Irish racisms demand responding anti-racisms. There is, unfortunately, enough work for everybody committed to developing anti-racism in Ireland.

References

All Different/All Equal Youth Campaign. 1995. (Researched and written by Adrienne Collins). *Racism and Intolerance in Ireland*. Dublin: All Different/All Equal Youth Campaign. National Youth Council of Ireland.

Ballagh, Robert. 2001. 'Riverdance and the birth of Le Chéile/Together: Irish Artists Against Racism', *Focus on Ireland and the Wider World*. Issue 64, spring/summer. Dublin: Comhlamh.

Ben Tovim, Gideon, J. Gabriel, I. Law and K. Stredder. 1986. *The Local Politics of Race*. London: MacMillan.

Bonnett, Alastair. 2000. *Anti-Racism*. London: Routledge.

Boucher, Gerard. 1998. *The Irish are friendly, but...: A Report on Racism and International Students in Ireland*. Dublin: Irish Council for International Students.

Commission of the European Communities. 1998. *An Action Plan Against Racism*. Brussels: EU Consultative Commission on Racism and Xenophobia (1995) (Kahn Commission)

Crowley, Niall and Ronnie Fay. (n.d.) *Travellers and Community Work*. Dublin: Dublin Travellers Education and Development Group.

Donovan, Katie. 1998. 'Ireland's young Blooms', *The Irish Times*, 7 January 1998: 13.

Drury, Beatrice. 1994. 'Ethnic mobilisation: Some theoretical considerations', in John Rex and Beatrice Drury (eds.) *Ethnic Mobilisation in a Multi-Cultural Europe*. Aldershot: Avebury.

Equality Studies Centre. 1995. 'A Framework for Equality Proofing'. Paper prepared for the National Economic and Social Forum.

Evrigenis, Dimitrios. 1985. *Committee of Inquiry into the Rise of Fascism and Racism in Europe*. European Parliament.

Fitzgerald, Gretchen. 1992. *Repulsing Racism*. Dublin: Attic Press.

Focus on Ireland and the Wider World. 2001. Issue no. 64. *Special Edition on Challenging Racism - Respecting Difference*. Dublin: Comhlamh.

Hainsworth, Paul (ed.) 1998. *Divided Society: Ethnic Minorities and Racism in Northern Ireland*. London: Pluto Press.

Harmony. 1990. *Racial Discrimination in Ireland - Realities and Remedies*. Dublin: Harmony.

Irish National Committee of the European Year Against Racism (1998) *European Year Against Racism 1997: Ireland Report*. Dublin: Stationery Office. (Official Publication J/153)

Ford, Glynn. 1991. *Committee of Inquiry on Racism and Xenophobia*. Luxembourg: Office for Official Publications of the European Community.

hooks, bell. 1990. *Yearning: race, gender and cultural politics*. London, Turnaround.

Keith, Michael and Steve Pile. 1993. *Place and the Politics of Identity*. London: Routledge.

Kirby, Peadar. 1981. 'Minorities in Ireland: an interview with Sean McBride'. *Crane Bag* Vol. 5, No. 1 (special issue on minorities in Ireland).

Lentin, Alana. 1997. *Effective Anti-Racism Strategies: New Social Movements as a Potential for Ethnic Mobilisation*. Masters Dissertation. London: Department of Sociology, London School of Economics and Political Science.

Lentin, Ronit. 1998. '"Irishness", the 1937 Constitution and citizenship: a gender and ethnicity view', *Irish Journal of Sociology*. Vol. 8: 5-24.

Lentin, Ronit (ed.) 1999. *The Expanding Nation: Towards a Multi-ethnic Ireland*. (Proceedings of a conference held at TCD September 1998 in association with the Refugee Agency). Dublin: MPhil in Ethnic and Racial Studies, TCD.

Lentin, Ronit (ed.) 2000. *Emerging Irish Identities*. (Proceedings of a conference held at TCD, November 1999 in association with the National Federation of Campaigns against Racism). Dublin: MPhil in Ethnic and Racial Studies, TCD.

Lynch, Kathleen. 1999. 'Equality Studies, the academy and the role of research in emancipatory social change'. *The Economic and Social Review*. Vol. 30, No. 1.

Lynch, Kathleen, John Baker and Sarah Cantillon. 2001. *Equality: Frameworks for Change* (Paper presented at the NESF for the Plenary Meeting on 30 January 2000). Dublin: Equality Studies Centre.

Mac an Ghaill, Mairtin. 1999. *Contemporary Racism and Ethnicities*. Buckingham: Open University Press.

MacGréil, Mícheál. 1980. *Prejudice and Tolerance in Ireland*. New York: Praeger.

McVeigh, Robbie. 1996. *Racism and Anti-Racism in Ireland: The Racialisation of Irishness*. Belfast: Centre for Research and Documentation (CRD).

McVeigh, Robbie. 1999. 'Is sectarianism racism? The implications of sectarian division for multi-ethnicity in Ireland', in Ronit Lentin (ed.) *The Expanding Nation: Towards a Multi-Ethnic Ireland*. Dublin: MPhil in Ethnic and Racial Studies. Department of Sociology TCD.

McVeigh, Robbie and Alice Binchy. 1998. *Travellers, Refugees and Racism in Tallaght.* Dublin: European Year Against Racism and the Combat Poverty Agency. (Official Publications JX/II)

Melucci, Alberto. 1992. 'Frontier land: Collective action between actors and systems', in Mario Diani and Ron Eyerman (eds.) *Studying Collective Action.* London: Sage.

Pavee Point. 1995). *Strategic Plan: A Framework for Projected Activities 1995-1999.* Dublin: Pavee Point.

Phillips, Ann. 2000. *Inequality between Individuals, Injustice Between Social groups: Remaking the connection* (Paper presented at the 10th Anniversary conference Equality and Social Justice, Local and Global Issues). Equality Studies Centre, UCD, 15 December 2000.

Rex, John. 1994. 'Conclusion: The place of ethnic mobilisation in West European democracies', in John Rex and Beatrice Drury (eds.) *Ethnic Mobilisation in a Multi-cultural Europe.* Aldershot: Avebury.

Schneider, C.G. 1998. *Core Missions and Civic Responsibility: Toward the Engaged Academy.* Washington, DC: Association of American Colleges and Universities.

Smith, S. and F. Mutwarasibo. 2000. *Africans in Ireland: Developing Communities.* Dublin: African Cultural Project.

Tannam, Marian. 1991. *Racism in Ireland: Sources of Information.* Dublin: Harmony.

Tannam, Marian. 1996. *At Home from Abroad: A Study of Migrant Women in Ireland.* Unpublished. Available from Dublin City University library or the National Committee for Development Education.

Tannam, Marian, Suzanne Smyth and Suzie Flood. 1998. *Anti-Racism: An Irish Perspective.* Dublin: Harmony.

Taylor, Paul. 1997. 'Overcoming barriers to higher education entry', in Orla Egan (ed.) *Minority Ethnic Groups in Higher Education* (Proceedings of conference held on 27 September 1996 in St. Patrick's College Maynooth). Cork: Higher Education Equality Unit.

Walsh, David. 2000. 'Policing pluralism', in Malcolm MacLachlan and Michael O'Connell (eds.) *Cultivating Pluralism: Psychological, Social and Cultural Perspectives on a Changing Ireland.* Dublin: Oak Tree Press.

Young, Iris Marion. 1990. *Justice and the Politics of Difference.* Princeton: Princeton University Press.

Yuval-Davis, Nira. 1997. *Gender and Nation*, London: Sage Publications.

14.

Is there an Irish anti-racism?
Building an anti-racist Ireland

Robbie McVeigh

Introduction

Contemporary racism and anti-racism in Ireland are characterised by two factors. *First*, numbers of minority ethnic people are rising markedly - albeit from a very low base. With the exception of the Jewish community,[1] every minority ethnic group is increasing in size. *Second*, Irish racism is also on the rise. There is a widely accepted recognition of an exponential increase in racism in Ireland over the past decade. Some 55 per cent of Irish people regarded themselves as 'racist' in a European Commission poll. A quarter of Irish people said they were 'quite' or 'very' racist while a third said they were 'a little' racist. Nine per cent of Irish people believed that immigrants should be repatriated; 25 per cent said that legal immigrants who were unemployed should be repatriated; 50 per cent said that 'illegal immigrants' should be automatically repatriated (Smith, 1997:6). This increase in racism has also, however, been accompanied by a widespread opposition to racism and an increasing awareness of both the necessity and value of new minority ethnic communities. There has been a much publicised and self-conscious examination of this new racism. This reaction to Irish racism is at the core of the challenge of building an anti-racist Ireland.

This notion of building an anti-racist Ireland is a relatively new project. Beyond the sectoral influences of the minority ethnic organisations, the Traveller Support Movement and Majority World Solidarity, there has been little organic anti-racism in Ireland. Most elements in the state and civil society have been neither actively racist nor anti-racist. Historically racism was seen as something that happened elsewhere and therefore not something to mobilise either around or against. In the south there has been a relatively successful wooing of major political parties to a liberal 'non-racist' position - although vitriolic racism still obtains in many local political

211

situations where there are votes to be mobilised around populist racism - especially directed against Travellers and refugees. In the north sectarian political divisions further complicate the situation but there is little history of a grounded anti-racism.

In both parts of Ireland, there has been a recent institutionalisation of anti-racism through state legislation on racism and the establishment of the Race Directorate of the Equality Commission (formerly the Commission for Racial Equality Northern Ireland) in the north and the Equality Authority in the south. There has been a related growth in grass roots and minority ethnic anti-racism, which has increasingly focused on state racism. This social movement emphasises that the commitments of both states on equality and diversity sit uneasily with their institutionally racist policies on refugees, immigrants and Travellers. This tension between state-led and community-led initiatives marks a new phase of Irish anti-racism and will characterise the development of anti-racism over the next few years.

Historical 'anti-racism' in Ireland

Ireland's experience of colonial racism encouraged solidarity with other colonised peoples and other victims and survivors of racism. This means that there has been a long-standing anti-racist tradition that can be drawn upon to support and inform contemporary anti-racism in Ireland. This tradition challenged the racist stereotypes and practices attendant with colonialism and drew on Ireland's anti-colonial struggle to show solidarity with other such struggles. This was, of course, far from universal - the racist views of nationalist icons like Arthur Griffith and John Mitchel are notorious (McVeigh 1995). Mitchel's anti-imperialism sat comfortably alongside his support for slavery, but United Irish leader Jemmy Hope illustrates how an opposing anti-racist strain could exist at the same time among other Irish republicans. While George M. Cohan (Irish American writer of such hits as 'Yankee Doodle Dandy') may have put Irishness at the heart of American chauvinism with songs like, 'It's a Grand Old Flag', Hope's 'Jefferson's Daughter' remains a stirring repudiation of slavery and continues to speak powerfully against racism in the US:

> When the incense that glows before Liberty's shrine
> Is unmixed with the blood of the galled and oppressed,
> Oh, then, and then only, the boast may be thine
> That the star spangled banner is stainless and blest (cited in Madden, 1887: 102).

Likewise, Daniel O'Connell was, 'the single most important supporter that American anti-slavery had in Europe' (Riach, 1977). He was instrumental in drawing up an *Address from the People of Ireland to their Countrymen and Countrywomen* in America in the summer of 1841 that was signed by some 60,000 Irish people:

> America is cursed by slavery! We call upon you to unite with the abolitionists and never to cease your efforts until perfect liberty be granted to every one of her inhabitants, the black man as well as the white man... Join with the abolitionists everywhere. They are the only consistent advocates of liberty. Tell every man that you do not understand liberty for the white man, and

slavery for the black man; that you are for liberty for all, of every color, creed, and country... Irishmen and Irishwomen! Treat the colored people as your equals, as brethren. By your memories of Ireland, continue to love liberty - hate slavery - cling by the abolitionists - and in America you will do honor to the name of Ireland (cited in Ignatiev, 1995: 9-10).

O'Connell was able to draw on 'Irish anti-slavery traditions' in his debates with pro-slavery Irish Americans:

He once referred to St. Patrick, for example, as the first Irish abolitionist, and frequently alluded to the council of Armagh which in 1177 had prohibited Irish trade in English slaves. O'Connell was also on many occasions to boast that no slave ships had left or entered an Irish port, though it seems clear that Irish merchants were heavily involved in the eighteenth century triangular trade, with its horrible implications for captive Africans (Riach, 1977).

As this illustrates, Ireland was not a model of emancipatory practice but neither should Irish contributions to the struggle against racism be denied or ignored. For example, antisemitism has been commonplace in Ireland but the 1937 Irish constitution - in many ways the embodiment of sectarian and patriarchal reaction - was also the first anywhere in the world (according to Hyman, 1972) to recognise specifically the place of the Jewish community within the nation. In short, there are positive aspects of Irish 'tradition' that need to be critically celebrated as part of the development of anti-racism in Ireland.

The development of Irish anti-racism

Not surprisingly, it was minority ethnic individuals and groups themselves who first began to challenge racism in Ireland itself. Of course, racism was rarely named in this way - and interventions were never named or theorised as 'anti-racism'. Nevertheless, this was the start of anti-racist struggle in Ireland. As soon as minority ethnic community or religious associations developed they recognised that racism - or 'race relations' or 'race prejudice' - was one of the issues that they had to address. These interventions were often low-key and carefully worded. They rarely characterised themselves as anti-racist and were more likely to talk in terms of the contribution of minority ethnic groups to society. For example, during the Limerick pogrom, Marcus Blond, a Jewish refugee from Lithuania who had become a shopkeeper wrote:

All of a sudden, like a thunderstorm they spoke hatred and animosity against the Jews, how they crucified Lord Jesus, how they martyred St. Simon, and gradually in one month's time I have none of my previous customers... I defy anyone in this city to say whom I have wronged, what did I overcharge? (cited in O'Clery, 1986: 32).

There were also non-Jewish Irish people willing to challenge different manifestations of racism. Michael Davitt spoke out strongly during the pogrom:

I protest, as an Irishman and a Christian, against this spirit of barbarous malignity being introduced into Ireland, under the pretended form of material regard for the welfare of our workers. The Jews have never done any injury to Ireland. Like our own race, they have endured a persecution, the records of which will forever remain a reproach to the 'Christian' nations of Europe (cited in O'Clery, 1986: 32).

This early example of racism, and reactions to it, set the pattern for much of what was to follow for the next century. An outburst of racism was followed by a cautious challenge from minority ethnic people and the intervention in solidarity by some members of the majority ethnic community.

Anti-Traveller racism assumed new forms with the establishment of the two states on the island following the Government of Ireland Act 1920 and the Tan War. Almost immediately, politicians in both jurisdictions were keen to make political capital out of attacking Travellers. In the north, different politicians including Cahir Healy and Sheila Murnaghan defended Travellers. In the south Victor Bewley and others raised objections to the hegemonic anti-Traveller discourse. English Traveller rights activist Grattan Puxon also spent time in Ireland in the 1960s and began to offer alternative analyses of Traveller inequality (Puxon 1967). These challenges to racism were never couched in terms of racism or anti-racism but they did begin to recognise the Travellers' right to difference, albeit in a way that was in itself sometimes stereotyping of Travellers (McVeigh, 1998). Beyond this kind of cultural solidarity and identification of 'positive images', however, there has been much more specific work in Ireland on constructing an anti-racist politics. This has been inseparable from the development of the 'Traveller Support Movement'.

From assimilation to anti-racism: The development of the Traveller Support Movement

To some extent the recognition of Traveller difference took a step backwards as settled people began to intervene more actively in 'support' of Travellers. The 1963 Irish Government Commission on Itinerancy marked a nadir in the emerging consensus that 'something' had to be done for Travellers. Across Ireland, the Traveller Support Movement developed as an expressly assimilationist movement through *itinerant settlement committees* - the 'final solution' to the Traveller problem would be assimilation into the sedentary community (Commission on Itinerancy 1963). Noonan (1998) provides a fine overview of the similar dynamic in the north. Travellers and settled activists uncomfortable with the assimilationist tone of early practice began to develop an analysis of Traveller oppression which explained Traveller disadvantage in terms of ethnicity and racism. The Dublin Travellers Education and Development Group (DTEDG) was established in response to a virulent outbreak of anti-Traveller racism in the west Dublin area of Tallaght and began to develop an analysis of Traveller disadvantage that was explicit in terms of the use of both ethnicity and racism as core explanatory tools. Eventually the key national organisation of the Traveller Support Movement - the National Committee for Travelling People - split over this issue. Groups and individuals supporting the use

of the terms ethnicity and racism drew on the analysis of the DTEDG (now Pavee Point) and formed the Irish Traveller Movement. The rump of the old National Committee for Travelling People reconstituted as the National Federation for Travelling People. In the north, groups like the Northern Ireland Council for Travelling People (now Traveller Movement NI) and the Belfast Travellers Education and Development Group followed the DTEDG model and started to popularise the use of racism when explaining anti-Traveller prejudice and discrimination (Noonan, 1998: 162).

This intervention by the Traveller Support Movement in the 1980s was the first time that racism had been used in a sustained way in the Irish context. It marked the first formal anti-racism in Ireland. From this point on, 'racism' was held to offer some explanatory function in Irish society. It was now a term that would increasingly permeate popular discourse - however much the received wisdom that there was 'no racism in Ireland' continued. From the early 1980s onwards this response begins to develop a distinctive Irish anti-racism. It was not coincidental that this developed alongside the emergent analysis of anti-Irish racism in Britain (Curtis, 1984). Comparison of the racialisation of Irish people with the racialisation of minority ethnic groups in Ireland was central to anti-racism in Ireland from this point on.

In both the north and south of Ireland, much subsequent anti-racist campaigning focused on the introduction of legislation on discrimination. This was to some extent simply a consequence of the absence of any legislation. In the 1980s the Republic of Ireland had no protection at all - it was the only Western European country not to have signed up to the United Nations Convention on the Elimination of Racial Discrimination (CERD) (finally ratified in 2001). Although the north was covered by CERD, no domestic British legislation on racism had been extended. Thus the north had eschewed the British Race Relations Acts of 1965, 1968 and 1976. (There was one anomaly in that racial hatred was prohibited in the north in the Incitement to Racial Hatred Order of 1969. This was, however, more by accident than design and this legislation was never used to address racial hatred.) The demand for legislation was also, crucially, one with which minority ethnic communities were comfortable. There was little demand emanating from minority ethnic communities, north or south, for a more radical anti-racism that might begin to critique state racism. In other words, the aspiration was to bring the state 'on board' in terms of a broader anti-racist project rather than to confront the state on issues like 'institutional racism'.

While this project carried with it the kernel of the project of an anti-racist Ireland, it was crucially structured by the states within which it had to operate. In the north, engagement was with the British state and regional institutions at Northern Ireland level; in the south, engagement was with the Dáil. In this sense we saw the development of distinct, if parallel and connecting, anti-racisms, north and south.

South of Ireland

As we have seen, minority ethnic organisations in Ireland have always been key to the process of developing anti-racism. Organisations like *Micéir Misli* (the autonomous

Traveller group) and Harmony in Dublin highlighted the specific concerns of minority ethnic people and ensured that Irish racism was named as such (Harmony, 1990; Tannam, 1991). The work of the Traveller Support Movement - notably Pavee Point (formerly Dublin Travellers Education and Development Group) and the Irish Traveller Movement - was also central to this process. The Traveller Support Movement was the first organised political lobby to use the term racism widely in the context of Irish society. It also developed a specific model for anti-racist work around the notion of *partnership* between Travellers and settled people (DTEDG, 1994). The Task Force Report of 1995 marked the most significant advance for this work by the Traveller Support Movement. This was followed by strong commitments by the government to implement the recommendations of the report. The report addressed the failure by the Irish state to service properly the Traveller community. It was the first serious attempt by either state in Ireland to 'mainstream' the needs and demands of *any* of the minority ethnic communities.

Irish people in the south of Ireland have also stood in a particular solidarity with liberation struggles in other countries. The victory in 1986 of the Dunnes Stores strikers who refused to sell goods from apartheid South Africa is one example. The profile and success of the Ireland East Timor Solidarity Campaign is another more recent case. Many Irish people have chosen to involve themselves in international solidarity work because they are Irish. In turn, this solidarity has its influence on anti-racism in Ireland. For example, the work of the *Comhlámh* group of returned development workers has been key in developing anti-racism in Ireland. The Anti-Racist Coalition grew out of this group. Irish people working more specifically on civil liberties and human rights have also played a key role in raising racism as a rights issue. Groups like the Irish Council for Civil Liberties (ICCL) in the south have campaigned in support of effective anti-racist legislation.

There were also other early examples of institutional anti-racism. The 'Youth Campaign Against Racism, Xenophobia, Anti-Semitism and Intolerance' was probably the best example of this. The project involved young people in Ireland, north and south, in a wider European campaign against racism but this responded to the availability of resources from the Council of Europe rather than being initiated by any element in the anti-racist movement in Ireland (All Different All Equal, 1995).

In combination these organisations and processes saw a strong and fairly focused analysis of racism grounded in the specific experience of anti-Traveller racism coming out of the Traveller Support Movement alongside a looser and less focused concern with other racisms coming out of organisations like Harmony (CWC, 1990). There was some cross-fertilisation between these groups - and one usually made reference to the issues of the other. There was, however, little organic synthesis of these strands. This arguably planted the seeds of future contradictions and tensions within the broad Irish anti-racist movement. A loose alliance from these sectors came together in 1997 in the Platform Against Racism. For the first time this anti-racism began to make inroads into government policy. After 1997 was designated European year Against Racism by the European Council of Ministers and member states, a National Coordinating

Committee of government departments/agencies and non-government organisations was established by the Department of Equality and Law Reform to coordinate the Irish response to the EYAR. This developed into the National Consultative Committee on Racism and Interculturalism, a partnership of government departments, agencies and non government organisations. It was established by the Department of Justice, Equality and Law Reform in July 1998. The aim of the Committee was to 'provide an ongoing structure to develop programmes and actions aimed at developing an integrated approach against racism and to act in a policy advisory role to the government. The development of such an approach goes hand and hand with the promotion of a more participative and intercultural society which is more inclusive of groups such as refugees, Travellers and other minority ethnic groups' (NCCRI, 2001).

The mainstreaming of anti-racism in the south synthesised with the gradual introduction of legislation on racism. The first victory in terms of legislation was when minority groups including Travellers were included in the 1989 Incitement to Hatred legislation. This proved to be almost as weak as the northern legislation - the first successful prosecution occurred only in September 2000 with the conviction of a Dublin bus driver who referred to a Gambian passenger as a 'nig nog' and told him to go back to his own country (Crosbie, 2000a: 1). The conviction, however, was quashed on 13 March 2001 on appeal, the judge having ruled that, appalling as they were, the bus driver's words 'were not likely or intended to stir up hatred under the strict interpretation of the law' (*Irish Independent*, 13 March 2001). Nevertheless, the inclusion of racism - particularly the specific naming of Travellers - was an advance and set an important precedent for future, more comprehensive legislation. The Employment Equality and Equal Status Acts - which outlaw racial discrimination alongside other discriminations - became law in 1998 and 2000 respectively. These established the Equality Authority (2001) in 1999 and a whole new sector of anti-racist work emerged. The ratification of CERD in January 2001 also marked a significant step forward.

With the advent of state-led anti-racism, there has also been a development of grass roots anti-racist organisations like ARC, Immigrant Solidarity and Residents Against Racism:

> The Anti Racism Campaign (ARC) is an open and democratic alliance of people who came together to combat the anti-refugee and anti-immigrant hysteria initiated and encouraged by many politicians and sections of the media. We are non-party political. We support equal rights for refugees and immigrants: work, welfare, housing and entry into Ireland. We welcome the advent of greater ethnic diversity as a positive development for Irish society. We also oppose the racist treatment that has been experienced by Travellers (an Irish ethnic minority) (ARC, 2001).

In particular, these organisations have a focus on 'state racism' and adopt a more radical and overtly political analysis than institutionalised anti-racism. This marks a new dynamic in terms of the state and anti-racism (see Tannam, chapter 13 in this volume for a detailed survey of anti-racism in the south).

North of Ireland

The Traveller Support Movement in the north drew on the analyses of its southern counterparts as it too began to identify and challenge anti-Traveller racism in the late 1980s. There were also, however, parallel developments in other communities in the north - both within the majority white communities and the minority ethnic communities. In particular, the Chinese Welfare Association emerged as a key organisation representing the largest minority ethnic community in the north and became one of the first spaces in which racism could be addressed.

The key structural factor in the north was its particular relationship to the British state and British civil society. This sometimes threatened to create a 'dependency anti-racism'. It has been emblematic of anti-racist organisations in the north that their practice is informed - indeed sometimes directly caused by - anti-racism elsewhere. In this sense, and with the notable exception of Travellers, *majority* ethnic anti-racism was rarely organic to the north. Trotskyite groups set up anti-racist organisations because their 'sister' organisations were doing the same in Britain; social workers became anti-racist because social work practice in Britain demanded that they take racism seriously; and so on. There was often nothing wrong in these developments and they gave anti-racist work a new impetus. They did, however, carry with them the danger of simply importing anti-racist practice wholesale. Even when this had been successful elsewhere there was no guarantee of its efficacy or appropriateness in the context of the Northern Ireland state. Worst of all, this could often be anti-racism without local minority ethnic involvement. In other words, white people rarely stopped to ask whether local minority ethnic people - who were, after all, the targets of racism - wanted this anti-racist work in the forms it took. This practice ignored the cardinal rule of majority ethnic engagement with racism - if white and settled anti-racist practice is to avoid becoming itself racist, it must be rooted in the analysis and demands of the minority ethnic population it claims to protect.

In contrast to formally anti-racist groups, minority ethnic organisations adopted a more gradualist approach. This produced an alliance of interests working through the Committee on the Administration of Justice (CAJ) - a Belfast-based human rights and civil liberties group. The CAJ, in alliance with minority ethnic organisations, took a lead role in demanding effective anti-racist legislation for Northern Ireland. The campaign for effective legislation was given definitive expression in a groundbreaking conference on *Racism in Northern Ireland* and the subsequent conference report (CAJ 1992). These groups campaigned successfully for the extension of the British Race Relations Act 1976. While groups in the north were often wary of addressing the same agendas as the Black British community, the campaign for anti-racist legislation had the backing of all the main minority ethnic organisations. This campaign culminated successfully in the Race Relations (Northern Ireland) Order 1997 which created the Commission for Racial Equality (Northern Ireland). This was the first statutory anti-racist institution on the island of Ireland.

Out of the campaigns and alliances around legislation came the development in 1994 of NICEM (the Northern Ireland Council for Ethnic Minorities). NICEM was the first body rooted in the different minority ethnic organisations to take a strategic cross-ethnic alliance. So the setting up of NICEM represented an important step forward as a representative alliance of minority ethnic groups in Northern Ireland with racism a central concern in their work. The alliance between the Traveller Support Movement and other anti-racist groups has been particularly strong in the north of Ireland (McVeigh, 1998). NICEM also began to play a part in developing an all-Ireland alliance through membership of the Platform Against Racism and the European Year Against Racism.

In the wake of the Good Friday Agreement, the Commission for Racial Equality Northern Ireland (CRENI) was amalgamated with other equality bodies in the north and integrated into the new Equality Commission. The powers of the new body *vis-à-vis* racism, however, remained broadly unchanged. While this marks a significant development in state anti-racism, there has been less grass roots anti-racism organising in the north than the south. The alliance of groups around NICEM remains the dominant voice of anti-racism in the NGO sector and there has been no northern equivalent of the new grass roots anti-racist coalitions emerging in the south.

The Good Friday Agreement of 1998 created a new, all-Ireland dynamic to the politics of anti-racism and racial equality. The new institutions created or encouraged by the Agreement - like the human rights commissions, north and south, and the two equality commissions - created new powers and responsibilities in terms of challenging racism. More specifically, they also carried an explicit all-Ireland dimension. This implies the integration of anti-racism across the island - in terms of state-led anti-racism at least. Cooperation between these institutions may integrate institutional responses to racism across Ireland despite the reality that grass roots organising against racism remains effectively divided on a north/south basis.

The role of the Traveller Support Movement

The defining feature of the development of anti-racism in Ireland has been the key role of the Traveller Support Movement. In Ireland, north and south, the experience of Travellers has always been central to anti-racist analysis and struggle and the alliances between Travellers and other minority ethnic groups have been relatively strong. In other situations the Traveller experience has often been left out of anti-racism. Thus, whatever the other limitations of Irish anti-racism, the strength of the political and analytical alliance between anti-racists, Travellers and other minority ethnic people is something to be celebrated and developed.

From this perspective, Irish anti-racism is probably the only anti-racism in the world grounded in the experience of *any* group of Travellers. There are, of course, countries where Travellers form a much larger proportion of the population - like Romani people in Romania or Slovakia - and countries where Travellers are much more central to dominant national cultural identity - like Gitanos in Spain or Travellers in Scotland. Even in these countries, however, anti-racism has not been constructed around anti-Traveller racism. This has created very different dynamics in Ireland in comparison to other anti-racist struggles. For example, anti-racism in the US is grounded in African American experience and extends to include other people of colour. Anti-racism in Britain is grounded in African Caribbean and South Asian experience and extends to include other minority ethnic people (including Irish people). Anti-racism in Germany is grounded in antisemitism and the specific experience of the Holocaust. So Irish anti-racism in unique in the sense that it is grounded in the experience of an indigenous, nomadic group. It bears emphasis that there are both positive and negative aspects of this.

Most importantly, on the positive side, anti-Traveller racism has been prioritised in this process - it is neither footnote nor afterthought but central to the whole development of Irish anti-racism. In other situations the Traveller experience has often been left out of anti-racism. For instance, in Britain political solidarity around racism has been strong between the sedentary Irish population and other minority ethnic groups but the specific experience of Irish Travellers (and 'Gypsies') is often missing from this anti-racist alliance. Across Europe, the experience of Roma and other Travellers is often missing from any analysis of racism. The recent commemoration of 'Holocaust Day' across Europe was a prime example of this. These events took place in 16 European countries and yet often failed even to mention the *Poraimos* or 'great devouring' - the holocaust of Roma and other Travellers under the Nazis. This is only the most shocking example of the ability of anti-racism to marginalise or ignore Travellers' experience of racism. In this context, the centrality of anti-Traveller racism in the theory and practice of anti-racism in Ireland has been quite remarkable and carries with it an importance beyond Ireland. At a theoretical level the focus on anti-Traveller racism has also foregrounded a whole series of issues that have made important contributions to wider European anti-racism. For example, few other states are engaging with questions of nomadic identity and sedentarism as part of work around racism. In terms of practice, initiatives like Pavee Point remain inspirational at a European level in terms of work with Travellers.

More negatively, however, all this foregrounding has not transformed the experience of Travellers in Ireland, north or south. It is striking to return to some of the old photographs of the earliest Traveller Support Movement. The billboards demand 'Rights for Itinerants' as the Gardai evict a Traveller family. Nobody, of course, would use the term 'itinerants' anymore - this is one symbol of the success of anti-racism. The core issues remain, however, depressingly similar. Traveller families are still living on illegal and un-serviced sites under constant threat of eviction from those sites. Anti-Traveller prejudice appears to have increased rather than decreased (O'Keefe, 2001). Anti-racism may have moved from the margins to the centre of government, but most Travellers remain on the margins. So the continuing social exclusion of Travellers provides a depressing background to the limitations of Irish anti-racism. While this remains broadly true in terms of other situations - like those of African Americans or African Caribbeans in Britain - the absolute exclusion of

Travellers still compares unfavourably. In terms of the meter of equality, Irish anti-racism has not worked for most Travellers.

In addition to this problem, the central role of the Traveller Support Movement allowed the development of a particular model of 'partnership' within Irish anti-racism. At its worst this was no more than a fig leaf for the non-participation of Travellers in projects that were supposed to resource Travellers. This notion of 'partnership' had certain logic - it was much more than a cynical attempt to reproduce dependency. Nevertheless, the *outcomes* were limited and problematic - posts created in the Traveller industry were overwhelmingly filled by settled people because it was argued Travellers did not have the qualifications to do the jobs; the movement was led by settled people because it was argued Travellers did not have the skills to provide leadership; the writing and analysis was done by settled people because it was argued most Travellers were non-literate; the trips around the world were undertaken by settled people because it was argued Travellers did not want to travel.

The core problem here was that the Traveller Support Movement created a dynamic to anti-racism that theorised a specific place for settled people in the struggle against anti-Traveller racism. It was argued that, as a consequence of Traveller inequality, Travellers needed the support of settled people through the notion of 'partnership'. The dominance of anti-racism by majority ethnic people was and is not unusual - if anything, broader European anti-racism has been characterised by the over-representation of white Europeans. The specific theoretical justification for the role of majority ethnic people *vis-à-vis* Travellers was, however, unique. This of course begged specific questions in terms of Travellers - Who had a right to speak for Travellers? Who were the experts on Travellers? Who had the right to represent Travellers? And so on.[2] This dynamic was even more problematic, however, in terms of other victims and survivors of racism in Ireland - like refugees or people of colour. None of them had ever posited the notion of needing 'partnership' in this sense. None of them endorsed this model. Thus the partnership model is even more problematic when it attaches to other minority ethnic groups.

The ownership of anti-racism elsewhere has been problematised because it did not have partnership as an excuse. While white dominance of anti-racism continued, it was at least challenged because of the continued exclusion of people of colour. After a while the absence of people of colour became, in itself, a key measure of a failed anti-racist project. In Ireland, however, the partnership model allowed this situation not only to obtain but also to be regarded as a positive part of anti-racism. The failure to transfer power and resources towards minority ethnic people was itself the symbol of 'partnership'. This model became even more dangerous once it began to inform work with refugees and other minority ethnic groups. These groups too could be brought into partnership and here too their non-involvement at a leadership level could be excused as an example of partnership. This is simply untenable - people of colour must lead people of colour organisations - the victims and survivors of racism must lead and define the struggle against racism. The way that the Traveller Support Movement, north and south, deals with this core contradiction will define Irish anti-racism over the next few years - both in terms of the specificity of anti-Traveller racism and the more general issue of racism against other groups like refugees, migrant workers and people of colour.

Racism, anti-racism and future developments

There has been an exponential rise in racism in Ireland over recent years. More positively, however, anti-racism in Ireland has also entered a new phase. The advent of institutionalised, state-led anti-racism was an important historical step forward for minority ethnic groups in general and anti-racism in particular. There are now institutions in place, north and south, with specific responsibility to address racism at all levels. These attract resources that are insignificant in relation to other government expenditure. Nevertheless they are much better resourced and empowered than minority ethnic and anti-racist NGOs. The rise in racism has inspired the growth of a number of new, radical anti-racist organisations. Most of these sit outside the formal, state-led institutions. The tensions in the triangular relationship between the state, the statutory anti-racist sector and the NGO sector will characterise the development of Irish anti-racism over the next decade.

Other developments will probably broadly mirror similar earlier processes across Europe. There will be a movement away from the campaign for an effective legislative framework against racism towards more specific demands for equality in a whole range of service provision. The focus will switch from the broad concerns of the whole minority ethnic community towards addressing the specific needs of different groups of community members - women, young people and so on. Just as there are multiple identities within the majority ethnic community, so are similar multiple identities with minority ethnic communities. These changes of political focus are likely to be accompanied by changes in the politics of identity. As the present first-generation migrant leadership is succeeded by more and more second- and third-generation people, there will be developments around newer, ever more complex identities. Younger people of colour have to decide how this connects with their minority ethnic identity - do they become 'Black Irish' or something else instead? (This is even more complicated in the north where people may also choose to be 'Black Northern Irish' or 'Black British').[3] For example, Black Irish pop star, Samantha Mumba represents a completely new cultural space:

> 'I'm black and I'm from Ireland,' smiles Samantha. 'It's kinda like, uh-oh …
> but it means I'm something totally different. There are a lot of female artists
> my age around at the moment, but they're all American and blonde and blue-
> eyed and smiley. I'm totally the opposite of that. I want to show a bit more
> attitude and I have an opinion…. (cited on the Samantha Mumba Website).

The future of this kind of Black Irishness is unwritten. In the 1970s Phil Lynott of Thin Lizzy famously identified himself as the 'first Black Irishman'; African Irish singer Martin Okasili's 1997 record, was called 'The Secret History of the Black Celt'. Yet only a few years later, Samantha Mumba is reaching Number One in the charts in USA and Britain and around the world. Black Irishness begins to raise profound questions about both Blackness and Irishness. With this goes a whole range of new questions about racism, anti-racism and identity. Refugees and asylum-seekers in Ireland face similar questions. This is especially true for white people in these categories since they occupy contradictory locations in terms of traditional ethnic characterisation in Ireland. Although the question is not as novel for them, Irish Travellers and Irish Jewish people face similar decisions. This process has hardly begun for most of the minority ethnic communities but it will involve a different emphasis in terms of the role that racism plays in structuring each of these identities.

The empowering of minority ethnic communities will also entail anti-racism being more directed and controlled by minority ethnic people. There is a specific requirement in the Traveller Support Movement for Traveller involvement and control but this is mirrored in terms of broader anti-racist work and interventions. There is a need, north and south, for more minority ethnic ownership and control of both minority ethnic organisations and anti-racist organisations. In response to this, we are likely to see minority ethnic people taking control of minority ethnic organisations and setting the agenda in terms of the struggle against racism.

Building an anti-racist Ireland

It is useful to begin to suggest how best to develop anti-racism in Ireland by way of conclusion. There are a number of clear objectives in terms of strengthening anti-racism and recognizing the important contribution of minority ethnic groups. *First*, opposing anti-Irish racism (which most Irish people support) has to be connected to opposing racism in general (which most Irish people remain equivocal on). *Second*, anti-racism has to be grounded in the agendas of minority ethnic Irish people. If anti-racism in Ireland is not responsive to the specific demands of the people who are disadvantaged by racism, it will be limited in effect and may be counterproductive. *Third*, anti-racism must be supported by strong and effective legislation. While legislation is never a panacea, it makes it clear that racism is no longer sanctioned by the state. It must, however, be legislation that works - the only meter of success in terms of ending minority ethnic disadvantage is equality of outcome. *Fourth*, the anti-racist alliance that sees the Traveller Support Movement work alongside other ethnic groups must be both valued and strengthened. The need to promote the issues of people of colour should not be an excuse to demote the issues of Travellers. *Fifth*, it is not enough to simply create a space for 'ethnic politics'. Challenging racism means centring anti-racism in every progressive struggle - the women's movement, the trade union movement, the anti-imperialist movement, the Lesbian and Gay movement, the disabled movement and so on. *Finally*, anti-racism must, even as it opts to sometimes work in partnership with state and statutory bodies, work to name and stem state and institutional racism and make visible the contradictory link between immigration and asylum policies and state-sponsored anti-racism.

Anti-racism must be forged out of an alliance across sectors of Irish society. It bears emphasis that this anti-racist alliance should be forged out of self-interest as much as solidarity. If the history of European racism teaches us anything, it is that racism can be a catalyst for reaction that disadvantages every disempowered group in society. In this sense, anti-racism is not an act of charity but rather one of self-preservation for most people. In the Irish context, racists have already mobilised to attack Jews and Travellers and refugees; it is imperative that we challenge Irish racism and stop this process now before it envelops everyone in a carnival of reaction. Building an anti-racist Ireland is not only in the interests of people of colour and refugees and Travellers but also in those of everyone who believes in democracy and equality and human rights.

References

All Different/All Equal. 1995. *Racism and Intolerance in Ireland*. Dublin: National Youth Council of Ireland.

ARC (Anti-racism Campaign). 2001. http://flag.blackened.net/revolt/arc.html

Caherty, Therese (ed.) 1992. *Is Ireland a Third World Country?* Belfast: Beyond the Pale.

CAJ (Committee on the Administration of Justice). 1992. *Racism in Northern Ireland*. Belfast: CAJ.

CCRU (Central Community Relations Unit). 1992. *Race Relations in Northern Ireland*. Belfast: CCRU.

Commission on Itinerancy. 1963. *Report of the Commission on Itinerancy*. Dublin: Stationary Office.

CRD (Centre for Research and Documentation). 1997. *Minority Ethnic Groups and Racism*. Belfast: CRD.

CRE (Commission for Racial Equality). 1997. *The Irish in Britain*. London: CRE.

Crosbie, Judith. 2000. 'Bus driver guilty of racial hatred,' *The Irish Times*, 15 September 2000: 1.

McCann, May, S. O'Siochain and J. Ruane (eds.) 1994. *Irish Travellers: Culture and Ethnicity*. Belfast: Institute of Irish Studies.

Curtis, Liz. 1984. *Nothing But the Same Old Story: The Roots of Anti-Irish Racism*. London: Information on Ireland.

CWC (Community Workers Co-op). 1990. *Co-options 2: Racism*. Dublin: CWC.

DTEDG (Dublin Travellers Education and Development Group). 1994. *DTEDG File: Irish Travellers, New Analysis and New Initiatives*. Dublin: DTEDG.

Equality Authority. 2001. http://www.equality.ie/aboutus.shtml

European Parliament. 1991. *Committee of Inquiry on Racism and Xenophobia*. Luxembourg: Office for Official Publications of the European Communities.

Fanon, Franz. 1967. *The Wretched of the Earth*. London: Penguin.

Fitzgerald, Gretchen. 1992. *Repulsing Racism: Reflections on Racism and the Irish*. Dublin: Attic Press.

Hainsworth, Paul. 1998. *Divided Society: Ethnic minorities and racism in Northern Ireland*. London: Pluto.

Harmony. 1990. *Racial Discrimination in Ireland: Realities and Remedies*. Dublin: Harmony.

Hickman, Mary and Bronwen Walter. 1997. *Discrimination and the Irish Community in Britain: A report of research undertaken for the Commission for Racial Equality*. London: CRE.

Hyman, Louis. 1972. *The Jews of Ireland*. Shannon: Irish University Press.

Ignatiev, Noel. 1995. *How the Irish became White*. New York: Routledge.

Madden, R. R. 1887. *Literary Remains of the United Irishmen*. Dublin: Duffy.

Mann-Kler, Deepa. 2000. 'Panel discussion: Beyond identity politics - Irish identity formation and anti-racism', in Ronit Lentin (ed.) *Emerging Irish Identities*. Dublin: MPhil in Ethnic and Racial Studies, Department of Sociology, Trinity College, Dublin.

McDonagh, Rosaleen. 2000. 'Talking back', in Anne Byrne and Ronit Lentin (eds.) *(Re)searching Women: Feminist Research Methodologies in the Social Sciences in Ireland*. Dublin: Institute of Public Administration.

McVeigh, Robbie. 1992a 'The Specificity of Irish Racism'. *Race and Class* 33 no. 4.

McVeigh, Robbie. 1996. *The Racialisation of Irishness: Racism and anti-racism in Ireland*. Belfast: CRD.

McVeigh, Robbie. 1998. 'There's no racism because there's no Black people here: Racism and Anti-Racism in Northern Ireland' in Paul Hainsworth (ed.) *Divided Society: Ethnic Minorities and Racism in Northern Ireland*. London: Pluto.

McVeigh, Robbie. 1999. 'Is sectarianism racism? The implications of sectarian division for multi-ethnicity in Ireland', in Ronit Lentin (ed.) *The Expanding Nation: Towards a Multi-ethnic Ireland*. Dublin: MPhil in Ethnic and Racial Studies, Department of Sociology, Trinity College, Dublin.

National Consultative Committee on Racism and Interculturalism (NCCRI). 2001. homepage.eircom.net/~racismctee/index

NICEM (Northern Ireland Council for Ethnic Minorities). 1996. *Mission Statement*. Belfast: NICEM.

Noonan, Paul. 1998. 'Pathologisation and Resistance: Travellers, Nomadism and the State' in Paul Hainsworth (ed.) *Divided Society: Ethnic Minorities and Racism in Northern Ireland*. London: Pluto.

O'Clery, Conor. 1986. *Phrases Make History Here: Political Quotations on Ireland*. Dublin: O'Brien Press.

O'Keefe, Cormac. 2001. 'Travellers face eviction and bias'. *Irish Examiner*. 28 February 2001.

Puxon, Grattan. 1967. *The Victims: Itinerants in Ireland*. Dublin: Aisti Eireannacha.

Race Relations (Northern Ireland) Order. 1997.

Riach, D.C. 1977. 'Daniel O'Connell and American Anti-Slavery' *Irish Historical Studies*, vol. 27, no. 77.

Samantha Mumba Official Website. 2001. http://www.samanthamumbausa.com/biog/index.html

Smith, Patrick. 1997. 'More than half of Irish see themselves as racist.' *The Irish Times*, 20 December 1997: 6.

Tannam, Marian. 1991. *Racism in Ireland: Sources of Information*. Dublin: Harmony.

Task Force. 1995. *Report of the Task Force on the Travelling Community*. Dublin: Stationary Office.

15.

Anti-racist responses to the racialisation of Irishness: Disavowed multiculturalism and its discontents[1]

Ronit Lentin

Introduction

In January 2001 the Immigration Control Platform issued a call on the government to opt out of the 1951 United Nations Geneva Convention Relating to the Status of Refugees. The ICP spokesperson Áine Ní Chonaill told a press conference that 'everybody except a handful of anarchists accept that we cannot have an open borders policy'. Arguing that the low level of deportations of asylum-seekers, ranging from one to 32 per month, means that Ireland is 'overrun by foreigners', Ní Chonaill, evoking Irish cultural authenticity, said that Ireland, like other European countries, colludes in the 'invasion of its own culture' (Haughey, 2001a: 4). 'Culture', and more specifically 'Irish culture', is constructed by rightist spokespersons such as the ICP as immutable, and 'already there', ignoring the less than homogeneous nature of Irishness (as argued, among others, by McVeigh, 1996, Lentin, 2000a, O'Toole, 2000). The only public response to the ICP call was the reassurance, the following day, by the Minister for Justice, Equality and Law Reform John O'Donoghue, that the Irish government remains 'committed to offering asylum to refugees fleeing persecution' (Haughey, 2001b: 6). What the Minister neglected to mention was that in 2001 the number of deportations of unsuccessful asylum-seekers was beginning to seriously increase while the number of asylum-seekers actually reaching our shores was on the decrease because many were being prevented from landing in Ireland already on the Rosslare ferry.[2]

It is not wholly surprising that the only response to the ICP came from the government. The exchange indicates a shift in the racism/anti-racism discourse in Ireland at the beginning of 2001. On the one hand, public sector bodies such as the National Committee on Racism and Interculturalism (NCCRI), the Equality Authority and the Human Rights Commission were beginning to work on enforcing the equality legislation; the government's National Anti-racism/Interculturalism Public Awareness Programme was being planned by appointing yet another 'High Level Steering Group' to handle it (thus neutralising the NCCRI, the government's own advisory body on racism and interculturalism, whose brainchild the awareness programme was and who had expended a lot of time and effort researching and constructing it). Thus a veritable Irish 'race relations industry' was being constructed, while at the same time the government was implementing strict immigration restrictions. On the other hand, grassroots anti-racism organisations - most of them under-funded and unsupported - were finding it increasingly difficult to do their work in an atmosphere of municipal (as well as corporate) multiculturalism which, imposing an integrationist agenda, tends to deny the experiences of racialised sections of Irish society. This shift in the anti-racism discourse towards top-down initiatives inadvertently cleared new spaces for bottom-up racialised ethnic groups to begin to form their own agendas, but it was unclear as to what shape these agendas and these spaces would take.

While discussions of 'new racism' (e.g., Barker, 1981), and of the need to theorise racism beyond 'race' have characterised recent debates on racism in Europe (e.g. Miles, 1989; Mac an Ghaill, 1999; Gilroy, 2000), discourses of racism in contemporary Ireland have until recently been considered both 'new' and 'part of human nature', as is argued throughout this volume. In contemporary Ireland, the 'semantic of race' (Goldberg, 2000: 362-77) is linked first and foremost to the racialisation of Travellers, asylum-seekers, refugees and migrants, despite the well-sustained arguments that Irish racism is neither 'natural', 'new', nor caused by in-coming out-groups. A conference organised by the Encounter group in Limerick in September 2000 asked whether prejudice is part of what 'we' are. To answer this question, we need firstly to problematise that 'we' and put paid to the notion of Ireland as a monoculture, as this volume is trying to do.

Disempowered ethnic groups in Ireland - Black-Irish people, members of African and Asian communities, Jewish people, but not Travellers, Ireland's largest racialised ethnic group- have been largely invisible in the Irish 'imagined community'. Yet, there is no doubt that the Irish ethnic landscape has been changing in the 1990s, not only because of changing migration patterns, or the internationalisation of labour, but also because of the politicisation of ethnic communities in their struggle against multi-racisms which inevitably accompany Ireland's increasing multiculturality. Ethnic difference, historically constructed as religious difference - in relation, for example, to the narrow definition of ethnicity in the Irish Constitution (Lentin, 1998) - is now being articulated more explicitly in government and NGO policy initiatives to combat racism and support migrant communities (see, for example, European Year Against Racism, 1997; Platform Against Racism, 1997; Tannam *et al.*, 1998; NCCRI, 1999; Tannam, chapter 13 in this volume). However, I would suggest that behind these initiatives is a 'disavowed multiculturalism': what is disavowed is the official version of the Irish nation, which constructs a non-national 'other' as both 'difference' and 'pathological' (c.f. Hesse, 1999: 215).

Despite the 'moral panic' of the late 1990s, racism is not new to Ireland as the experiences of Travellers, Jews, Black-Irish people and other racialised groups attest. As Brah argues (2000: 443), 'social phenomena such as racism seek to fix and naturalise "difference" and create impervious boundaries between groups'. The specificities of Irish racism are discussed elsewhere in this volume. This chapter focuses on the now ubiquitous discourse of multiculturalism. I begin by trying to define the contested concept of multiculturalism and critique multiculturalist and top-down anti-racism policies. I will argue that Irish multiculturalist policies are anchored in a liberal politics of recognition of difference, which do not depart from western cultural imperialism (cf Hesse, 1999) and are therefore inadequate in terms of deconstructing ethnic power relations. The multiculturalist approach to anti-racism results in a climate, on the one hand, of a growing tendency towards separatist identity politics groupings, and on the other, the top-down ethnicisation of Irish society which includes, among other things, government initiatives which operate - contradictorily - side by side with restrictive immigration measures. The multiculturalist approach is failing to intervene in the uneasy interface of minority and majority relations in Ireland. This problematic interface, which reduces the problems of unequal power relationship to one of numbers, with the effect of naturalising, rather than challenging the power differential (Brah, 1996: 186-7) has already been mentioned in the introduction. I therefore use the terms 'ethnic minorities' and 'racialised ethnic groups' interchangeably. I conclude the chapter by developing Barnor Hesse's (1999) idea of a 'politics of interrogation' of the 'we' of the 'part of what we are' to propose that disavowed multiculturalism is a more appropriate way of theorising Irish responses to ethnic diversity. Interrogating the Irish 'we' cannot evade interrogating the painful past of emigration, a wound still festering because it was never tended, and which is returning to haunt Irish people through the presence of the immigrant 'other', as the examples I bring from contemporary works of art illustrate.

Multiculturalism and its discontents

Multiculturalism is a 'portmanteau term' for anything from minority discourse to postcolonial critique, from municipal and governmental anti-racism programmes to ethnic diversity as prominently manifested in food scapes (as in Thai curries and Japanese sushi joining burgers, pizzas and Indian and Chinese takeaways as quintessentially 'Irish' foods in contemporary Ireland), from black music to the commercial appropriation of 'the black' and 'the east'. Multiculturalism is not a single doctrine, does not characterise one political strategy, and does not represent an already achieved state of affairs. It is not a covert way of endorsing some ideal, utopian state. It describes a variety of political strategies and processes that are everywhere incomplete.

Stuart Hall (2000) describes several varieties of multiculturalism:

Conservative multiculturalism insists on the assimilation of difference into the traditions and customs of the majority.

Liberal multiculturalism seeks to integrate the different cultural groups as fast as possible into the 'mainstream' provided by a universal individual citizenship, tolerating only in private certain particularistic cultural practices.

Pluralist multiculturalism formally enfranchises the differences between groups along cultural lines and accords different group-rights to different communities within a more communal or communitarian political order.

Commercial multiculturalism assumes that if the diversity of individuals from different communities is recognised in the marketplace, then the problems of cultural different will be (dis)solved through private consumption, without any need for a redistribution of power and resources.

Corporate multiculturalism (public or private) seeks to 'manage' minority cultural differences in the interests of the centre.

Critical or 'revolutionary' multiculturalism foregrounds power, privilege, the hierarchy of oppressions and the movements of resistance. It seeks to be insurgent, polyvocal, heteroglossial and anti-foundational (Hall, 2000: 210).

Wieviorka (1998a) divides multicultural policies into *relatively integrated multiculturalism* - as practiced in Canada, Australia and Sweden, where economic integration is linked to cultural integration (albeit often catering to the economic interests of the majority, such as the wish, in Australia, to integrate immigrants from Asia and the Pacific rim to enable Australia to trade with these regions); and *disintegrated multiculturalism* - such as practiced in the USA and Britain, where cultural and economic integration are separate practices. In both cases, the debates are always about the interests of the majority; immigrant and minority cultures are required to assimilate, integrate or otherwise opt to live separately according to the dictates of the hegemonic majority.

From a policy standpoint, multiculturalism is but one response to cultural diversity which assumes that racism is caused by the 'strangeness' of incoming immigrant groups (rather than by the 'host' society) and that by integrating and eventually assimilating out-groups, the 'problem' would disappear. In Britain, multiculturalist policies gave birth to various 'race relations' and 'community relations' initiatives, which claim to bridge the gap between the 'host' society and minority ethnic and religious groups. However, Phil Cohen reminds us:

> The multicultural illusion is that dominant and subordinate can somehow swap places and learn how the other half lives, whilst leaving the structures of power intact. As if power relations could be magically suspended through the direct exchange of experience, and ideology dissolve into the thin air of face-to-face communication (Cohen, 1988: 13).

Kenan Malik (1998) argues that the celebration of difference, far from being an anti-racist principle, has from the start been at the heart of the racial agenda. The ideology of multiculturalism was developed as an accommodation of the persistence of inequalities despite the rhetoric of first assimilation, then integration, and currently equality. In his edited collection *Un/settled Multiculturtalisms: Diasporas, Entanglements, Transruptions*, Barnor Hesse (2000: 8-10), describing the history of British multiculturalism, argues that multiculturalism was 'the culmination of liberal attempts to address the social accommodation of racially marked white/"non-white" cultural differences in terms that enshrined the values of liberty and tolerance for both the "British" self and the Caribbean, Asian and African "others"', which meant that the question of racism remained untouched.

In an earlier article, Hesse (1999: 210-1) suggests that the multicultural meaning of the Western nation emerges in relation to the racialisation of modernity. Deriving from Charles Taylor's (1992) argument that multiculturalism was an outcome of the 'politics of recognition' demanded by 'minority and subaltern groups', multiculturalism is anchored in two contradictory discourses: on the one hand, a universalist demand for equal dignity to all citizens, and on the other, a politics of difference. Criticising Taylor's universalism, Hesse reminds us that until the advent of the Black Power, women's and gay movements, discourses of equality for all citizens initially excluded everyone but white Americans, since the principle of universalism and equal dignity was formed in articulation with European racism and white masculinity. Taylor's theory, Hesse argues, poses the quandary of whether 'the desire to preserve the sanctity of the universal, which gives rise to an unmarked politics of recognition... (can) be reconciled with the desire to defend the integrity of difference'. The question is - and here we return to interrogating the 'we' of 'part of what we are' - *whose* recognition is sought and what is involved in the power to confer recognition and value'? (Hesse, 1999: 212). Instead of a politics of recognition, Hesse posits a politics of interrogation, a subversive circumvention of western culture, or, in relation to anti-racist possibilities, a subversive inscription of racialised spaces in white, settled Ireland, by Traveller, African and Asian people, asylum-seekers and anti-racism activists.

In Ireland the debate on the limits of multiculturalism[3] is still in its infancy. There is no doubt that the Irish government's contradictory messages in relation to asylum and immigration, together with media responses (see Guerin and White, chapters 5 and 6 in this volume respectively) are major causative factors in contemporary Irish racisms. On the one hand, the Minister for Justice, Equality and Law Reform has called on regional communities to be hospitable to dispersed asylum-seekers, and has announced the £4.5 million three-years government-sponsored Anti-racism/Interculturalism Public Awareness Programme (Haughey, 2001c). On the other hand, in the Illegal Immigrants (Trafficking) Bill (2000), the government has clearly legislated for deportations. Thus, the Irish government's racist immigration and asylum policies (Tracy, 2000) sanction racist violence by the citizenry, just as its past assimilationist policies towards Travellers sanctioned violent sedentarism by the citizenry. In both cases, the official version of the Irish nation constructs otherness as pathological and in need of top down intervention to ensure integration on the majority's terms.

Whilst the fight against racism must begin from the top, I would argue that the top-down responses to racism, including partnerships between racialised ethnic and refugee groups (particularly Traveller organisations; see McVeigh, chapter 14 in this volume, for an extended discussion of the partnership approach) and government-funded bodies (such as the NCCRI) build on Westocentric multiculturalist assumptions. This, despite the NCCRI substituting the term 'multiculturalism' with 'interculturalism', supposedly assuming a 'parity of cultures', but in reality not deconstructing the power relations between 'majority' and 'minority' ethnicities.

In implementing multiculturalist policies, and in the absence of democratic consultation processes, the state largely negotiates with *leaders* of already constituted racialised ethnic groups. Therefore, a contradiction arises between group rights and individual rights. Multiculturalist policies assume that all members of ethnic minority groups are equally committed to their group's 'culture', which is understood as fixed and unchanging, while, in reality, culture is a set of fluid and shifting discourses and practices. Leaders of racialised ethnic groups (who are rarely elected and who may or may not be fundamentalist leaders) often do not represent the interests of groups *within* racialised ethnic groups such as women, young people, disabled people or gays. Indeed, as Minh-ha (1991: 107) argues: 'Multiculturalism does not lead us very far if it remains a question of difference only between one culture and another. Differences should also be understood within the same culture' (cited by Hesse, 1999: 205).

One example of the discontents of multiculturalism relates to gender. The multiculturalist response to ethnic diversity leaves the question of gender equality and the power issues involved within racialised ethnic groups un-addressed. Advocates of group rights give little attention to the domestic sphere, despite the fact that religious and ethnic groups often centre on gendered aspects of 'personal law' in relation to marriage, divorce, procreation and inheritance. According to Suruchi Thapar-Bjorkert (2000), agents of multiculturalist policies tend to perceive violence against racialised women as 'part of their culture' and as a result, service providers often do not intervene out of an ethnocentric assumption that violence is part of racialised ethnic culture and that to intervene would be to fracture the already difficult relations between these agencies and the leaders of racialised ethnic communities. This means that the multiculturalist approach can, in practice, nurture physical violence, but also 'symbolic violence' which Thapar-Bjorkert sees as being caused by cultural relativism, the separation between the public and private spheres and by silencing the voices of victims and survivors of intra-community violence.

An Irish example of the uneasy relationship between group rights and the rights of women within a racialised group is the first ever project on violence against women in the Irish Traveller community (Pavee Point, 2000). This project demonstrates just how reluctant women members of racialised ethnic groups are to report violence to the police, or to use refuges, where racism and ethnocentrism combine to emphasise their vulnerability. But it also demonstrates the power of the racialised group, who, by training Traveller women as outreach workers and by making clear policy recommendations, is naming its own demands, in its own words, charting new ethnicised gendered spaces in a sedentary Ireland.

Multiculturalist approaches are also evident in the research agenda in relation to racialised ethnic groups. Multiculturalism means social scientists often regarding research 'on' racialised ethnic groups - largely without consultation as to what members of these groups wish them to research - as progressive, despite concerns voiced by members of racialised groups - their research 'subjects'. Indeed, social scientists, in their anxiety to use categories and sub-divisions, and by presenting 'race' as a category 'whereby social structure, social change or the movement of history could be understood' have contributed a great deal to the invention of racism, to its formulation as doctrine and scholarly theory (Wieviorka, 1995: 3).

In contemporary Ireland members of racialised ethnic groups are beginning to question seriously social scientists' research agendas. Travellers and refugees have begun to articulate their reluctance to be interviewed for yet another undergraduate, postgraduate, doctoral dissertation or academic research project. In a paper titled 'Talking back', Rosaleen McDonagh (2000) identifies herself as a 'Traveller feminist' who had been 'used' and 'exploited' by researchers. Focusing on her experience of racism within the research process, McDonagh addresses the power inequalities in the researcher-researched relationships and questions the context, the use and value of social research - which is rarely constructed as collaborative and emancipatory - which benefits the researcher but which does not benefit and is often harmful to the researched. In a similar vein, Katrina Goldstone (2000) cautions against representing the other in simplified and reductionist terms and argues that academic research and academic and journalistic writing can be used 'as a means of legitimising continued oppression or condoning past injustices'. She exhorts researchers and writers to question their motives when setting out to research racialised ethnic groups and says that 'the colonisation of the images and experiences of blacks, Jews, Muslims or any group outside the golden circle of western Eurocentrism contributes to continued subjugation' (Goldstone, 2000: 313). Like many top-down anti-racism projects, academic research projects are often conceived and designed without consultation with those being researched or aimed at.

Disavowed multiculturalism

Anti-racism in Ireland has a relatively short history (Tannam *et al*, 1998; see also Tannam in this volume and McVeigh, chapter 14 in this volume), and anti-racism legislation is in its infancy. Racism Irish-style owes to the strength of a sense of community (as argued by McVeigh, 1992), as can be seen in the opposition by local communities to permanent halting sites for nomadic Travellers or to hostels for asylum-seekers,[4] although many regional communities are reported to have befriended 'their' local asylum-seekers (see Dooley, 2000: 2), probably because they are increasingly filling vacant positions in tourism and catering, albeit as part of an informal 'black' economy. Anti-racism Irish-style arguably derives from the same sense of community, in that top-down partnership anti-racism initiatives stress, with all the attended goodwill, integration on the majority's terms. Call it integration, interculturalism or what you will, all these initiatives are ultimately based on a multiculturalist politics of recognition, not a politics of interrogation. A politics of interrogation interrogates the relations between the visible 'civilised grandeur' of the majority and the invisibility of minority dehumanisation in western culture: 'interrogating … so that something can be seen…' (Hesse, 1999: 213). This means not only recognising ethnic difference, but also the active participation of and leadership by members of racialised ethnic groups in all public sector and community anti-racism initiatives.

Following Hesse, I propose that a political theory of Irish multiculturalism must begin with an interrogation of the nation. But, as Zizek (1989) suggests, in order to engage the multicultural we need to work through 'the symbolic reality of the past, long forgotten traumatic event, that can no longer evade interrogation'.

Multiculturalism, in other words, is the return of the national repressed. In the Irish case, I would suggest this national repressed is the pain of emigration, returning to haunt the Irish, through the presence of the immigrant 'other' and in its wake invoking the unseemly presence of the 'less than fully Irish' indigenous and non-indigenous racialised ethnic groups, such as the Traveller, the Asian, the Black, the Jew. Making the link between past (and present) Irish emigration and present immigration into Ireland, Fintan O'Toole (2001: 16) writes about the treatment of 19 Moldovan workers who arrived in Ireland in January 2001 with valid passports, visas and work permits but who, nonetheless, were jailed once it was found that the firm they were supposed to work for had closed. He compares this with the Irish Immigration Centre in Boston, set up to assist contemporary Irish emigrants. The IIC, catering for Irish 'economic migrants' - the same migrants derided in today's Ireland as 'illegal' - is financially supported by the Irish government, although, as O'Toole reminds us, anyone going to the US looking for work is just as much an 'illegal immigrant' as anyone coming into Ireland in search of a better economic existence.

Emigration is more tangibly linked to in-migration in other ways too. According to a document underlying the Irish government's immigration policy released in January 2001, 336,000 people were expected to immigrate into the Republic of Ireland in the six years to 2006, to fill job vacancies arising during the six-year life of the £41 billion National Development Plan. The largest group of these new workers are expected to fill vacancies created as a result of the continued emigration by Irish people: a total of 112,000 people (an average of 16,000 a year) are expected to leave Ireland by 2006 (McManus, 2001: 1). Immigrants continue to be objectified and conceptualised by the Irish government as either problem (causing racism), or as economic stopgaps. While questioning the wisdom - in terms of costs and benefits to the economy - of encouraging such an influx into the state, placing 'additional pressure on domestic and social physical infrastructure', little attention has been drawn to the social price that in-coming labour migrants would have to pay in a multiracist Ireland.

Another link between Irish economic migrants and economic migrants into Ireland has also been made by Minister of State in the Departments of Foreign Affairs and Justice Liz O'Donnell, who, in autumn 1999 called her government's asylum policy 'a shambles'. The Minister links the dire need for workers with what she calls the Department of Justice 'security-led' attitude to asylum and immigration:

> If only 12 per cent of asylum-seekers are being given [refugee] status, it would suggest that large groups of them are economic migrants. What's wrong with that? We were all economic migrants, but using the asylum process is the

wrong way to go. There should be a route for economic migrants to come here (Haughey, 2001d: 7).

A couple of days later, another minister of state, this time Eoin Ryan, made a similar statement, only according to his version, only 7 per cent of asylum-seekers were granted refugee status last year. He too suggests that this means that 'many who come to Ireland are in fact economic migrants, as were so many Irish over the past 100 years' (Haughey, 2001e: 4). Note the circular argument: both ministers are suggesting that since *we, the state* have decided to grant only 12 (or is it 7?) per cent of asylum-seekers refugee status, we are relegating the rest to the lesser rank of economic migrants, thus replacing the erstwhile 'bogus refugee' tag with the current, more objectified, 'economic migrants' tag. Neither one was questioning the low rate of granting refugee status.

However, invocations of the pain of emigration are beginning to seep through Irish celebrations of affluence in recent cultural interrogations of emigration. One example is Tom Murphy's Abbey play *The House*, in which Christy, the returning poor emigrant boy who made money illicitly in London, buys up 'the house' in his home town to assuage the pain of the dispossessed. Susanne, the daughter of 'the house', herself a returned emigrant, expresses the pain of emigration when she pleads with her mother and sisters not to sell the old place: 'I'm saying, even if I'm away, I belong here. I'd like to have some - standing! Somewhere! I'm saying, I'm saying... Standing! What else is there...' (Murphy, 2000: 42).

Another example is *I Could Read the Sky* (O'Grady and Pyke, 2000), in which the main character, a middle-aged Irish construction worker, draws a picture of the emigrant's loneliness when he speaks of what is left after the untimely death of his beloved wife with whom he had known short-lived happiness:

> I'll not be leaving Kentish Town now except in a brown box and when I do I'll be going to Labasheeda to lie with Maggie. I've left the instructions. The girl who lives in the flat downstairs knows what to do. The governor of the Gloucester Arms. The woman whose dog I walk on weekday afternoons. And I've written it all out on a paper that's on the table beside the bed. There's the key to the box that has the money. How many feet of tunnelling to buy a coffin? How many to send me to Labasheeda? These hands. Battered and scarred like all of our hands. What travels through the tunnels? Who drives over the roads? What happens within the brick walls? Do the people there think of the men who built them? (O'Grady and Pyke, 2000: 152).

Nicola Bruce's film (2000) turns the novel into a cinematic rendition of the exilic memory patterns of the middle-aged emigrant played by the novelist Dermot Healy, whose face, furrowed as the land he had tilled and had left, keeps dissolving into bloodstained home and exile landscapes and back again.

These contemporary interrogations which subvert the dividing lines between hegemonic and subordinate through temporal and spatial enactment of migration are but two recent, feeble voices interrogating the disavowed migratory past just when boom and doom compete in responding to the racialisation of Irishness.

Breda Gray, in her study of hegemonic discourses of Irishness (1999), compares the negative portrayal of the immigrant 'other' with the positive images of the Irish 'us'. Gray suggests that discourses of Irishness as 'diasporic', as evident in former President Mary Robinson's speeches, emphasise the expansion and enrichment of Irishness through the diaspora, thus expanding the boundaries of Irishness. She cites Wieviorka, who argues that:

> Contemporary diasporic identities provide a strong basis from which to oppose contemporary expressions of racism. Immigrant and mobile populations have been able to construct images of identity that are based neither on the assimilationist model nor defensive strategies against assimilationism. Rather, the older, internal relation between racism and diasporisation has been broken by the ability of groups to claim a diasporic status on the basis of a public and not private articulation of self-identity (Wieviorka, 1998b: 69).

Indeed, as well as getting involved in racialised encounters in their countries of the diaspora, Irish emigrants have organised economic and cultural networks, which, among other things, succeeded in incorporating anti-Irish racism into the British racial equality paradigm. A case in point is the recent work on anti-Irish racism commissioned by the British Commission of Racial Equality (Hickman and Walter, 1997). However, despite nascent diasporic organisations such as the Association of Refugees and Asylum-seekers in Ireland (ARASI), the Association of Nigerian Asylum-seekers in Ireland (ANASI), the African Refugee Network, the Pan-African Organisation, etc., anti-racism in Ireland is still largely orchestrated by well-meaning white, settled, Christian Irish people, often in partnership with government departments and statutory agencies.

Multiracist Ireland is indeed being normalised, not only through the continuing daily harassment of members or racialised ethnic groups, as evidenced, for example, in testimonies by participants in the conference 'Ireland - Pluralism or prejudice?' organised by the Pan-African Organisation and the Irish Council for Civil Liberties on January 27, 2001 (see Donnellan, 2001: 13). Take for example a 2001 tutorial in Criminal Law at University College Dublin in which students are asked to assess the criminal liability of R, a 'Romanian refugee... (who), depressed and disillusioned, meets his son who tells him that there is a youth around the corner who yelled "Refugees go home" at his wife. Enraged at this insult to his wife, R picks up a stick, locates the youth and, without saying a word, viciously beats him about the head...' R then proceeds to beat his wife who 'knifes him through the heart' when he is asleep.[5] The racialisation and demonisation of Romanian refugees routinised in this tutorial exercise is another example of the normalisation of multiculturalism, which often means not conceptualising racism as part of the multicultural equation (Hesse, 2000: 8).

As 'we' the nation celebrate 'our' sameness through Riverdancing Irish culture,[6] 'we' expel otherness. The 'other' threatens the newly regained national voice of contemporary Ireland not only because her/his habits, rituals and discourses interfere with the nation's enjoyment of itself. It also threatens this regained national voice because it reminds it of its not-too-distant past pain.

Conclusion

Multiculturalist responses mean, above all else, not having to tend the wound, as top-down government racial awareness campaigns pretend that the exclusionary immigration policies of the same government do not exist. What is paradoxical about the politics of multiculturalism is that on the one hand it re-rehearses hegemonic power relations while on the other it pretends to deconstruct, or at least re-arrange them.

Anti-racist action is faced with fundamental structural and theoretical problems. It cannot be satisfied either with the easy conscience that moralising speeches or expressions of goodwill induce, or with the idea that racism, which has no scientific basis, ought to decrease with education or awareness programmes. Anti-racism is often beset by all sorts of exaggerations, and runs the risk of being inefficient and counterproductive. But this is true not only of anti-racism, but of all collective action (Weiviorka, 1997). Of course, we should be careful when we criticise anti-racism initiatives lest we feed into the hands of the anti-foreigner lobbies. My criticism of top-down initiatives aims to be constructive and enhance the capacity for action of participants in the intellectual and practical struggle against racism, rather than indicate a pessimism that ultimately might leave the terrain to the forces of reaction.

Disavowed, discrepant multiculturalism is, however, not the only way. Nor is multiculturalism a unitary discourse or practice. If multiculturalism is to offer a hope of pluralism, it would be through new social and cultural articulations by, among other performative possibilities, artists such as Ursula Rani Sarna, the Clare Irish-Indian playwright whose plays deal with Irish, rather than Indian life. It would be through pop stars such as Samantha Mumba, the black-Irish diva currently occupying a space for Ireland in the US charts, who presents a completely new cultural space (see www.samathamumbause.com/biog/index.html). It would be through the increasing numbers of dual heritage Irish couples, whose children will be speaking in Dublin, rather than Lagos or Bucharest accents. It would also be through racialised anti-racism activists creating their own anti-racism agendas despite the daily harassment. Hopefully such agendas would be established before 'there are race riots on Irish streets', as Gabriel Okenla of the Pan-African Organisation warned the 'Ireland: Pluralism or Prejudice' conference in January 2001. In occupying new ethnic spaces outside the official multiculturalist initiatives, spaces which at once attempt integration into the multiculturalist enterprise and at the same time subvert it, racialised out-groups are telling 'us' what 'we' already know: Ireland, untended wounds and all, is no longer what it was, as new ethnic landscapes are changing its geographies of exclusion. But these new ethnic landscapes are not univocal; they are gendered, sexualised, politicised in diverse ways which render the 'we' of contemporary Ireland obsolete as an 'authentic' (mono) cultural voice.

References

Barker, Martin. 1981. *The New Racism*. Brighton: Junction.

Brah, Avtar. 1996. *Cartographies of Diaspora : Contesting Identities*. London : Routledge.

Brah, Avtar. 2000. 'Different, diversity, differentiation: Processes of racialisation and gender', in Les Back and John Solomos (eds.) *Theories of Race and Racism*. London: Routledge.

Bruce, Nicola. 2000. *I Could Read the Sky*. Film based on Timothy O'Grady and Steve Pyke's novel (1998).

Cohen, Phil. 1988. 'Perversions of inheritance: studies in the making of multi-racist Britain,' in Phil Cohen and H. Baines (eds.) *Multi-Racist Britain*. London : Macmillan.

Cohen, Phil. 1993. *Home Rules: Some Reflections on Racism and Nationalism in Everyday Life*. London: New Ethnicities Unit, University of East London.

Donnellan, Eithne. 2001. 'Government accused of not dealing with racism', *The Irish Times*, 27 January 2001: 13.

Dooley, Chris. 2000. 'Reversal of fortune for asylum-seekers as village overcomes its "fear of the unknown"', *The Irish Times*, 15 August, 2000: 2.

European Year Against Racism. 1997. *Travellers in Ireland: An Examination of Discrimination and Racism. A Report to the Irish National Co-ordinating Committee for the European Year Against Racism*. Dublin: EYAR.

Gilroy, Paul. 2000. *Between Camps: Nations, Cultures and the Allure of Race*. London: Allen Lane.

Goldberg, David Theo. 2000. 'Racial knowledge,' in Les Back and John Solomos (eds.) *Theories of Race and Racism*. London: Routledge.

Goldstone, Katrina. 2000. 'Re-writing you: Researching and writing about ethnic minorities', in Malcolm MacLachlan and Michael O'Connell (eds.) *Cultivating Pluralism: Psychological, Social and Cultural Perspectives on a Changing Ireland*. Dublin: Oaktree Press.

Gray, Breda. 1999. '"Multiculturalism" and "Diaspora": Interrupting discourses of "Irish national identity"?' in Ronit Lentin (ed) *The Expanding Nation: Towards a Multi-ethnic Ireland*. Dublin: MPhil in Ethnic and Racial Studies, Department of Sociology, TCD.

Hall, Stuart. 2000. 'Conclusion: The multi-cultural question', in Barnor Hesse (ed.) *Un/settled Multiculturalism: Diasporas, Entanglements, Transruptions*. London: Zed Books.

Haughey, Nuala. 2001a. 'Group wants asylum laws to be tightened' and 'Nations supposed to be selfish - Ní Chonaill', *The Irish Times*, 5 January 2001: 4.

Haughey, Nuala. 2001b. 'Minister says refugee policy will not change', *The Irish Times*, 6 January 2001: 6.

Haughey, Nuala. 2001c. 'Rights activist received namesake's hatemail,' *The Irish Times*, 15 January 2001: 4.

Haughey, Nuala. 2001d. 'O'Donnell still unhappy with asylum policy pace', *The Irish Times*, 20 February, 2001: 7.

Haughey, Nuala. 2001e. 'Racist incidents will be monitored under new system', *The Irish Times*, 23 February, 2001: 4.

Hesse, Barnor. 1999. 'It's your world: Discrepant M/multiculturalism', in Phil Cohen (ed.) *New Ethnicities, Old Racisms*. London: Zed Books.

Hesse, Barnot. 2000. 'Introduction: Un/settled multiculturalism', in Barnor Hesse (ed.) *Un/settled Multiculturalism: Diasporas, Entanglements, Transruptions*. London: Zed Books.

Hickman, Mary and Bronwen Waters. 1997. *Discrimination and the Irish in Britain: A Report of Research Undertaken for the Commission for Racial Equality*. London: CRE.

Lentin, Ronit. 1998. '"Irishness", the 1937 Constitution and citizenship: a gender and ethnicity view', *Irish Journal of Sociology*, vol. 8: 5-24.

Lentin, Ronit. 2000a. 'Introduction: Racialising the other, racialising the "us": Emerging Irish identities as processes of racialisation', in Ronit Lentin (ed.) *Emerging Irish Identities*, Dublin: MPhil in Ethnic and Racial Studies, Department of Sociology, TCD.

Lentin, Ronit. 2000b. 'Multiculturalism or interculturalism? Educational challenges for all.' Paper presented to the Intercultural Ireland: Identifying the Challenges for the Police Service Conference, Dublin Castle, 4-6 April 2000.

Lentin, Ronit. 2001. 'Responding to the Racialisation of Irishness: Disavowed Multiculturalism and its Discontents' *Sociological Research Online*, vol. 5, no. 4, http://www.socresonline.org.uk/5/4/lentin.html

Mac an Ghaill, Máirtín. 1999. *Contemporary Racisms and Ethnicities: Social and Cultural Transformations*. Buckingham: Open University Press.

MacLachlan, Malcolm and Michael O'Connell (eds.) 2000. *Cultivating Pluralism: Psychological, Social and Cultural Perspectives on a Changing Ireland*. Dublin: Oak Tree Press.

McDonagh, Rosaleen. 2000. 'Talking back', in Anne Byrne and Ronit Lentin (eds.) *(Re)searching Women: Feminist Research Methodologies in the Social Sciences in Ireland*. Dublin: Institute of Public Administration.

MacManus, John. 2001. '336,000 immigrants predicted over next 6 years', *The Irish Times*, 24 January 2001: 1.

McVeigh, Robbie. 1992. 'The specificity of Irish racism'. *Race and Class*, 33/4

McVeigh, Robbie. 1996. *The Racialisation of Irishness: Racism and Anti-racism in Ireland*. Belfast: CRD.

Malik, Kenan. 1998. 'The perils of pluralism', *Index Online*.
    http://www.indexoncensorship.org.issue397//malik.htm

Miles, Robert. 1989. *Racism*. London: Routledge.

Minh-ha, Trinh T. 1991. *When the Moon Waxes Red: Representation and Cultural Politics*. London: Routledge.

Murphy, Tom. 2000. *The House*. Play, Abbey Theatre.

NCCRI (National Consultative Committee on Racism and Interculturalism). 2000. *Addressing Racism and Promoting a More Inclusive, Intercultural Society*. Dublin: NCCRI.

O'Grady, Timothy and Steve Pyke. 1998. *I Could Read the Sky*. London: The Harvill Press.

O'Toole, Fintan. 2000. 'Green, white and black: Race and Irish identity,' in Ronit Lentin (ed.) *Emerging Irish Identities*, Dublin: MPhil in Ethnic and Racial Studies, Department of Sociology, TCD.

O'Toole, Fintan. 2001. 'Immigrants at home and abroad', *The Irish Times*, 30 January 2001: 16.

Pavee Point. 2000. *Pavee Beoirs Breaking the Silence: Traveller Women and Male Domestic Violence*. Dublin: Pavee Point in association with the Eastern Health Board and Women's Aid.

Platform Against Racism. 1997. *Platform against Racism*. Dublin.

Tannam, Marian, Suzanne Smith and Suzie Flood. 1998. *Anti-Racism: An Irish Perspective*. Dublin: Harmony.

Thapar-Bjorkert, Suruchi. 2000. 'Private lives/public debates: social exclusion, violence and health of Muslim women in Britain,' paper presented at the 'Women, Violence and Reconciliation' Euroconference, Centre for Women's Studies, Trinity College Dublin, 10-12 March 2000.

Taylor, Charles. 1992. 'Multiculturalism and the politics of recognition', in A. Gutman (ed.) *Multiculturalism and the Politics of Recognition*, Princeton, New Jersey: Princeton University Press.

Tracy, Marshall. 2000. *Racism and Immigration in Ireland: A Comparative Analysis*. Dublin: MPhil in Ethnic and Racial Studies, Department of Sociology, TCD.

Wieviorka, Michel. 1995. *The Arena of Racism*. London: Sage.

Wieviorka, Michel. 1997. 'Is it so difficult to be an anti-racist?' in Pnina Werbner and Tariq Modood (eds.) *Debating Cultural Hybridity: Multi-cultural Identities and the Politics of Anti-racism*. London: Zed Books.

Wieviorka, Michel. 1998a. 'Is multiculturalism the solution?' *Ethnic and Racial Studies*, vol. 21, no. 5: 881-910.

Wieviorka, Michel. 1998b. 'Racism and diasporas,' *Thesis Eleven*, 52.

Zizek, Slavoj. 1989. *The Sublime Object of Ideology*. London: Verso.

Endnotes

Chapter 1:

1. The majority-minority interface in relation to ethnic groups is in extremely problematic, because it reduces issues of unequal power relationship to one of numbers, with the effect of naturalising, rather than challenging the power differential, as argued by Avtar Brah (1996: 186-7). Terms are important, not only for academics, because they often set the tone of the debate; therefore in this introduction, we use 'minority ethnic groups' and 'racialised ethnic groups' interchangeably.

2. The reason for choosing to refer to 'antisemitism' rather than 'anti-Semitism' is that there is no Semitism (see Lentin chapter 10 in this volume).

3. In the name of the Most Holy Trinity, from Whom is all authority and to Whom, as our final end, all actions both of men and States must be referred, We, the people of Éire, Humbly acknowledge all our obligations to our Divine Lord, Jesus Christ, Who sustained our fathers through centuries of trial... Do hereby adopt, enact and give to ourselves this Constitution' (Bunreacht na hÉireann, 1937).

4. Of interest here is Tanya Ward's (2001) report on the different forms of legal residency and types of citizenship in which she notes the lack of reliable statistics on the numbers of EU and EEA nationals since, unlike non-EU and non-EEA nationals, they are not obliged to inform the Department of Justice of their presence in the State.

5. On 19 December 2000, the Minister for Justice announced a second £100,000 grant to the Irish Refugee Council.

6. The ICP's spokesperson, Áine Ní Chonaill, stood for the 1998 elections on an anti-immigration ticket, receiving 293 votes in Cork South-West (Cullen, 1998b). In February 2000, the IPC distributed 5,000 leaflets demanding AIDs tests for all African asylum-seekers (Haughey, 2000).

7. The first successful prosecution occurred only in September 2000 of a Dublin bus driver who referred to a Gambian passenger as a 'nig nog' and told him to go back to his own country (Crosbie, 2000: 1). However, on 12 March 2001, the bus driver, Gerry O'Grady, was cleared on appeal, the judge having ruled that Mr O'Grady's words, however appalling, 'were not likely or intended to stir up hatred under the strict interpretation of the law' (*Irish Independent*, 13 March 2001).

8. Daithí Mac Síthigh (2001) points out that the absence of a hate crime statute, dealing specifically with physical crimes against racialised people, is a serious gap in the legislation in the south.

Chapter 2:

1. This chapter was first published as a report from the Irish National Co-ordinating Committee for the European Year Against Racism, 1997

Chapter 3:

1. Irish for 'One hundred thousand welcomes'!

Chapter 7:

1. Recognising that there are, of course, no 'race' distinctions between humans, the term is used here to identify that part of our identity which is racialized by majority society.

2. In a similar fashion, it is necessary to frame the experience of privilege within the self - a task I do not undertake here.

3. This forum took place on June 4, 1998. The report is available through the Platform Against Racism.

Chapter 10:

1. Keogh notes that Mac Gréil's 1978 survey was conducted after the Catholic document Nostra Aetate which repudiated displays of antisemitism was signed in 1965 and adopted in Ireland in 1974 (Keogh, 1998: 236).

2. There are seveal estimates: Karpf (1997: 175, 198) cites Britain admitting 40,000 Jews between November 1938 and the outbreak of war in 1939 compared with 11,000 in the previous five years, but only 1,200 Jewish refugees between 1945 and 1949 . Wasserstein (1997: 71) cites Britain admitting 50,000 Jewish refugees, including 10,000 unaccompanied children, between 1933 and 1939 and 'several thousands' more during and after the war.

Chapter 12:

1. Worth quoting here, precisely because imperial pursuit of self-interest is palatably formulated as noble self-sacrifice:

   'Take up the White Man's burden,
   Send forth the best ye breed.
   Go bind your sons to exile
   To serve your captives' need;
   To wait in heavy harness,
   On fluttered folk and wild,
   Your new-caught, sullen peoples,
   Half-devil and half-child.' (Rudyard Kipling)

2. From Edward Spenser's, *A View of the Present State of Ireland* (1596), quoted in Harrington (1991: 14).

3. From John Stevens' *A Journal of my Travels in Ireland Since the Revolution*, Containing a Brief Account of the War in Ireland (journal entries 1689-1691), cited in Harrington (1991: 137-8).

4. A notion developed at great length in Johannes Fabian's *Time and the Other: How Anthropology Makes its Object* (1983).

5. George Cooper, *Letters on the Irish Nation Written During a Visit to that Kingdom in the Autumn of the Year 1799*, cited in Harrington (1991: 190-1).

6. It should be noted that, at the time, 'Hottentot' was the colloquial shorthand for 'alien primitive'.

7. Or, as L. Perry Curtis (1968:,68) puts it, 'The conviction that race rather than environment or climate determined human behaviour, and... that membership in any race could be ascertained by merely examining the skull or head shape, the colour of hair and eyes, the pigmentation and the degree of prognathism or orgnathism, and the stature or carriage of the specimen in question.' He goes on to describe how these eminently quantifiable characteristics were meticulously measured and charted; this was hard science.

8. For a discussion of the interchangeability of physical characteristics, sex and class in 'scientific racism', see Gould (1981).

9. These images merit detailed analysis, particularly in gender terms. While Ireland is both 'good' (feminine) and 'bad' (masculine/simian), Britannia - always good, of course - is portrayed both as a female who is rarely feminine (in 'classical' garb of toga and sandals, with Athenian head-dress, she is markedly taller and more muscular than the cowering Hibernia, whom she shelters as she courageously confronts the Irish male) and as a male: the mild-mannered, middle-aged, middle-class, prosperously stout John Bull, or as the national saint - George - chivalrously rescuing the helpless Hibernia from a simian dragon/sea monster. Occasionally this theme is reversed, and Britannia swaps her modest toga for a Roman miniskirt to assume a sexually suggestive, supine pose as she is impaled by a Hibernian 'St. Dragon'. It should be noted that Hibernia - so bland that she must always be labelled as such, and/or supplied with an accoutrement such as a harp - is a generic 'comely maiden' with no distinct existence or personality of her own: in contrast to personifications of Britain/England, her face is rarely seen full on, and may be obscured altogether as she cowers. The Irish male, by contrast, is so unmistakable in his simianism that he is never labelled by nationality, always in political terms ('anarchy', 'rebellion', 'treason') - see Curtis 1997 for examples and discussion.

10. See, for example, Corkery (1977 [1924]), *The Hidden Ireland*, for discussion of collective terms applied by the English to the native Irish.

11. The Statutes of Kilkenny (1366) had already forbidden intermarriage, the Irish language, costume, sports and customs, and barred the native Irish from religious institutions - and this when England and Ireland were both Roman Catholic. After the Reformation, repressive legislation was always expressed in religious terms: from 1691 a series of 'penal' laws was passed restricting the rights of Catholics - in practice a synonym for the native Irish - to vote, own land or horses, access education or government jobs, etc.

12. For example, geographer and folklorist E.E. Evans (1942) notes the existence of dozens of different spade designs, each exclusive to a tightly confined area of Ireland.

13. Curtis (1968: 23), summarizing the attributes habitually imputed to the Irish by the English.

14. *JGLS* vol. 1, no. 4 April 1889, Notes and Queries, p. 248; vol. 2, no. 1 January 1880 , Notes and Queries, p. 7; vol. 3, p. xi.

15. And remains so. 'Real Gypsies' must be totally different, exotic, bizarre; colloquially, they practise magic and cannibalism; in academia, they are racial, linguistic and cultural Indians, geographically displaced in a time warp. Irish Travellers, by contrast, cannot be different at all; they are racially, linguistically and culturally mainstream, albeit with a timewarp. In fact the only thing they are deemed to hold in common is what Fabian in *Time and the Other* identifies as 'allochronism': neither coexists with 'us' in time. Travellers are 'as we were' while Gypsies are 'as they were'. Current Gypsy/Traveller realities are a mere veneer over their true identity, which is whatever their great great... grandparents are defined as having been (Indian nomads on the one hand, Irish peasants on the other). Virtually all observers impatiently brush aside the present tense veneer (the fact that English Gypsies are by and large pale-skinned, and have a limited Anglo-Romani vocabulary; the fact that Irish Travellers are nomadic, and speak Hiberno-English in an absolutely unique and distinctive way) to focus on determinant past tense 'realities'. Gypsy/Traveller contemporaneity is systematically belittled. This is ironic because these very observers by and large insist that Gypsies/Travellers live in an 'eternal now', while themselves dismissing the Gypsy/Traveller 'now' as irrelevant and misleading.

16. This polarisation into Romani/British/genuine versus Traveller/Irish/bogus was adopted as conventional wisdom at the time and, far from being questioned since, is routinely

reaffirmed as a statement of what Irish Travellers are not, as a preface to defining who or what they purportedly are. For example the 1963 Report of the Commission on Itinerancy tells us, in paragraph 1 regarding 'Origins', that 'Few of the itinerants in Ireland are of Romany or Gypsy origin' before going on, in paragraph two, to speculate as to the 'causes' of 'the existence of itinerants in Ireland' (p 34); Barnes (1975) tells us in Chapter Two and is in turn quoted by Mac Laughlin (1995: 14). The assertion is equally standard in popular works, viz. Levy 1996: 206, while Lalor (1997:169) informs us that 'travellers' are 'not Romany but merely dislodged and landless Irish wanderers of some earlier epoch' - note the chronological othering.

17. Note that, at this point, there is still recognition of the existence of indigenous English Travellers alongside Genuine Romanies and Irish Tinkers, compared to both of whom they are mere 'half breeds'. Academia subsequently - most particularly in the wake of Thomas Acton's seminal *Gypsy Politics and Social Change* (1974) - extended the Romani mantle to all English and Welsh Travellers, though the grassroots English have not followed suit. In academic circles, meanwhile, so heretical is the notion that British Gypsies may be more indigenous than Indian that Judith Okely, the one scholar to suggest this, has been repeatedly subject to unedifying, often personalised, attack in internet discussion groups. One of her more sober opponents, Ian Hancock (1998) 'emphasises' that she never 'denies an ethnic identity (or series of identities) for Gypsies; the argument is simply that Romani origins are ultimately mixed and mainly European' - an outrage. Hancock's counterclaim is that 'the Indian origin is beyond dispute, not only on the basis of linguistic but also of cultural and serological [blood] evidence.' It is not only in Ireland that the origins question is both passionate and political! The one largely undisputed point is that a people's present identity is identical to that of a select core group of ancestors, yet that an unspecified proportion of genetic admixture would dilute this into insignificance. 'Blood' has gone from the metaphor of Victorian times to laboratory analysis of albumen and DNA - hard science - on the unspoken assumption that these literally embody culture.

18. For a detailed discussion of this topic see ní Shuinéar (forthcoming).

19. Almost certainly Dinneen 1927, which uses pre-reform Irish orthography in the Irish alphabet, and is widely available.

20. On the same page, the author explains 'the importance of extending kinship to the siblings of the third cousins to include fourth and fifth cousins', clearly unaware that 'sibling' means brother or sister - the siblings of third cousins are also third cousins.

21. For a discussion of official policy towards Travellers as expressed in government reports, see ní Shuinéar 1999.

22. Gmelch expresses special thanks to sixteen named individuals 'all of whom are involved in itinerant settlement work' (1985: xi).

23. Charles Godfrey Leland (1881; these quotes from 1907 *JGLS* reprint) describes his first encounter with speakers of 'Shelta': an English tramp - an 'eccentric and most miserable fellow' (169), a 'grotesque figure' (170) accompanied by 'a woman tramp of the most hardened and audacious kind' (173). The male tramp claimed to have been 'kicked out of the lowest slums in Whitechapel because I was too much of a blackguard for 'em' (171). Leland, however, suspects him of 'romancing... to make himself of value or interesting' (*ibid*). By alleging such negatively tinged impression management, the author is in fact admitting that 'blackguards' in the 'lowest slums' were indeed 'of value or interesting' to him, thus revealing his expectations of speakers.

24. Cited as a quote from an unnamed 1980 publication on fieldwork by the author's wife and co-researcher Sharon Bohn Gmelch.

25. A particularly poignant insight into Gmelch's vision of Travellers, and his relationship to them, is his description of the barrel-top he and his wife shared on a Traveller site as a

'covered wagon' (Gmelch 1985:7), a Wild West allusion that evokes white pioneers surrounded by savage natives (whose identical dwellings are never described in this way) and leaves no doubt which side the author identifies with. Similarly, his fellow American Scheper-Hughes describes the currach - an indigenous Irish seagoing rowboat - as a 'canoe' (Scheper-Hughes 1982:10) - another 'Indian' image.

26. The first paragraph of the first page of the book states that Gypsies were 'only occasional visitors' to Ireland, and so did not intermarry with indigenous Travellers, who have remained sharply demarcated; the only overlap he concedes is in similarly 'predatory' behaviour (Gmelch 1985: 79) and fortunetelling, which Irish Travellers possibly 'copied' from Gypsies (Gmelch 1985: 21). Gmelch's bibliography lists Adams *et al*'s groundbreaking *Gypsies and Government Policy in England* (1975) but his text makes no reference to it or to its matter-of-fact pooling of Irish Travellers with British - Romani - Travellers generally.

27. An unconscious echo of 18th century English commentator Richard Twiss' observation that 'what little the men can obtain by their labour... is usually consumed in whiskey...' This bestseller so enraged the Irish that a chamberpot with Twiss' image on the bottom became a Dublin bestseller in its own right. (From Richard Twiss, *A Tour of Ireland 1775*, quoted in Curtis (1984: 38.)

28. Travellers continue to represent 'otherness' in the most varied and unexpected of ways. Two recent examples: Brian Lalor describing Traveller children's drawings, notes that 'something is always missing, which anybody who has taught art to settled Western children will recognise as ubiquitous. There are no dinosaurs' (1997: 165), while anthropologist Dr. Christopher Griffin solemnly ponders why 'some [Irish Traveller] men refused to wear underpants...' (1999: 15).

29. For a detailed discussion of historical trends in mainstream attitudes towards Irish Travellers see ní Shuinéar (1997).

30. See Gmelch (1985: 8-11) 'A Note on the Origins of Tinkers', for a summary of existing theories; the author did no original research on this topic, but is often quoted as if he had established that which he merely reports. For an overview of origins hypotheses and their plausibility, see ní Shuinéar (1994).

31. McCarthy very quickly rejected this original assessment, and was much dismayed to see it evoked in justification of policies she found ill-advised and objectionable. See McCarthy 1994.

32. viz. ATTP 38: 9, in a survey of sixty Travellers and sixty Middle Class Children...' [sic caps], while Gmelch (1985: 151) coins the oxymoron 'middle class County Council estate' (to emphasise that Travellers there are living among non-Travellers). Ethnonyms applied to differentiate the mainstream Irish from Irish Travellers merit detailed study in their own right. The latter may be utterly stripped of humanity and simply termed 'the problem', while 'residents' and 'people' apply solely to the former.

33. For example, one teacher of an all-Traveller class recently noted that 'Unemployment in the area [where the school is situated] is estimated to be as high as 80 per cent' (*Glocklaí*, 1995: 8).

34. The Parish of the Travelling People submitted a discussion document to the Bishops' Conference meeting in October 1993, expressing their 'pastoral concerns' about the 'health risks' posed by consanguineous marriage and recommending a 'review of current practice' pending which 'requests for dispensations be discouraged and only very exceptional cases be presented to the Bishop for consideration'. In practice, each Bishop has discretion over this matter within his own diocese. Where Traveller applicants fail to obtain the dispensation - essential to the equally essential church wedding - in one

diocese, they simply apply in another and another until it is obtained. To my knowledge only one bishop - the one who appears in the video mentioned above - refuses point blank to issue dispensations to Travellers (and only to Travellers).

35. Even if the family is settled in standard housing, the child nearly always suffers from lack of early training, inability to socialise, poverty of vocabulary because travelling parents rarely teach their children to speak, general lack of support from the older members of the family who have not themselves received any education [sic] at all' (Dwyer ATTP 11: 13).

36. British home secretary Jack Straw notoriously made this comment in an interview with Annie Oathen on Radio West Midlands, 22 May 1999. It is worth reproducing because it encapsulates conventional wisdom, contrasting a dwindling minority of harmless, legitimate Romanies versus hordes of criminals 'masquerading as travellers or Gypsies':

'Now the first thing we have to say is that people have got to stop being sentimental about so-called travellers. There are relatively few Romany Gypsies left, who seem to be to able to mind their own business and don't cause trouble to other people, and then there are a lot more people who masquerade as travellers or gypsies, who trade on the sentiment of people, but who seem to think because they label themselves as travellers that therefore they've got a licence to commit crimes and act in an unlawful way that other people don't have. In the past there has been rather too much toleration of travellers and we want to see the police and local authorities cracking down on them... Many of these so-called travellers seem to think that it's perfectly OK for them to cause mayhem in an area, to go burgling, thieving, breaking into vehicles, causing all kinds of other trouble including defecating in the doorways of firms and so on, and getting away with it, then their behaviour degenerates.'

It should be noted, because not apparent from the wording, that this interview took place in the aftermath of calling out police reinforcements on the occasion of an Irish Traveller wedding. This senior politician took the opportunity to reaffirm stereotypes about Irish Travellers and to apply them to the Traveller population of Britain in general.

The long-established counter image of the harmless legitimate Romani is currently crumbling on both sides of the Irish Sea as these mythical creatures appear as flesh and blood asylum-seekers.

37. It was never my intention to be derogatory or abusive or insulting - quite the contrary - I have been a member of the Itinerant Settlement Committee for 17 years.' Councillor John Flannery in evidence at his trial, as reported in *The Irish Independent* 2/3/99. Note that the 'Itinerant Settlement Committee' changed its name to the 'National Council for Travelling People' in 1975, and ceased to exist in 1990.

Chapter 13:

1. Whilst recognising the differing categorisation of the terms 'voluntary' and 'community' and acknowledging the overlap of activities within these sectors, for the purpose of this chapter the terms 'voluntary' and 'community' are being used interchangeably.

2. Part of this chapter is based on research carried out in 1997/98. This included interviews with representatives of organisations working in the area of anti-racism in both the south and north of Ireland.

3. According to Ronit Lentin (personal communication, January, 1998) any official Jewish mobilisation has originated from the Jewish Representative Council of Ireland and its Public Affairs Committee. The Jewish community has apparently opted not to take part in any public anti-racism coalitions.

4. The situation is slightly different in Northern Ireland where the two key minority ethnic organisations - the Northern Ireland Council for Ethnic Minorities (NICEM) and the Multicultural Resource Centre - are arguably more obviously minority ethnic led and run. Both have played a key part in setting an anti-racist agenda in the north. NICEM - as a grassroots movement - has identified capacity building as a key task. It is a dynamic, active and organised minority ethnic alliance whose agenda is set by minority ethnic groups themselves.

Chapter 14:

1. And Irish Protestants, if they are included. See McVeigh, 1999, for the discussion of sectarianism as racism.

2. See McDonagh, 2000, on the conceptual problems involved in settled researchers researching and speaking for Travellers.

3. See Mann-Kler, 2000, for a discussion of the multi-layered construction of black / Irish / British identities.

Chapter 15:

1. Thanks to Alana Lentin for helpful comments on earlier drafts and to Robbie McVeigh for reminding me to retain my optimism about the anti-racism potential of Irish society.

2. See the introduction for a discussion of deportations.

3. See Lentin, 2000b, 2001, and MacLachlan and O'Connell, 2000, for a preliminary discussion of multiculturalism in Ireland.

4. Gerry Stembridge's television play 'Black Day in Black Rock', produced by Venus Productions and broadcast on RTE 1, 29 January 2001, offers a comic, yet depressing, view of the reactions of the residents of a rural village to the proposed arrival of 30 asylum-seekers at the local hostel.

5. This tutorial exercise is taken from 2 BBLS Criminal Law 2000/2001, Dr Paul Anthony McDermott, University College Dublin.

6. However, I accept Robbie McVeigh's challenge that the tap/Irish dancing interchange of Riverdance is 'as good a bit of anti-racism as can be seen' (personal communication).

Contributors' biographies

Katrina Goldstone is a freelance researcher. She completed a Masters dissertation in history in St Patrick's College, Maynooth on 'Irish responses to the Jewish refugee crisis: policy and public opinion 1933-1945'. She researched and co-wrote the script for *No More Blooms: Ireland's Attitudes towards Jewish Refugees 1933-46*, produced by Louis Lentin and broadcast on RTE 1 in December 1997. She has published book chapters about writing about ethnic minorities and about Ireland's reaction to Jewish refugees. Kartina has served as a board member of the Irish Refugee Council and member of the sub group on Asylum with the National Consultative Committee on Racism and Interculturalism. She has been involved in anti racism work and given workshops and talks on this theme and is an associate member of Harnett Tannam Anti Racism Consultancy.

Pat Guerin has been involved voluntarily in campaigning against racism and for immigrant rights in Ireland for the past four years as a member of the Dublin-based Anti-Racism Campaign (ARC). He completed an MPhil in Ethnic and Racial Studies at Trinity College Dublin in 2000 and is now working with the Irish Refugee Council and as a freelance researcher on asylum/refugee issues.

Ronit Lentin, an Israeli Jew who has lived in Ireland since 1969, is course coordinator of the MPhil in Ethnic and Racial Studies, Department of Sociology, Trinity College Dublin. Among her books are *Conversations with Palestinian Women* (Jerusalem, 1982), and *Israel and the Daughters of the Shoah: Re-occupying the Territories of Silence* (Oxford and New York, 2000). Ronit is the editor of *Gender and Catastrophe* (London, 1997), *The Expanding Nation: Towards a Multi-Ethnic Ireland* (Dublin, 1999) and *Emerging Irish Identities* (Dublin, 2000). She is co-editor, with Anne Byrne, of *(Re)searching Women: Feminist Research Methodologies in the Social Sciences in Ireland* (Dublin, 2000), and with Nahla Abdo, of *Women and the Politics of Militry Confrontation: Palestinian and Israeli Gendered Narratives of Dislocation* (Oxford and New York, 2002). She has published extensively on racism in Ireland, gender and genocide, and Israeli feminist peace activism. She was founder member of the Irish Association of Minority Ethnic Women and member of NCCRI's Women's Sub-Committee.

Deepa Mann-Kler is an Indian woman born in England. She completed a BSc at the London School of Economics and an MSc at Bath University. Both degrees focused on black and minority ethnic children in education. She settled in Northern Ireland in 1996 and is the author of several works on racism in Northern Ireland. She was employed as equality officer with the Northern Ireland Council for Ethnic Minorities and is currently employed as research officer with the Belfast City Council. She specialises in anti-racism training, anti-discriminatory practice and equality proofing.

Rosaleen McDonagh is a feminist activist, academic, performer and writer. Her politics involve human rights, Traveller rights and disability rights. She is a development worker with the National Traveller Women's Forum and has recently completed a Master's degree in Ethnic and Racial Studies. She is also the chair of the Centre for Independent Living. She has brought a perspective of the issues involved in the possession of multiple identities to bear on her activism.

Robbie McVeigh is a researcher and activist. He has taught on racism and anti-racism at Queen's University Belfast and the University of Ulster and was course convenor of the module on racism and anti-racism at the Masters in Equality Studies, UCD. He has pioneered research about racism in Irish society and is the author of *The Racialisation of Irishness: Racism and Anti-Racism in Irish Society* (Belfast, 1996), and *Theorizing Sedentarism: The Roots of Anti-Nomadism* (Hertfordshire, 1997) and *Travellers, Refugees and Racism in Tallaght* (Dublin, 1998). He has published extensively on racism and anti-racism in Ireland north and south, and is active in a number of anti-racism organisations. In 2000 he appeared as expert witness in *P. O'Leary and others vs. Allied Domecq and others* in the Central London County Court - the test case that established that Travellers in Britain are protected under the Race Relations Act (1976).

Sinéad Ní Shuinéar has for decades promoted recognition of Irish Traveller ethnicity, the topic of her thesis for a Master's degree in Cultural Anthropology from the Jagiellonian University, Cracow (1979), in both published work and conference contributions. She is currently researching a doctorate on Irish Traveller social structure and social control with the University of Greenwich.

Drazen Nozinic is a former asylum seeker to Ireland from Yugoslavia. He was an occasional Lecturer in Anthropology at NUI Maynooth and worked for the Irish Refugee Council on educational issues. He has published on Balkanology, South-East European and Slavic Ethnology as well as on refugee issues.

John O'Connell, BA, MA, was Director of Pavee Point Traveller Centre, Dublin. He had been actively involved in Traveller/Gypsy issues at national and European levels and in the European Anti-Poverty Network (EPAN) since its establishment. He was a member of the National Committee of the European Year Against Racism and an active member of the Platform Against Racism. John passed away in November 1999 after a long illness.

Shalini Sinha is an antiracism and equality trainer in Ireland. She has provided consultation and training for government departments, unions, concerned businesses and non-governmental organisations. She undertakes research and lectures in the areas of gender and racism in Ireland with the Women's Education Research and Resource Centre, University College Dublin. Her research has included characterising the experiences of women of colour and examining institutional racism in Ireland. In addition to publishing on issues of gender, racism, and privilege, Shalini continues to contribute personal pieces reflecting her life experiences as a woman and product of an increasingly globalised world. She has a long history of activity with the anti-racism movement, and is a founding member of the Black Collective Ireland. She is a co-presenter of MONO, RTE Television's intercultural magazine programme.

Marian Tannam is a consultant, trainer and researcher who specialises in intercultural communication, anti-racism and diversity management. She has a B.A. in Communications and a Masters in Equality Studies. She has been actively involved in anti-racist work for many years and was one of four founder members of Harmony (1986-98), an anti-racist/intercultural organisation set up by people in inter-cultural marriages and relationships. She is an executive committee member of Comhlamh and also serves on a number of other related committees. She has a number of publications in the area and is co-author of *Racism in Ireland: Sources of Information* (1992) and co-author of *Anti-racism: An Irish Perspective* (1998). Her experience of being in an intercultural family has given her insight into issues of culture and racism in Irish society.

Elisa Joy White is a PhD candidate in African Diaspora Studies at the University of California at Berkeley. She received an MA in Media Studies at the New School University and MA in African-American Studies at the University of California at Berkeley. She has lectured in communications, theatre, and African-American studies, as well as written and produced theatre, radio, and film projects. She received a Fulbright Fellowship in 2000 to conduct research in Ireland for her PhD thesis on culture and identity in the emerging African Diaspora communities of Dublin.